Responsibility as Emmanuel Levinas's Mission to the Gentiles

John Turner Kilzer

EMETH PRESS
www.emethpress.com

Copyright © 2012 John Kilzer
Printed in the United States of America on acid-free paper

All rights reserved. No part of this book may be reproduced, or stored in a retrieval system or transmitted in any form or by any means, electronic, mechanical, photocopying, recording, scanning or otherwise, except as permitted by the 1976 United States Copyright Act, or with the prior written permission of Emeth Press. Requests for permission should be addressed to: Emeth Press, P. O. Box 23961, Lexington, KY 40523-3961. http://www.emethpress.com.

Library of Congress Cataloging-in-Publication Data

Kilzer, John Turner.
 Responsibility as Emmanuel Lévinas's mission to the Gentiles / John Turner Kilzer.
    p. cm.
 Includes bibliographical references and index.
 ISBN 978-1-60947-024-1 (alk. paper)
 1. Lévinas, Emmanuel. 2. Responsibility. 3. Christian ethics. I. Title.
 B2430.L484 K55
 194--dc23
                               2011040029

Cover Photograph used by permission
Emmanuel Levinas at his home, Paris 1984 by Marion Kalter

Contents

Acknowledgments / v

Introduction: Ethical Exigency / 1

Chapter One: Influence and Escape / 23

Chapter Two: Positioning / 49

Chapter Three: Upon Transcendence / 65

Chapter Four: Ethical Optics / 87

Chapter Five: From Stranger to Neighbor / 115

Chapter Six: This Strange Mission / 139

Chapter Seven: Waging Peace / 167

Conclusion: The Least of These / 191

Bibliography / 209

Acknowledgments

I want to thank Dr. Robert Bernasconi for his invaluable insight and encouragement regarding my work with Emmanuel Levinas. And to Dr. Larry Wood and Dr. Graham McFarlane, my thesis supervisors, I owe heartfelt gratitude for their incisive advise and unyielding call to rigorous scholarship. And for my wife Stacey, God's amazing gift, many thanksgivings. And to Levinas, for calling me to the other through the face of Christ.

Introduction

Ethical Exigency

In his conversations and writings, Emmanuel Levinas (1906-1995) spoke at times directly to Christians, challenging them to probe more deeply into the ethical nuances of responsibility. A Talmud scholar as well as Jewish philosopher trained in phenomenology, Levinas was constantly in search of an ideal of holiness, one that would become an 'absolute value (in) the human possibility of giving the other priority over oneself.'[1] This priority became real whenever the search for God was focused into a concern for the other, a concern Levinas shared with Christians: 'When I speak to a Christian, I always quote Matthew 25; the relation to God is presented there as a relation to another person. It is not a metaphor: in the other, there is a real presence of God. In my relation to the other, I hear the Word of God.'[2] Elsewhere Levinas mentions how he was led to this same passage in the Gospel 'where the people are astonished to hear that they have abandoned and persecuted God. They eventually find out that while they were sending the poor away, they were actually sending God himself away.' Later commenting on the theological motif reflecting God's descent to earth, and how this movement is commensurable with helping the poor and feeding the hungry, Levinas brings one's attention to 'the authentic Eucharist . . . when the other comes to face me.'[3]

For one notoriously difficult to read, Levinas essentially spent his life expounding one simple idea: the other is precedential.[4] Finding thought in general, and Western philosophy in particular, beggared when faced with the exigencies of the other, Levinas assumed a moral stance reverential to those the Bible calls widows, orphans, and strangers. According to Levinas, 'the Other's hunger — be it of the flesh, or of bread — is sacred.'[5] One called to the other's hunger is thus elected to serve the other. 'This election is made up not of privileges but of responsibilities. . . . I see myself *obligated* with respect to the Other; consequently I am infinitely more demanding of myself than of

1

others.'⁶ Moreover, Levinas regarded this election as a 'particularism that conditions universality,' thus establishing it as *'a moral category rather than historical fact to do with Israel.'*⁷

Reflecting on this authentic obligation for the other whose sacred hunger one is elected to serve provoked Hilary Putnam to claim that 'Here and elsewhere, Levinas is universalizing Judaism. To understand him, one has to understand the paradoxical claim implicit in his writing that, in essence, all human beings are Jews.' Putnam further claims that 'Levinas's audience is typically a gentile audience. He celebrates Jewish particularity in essays addressed to Christians and to modern people in general. *He is fully aware of this.*'⁸ What is more, these addresses are called 'Levinas's Mission to the Gentiles.'⁹

This thesis will reference many of Levinas's essays and works, focusing on themes and concepts and ways they convolve with responsibility. Peripheral to the presentation will be the steady question of how analyses of responsibility address Christians. Most chapters will adumbrate this peripheral relevance, with the concluding chapter bringing these horizons into specific focus. Patience is requested of the reader as the multifarious permutations of responsibility in works of Levinas are parsed. It is through the painstaking exegesis of responsibility, however, that Levinas's mission to the Gentiles assumes specific shape. And by detailing Levinas's unusual nomenclature signifying responsibility, terms and idioms assumed from both phenomenological and theological fields will be utilized in arrangements deferential to ethical thought.¹⁰ Modes of analysis will aim towards a transparency regarding Levinas's work, letting his writing carry the burden of its own proof.

The objective herein involves presenting these themes and concepts of Levinas clearly and precisely, noting particularly ways these motifs constellate around Levinas's ethical hermeneutics. Charting responsibility through the writings of Levinas will in essence clarify his vision of eschatology, one that 'institutes a relation beyond the totality.' Regarding this institution, one finds that

> it is a relationship with a *surplus always exterior to totality*, as though the objective totality did not fill out the true measure of being, as though another concept, the concept of *infinity*, were needed to express this transcendence with regard to totality, non-encompassable within a totality and as primordial as totality. This "beyond" the totality and objective experience is, however, not to be described in a purely negative fashion. It is reflected *within* the totality and history, *within* experience. The eschatological, as the "beyond" of history, draws beings out of the jurisdiction of history and the future; it arouses them in and calls them forth to their full responsibility. . . . The eschatological vision breaks with the totality of wars and empires [and reveals] the possibility of a signification without a context. The experience of morality does not proceed from this vision – it consummates this vision; ethics is an optics.¹¹

Totality for Levinas is anything that militates against the other.¹² Putting into practice the above optics, what Levinas calls a 'vision without image,' calls one to a severe obligation for the other marked by a concern both vigilant and sober.[13] Taking into account Levinas's emphasis on obligation, John D. Caputo notices that it 'is what is important about ethics.... It gives: without referring to something entitative, the "it" points to a deep anonymity in things, in the world, in the stars as in ourselves.' Caputo, moreover, senses a metaphysical urge in Levinas's eschatological vision, noting its 'attempt to shatter anonymity, to affirm "something" (which is not some thing at all but the Other person) that transcends anonymity, that infinitely surpasses it. I see this metaphysicality as prophetic hyperbole, as a great "as if": act as if the Other were an Infinity that surpasses the totality, an infinity "as it were."'[14]

For Levinas the ethical relation is irreducible to a theme. Yet he spent his whole life straining for concepts ingredient to this relation. Beginning from the elementary premise 'ethics happens,' Levinas strives for a circumambient purview loyal to the grandeur of the other. Endemic to this loyalty is a relentless responsibility opposing the machinations of totality with a moral force not stronger — but better. According to Richard A. Cohen,

> Ethics is forceful not because it opposes power with more power ... but rather because it opposes power with what appears to be weakness and vulnerability but is responsibility and sincerity. To the calculations of power, ethics opposes *less* than power can conquer.... Moral force is not stronger than the powers of being and essence, the totalizing, synthesizing powers, it is *better*, and this is its ultimate strength.[15]

Ever mindful of what he called the surplus exterior to totality, Levinas's writings confront openly the avaricious systems of ontology he felt were biased and egocentric, reducing heterogeneous experience into banal neuters.[16] For Levinas, the only true way to obviate this reductive systematizing was through communication with the other, a communion suggestive of the aforementioned authentic Eucharist. This communion suggests, as Jan De Greef points out, an ethical event where 'one must act before understanding, ' and where, moreover, the agency involved 'does not *represent* what it accomplishes but *presents* it' -- exhibiting a performative agency marked by 'an identification between the expression, what is expressed, and the act accomplished by these.'[17]

Asymmetry

Fundamental to our analysis of responsibility in the works of Levinas is its asymmetrical nature. Speaking of the relation with the other, Levinas notes 'that the intersubjective relation is a non-symmetrical relation. In this sense, I am responsible for the Other without waiting for reciprocity, were I to die for it. Reciprocity is his affair.' Concerning another central motif, subjectivity, Levinas adds: 'It is precisely insofar as the relationship between the Other and me is not reciprocal that I am subjection [*sic*] to the Other; and I am "subject" essentially in this sense. It is I who support all.'[18] Edith Wyschogrod is corroborative, noting that 'when we look at the face of the other we know that we are commanded to honor the alterity of the Other by recognizing an asymmetry between us. We also know that something has "happened" in the intersubjective "space" between us that transcends any knowledge we may have of it.'[19]

Severe though it may sound, understanding asymmetrical responsibility is a key in understanding Levinas.[20] In a seminal passage concerning asymmetry and the movement towards transcendence, Levinas notes that '*correlation does not suffice as a category for transcendence*. . . . What I permit myself to demand of myself is not comparable with what I have the right to demand of the Other. This moral experience, so commonplace, indicates a metaphysical asymmetry.'[21]

Properly speaking, reciprocity with regards to the other would be assumable by ontological schemata. Falling into the wiles of this schema for Levinas would be equivalent to being duped by morality. In fact, relationships contingent on reciprocity suspend morality into permanent possibilities of war.[22] These possibilities for war subtend ontological events while mobilizing antagonistic forces. Moreover, these volatile forces also pervert true otherness. According to Levinas, this was 'the test of the real, (since) violence does not consist so much in injuring and annihilating persons as in interrupting their continuity, making them play roles in which they no longer recognize themselves, making them betray not only commitments but their own substance, making them carry out actions that will destroy every possibility for action.'[23] For those playing unrecognized roles, oblivious yet complicit, war preponderates.[24] It is the natural, ineluctable result of conditional symmetry, one Levinas felt could only be surmounted 'when the eschatology of messianic peace will have come to superpose itself upon the ontology of war.'[25] Only then would one be beyond the totality.

The asymmetrical nature of the ethical relationship means that my obligation to the other is incumbent upon no one else but me, and hence unique.[26] No coercion prompts me to respond to the other and no rule or regiment orders me. In addition, as notes James Olthuis, 'in insisting on ethical asymmetry, Levinas emphasizes the movement of the other to the self at the cost of minimizing the corresponding movement of the self to the other. The result is that, ethically, instead of a two-directional interplay of mutuality, there is uni-directionality.'[27] This relationship cannot be singularized into moral precepts or formulated into procedures. Levinas, when depicting this asymmetric relationship, repeatedly quotes Alyosha in Dostoevsky's *The Brothers Karamazov*: 'Each of us is guilty before everyone for everyone, and I more than the other.'[28]

Alain Toumayan feels that 'Levinas alludes to this particular quote, modifying it occasionally and elaborating certain of its features in order to illustrate saliently various dimensions of his concepts of subjectivity and ethics, most often the notion of asymmetry or nonreciprocity that it expresses so radically and so strikingly.'[29] Just as important is the way the accusative 'I more than others' isolates the subject, riveting it to itself with an ethical servitude noncompliant to ontological wiles. Here the infinite overflows being, disaffecting one from adopting postures congenial to symmetric exchange.³⁰ More to the point (in effect to the point of obsession) would be an assumed posture of watchfulness, one taken on with what Levinas calls a spirit of sobriety 'because it is a perpetual duty of vigilance and effort that can never slumber.'³¹ Asymmetrical, nonreciprocal responsibility in essence reconfigures subjectivity, obliging one – on an ethical level – to acknowledge that the self, true to its nature, is selfish. This acknowledgement implies what Levinas calls a difficult freedom, one preceded by an obligation to the other.³²

The Same and the Other

This analysis focuses specifically on responsibility in works of Levinas. Through critical expositions of works of Levinas, it will constantly keep in the foreground the following questions: how do these analyses bring attention to what Levinas calls an authentic Eucharist when the other comes to face me? And how are these questions addressed by exegeting responsibility?³³ Presenting Levinas's mission to the Gentiles (Christians and modern people in general) through key terms in his writings, it is anticipated that his statement 'all human beings are Jews' will resonate universally with the genuine, experiential obligation honoring what Levinas called the other's hunger. The other for Levinas, according to B. C. Hutchens, is 'different in every relevant sense, and not only in its characteristics and comportment. Despite being naked, foreign, a stranger, a widow, an orphan or, in general, destitute and needy, it is also lord and master precisely because of the effect it has on the self.'³⁴

A distinction must be applied delineating the same (totality) and the other (infinity), however, before this hermeneutic can be properly initiated.³⁵ For Levinas, totality was tantamount to assimilative violence.³⁶ Co-categorized with such terms as the "I," the ego, and the same, the operations of totality operate systemically and synoptically: 'vision is an adequation of the idea with the thing, a comprehension that encompasses.'³⁷ For Levinas, totality's comprehensive violence was manifested in large part due to its relative existence. He had reflected on Plato's dialogue the *Sophist*, where the exposed aspects of multiform being contradict the edicts of Parmenidean monism, and where the Eleatic Stanger shows 'that "not-being" cannot exist in absolute terms (but can only) have *relative* existence in the sense that something can be *other than* something else. . . . These two ways of speaking correspond to the two "forms" or categories of Being that Plato calls "same" and "other."'³⁸ Levinas felt there was no real concept depicting what was contrary to Being that could distinguish it from a diffuse categorical mélange. 'To Levinas's mind,' notes Atterton, 'this meant that we still lack the proper philosophical tools necessary to think the otherness of the Other. We have not yet left the climate of Parmenidean Being. Indeed, over two millennia later . . . we would still appear to be living in its shadow.'³⁹ This meant, moreover, that we were still living in the shadow of the same.

For Levinas, questioning the same was an ethical endeavor. And since the same, or totality, claims only a relative existence, it tends to hide in the shadows of *tertium quid*, or neutral thirds. According to Levinas, philosophy has 'most often been an ontology: a reduction of the other to the same by interposition of a middle and neutral term that ensures comprehension of being.'[40] And this coinage usually betrays its provenance. Spinoza clumped everything in substance; Hegel in Spirit; Heidegger in Being.[41] Levinas challenged these radical assimilative procedures by critically calling them out:

> Critique does not reduce the other to the same as does ontology, but calls into question the exercise of the same. A calling into question of the same – which cannot occur within the egoist spontaneity of the same – is brought out by the other. *We name this calling into question of my spontaneity by the presence of the other ethics*. The strangeness of the other, his irreducibility to the I, to my thoughts and my possessions, is precisely accomplished as a calling into question of my spontaneity, as ethics. Metaphysics, transcendence, the welcoming of the other by the same, of the Other by me, is correctly produced as the calling into question of the same by the other, that is, as the ethics that accomplishes the critical essence of knowledge. And as critique precedes dogmatism, metaphysics precedes ontology.[42]

Here Levinas's torturous style enacts what it proposes, effectively leaving and returning to mimetically contextualize the semantic event. Through the recurrent calling of the same into question, Levinas disabuses ontology from its biased and categorical status. He also engages in what Colin Davis calls a 'paradoxical intellectual project' by arranging his texts so that 'they are articulated around a self-challenging double movement: the texts make propositions but simultaneously endeavor to avoid being reducible to such propositions. The process of thought remains fluid, whilst sometimes crystallizing in the form of analyzable themes and ideas.'[43] Here Levinas also discloses a provocation towards transcendence, one investing a strange nobility to the other that, as Critchley notes, 'is very much of this world and not part of some other-worldly mysticism.'[44]

Encapsulated in this passage is a key to Levinas's thought: the relationship between the same and the other volatizes knowledge.[45] What is more, this 'calling out' by Levinas underscores his contention that 'ethical exigency is not an ontological necessity.'[46] In fact, Levinas here is inviting thought to break away from dogmatic givens, to abscond from the regulative idea where intelligibility is reduced to comprehension, where knowledge naturalizes being as its object. What is also striking is Levinas's contention that ethics 'accomplishes the critical essence of knowledge.' Again, the relationship between same and the other, productive of transcendence, prompts this critique by inciting what Levinas elsewhere calls the 'ethical significance of a past that concerns me, that regards me, that is my business outside all reminiscence, all retention, all representation, all reference to a remembered present.'[47] In an odd turn the other's presence, inflecting the ego's spontaneity, invests 'significance in the ethics of a pure past, irreducible to my present, and thus, of an originary past.' And upon what is this significance based? As will be addressed, it is 'based on the responsibility for the other man.'⁴⁸

In many ways Levinas's passage above will model the methodology of this analysis. The other will be origin and destination. Themes and concepts will be taken apart, examined, and then reconfigured around a Levinasian notion of responsibility. Exposition of his works will be guided by his ethical thought, registering what is topical in its symbiotic relation with moral exigency and obligation. This registering will reduce each assumption to what Levinas calls the 'ethical significance of a past that concerns me.' Assumed in this reduction is a hermeneutic of sobriety, a vigilance Levinas collates with a difficult freedom.⁴⁹ Moreover, difficult freedom herein will be equivalent with the severe obligation Levinas calls all to pursue that devote themselves 'to service with no thought of reward' as it relates to a 'burden carried out at its own expense.... This is the original and incontestable meaning of the Greek word *liturgy*.'⁵⁰ Perhaps, for Levinas, the authentic Eucharist is this service with no thought of reward – and the burden carried would be as bread for the other.

A Self Enclosed

At the base of Levinas's thought is a phenomenology of engagement, descriptions depicting the encounter with the other. These engagements exhibit distinct traits unique to what Levinas calls the humanism of the other, features irreducible to objects. The phenomenological descriptions employed portray interhuman experiences manifest in the various existential modalities inherent in the banalities of everyday life.⁵¹ Ingredient in these modalities are what Levinas calls enjoyment and nourishment. Through enjoyment and nourishment the ego consumes the fruits of the world, basking in a medium too rarified for representation.⁵² In preliminary fashion enjoyment and nourishment provide Levinas with a paradigm employed in analyses of need and desire, implementing a model for what in essence is contrary to totality:

> In enjoyment the things are not absorbed in the technical finality that organizes them into a system. They take form within a medium [milieu] in which we take hold of them. They are found in space, in the air, on the earth, in the street, along the road. The medium remains essential to things.... This medium is not reducible to a system of operational references and is not equivalent to the totality of such a system, not to a totality in which the look or the hand would have the possibility of choosing, a virtuality of things which choice would each time actualize. The medium is its own density... To tell the truth the element has no side at all. One does not approach it. The relation adequate to its essence discovers it precisely as a medium: one is steeped in it; I am always within the element.⁵³

Levinas depicts here economic transactions antecedent to representation, closer in fact to affective events.⁵⁴ He utilizes, moreover, descriptions establishing precedence for an interpretive phenomenology militating against the empirical biases prevalent in systems of totality.[55] Inherent in this passage is an incipient analysis of need that, along with desire, reveal two contradictory positions assumed in Levinas's writings. 'The first,' states Wyschogrod, 'assumes that need is not demolished with the satisfaction of need, that there is a pressure that we experience when need is satisfied, a pressure whose source remains inexplicable. The second assumes the adequacy of intention to what is given, of desire to the desirable, and therefore presumes genuine satiety.'[56] Concentrating on these affective modalities originary to intersubjective discourse affords Levinas a fundamental intuition addressing multiple perspectives of objects prior to cognitive assimilation. These intuitions in fact compel Levinas 'to affirm either that there are some things that we can think that are totally formless or to claim that there are objects of need and desire that transcend ontology and therefore do not have to meet the requirement for all thought, namely, that they have form in order to be thinkable.'[57] Levinas chose the latter alternative, finding transcendence fulfilled through obligation to the other.

For all practical purposes, the enjoyment of things ('in the air, on the earth, in the street, along the road') illustrates a sufficiency and accommodation to form. Consigned to the solipsism and complacency of enjoyment, the ego is in fact tied to its needs. According to Levinas, 'in enjoyment I am absolutely for myself. Egoist without reference to the Other, I am alone without solitude, innocently egoist and alone. Not against Others, not "as for me . . ." — but entirely deaf to the Other, outside all communication and all refusal to communicate — without ears, like a hungry stomach.'[58] Living off the elements, basking in the satisfaction provided by the milieu, the self nonetheless experiences an insatiable longing interrupting the alimentary contentment. Things become cloying, redundant, reverting into a plastic art. Objects graspable soon become clinging: 'Tools and implements, which themselves presuppose enjoyment, offer themselves to enjoyment in their turn. They are playthings: the fine cigarette, the fine car. They are adorned by the decorative arts; they are immersed in the beautiful, where every going beyond enjoyment reverts to enjoyment.'[59]

At this juncture the phenomenology of need has reached its term. One now finds the mode of enjoyment self-referential, blocked in resistance, and relegated to destiny.[60] According to Levinas, this condition depicts the ego rapt in rudimentary duration — lost in what he calls 'the nowhere.' Noteworthy here is Levinas's belief that this elemental existence, bounded by nothingness on all sides, is ironically the point of ingress for the chthonic gods prevalent in mythology and paganism. He considers it a place where one could have 'recourse to totemism (where) animal energy would control the secret of the social' and leave one 'indifferent to all justification and all accusation.'[61] It is a place where fate intercedes, and the I, sufficient unto itself, enrooted in itself, is still nonetheless menaced by uncertainty, by a destiny that contravenes sovereignty.

The elemental now is experienced as pleasure, an indeterminacy extended yet without perspective. As Adriaan Peperzak notes, for Levinas 'elements are not things, because they are too independent for that, too formless. Therefore, they cannot be possessed. Without limitations, without beginning or end, they come from nowhere.'⁶² Nothingness has assumed dimension. And the self, through the agency of feeling, does not know things – but lives things. Indeed, feeling establishes the relation with the elemental. What is more,

> the elemental as Levinas describes it is Janus-faced: it both gives itself and escapes through its very insubstantiality in the giving. What is offered by the elemental disappears without explanation. The future is thus lived as insecurity, an insecurity that is expressed concretely in the mythical divinity of the elemental gods. But for Levinas these gods are without face; one therefore cannot address them: they lack the fundamental prerequisite for *religio*. They stand as the nothingness that marks the limit of enjoyment. Consciousness as separated being is pagan consciousness.⁶³

The limit of the elemental is this dimension pressed against itself, confronted with the transmogrified gods determined by this indeterminacy. For Levinas, however, there is a place even more primordial than the elemental exhibiting 'the dimension of a completely contourless and dangerous protoworld, the anonymous underworld of faceless monstrosity, a chaos in which there are no facts, no data, no givens, a neuter without any giving, the contrary of generosity.'⁶⁴ There is a name for this proto-place: the *there is*, (*il y a*).

For Levinas the *il y a* expresses the phenomenal haunting of impersonal being. He likens this haunting to reflections on childhood memories where, sleeping alone, one experiences the impersonal silence as if it were alive, as if it were rumbling. 'It is something resembling what one hears when one puts an empty shell close to the ear, as if the emptiness were full, as if the silence were a noise. It is something one can also feel when one thinks that even if there were nothing, the fact that "there is" is undeniable.' Indeterminacy here is as real presence, a concrete nothingness: 'not that there is this or that; but the very scene of being is open: there is. In the absolute emptiness that one can imagine before creation – there is.'⁶⁵ Disturbingly this presence folds about, tarries with, and clings to – leading one to an unrelenting anxiety. 'And this despair, this fact of being riveted,' notes Jacques Rolland, 'constitutes all the anxiety of nausea. In nausea – which amounts to an impossibility of being what one is – we are at the same time riveted to ourselves, enclosed in a tight circle that smothers.'⁶⁶ Haunted by this anonymous rumbling, this full emptiness, 'we are there, and there is nothing more to be done, nor anything to add to the fact that we have been entirely delivered up, that everything is consumed.'⁶⁷ Being delivered up is being consumed. And the only way out is to escape.

Nightwatch

For Levinas, to be embodied is to battle, to question while struggling against the limits of one's being and situation.⁶⁸ Not only is everything human belabored with the comprehension of being human, but contingencies and brute facts of existence disturb each ontological adventure. Moreover, in the drama of consciousness obligation is not rationally motivated. Prior to the ethical event only a diffuse concern for things coerces consciousness: 'the love of life does not resemble the care for Being, reducible to the comprehension of Being, or ontology. The love of life does not love Being, but loves the happiness of being.'[69] Yet this happiness is still contingent on a something that is neither nothing nor being; for according to Levinas, 'one cannot say of this "there is" which persists that it is an event of being. One can neither say that it is nothingness, even though there is nothing.'[70]

Irreducible to reason, the *il y a* is engaged via a strewed intuition — an inchoate, brute fear bordering on apprehension. Comparing its presence to a field of forces, to nocturnal space, Levinas says that 'darkness fills it like a content; it is full, but full of the nothingness of everything. Can one speak of its continuity? It is surely uninterrupted. But the points on nocturnal space do not refer to each other as in illuminated space; there is no perspective, they are not situated. There is a swarming of points.'[71] According to Jeffrey L. Kosky, 'for Levinas, the *il y a* explains the way in which, even after the negation of all beings, there still remains the void or horrifying darkness which there is in the absence of each and every being. The *il y a* thus designates the irremissibility and anonymity of what Levinas calls "being in general."'[72] Here is a veritable haunting, one where the scarcity of acumen fuels anxiety — even though 'nothing approaches, nothing comes, nothing threatens; this silence, this tranquility, this void of sensations constitutes a mute, absolutely indeterminate menace.'[73] The indeterminateness is astringent: and though the menace is pure and simple to the point of being ambiguous, it is still invasive — threatening with the blunt edge of anonymity.

The situation suggests a reducing darkness where 'illuminated objects can appear to us as though in twilight shapes. Like the unreal, inverted city we find after an exhausting trip, things and beings strike us as though they no longer composed a world, and were swimming in the chaos of their existence.'[74] Levinas now gives us a hermeneutic term in order to collect and categorize what he calls this rustling horror of darkness: insomnia.

Denoting an impersonal vigilance — more like a mystical, depersonalized involvement in this pre-elemental haunting — still in insomnia there is an ambient awareness suggestive of the shape-taking of anxiety presaging agency.[75] Yet strangely anxiety here is inverted, resulting in the peculiar notion that the ambient itself is peering in on being. Thus insomnia is suspended in an anonymous wakefulness, one where 'it is the night itself that watches. It watches. In this anonymous nightwatch where I am completely exposed to being, all the thoughts which occupy my insomnia are suspended on *nothing*. They have no support. I am, one might say, the object rather than the subject of an anonymous thought.'[76]

Claire Elise Katz believes that 'the nothingness to which Levinas refers is not yet substantive, is not yet attached to being, but is itself "the very work of being." Thus he refers to it as anonymous. He compares existing without existents to the absolute nothingness before creation, to an inability to escape sleep.'[77] Menacingly, here is an existence independent of the existent. And while description tends to follow seriatim the logistics of narrative, in this situation time, like the milieu, is deformalized into anonymous presence. What is more, in the *il y a* it is as though what is indeterminate assumes categorical status, as though its lack of attachment to anything was its *modus operandi*.[78]

Levinas is acutely aware of the difficulty involved in expressing what is essentially inexpressible, of finding words for what is refractory to description:

> How are we going to approach this existing without existents? Let us imagine all things, beings, and persons, returning to nothingness. What remains after this imaginary destruction of everything? What remains after this imaginary destruction of everything is not something, but the fact that there is [*l y a*]. The absence of everything returns as a presence, as the place where the bottom has dropped out of everything, an atmospheric density, a plentitude of the void, or the murmur of silence. There is after this destruction of things and being, the impersonal "field of forces" of existing. There is something that is neither subject nor substantive. The fact of existing imposes itself when there is no longer anything. And it is anonymous: there is neither anyone nor anything that takes this existence upon itself . . . Existing returns no matter with what negation one dismisses it. There is, as the irremissibility of pure existing.[79]

The hermeneutic impasse confronted as one attempts to negate this infra-presence frustrates most logical expositions.[80] It is the interminable pop-up 'that imposes itself because one cannot deny it. Behind every negation this ambience of being . . . reappears as the field of every affirmation and negation. It is never attached to an *object that is*, and because of this I call it anonymous.'[81] This anonymity however does nothing to diminish the burgeoning anxiety resulting from the fundamental absurdity the situation constitutes.[82] Again, the only way out is to escape.

The True Exit: A Lived Adventure

There is a way out of the *there is*. It involves consciousness – but consciousness understood both typically and atypically. Significantly a unique understanding of vigilance collates with escape as it dramatizes the rending effort involved in leaving the *il y a*. This coming to consciousness unique to Levinas parallels the difficult freedom he calls all to pursue who devote themselves to service with no thought of recompense – particularly as it relates to a burden carried out at its own expense. Again Levinas calls this service a liturgy.[83] This service, moreover, is from responsibility, through responsibility, to responsibility. And responsibility is the way to the other.[84]

Thus it is here, approaching a situation where brute existence is singularized into existents – where metaphysics and physics meet – that the beginning of consciousness is a consciousness of beginning.[85] For Levinas, 'consciousness is a rupture of the anonymous vigilance of the *there is*; it is already hypostasis; it refers to a situation where an existent is put in touch with its existing.'[86] Referring to this hypostasis, Katz suggests that for Levinas it is a dramatization of a 'time' before existents, and 'his focus is on the point before the solitude of existing, the point before subjectivity took hold. That is, Levinas wants to go back to the events by which the existents contracted their existing, what he calls the hypostasis. . . . He wants to interrogate the possibility of going back to the hypostasis' by asking the question 'what prompts the existent to contract existence?'[87]

Levinas here is declaring affective modes of intentionality open to descriptive analysis and hence susceptible to meaning. He is also concerned with approaching these modalities artlessly, devoid of the psychological nomenclature that tends to intellectualize affectivities – thus denaturing them. Decontextualized yet sensible, there is a sense that Levinas is as intent on conserving the anonymity of the presence as he is in identifying the present, in effect singularizing the moment into consciousness as he punctuates it into time.

Hypostasis signals for Levinas an exit from what he characterizes as a 'process of being, without a bearer, without a subject,' something he also calls an 'anonymous "nonsense."' Moreover, hypostasis entails a 'getting out . . . by the subject who is bearer and master of being, of his being. The *there is* first proceeds from a phenomenology of fatigue, of laziness; then the search for being, hypostasis.'[88] This laziness, however, this inverted vigilance, is only mitigated through 'the true exit from the *there is* (that) is in obligation, in the "for-the-other" which introduces a meaning into the nonsense of the *there is*.'[89]

In other words, for Levinas the provenance of meaning is in this obligation for the other – in responsibility. What is more, this obligation is unique to each self, is in fact what authenticates the awakening to ethical responsibility. As Leora Batnitzky notes, 'this responsibility is mine alone and I am uniquely defined by it. I do not possess this responsibility; rather, this responsibility *is* me.'[90]

True exit from the *il y a* situates one at the crossroads of Levinasian studies. At this crossroads the 'I' or ego is obedient to the other to the point of submission. In an interview, Levinas calls this moment 'the ethical event,' noting that it 'is the kernel of all I would say later.'[91] And when Levinas is asked 'So what is at stake to leave oneself?' the response is noteworthy: 'now we are getting to the fundamental themes.' Richard A. Cohen corroborates when he notes that 'Levinas insists on ethics, on metaphysical responsibility, an exorbitant and infinite responsibility for other human beings, to care not for being, for the unraveling of its plot, but for what is beyond and against being, the alterity of the other person.'[92] Levinas's detailed response reflective of these themes is significant and will concatenate throughout this analysis. It speaks of a true exit, of an escape suggesting perpetual leave-taking and incessant non-arriving. Levinas begins by speaking of the importance of leaving oneself, that is, being occupied with the other, that is, with his suffering and death, before being occupied with one's own death. . . . I'm not afraid of the word *good*: the responsibility for the other is the good. It's not pleasant, it is good. . . . But in sum, the true, the incontestable value, about which it is not ridiculous to think, is holiness. This is not a matter of privations, but it is in the certitude that one must yield to the other in the first place in everything, from the *après vous* ["after you"] before an open door right up to the disposition – hardly possibly, but holiness demands it – to die for the other. In this attitude of holiness, there is a reversal of the normal order of things, the natural order of things, the persistence in being of the ontology of things and of the living. For me that is the moment where, through the human, the beyond being – God – comes to mind. . . . The shock of the divine, the rupture of the immanent order, of the order that I can embrace, of the order which I can hold in my thought, of the order which can become mine, that is the face of the other.[93]

Levinas here delineates his life's work *in nuce*. He also offers what can be presented as a vision statement for his 'mission to the Gentiles.' He enjoins one to suffer, to leave oneself for the only journey worthy of one's departure: the journey to the other.[94] He is quick to note the gravitas of the mission, and seems to insinuate that a willingness to die for the other ruptures being's menacing grip. He accentuates again the goodness beyond being – a goodness better, not stronger.[95]

Implied as well is the notion that goodness and responsibility are cognate, and that harnessed together they yield an 'incontestable value' – that of holiness. Naturally one is now in the realm of the transcendent, yet Levinas was as intrepid in the face of the transcendent as he was obeisant in the face of the other. As will be submitted, it is here in the overlapping – in the locus where the stranger's needs refract the gravity of quotidian life – that space for holiness opens upon the holiness of space.[96] And it is here that the shock of the divine bursts the bustling nothingness bounded by anonymity, revealing the face of the other.

In this seminal interview, where in conversation Levinas pared much of his thought into smaller bites, one is introduced again to his contention that the relation with the other is intractably ethical, hence contextually confirming this overlapping of immanence and transcendence and its betrayal in the face. Here Levinas notes that 'the face is not of the order of the seen, it is not an object, but it is he whose appearing preserves an exteriority which is also an appeal or an imperative given to your responsibility: to encounter the face is straightaway to hear a demand and an order.' Later this imperative becomes 'the commandment to take the other upon oneself, not to let him alone; *you hear the word of God.*'[97] This is the plexus of Levinas, an interwoven structure where the 'stranger-ness' of the other links one ethically to the idea of transcendence. And it all hinges on one word: courtesy.

For Levinas courtesy implies 'ethics before everything else.' It means 'when I say to you, *bonjour,* I have blessed you before knowing you.' It also means that 'there is a holiness in the face but above all there is holiness or the ethical in relation to oneself in a comportment which encounters the face as face, where the obligation with respect to the other is imposed before all obligation: to respect the other, to take the other into account, to let him pass before oneself.'[98] This excessive obligation, this hyperbolic concern, ruptures reality with holiness: 'The human is the possibility of holiness. . . . To be for the other, to respond to the other, to love!'[99]

In his preface to the German edition of *Totality and Infinity*, Levinas, less extemporaneously yet just as rigorously, ties the exigency of holiness once more to hearing the word of God. As Robert Gibbs comments, for Levinas 'holiness, which seems to relate the human and the divine, is translated as a relation between human beings. . . . The desacralization of the world is what allows that full translation of the relations to God to become realized in our relations with other people.' [100] Again the transcendent and embodied merge in responsibility, in what Levinas calls 'the word of God and the verb in the human face' conveying 'a message of difficult holiness, of sacrifice (through) the language of the unheard of, the language of the non-said: Scripture!'[101] Moreover, in "The Other, Utopia, and Justice" Levinas writes of 'the adventure of a possible holiness' and the 'possibility for the human of signifying in it uniqueness, in the humility of its nakedness and mortality, and the Lordship of its recall – word of God – of my responsibility for it, and of my chosenness *qua* unique to this responsibility.'[102]

There is a difficult holiness assumed in works of Levinas where responsibility for the other entails a willingness to substitute oneself for the other.[103] This assumed responsibility is as if an authentic Eucharist, a liturgy for a stranger. In this liturgy there is a possibility for rupturing the enclosed self, for creating a space where obligation can be purified in love. In this space 'Scripture' is the commandment to take the other upon oneself, where the word of God and the verb of the face become one.

Notes

[1] Levinas, *Entre Nous: Thinking-Of-The-Other*, trans. Michael B. Smith and Barbara Harshav (New York: Columbia University Press, 1998) 109.

[2] Ibid., 110. See also Levinas, *Difficult Freedom: Essays on Judaism*, trans. Sean Hand (Baltimore: The Johns Hopkins University Press, 1990) 87; Levinas, *In The Time Of Nations*, trans. Michael B. Smith (Bloomington, Indiana: Indiana University Press, 1994) 153f.; Levinas, *Outside The Subject*, trans. Michael B. Smith (Stanford, California: Stanford University Press, 1993) 51f.

[3] *Is It Righteous To Be? Interviews With Emmanuel Levinas*, ed. Jill Robbins (Stanford, California: Stanford University Press, 2001) 255f.

[4] B. C. Hutchens notes that Levinas 'delights in contradiction, paradox, and circular reasoning . . . intend(ing) to be abstruse and elusive in order to present his ideas in what he regards as the only truly disputatious fashion,' *Levinas: A Guide For The Perplexed* (New York: Continuum, 2004) 3f; See also Colin Davis, *Levinas: An Introduction* (Notre Dame, Indiana: University of Notre Dame Press, 1996), who asserts

that 'much of the difficulty of Levinas's writing derives from the complexity of his prose and the deceptive familiarity of his key terms,' 35.

[5] Levinas, *Difficult Freedom*, xiv.

[6] Ibid., 21f., emphasis in text. This thesis, like most translations, follows the rule of translating Levinas's *"autrui"* as the personal Other, the you – and translating *"autre"* as simply other.

[7] Ibid., emphasis added. Regarding the particular and the universal, Robert Bernasconi notes that 'one can see what Levinas is attempting to do when he looks to Judaism to negotiate the relation between the particular and the universal. Judaism is a particularity that promotes universalism, conditions it. . . .' Bernasconi later warns, however, that 'Levinas is not always Levinasian,' "Only the Persecuted . . ." in *Ethics as First Philosophy: The Significance of Emmanuel Levinas for Philosophy*, Literature, and Religion, ed. Adriaan T. Peperzak (New York: Routledge, 1995) 83f.

[8] "Levinas and Judaism," in *The Cambridge Companion to Levinas*, eds. Simon Critchley and Robert Bernasconi (Cambridge: Cambridge University Press, 2002) 33f, emphasis mine. Consonant with these impressions are thoughts of Levinas from *In the Time of the Nations*, trans. Michael B. Smith (Bloomington In.: Indiana University Press, 1994) 151f. : 'From these insights is derived in particular the astonishing idea of absolute truth splitting, by its very essence, into Christianity and Judaism – two adventures of the spirit that are both . . . necessary to the veracity of the True.' For a perspective, however, on the 'twin dangers' of universalism in Levinas, see Robert Bernasconi, "Who Is My Neighbor? Who Is The Other?" in *Emmanuel Levinas: Critical Assessments of Leading Philosophers*, ed. Claire Elise Katz, vol. 4 (London: Routledge, 2005) 20.

[9] Ibid., 33.

[10] For more on Levinas's heterodox approach to representation and signification, see Mark C. Taylor, *Alterity* (Chicago: The University of Chicago Press, 1987) 201f.

[11] Emmanuel Levinas, *Totalité et Infini: Essai Sur Extériorité, Quatrieme Edition* (La Haye: Martinus Nijhoff, 1971) xif; *Totality and Infinity: An Essay on Exteriority* (Pittsburgh, Pennsylvania: Duquesne University Press, 1969) 22f, emphasis in text.

[12] See Edith Wyschogrod, *Emmanuel Levinas: The Problem of Ethical Metaphysics*, 2nd ed. (New York: Fordham University Press, 2000), where it is noted that totality is 'that view of the whole that destroys the alterity of the Other and is therefore a primal act of violence,' 245. Contradistinctively, Rebecca Comay, through her paralleling Walter Benjamin's and Levinas' notions of proximity, numericalizes totality through a singularity commensurate with self-identity, one reducible to idolatry, "Facies Hippocratica," *Ethics as First Philosophy*, 225.

[13] For more on 'wakefulness as sobering,' see Levinas, "Philosophy And Awakening," in *Discovering Existence With Husserl* (Evanston, Illinois: Northwestern University Press, 1998) 178.

[14] *Against Ethics: Contributions to a Poetics of Obligation with Constant Reference to Deconstruction* (Bloomington, Indiana: Indiana University Press, 1993), 18.

[15] Introduction to *Emmanuel Levinas: Ethics and Infinity: Conversations with Philippe Nemo*, trans. Richard A. Cohen (Pittsburgh: Duquesne University Press, 1985) 13f, emphasis in text.

[16] Levinas even subtitles a section of *Totality of Infinity* "Against the Philosophy of the Neuter," where he likens totality's assimilative properties to materialism: 'We have thus the conviction of having broken with the philosophy of the neuter. . . . Materialism does not lie in the discovery of the primordial function of the sensibility, but in the primacy of the Neuter. To place the Neuter dimension of Being above the

existent which unbeknown to it this Being would determine in some way, to make the essential events unbeknown to the existents, is to profess materialism,' 298f.

[17] "Skepticism and Reason," *Face to Face with Levinas*, ed. Richard A. Cohen (Albany: State University of New York Press, 1986) 163, 172, emphasis in text.

[18] Levinas, *Éthique et Infini* (Paris: Librairie Artheme Fayard, 1982) 105 ; *Ethics and Infinity*, 98.

[19] *Emmanuel Levinas: The Problem of Ethical Metaphysics*, 224.

[20] One who takes a critical stance contra asymmetry in Levinas, however, is Jacques Derrida. In fact, it is Derrida's contention that asymmetry is impossible without symmetry, an assertion he makes clear as follows: 'That I am also essentially the other's other, and that I know I am, is evidence of a strange symmetry whose trace appears nowhere in Levinas's descriptions,' "Violence and Metaphysics: An Essay on the Thought of Emmanuel Levinas," *Writing and Difference*, trans. Alan Bass (Chicago: University of Chicago Press, 1978) 128. Interestingly, Paul Ricoeur voices the same concerns in *Oneself as Another*, trans. Kathleen Blamey (Chicago: University of Chicago Press, 1995) 335f. The most dismissive and caustic critique of Levinas, however, is reserved for Alain Badiou. In his *Ethics: An Essay on the Understanding of Evil*, trans. Peter Hallward (London: Verso, 2001) he calls to task Levinas' inability to convincingly establish the predominance of the other over the same. Badiou notes that 'the ethical primacy of the Other over the Same requires that the experience of alterity (otherness) be ontologically "guaranteed" as the experience of a distance, or an essential non-identity, the traversal of which is the ethical experience itself. . . . The other always resembles me too much for the hypothesis of an originary exposure to his alterity to be necessarily true,' 22f. Reduced, as B. C. Hutchens confirms, this criticism by Badiou essentially affirms that 'the other person resembles the self too much,' *Levinas: A Guide for the Perplexed*, 162.

[21] Levinas, *Totalité et Infini*, 24; *Totality and Infinity*, 53, emphasis in text.

[22] See Levinas, "Transcendence and Height," in *Basic Philosophical Writings*, eds. Adriaan T. Peperzak, Simon Critchley, and Robert Bernasconi (Bloomington, Indiana: Indiana University Press, 1996), 12.

[23] Levinas, *Totalité et Infini*, ix; *Totality and Infinity*, 21.

[24] For more on how Levinas exposes forces of reason that, through the machinations of the state, devolve into a 'repressive justice,' see Robert Gibbs, *Why Ethics: Signs of Responsibility* (Princeton: Princeton University Press, 2000) 97. Moreover, according to B. C. Hutchens, this violence may be traced back to an 'ethically negative technology,' *Levinas: A Guide for the Perplexed*, 132.

[25] Levinas, *Totalité et Infini*, x; *Totality and Infinity*, 22.

[26] Chapter Eight of this analysis focuses exclusively upon Christian implications involving asymmetrical responsibility in Levinas. Noteworthy here, however, is a fascinating parallel between evangelism and asymmetrical responsibility found in William J. Abraham's *The Logic of Evangelism*, (Grand Rapids: Eerdmans, 1989). Abraham, reflecting on the relational nature of evangelism, notes that 'the relation is not, however, reciprocal or symmetrical,' p. 183.

[27] "Ethical Asymmetry or the Symmetry of Mutuality?" *Knowing Otherwise: Philosophy at the Threshold of Spirituality*, ed. James H. Olthuis (Ney York: Fordham University Press, 1997) 141.

[28] Fyodor Dostoevsky, *The Brothers Karamozov*, trans. Andrew R. MacAndrew (New York: Bantam, 1970) 348.

[29] "'I More Than Others": Dostoevsky and Levinas," in *Yale French Studies: Encounters With Levinas* (New Haven, Connecticut: Yale University Press, 2004) 55.

Concerning Levinas's proclivity towards this selection from Dostoevsky, Toumayan notes Marie-Anne Lescourret's opinion that he suffered from a 'citation fetish,' ibid.

[30] For more on the difficulties inherent in circumscribing this overflow of being through language, particularly the ways Levinas's ethical language 'combines a negative and a positive function,' see Paul Davies, "On Resorting to an Ethical Language," *Ethics as First Philosophy*, 96f.

[31] Richard Kearney, *Dialogue with Emmanuel Levinas* in *Face to Face With Levinas*, 30.

[32] See Robert Gibbs, *Correlations in Rosenzweig and Levinas* (Princeton: Princeton University Press, 1992) 182f. As James Wm. McClendon, Jr. notes, from a Christian perspective this obligation to the other is rooted in a communal journey consisting of discipling, going, baptising, and teaching, *Systematic Theology: Ethics* (Nashville: Abingdon Press, 1986) 233.

[33] Michael Purcell, regarding these themes in Levinas, notes that 'Responsibility, as "for-the-other," has the same "for-structure" of the Eucharist. "This is my body which is 'for-you.'" He further notes that the Eucharist, as a work of justice, involves an extreme responsibility not unlike that depicted in works of Levinas, *Levinas and Theology* (Cambridge: Cambridge University Press, 2006) 158.

[34] *A Guide for the Perplexed*, 20.

[35] The same for Levinas is 'the possibility of suspending the otherness of the world by sojourning in it, by being at home with oneself in it. What is other is so only relative to the self. The reduction of the Other to the same occurs in a concrete relationship to the world and is not merely formal,' Wyschogrod, *Ethical Metaphysics*, 245.

[36] Cf. Paul Davies, " A Fine Risk: Reading Blanchot Reading Levinas," *Re-Reading Levinas*, eds. Robert Bernasconi and Simon Critchley (Bloomington: Indiana University Press, 1991) 221.

[37] Levinas, *Totalité et Infini*, 4; *Totality and Infinity*, 34.

[38] Peter Atterson and Matthew Calarco, *On Levinas* (Belmont, California: Thomson Wadsworth, 2005) 7, emphasis in text. See also Richard A. Cohen, *Elevations: The Height of the Good in Rosenzweig and Levinas* (Chicago: The University of Chicago Press, 1994) 164; Andrew Tallon, "Nonintentional Affectivity," in *Ethics as First Philosophy*, 110.

[39] Ibid. Cf. Levinas, "Without Identity," in *Humanism of the Other*, trans. Nidra Poller (Chicago: University of Illinois Press, 2006) 65. See also Ryan G. Duns, "Being in the Face of Nameless Mystery: Levinas and the Trace of Doctrine," *Heythrop Journal* 49, no. 1 (Jan 2008): 97f.

[40] Levinas, *Totalité et Infini*, 13 ; *Totality and Infinity*, 43. Ingredient in this reduction is the concealed difference or ambiguity in Heidegger's ontological difference, noted by Llewelyn as 'the difference between Being and a being present.' Levinas used the term amphibology to denote this difference, "Levinas and Language," *The Cambridge Companion to Levinas*, 126.

[41] See Michael B. Smith, *Toward The Outside: Concepts and Themes in Emmanuel Levinas* (Pittsburgh: Duquesne University Press, 2005) 150.

[42] Levinas, *Totalité et Infini*, 13; *Totality and Infinity*, 43, emphasis added.

[43] *Levinas: An Introduction*, 38.

[44] Introduction, *The Cambridge Companion to Levinas*, 26.

[45] See Merold Westphal, "Levinas's Teleological Suspension of the Religious." *Ethics as First Philosophy*, 153.

[46] Levinas, *Ethique et Infini*, 92 ; *Ethics and Infinity*, 87. In his conversation with Philippe Nemo, Levinas here is responding to the injunction from the face saying 'Thou shalt not kill.' By stating that 'the ethical exigency is not an ontological

necessity,' he still nonetheless concedes that 'murder is a banal fact: one can kill the Other.' Since violence is a key motif in Levinas, and since -- particularly in his later work -- there is a steady polemic between persecution and psychosis, this early disclosure of the emphatic mentioning of murder is essential. For more on this emphasis, see Elisabeth Weber, "Persecution in Levinas's *Otherwise than Being*," *Ethics as First Philosophy*, 73. For an atypical yet trenchant perspective on persecution in works of Levinas, particularly ways suffering 'takes the phenomenon of hatred to illustrate this fact' in light of the 'supreme ordeal of freedom,' see Noreen O'Connor, "Who Suffers?' *Re-Reading Levinas*, 231.

[47] Levinas, "Philosophy and Transcendence" in *Alterity and Transcendence*, trans. Michael B. Smith (New York: Columbia University Press, 1999) 32.

[48] Ibid.

[49] Freedom in Levinas is yoked with responsibility through ethics. As Jeffrey Bloechl point out, 'The themes of individual freedom and responsibility for the other person come together in what might be called the *ethics of respect*, where the term *respect* signifies a concern with that other person *as* other,' *Liturgy of the Neighbor*, 25.

[50] Levinas, *Difficult Freedom*, xiv, emphasis in text. Liturgy for Levinas is commensurate with ethics, as it 'designates the exercise of a function which is not only totally gratuitous, but requires on the part of him who exercises it a putting out of funds at a loss. . . . (As) a work that is effected in the complete dominations of and surpassing of my time, liturgy is not to be ranked alongside of "works" and ethics. *It is ethics itself,*' "Meaning and Sense," in *Collected Philosophical Papers*, trans. Alphonso Lingis (Pittsburgh, Pennsylvania: Duquesne University Press, 1998) 92f, emphasis in text.

[51] See Theodore De Boer, "An Ethical Transcendental Philosophy," *Face to Face with Levinas*, 88f.

[52] See John Llewelyn, *Appositions of Jacques Derrida and Emmanuel Levinas* (Bloomington: Indiana University Press, 2002) 224.

[53] Levinas, *Totalité et Infini*, 104f; *Totality and Infinity*, 130f.

[54] Two salient views regarding representation in Levinas fit here. Simon Critchley argues 'that Levinas's work offers a material phenomenology of subjective life, where the conscious ego of representation is reduced to the sentient self of enjoyment.' Key here is Critchley's claim that it is exactly this 'self of enjoyment' that can be questioned ethically by the other person, Introduction, *The Cambridge Companion to Levinas*, 20. Andrew Tallon adds that is incorrect to make Levinas's ethics depend on nonintentional affectivity solely, noting that the 'rejection of intentionality is a rejection of *representational* intentionality,' "Nonintentional Affectivity," *Ethics as First Philosophy*, 119, emphasis in text.

[55] See Bernhard Waldenfels, "Levinas and the Face of the Other," *Cambridge Companion to Levinas*, 66.

[56] *Emmanuel Levinas: The Problem of Ethical Metaphysics*, 22. See also Adriaan Theodoor Peperzak, *Beyond: The philosophy of Emmanuel Levinas* (Evanston, Illinois: Northwestern University Press, 1997) 29; Andrew Tallon, "Nonintentional Affectivity," *Ethics as First Philosophy: The Significance of Emmanuel Levinas for Philosophy, Literature, and Religion*, ed. Adriaan T. Peperzak (New York: Routledge, 1995). Tallon speaks of the ego's dethronement resulting from being driven out of the 'paradise of enjoyment,' 113.

[57] Levinas, *Totalité et Infini*, 104f; *Totality and Infinity*, 130f. Cf. Levinas's statement that "The other metaphysically desired is not "other" like the bread I eat, the land in which I dwell, the landscape I contemplate, like, sometimes, myself for myself. I can

"feed" on these realities and to a very great extent satisfy myself, as though I had simply been lacking them. . . . The metaphysical desire tends toward *something else entirely,* toward the *absolutely other,' Totality and Infinity,* p. 33, emphasis in text. See also Adriaan Peperzak, "Presentation," in *Re-Reading Levinas,* eds. Simon Critchley and Robert Bernasconi, 63.

[58] Levinas, *Totalité et Infini,* 107; *Totality and Infinity,* 134.

[59] Ibid., 114; 140.

[60] See Atterton, *On Levinas.* 18f.

[61] Levinas, *L'Au-Delà du Verset : Lectures Et Discours Talmudiques* (Paris: Minuit, 1982) 76f. ; *Beyond The Verse: Talmudic Readings and Lectures,* trans. Gary D. Mole (London: Athlone Press, 1994) 58.

[62] Adriaan Theodore Peperzak, *To The Other: An Introduction to the Philosophy of Emmanuel Levinas* (West Lafayette, Indiana: Purdue University Press, 1993) 155. Regarding the above assertion by Peperzak, Wyschogrod begs to differ, noting that 'the elemental *can be dominated or used* but remains essentially what it was before,' *The Problem of Metaphysical Ethics,* 68, emphasis added. We assume dominion to be synonymous with possession.

[63] Wyschogrod, *The Problem of Ethical Metaphysics,* 69, emphasis in text.

[64] Peperzak, *Beyond: The Philosophy of Emmanuel Levinas* (Evanston, Illinois: Northwestern University Press, 1997) 196. See also John *Sallis,* "Levinas and the Elemental," *Research in Phenomenology*28(1998). http://www3.baylor.edu/American_Jewish/everythingthatusedtobehere/resources/jphil_articles/levinas-elemental.doc. (accessed December 9, 2008).

[65] Levinas, *Éthique et Infini,.* 46; *Ethics and Infinity,* 48. See also Roger Burggraeve, *The Wisdom of Love in the Service of Love: Emmanuel Levinas on Justice, Peace, and Human Rights,* trans. Jeffrey Bloechl (Milwaukee: Marquette University Press, 2002), where the *Il y a* is described as 'the most threatening totality, the totality from which every other "totalitarian totality" is derived . . . the anonymous, nocturnal chaos in which everything is reduced to "no-thing" (not something) and "no-one" (not someone), but without there being pure nothingness. In the experience of the "there is," the ego is overpowered by the all-consuming mass of pure, undifferentiated being, through which it is "un-done" from itself. The ego can react to this brutal overwhelming by the "there is" only with horror, with a trembling shrinking form the threat of imminent "de-subjectivization,"' 47.

[66] "Getting Out of Being by a New Path," introduction to Emmanuel Levinas, *On Escape,* trans. Bettina Bergo (Stanford, California: Stanford University Press, 2003) 23.

[67] Levinas, *Éthique et Infini,.* 46; *Ethics and Infinity,* 48.

[68] See *On Escape,* Trans. Bettina Bergo (Stanford, California : Stanford University Press, 2003) 49; See also "Monotheism and Language," in *Difficult Freedom,* 179; *Is It Righteous To Be?,* 55; *Totalité et Infini,* ix; *Totality and Infinity,* 21.

[69] Levinas, *Totalité et Infini,* 118; *Totality and Infinity,* 145.

[70] *Ethique et Infini,* 46f. ; *Ethics and Infinity,* 48f.

[71] Levinas, *De l'existence a l'existant* (Paris : Librairie Philosophique J. Vrin, 1986) 95f. ; *Existence and Existents,* trans. Alphonso Lingis (Pittsburgh: Duquesne University Press, 1978) 53. See also Lars Iyer, *Janus Head, Journal of Interdisciplinary Studies in Continental philosophy, Literature, Phenomenological Psychology and the Arts,* "The Unbearable: Trauma and Witnessing in Blanchot and Levinas," 6 no. 1 (2003): 37-41.

[72] *Levinas and the Philosophy of Religion* (Bloomington: Indiana University Press, 2001) 193.

[73] Levinas, *De l'existence a l'existant*, 95 ; *Existence and Existents*, 53. John llewelyn notes that 'determinacy of being, limitation, is a function of negation, whereas the nothingness of the "there is" is not a nothingness that limits being, but is indistinguishable from being,' *Appositions of Jacques Derrida and Emmanuel Levinas* (Bloomington: Indiana University Press, 2002) 173.

[74] Ibid., 54. Lenka Karfikova sees this existence as an 'independent internal life' not yet liberated and 'called to responsibility and ethical behavior by the alterity of the other,' *Communio Viatorum*, 48 no 2 2006, 117.

[75] See Jeffrey Bloechl, *Liturgy of the Neighbor: Emmanuel Levinas and the Religion of Responsibility* (Pittsburgh: Duquesne University Press, 2000) 134f.

[76] Ibid., 63, emphasis in text.

[77] *Levinas, Judaism, and the Feminine: The Silent Footsteps of Rebecca* (Bloomington: Indiana University Press, 2003) 24.

[78] Some suggest that Levinas seems to 'subordinate the *Il y a* to a certain linearity; thinking it between ontology and "ethics," the ruin of the former and so entrance to – or expression for – the latter,' Paul Davies, "A Fine Risk: Reading Blanchot Reading Levinas," in *Re-Reading Levinas*, 214.

[79] Levinas, *Time And The Other*, trans. Richard A. Cohen (Pittsburgh: Duquesne University Press, 1987) 46f.

[80] For an excellent essay that reduces to formula these two essential statements operational in works of Levinas: *'The self (soi) does not proceed from the other; the other befalls the self,'* see Jean-Francois Lyotard, "Levinas's Logic," *Face to Face with Levinas*, 120f.

[81] Levinas, *Time And The Other*, 48, emphasis in text.

[82] Hent De Vries, in his essay "Adieu, a-Dieu," speaks of this seemingly fundamental absurdity when he comments upon how one 'runs up against a paradox' when attempting to limn the *il y a* in works of Levinas. De Vries further connects this haunting anxiety to the 'silent agony of Abraham' depicted in Kierkegaard's *Fear and Trembling, Ethics as First Philosophy*, 218.

[83] *Difficult Freedom*, xiv.

[84] See Wayne Froman, "Strangeness in the Ethical Discourse of Levinas," *Addressing Levinas*, eds. Eric Nelson, Antje Kapust, and Kent Still (Evanston, Ill.: Northwestern University Press, 2005) 54.

[85] This consciousness of beginning is a moral issue; hence it is critical of implicit models of knowledge that disregard consciousness as sincerity. See Smith, *Toward the Outside*, 189.

[86] *Time and The Other*, 51. See also Levinas, "Language et Proximite," *En découvrant l'existence avec Husserl et Heidegger* (Paris: Librairie Philosophique J. Vrin, 1967) 229 ; "Language and Proximity," *Collected Philosophical Papers*, 119.

[87] *Levinas, Judaism, and the Feminine*, 22.

[88] *Is It Righteous To Be?*, 45f. Cf. Claire Elise Katz, *Levinas, Judaism, and the Feminine*, 22f.

[89] Ibid.

[90] "Encountering the Modern Subject in Levinas," *Yale French Studies: Encounters with Levinas* (New Haven: Yale University Press, 2004) 13, emphasis in text.

[91] *Is It Righteous To Be?*, 77.

[92] Introduction to *Ethics and Infinity*, 3.

[93] *Is It Righteous To Be?*, 47f.

[94] To avoid reducing the relation with the other to another totalized perspective, Levinas resorts to paradoxical formulations designed to deflect ontologism. He thus

speaks of 'relation without relation' in *Totality and Infinity* (79f.), acknowledging the event of and encounter with the other while not situating the engagement in time; 'it is rather a structural possibility that precedes and makes possible all subsequent experience,' Davis, *Levinas,* 45.

[95] See Catherine Chalier, "Ethics and the Feminine," *Re-Reading Levinas,* 126f.

[96] In Levinas's later years there was no distinction between the ethical and the holy. Jacques Derrida tells of 'One day, on the rue Michel-Ange, during one of those conversations whose memory I hold so dear, one of those conversations illuminated by the radiance of his thought, the goodness of his smile, the gracious humor of his ellipses, he said to me: "You know, one often speaks of ethics to describe what I do, but what really interests me in the end is not ethics, not ethics alone, but the holy, the holiness of the holy." And then I thought of a singular separation of the curtain or veil that is given, ordered and ordained, by God, the veil entrusted by Moses to an inventor or an artist rather than to an embroiderer, the veil that would separate the holy of holies in the sanctuary,' *Adieu To Emmanuel Levinas,* trans. Pascale-Anne Brault and Michael Nass (Stanford, California: Stanford University Press, 1999) 4.

[97] *Is It Righteous To Be?,* 48, emphasis in text.

[98] Ibid., 49.

[99] Ibid., 55.

[100] *Correlations in Rosenzweig and Levinas,* 165.

[101] *Entre Nous: Thinking-Of-The-Other,* 199.

[102] Ibid., 231.

[103] Responsibility isolated as substitution is the theme of chapter seven.

Chapter One

Influence and Escape

Levinas's descriptions of the *il y a,* as well as the many other themes and concepts propounded in his works, employ phenomenological analyses. Much of the technical language used in these analyses reflects Levinas's direct tutelage under Edmund Husserl as well as the significant influence of Martin Heidegger.[1] Thus an understanding of these two men's impact on the thought of Levinas is essential. But first, however, Kant's influence on Chapter One

Levinas's descriptions of the *il y a,* as well as the many other themes and concepts propounded in his works, employ phenomenological analyses. Much of the technical language used in these analyses reflects Levinas's direct tutelage under Edmund Husserl as well as the significant influence of Martin Heidegger.[2] Thus an understanding of these two men's impact on the thought of Levinas is essential. But first, however, Kant's influence on Levinas's philosophical ethics, particularly as it relates to an ethics grounded in pure reason, needs to be addressed.

According to Hilary Putnam, within the purview of philosophical ethics in general one can make a distinction between two classes of moral philosophers, namely, legislators and those Stanley Cavell calls moral perfectionists. 'It is not,' Putman states, 'that the perfectionists deny the values of what the legislative philosophers are attempting to do; it is that they believe there is a need for something *prior* to principles or a constitution, without which the best principles and the best constitution would be worthless. Emmanuel Levinas is a 'moral perfectionists.'"[3] Among those listed by Cavell as exemplars of moral perfectionists, according to Putnam, are Emerson, Nietzsche, Mill, and Kant.[4]

Near the end of his 1951 essay "Is Ontology Fundamental," Levinas, in reference to his own 'sphere of relations,' notes 'that which we catch sight of seems suggested by the practical philosophy of Kant, to which we feel particularly close.'[5] In Levinas's case, this 'sphere of relations' is contingent upon what he deems an antecedent and asymmetrical obligation to the other. Because of Levinas's conviction of the a priori nature of this responsibility, he was convinced that ethics is first philosophy.[6] This credo, what Critchley calls Levinas's 'Big Idea,'[7] resonates sympathetically with ideas found in Kant's *Foundations of the Metaphysics of Morals*, particularly as these ideas involve Immanuel Kant's project of an ethics grounded in pure reason.

Kant felt that 'all philosophy, so far as it is based on experience, may be called empirical; but, so far as it presents its doctrines solely on the basis of a priori principles, it may be called pure philosophy.'[8] Moreover, concerning Kant's categorical imperative, particularly 'in accordance with this principle (where) man is an end for himself as well as for others . . . what, in relation of man to himself and others, *can* be an end *is* an end for pure practical reasons.'[9] From Levinas's perspective, this categorical imperative depicts a directive 'of the kind that Kant hastens . . . which finds its concrete realization in the relationship with the other.'[10] So there is in both Kant and Levinas a pure, anarchical, a priori obligation to the other. However, 'for Kant ethics is fundamentally a matter of principles and or reason. . . . For Levinas the indispensable experience is the experience of responding to another person, where neither the other person nor my response are seen at that crucial moment as instances of universals.'[11]

Husserl

Levinas's first major work, a published thesis titled *The Theory of Intuition in Husserl's Phenomenology* (1930), was an ambitious project presenting Levinas's interpretation of Husserl's *Ideas* (1913). According to Andre Orianne, 'One of Levinas's major theses in *Theory of Intuition* is that phenomenology transcends its apparently epistemological point to develop into a full-fledged ontology.'[12] Levinas's studies concerning intuition in works of Husserl inspired him to further pursue human experience as a viable object for phenomenological investigation, noting that as modes of intentionality these experiences were in essence meaningful. Concerned with certainty, Husserl in fact thought any philosophy worthy of the name should be scientific in scope, strictly adhering to the dictates of proof and probity. Robert Manning, moreover, believes that

> Husserl found the absolutely certain foundation for which he was searching in consciousness. We cannot be certain that the thing-out-there actually exists, but we are certain that we have consciousness of a thing-out-there. Like Descartes, Husserl indentified the *cogito*, or the consciousness, as that of which we can be absolutely certain. Unlike Descartes, however, Husserl did not stop there. He maintained that we can be certain not only that we have consciousness, but also that we have consciousness of something. That every

act of consciousness is always consciousness of something is what Husserl means by *intentionality of consciousness*.[13]

Husserl was reluctant to create one-dimensional models depicting unilateral truths, asserting instead that affective modes revealed in sense experience opened up events and horizons of meanings each with its own integrity. These occurrences, moreover, result from a certain 'state of affairs' where 'consciousness finds itself promoted to the rank of an "event" that in some manner unfolds in appearing.'[14] Moreover, Husserl had alluded in his *Ideas* 'to the pure regional essence' where there 'corresponds a regional eidetic science, or, as we can also say, a regional ontology.'[15] Reconfigured in his *Theory of Intuition*, Levinas notes that 'the Husserlian conception of ontology has the particular feature that the structure of being which is the object of ontology is not everywhere the same: diverse regions of being have a different constitution and cannot be thought of by means of the same categories.'[16] Husserl's thought introduced Levinas to a new way of thinking, different from the usual processes involving deduction, induction, and dialectic. Much of this thinking in fact can be attributed to a different philosophical attitude, one convinced of the importance of studying consciousness from a first-person point of view. This first-person perspective views objects of consciousness meaningfully, as a result allowing horizonal or regional phenomenon positions of significance.[17]

Phenomenology

Phenomenology, as Husserl conceived it, is the study of the objects of consciousness. Simon Critchley notes that 'A phenomenologist seeks to pick out and analyze the common, shared features that underlie our everyday experience, to make explicit what is implicit in our ordinary social know-how.'[18] This making explicit occurs by primarily focusing on intentionality as it operates in regions of being (horizons) gathered in peripheral modes of affectivity sometimes hidden in normal conscious activity. Levinas found these regions of being vital in understanding the complexities of meaning and its mode of access:

> Recalling the obscured intentions of thought, the methodology of phenomenological work is also at the origin of some ideas which seem to me indispensable to all philosophical analysis. It is the new vigor given to the medieval idea of the intentionality of consciousness: all consciousness is consciousness of something; it is not describable without reference to the object it 'claims.' The intentional aim which is not a *knowledge*, but which in sentiments or aspirations, in its very dynamism, is qualified 'affectively' or 'actively.' Another idea correlative to intentionality, and equally characteristic of phenomenology is that the modes of consciousness having access to objects are *essentially* dependent of the essence of the object.[19]

Husserl spent his philosophical career attempting to register as concisely as possible the assumed laws governing the relations between the myriad sorts of objects in these regions of being, and Levinas – who in 1928-29 took classes from Husserl — sensed in this new attitude a mathematical clarity as well as psychological acumen. Husserl called this new method phenomenology, as it dealt with *phenomena* (Greek for 'things appearing') in a descriptively rigorous manner. 'In our everyday dealing with the world,' notes Peter Atterton, 'we tend to make various assumptions about the world. We naively assume that the world exists outside us and that the objects it contains exist independently of consciousness. This so-called "natural attitude," according to Husserl, is the greatest obstacle in the way of achieving genuine scientific results in philosophy.'[20]

In order to philosophically contest this natural attitude Husserl utilized a method not unlike that used by Descartes in his *Meditations,* one employing hyperbolic doubt in order to suspend belief in external things.[21] This suspension in effect constituted what Husserl called the phenomenological or transcendental reduction, a process intent on neutralizing one's perspective on lived experiences, hence on intentions.[22] Levinas considered insight into the phenomenological reduction (technically called the *epoché*) seminal. Regarding this reduction, Levinas notes that 'the phenomenological reduction is precisely the method by which we are going back to concrete man. Because of it, we discover the field of pure consciousness where we can practice philosophical intuition. The characters of transcendental consciousness allow us to understand the meaning of this operation.'[23]

Noticing as well the resemblance with Descartes' method of radical doubt, Levinas further mentions that 'instead of positing the existence of the world as we do in the natural attitude, we are suspending our judgment, as Descartes does when he exercises his doubt with respect to all his assertions. But we posit neither the existence not the non-existence of the world. We "disconnect," we "bracket," the position of existence.'[24] In effect neither asserting nor denying existence, Levinas maintains here a neutral position, one essential in studies giving precedence to the ways and manners of things appearing.[25]

According to Husserl, it was not objects in the world per se that were accessible to investigation, but the contents of our consciousness.[26] Moreover, since Husserl insisted that consciousness was always consciousness of something (it was this 'of something' that manifested reality), the things appearing were thus elemental to the essential qualities ingredient to meaning. And as phenomenology sought the fundaments of these things appearing in human consciousness, it found itself persuaded by the notion that the mind was constitutive of meaning. Charting phenomenologically the coordinates of these things appearing in effect was commensurate with implementing a philosophical stratagem.[27] According to Levinas, 'Husserl brought a method to philosophy. It consists in respecting the intentions which animate the psychic and the modalities of the *appearing* which conform to these intentions, modalities which characterize the diverse beings apprehended by experience. It consists in discovering the unsuspected *horizons* within which the real is apprehended by representative thought but also apprehended by concrete, pre-predicative thought.'[28]

It became apparent as Levinas studied Husserl that features and structures relevant to objects of consciousness were not isometric but indeed displayed variable horizons irreducibly distinct.[29] These ontological horizons, moreover, were categorically different in each realm of being — dividing existence into regions, each the object of a regional ontology. These discoveries led Levinas to a radical assumption: 'diverse regions of being have a different constitution and cannot be thought of by means of the same categories.'[30] Essentially this means that there are different structures for these variant regions of being, leading Levinas to conclude that *'To exist does not mean the same thing in every region.'*[31]

Escaping Naturalism

Significantly, if existence is different in every ontological region, then philosophical systems based on epistemology betray at times a dogmatic yet naïve disposition. Essentially contra-poised to the intuitional ontological horizons, according to Levinas this disposition (what Husserl called the 'natural attitude') simply directs itself 'toward the world and posits it as existing.'[32] In this positing, facets of experience may be dubious and statements about them may even be disputed and gainsaid:

> For the purposes of understanding the natural attitude — not for analyzing the problem of cultural relativism — we may say that the truth of the claim to universality implicit in the belief of common-sense men is irrelevant to the phenomenological status of the natural attitude. Whether or not their faith is warranted by anthropological or historical fact, men simply accept the givenness of an intersubjective reality in which essentially the same world exists for all of us. If doubts arise about the world, they make sense only over and against the frame of the world *within* which they present themselves. Whatever the inconsistencies of experience, the natural attitude expects an underlying uniformity, a persistent texture. The bridge between what is given and what is anticipated is the indeterminate penumbra of association which surrounds perceptual experience.[33]

The naïve attitude simply and uncritically accepts things as existing without questioning the meaning of this existence. Furthermore, these constant relapses into underlying uniformity alerted Levinas to the need of sobering up, of constant vigilance against what he termed the 'embourgeoising' witnessed as 'a drowsiness within spontaneous truth.'[34] Regarding this Levinasian circumspection, Michael D. Barber notes that 'When the natural attitude's blinders to Otherness fall from our eyes, we can recognize some of our own intentionalities, including relevances, through which the world is given to us, as never before, as well as recognizing that other intentionalities are possible and that our own are not absolute.'[35] Anticipating later analysis, this vigilance for Levinas assumes ethical status in what he calls 'a permanent revolution.'[36] What is more, within the constraints of this thesis this permanent revolution may be reduced to ethical responsibility.[37]

Conclusions drawn from Husserl led Levinas to accuse naturalism of offering vague approximations of reality.[38] Missing in this hermeneutic, according to Levinas, were meanings intrinsic to the cognitive world, meanings prompting him toward the psychic phenomena implicit in the relations between intentionality and the self.[39] These promptings in turn convinced Levinas that the ego's awakening to its acts could be registered phenomenologically and that intentionality presupposed structures of consciousness:

> It is intentionality as such that coincides with the vigilance of the I affected and already waking. This I is *never numbed to the point of absence*. Even in the passivity of consciousness, where one cannot yet speak of knowledge proper, the I keeps watch. Even if this virtual intentionality must blossom into knowledge and into evidence that bring forgetfulness to the underlying life of the I or that put this life to sleep, the possibility of awakening already makes the heart of the I beat, from the disturbed and living interior, "transcendence in immanence."[40]

Levinas's appeal to the operational and vigilant I, whose passive watching precedes the totalization performed by synoptic knowledge, significantly suggests that Husserl's notion of intentionality so involves the conscious subject that its existence interfaces with things. One here, according to Cohen, witnesses Levinas challenging 'Husserl for his interpretation of the hidden horizons at the heart of intentionality, the intersection of constituting and constituted ... which reproduces and does not undercut the consciousness whose excess it discovered.'[41] In other words, for Levinas an intentionality whose *telos* assumes a blossoming into knowledge and evidence is essentially circumscribed by an irreducible intellectualism. What is more, this conviction led Levinas to conclude that 'for Husserl, being is correlative to theoretical intuitive life, to the evidence of an objectifying act. This is why the Husserlian concept of intuition is tainted with intellectualism and is possibly too narrow.'[42]

Escaping Theory

Much of this phenomenological thought seems inextricably bound in theory. And, even more problematic, it appears that in reality the only thing left after reducing the world is the solipsistic loop of one's own thoughts. This was indeed Levinas's conclusion as well, one that led him to reassume Husserl's famous *epoché*. Positively, the reduction invited one to a philosophical interrogation so extreme it neutralized one's existential place in the world, causing therefore a new perspective on one's life. Problematic in this reduction, however, was its obliviousness to interhuman sympathies. Levinas in fact closes his study on Husserl with a critically engaging comment: 'Consequently, despite the revolutionary character of the phenomenological reduction, the revolution which it accomplishes is, in Husserl's philosophy, possible only to the extent that the natural attitude is theoretical. The historical role of the reduction and the meaning of its appearance at a certain moment of existence are, for him, not even a problem.'⁴³ Then, anticipating his next philosophical venture, Levinas ends *The Theory of Intuition in Husserl's Phenomenology* with a question: 'But isn't the possibility of overcoming this difficulty or fluctuation in Husserl's thought provided with the affirmation of the intentional character of practical and axiological life?'⁴⁴

Levinas is foreshadowing here his disengagement from the scientism latent in Husserl's theoretical framework in quest of a more moral horizon. Intuiting in Husserl a blind spot occluding one's neighbor (Husserl's sociology was ingrown at best, viewing the other merely as an alter ego), Levinas transposed his mentor's phenomenological reduction into an ethical concern for the widow, orphan, and stranger.⁴⁵ Along these lines, Rudolf Bernet is also quick to note Levinas's criticism concerning Husserl's insufficient account of the 'novelty, unpredictability and impossibility' regarding ethical events, a lack of concern further naturalizing the encounter with the other.⁴⁶

By way of summation: Husserl in particular, and phenomenology in general, provided Levinas with an 'intentional analysis' focused solely on 'the search for the concrete (where) notions held under the direct analysis of the thought that defines them are nevertheless, unbeknown to this naive thought, revealed to be implanted in horizons unsuspected by thought; these horizons endow them with meaning.'⁴⁷ And while Levinas never disinherited the methodological implications and applications ingredient to phenomenological research, he did disengage himself philosophically from Husserl's 'theoreticism, intellectualism and overlooking the existential density and historical embeddedness of lived experience.'⁴⁸ Furthermore, notwithstanding the insight Levinas gained through Husserl's insistence on studying existence in all its multiplicity (including valuing the meaning consciousness attributes to objects of the world), there were still axiological lacunae in these investigations. In fact, De Boer argues the point that it is through Levinas's digging deeper into these gaps that a metaphysical dimension is reached, one disclosing a revelation involving 'the condition for the possibility of experience (that) is not experience itself.' ⁴⁹ Stated differently: exceeding a naturalist epistemology is simply not enough if historicity and time, the nexus of society, are subverted in order to accommodate theory and intellectualism. Missing is intersubjectivity and an agential consciousness implicated through time. According to Levinas, Husserl's fascination with things, with objects of consciousness, while involving perception 'in flesh and bones,' — thus privileging the intuitive act with ontological significance — still neglected the ethical significance yielded in responsibility.⁵⁰

For Husserl everything was reducible to the ego.⁵¹ That reduction absolved itself from intersubjectivity, an absolution Levinas found unforgivable. The world for Husserl, furthermore, was a world to be illuminated, comprehended, and possessed; it was chattels, a privileged custody. Worst of all, this possession, due to the monadic condition of its owner, could not be shared. Levinas found this problematic:

> There is another reason why the phenomenological reduction . . . does not reveal concrete life and the meaning that objects have for concrete life. Concrete life is not the solipsist's life of a consciousness closed upon itself. Concrete being is not what exists for only one consciousness. In the very idea of concrete being is contained the idea of an intersubjective world. If we limit ourselves to describing the constitution of objects in an individual consciousness in an ego, we will never reach objects as they are in concrete life but will reach only an abstraction. The reduction to an ego, the *egological reduction*, can be only a first step toward phenomenology. We must discover "others" and the intersubjective world. . . . Here again, the problems of the constitution of the world will arise.[52]

Husserl's reduction to the transcendental ego — his creative subject, his ideal I — thus cornered himself in himself, solitary and solipsist. He was not unaware, however, of this imbroglio: 'When I, the meditating I, reduce myself to my absolute transcendental ego by phenomenological epoche do I not become *solus ipse*? . . . What about other egos, who surely are not a mere intending and intended in me, merely synthetic unities of possible verification in me but, according to their sense, precisely others?'[53]

Finally, Levinas found the concept of freedom troubling in Husserl's phenomenology, particularly its reduction to idealism.[54] Emphasis on intention as aiming, as an accessing synoptic and comprehensive, when brought to light, presented representation as a paradigm of clarity.[55] Ironically the ego, reduced to itself through the operations of the phenomenological reduction, finds itself coinciding with itself, a coincidence felt as freedom. According to Levinas, 'Husserl's phenomenology is, in the final analysis, a philosophy of freedom, a freedom that is accomplished as, and defined by, consciousness. This freedom does not merely characterize the activity of being, but is placed prior to that being; it is that in relation to which that being constitutes itself.'[56] This freedom in being, defined by consciousness, betrays an expropriating predilection Levinas will liken to the domination of totality and the same. Converting involvement in the world into structures of consciousness consuming external objects, the reduction is a crucible of clarity — where freedom is reduced to truth and Being absorbs beings.[57] Later, in *Totality and Infinity*, Levinas extrapolates on this violence of freedom:

> To affirm the priority of Being over existents is to already decide the essence of philosophy; it is to subordinate the relation with someone, who is an existent, (the ethical relation) to a relation with the Being of existents, which, impersonal, permits the apprehension, the domination of existents (a relation of knowing), subordinates justice to freedom. If freedom denotes the mode of remaining the same in the midst of the other, knowledge, where an existent is given by interposition of impersonal Being, contains the ultimate sense of freedom. . . .Freedom comes from an obedience to Being: it is not man who possesses freedom; it is freedom that possesses man.[58]

In the closing pages of his book on Husserl, Levinas states that Husserl's theory-laden system is ill-equipped to face the problem concerning 'the meaning of the very *existence of being*.' He also announces another philosopher, Martin Heidegger, one whom he feels 'dares to face the problem deliberately.'[59] In fact, Heidegger spent his life's work engaging and addressing the problem of the meaning of existence.

From Husserl to Heidegger

An impasse had been reached concerning Husserl's philosophical system, one that seemed inextricably bound in theory. Yet Levinas was indebted to Husserl for teaching him a method, one he would implement throughout his career (but also transgress deliberately). Despite his excessive theoreticism and solipsism, Levinas still admired Husserl, for it was from him that he learned concretely a way of 'working in philosophy without being straightaway enclosed in a system of dogmas, but at the same time without running the risk of proceeding by chaotic intuitions. The impression was at once of opening and method; the sentiment of the suitability and legitimacy of a questioning and philosophical inquiry which one would want to follow "without leaving the ranks."'[60]

So the question at this juncture is how might Levinas escape the aforementioned problems endemic in Husserl and still be a strict follower of phenomenological truisms? Further, how might he implicate these truisms existentially, introducing consciousness into the arena of time and intersubjectivity? And how would these convolve with our theme of responsibilty? According to Robert Manning, Levinas had to be mindful that

> the true follower of Husserl will pursue Husserl's question of the meaning of being in a way that is not hampered or limited by the strictures resulting from Husserl's own excessive theoreticism. Only the one who analyzes human being in all its fullness and not merely in its cognitive aspect, only the one who takes seriously human being's rootedness in time and in history, only the one who tackles the existence of human being as it is actually lived, is really raising in its most comprehensive and profound sense the question of the meaning of Being.'[61]

It appeared that Levinas was now prepared to deliberately confront the problem of existence, the question of being – and that meant addressing Martin Heidegger.

Heidegger, who studied under Husserl as well, had begun to draw followers of his own, and his *Being and Time* (1927) was almost insurrectionary in the way it met and moved phenomenology both radically and irrevocably.[62] Extreme in this work is the shift of emphasis from objects present in consciousness to undetected regions of affectivity. Performing a revolutionary reduction of his own, Heidegger collapses these peripheral horizons onto an ontological ground, announcing this region inaccessible by scientific query yet open to more practical undertakings. 'What is essential about *Dasein* for Heidegger,' Critchley notes, 'is its capacity for disclosure, the revealing of a meaningful and familiar world full of things and persons. One of the most radical innovations of *Being and Time* is that this disclosure is not first and foremost rational, but affective, and achieved through moods and attunements.'[63]

Calling human existence *Dasein*, a modality where being is an issue for itself, Heidegger is keen on isolating these pre-cognitive affectivities.[64] This isolation rivets one concretely in existence, prompting an ambient awareness disabused of theory. 'For Levinas, the exceptional character of Heideggerian ontology is that it presupposes the factual situation, or existential facticity, of the human being. The comprehension of Being ... does not assume a merely intellectual attitude, but rather the rich variety of emotional life through which we relate to the Being of various beings.'[65] According to Levinas, Heidegger's redirection results from his unique contextualization of being: 'Ontology would be distinguished from all the disciplines which explore that which is, being, that is, the "beings," their nature, their relations — while forgetting that in speaking of these beings they have already understood the meaning of the word being, without, however, having made it explicit.'[66]

For Levinas this new thought provided more concrete insight and analysis of the regional ontologies implicit in Husserl. In fact, Levinas made the point in *The Theory of Intuition in Husserl's Phenomenology* that one pursuing Husserl would have to engage the meaning of being. By asserting his proposal thusly: 'We have interpreted the constitutional problems as ontological problems and we have seen their essential task: to throw light on the meaning of existence' — and by immediately following this proposal with the claim that 'Only Heidegger dares to face this problem deliberately, it having been considered impossible by the whole of traditional philosophy' — Levinas announces his involvement with the problem whose object is the meaning of existence.[67]

Levinas was aware that this shift of emphasis implied a renewed focus on the relationship between the embodied self and the ego, noting particularly how threadbare conceptions of vision and intentionality played out in this relationship. As noted by Merold Westphal, 'Levinas teleologically suspends a whole tradition that culminates in Husserl's account on intentionality and Heidegger's of disclosure, a tradition dominated by the metaphor of vision.' Westphal goes on to say that Levinas's lack of reverence regarding these phenomenologies is not a flight from reality 'but the ascent to a higher reality.'[68] This renewed focus, moreover, meant that the various modes of affectivity would be instrumental in providing insight into the practical doings involved in embodied existence. These new perspectives were dependent on more concrete, worldly approaches to existence, many of which Levinas would scrutinize under such affective states as need, shame, nausea, insomnia, and pleasure. A look at *On Escape*, an early work by Levinas, will serve to introduce many of these new perspectives.[69]

In the early essay *On Escape* (1935), Levinas issues forth phenomenological queries into human existence similar to those offered in Heidegger's analyses of *Dasein*. However, according to Manning, 'Levinas's philosophy will interpret human existence differently from the way Heidegger does in *Being and Time* and, accordingly, will offer distinctively different interpretations of the meaning of being.'⁷⁰ Engaging differently the ramifications latent in Heidegger's *ontological difference*, which distinguishes *what is* from the *being* of what is, Levinas in *On Escape* comes straight to the point by asserting that

> The elementary truth that *there is being* – a being that has value and weight – is revealed at a depth that measures its brutality and its seriousness. The pleasant game of life ceases to be just a game. It is not that the sufferings with which life threatens us render it displeasing; rather it is because the ground of suffering consists of the impossibility of interrupting it, and of an acute feeling of being held fast. The impossibility of getting out of the game and of giving back to things their toy-like uselessness heralds the precise instant at which infancy comes to an end, and defines the very notion of seriousness. What counts, then, in all this experience of being, is the very discovery not of a new characteristic of our existence, but of its very fact, of the permanent quality itself of our presence.⁷¹

Here are themes that will resonate throughout Levinas's career. Significant is the semantic play locating the *there is* proximally next to *being*, and the added detail of 'value and weight' to this being, as if quantity now is collateral with anonymous quality. This in essence sketches a definition of being, one revealed in the brutal depth of an inescapable game.⁷² Awakening to this game is an awakening to vigilance, a vigilance that will later modulate into a severe responsibility.⁷³

Another noteworthy theme involves *being* riveted to itself, or of being's tortuous clinging to the ego or self, one that manifests in the aforementioned shame, nausea, and insomnia. Cognizance of these modalities, insofar as there is an awareness that the implicated suffering is its own vehicle of egress, accentuates a methodology of interruption that retards the constant presence of manifold sensations, emotions, and states of mind.⁷⁴ This interruption fixes the ego in its situation, one where antipodal experiences of pleasure and suffering only make more riveting the privation inherent in one's ground of existence.⁷⁵ In a sense, interruption instantiates a pause wherein a retroaction may be effected, a turning away fully aware of the existential toys abandoned to their own juvenilia. 'In turning away from the weight upon the self, the self also turns away from its self. It is important to notice, however, that for Levinas the self flees itself not in the sense that it flees its possibilities, but that it flees itself as it actually is, as that which feels the weight of being upon it.'⁷⁶ François Raffoul comments, in fact, that 'One could approach Levinas's thought as a whole from this effort to exit, or go beyond, and go toward an other that does not come back, and in that sense is Absolute.'⁷⁷ Stated differently, interruption provides a creative pause, one where the intrigues of escape may be implemented. This creative pause is also a precursor of separation, another major motif Levinas will utilize in order to superimpose a temporality, a 'concretized conjuncture,' upon a transcendent milieu.⁷⁸

Being's Dead Weight

Thus we find in *On Escape* Levinas wrestling with both the need to escape and the futility of the endeavor. This situation is contextualized in 'a case in which the nature of the malaise appears in all its purity and to which the word "malaise" applies par excellence: nausea.'[79] Here, in the wrenching torment of nausea, Being in one of its most fundamental modalities portrays a menacing neutrality that further rivets the existent to existence. However, 'There is in nausea a refusal to remain there, an effort to get out.... And this despair, this fact of being riveted, constitutes all the anxiety of nausea. In nausea, which amounts to an impossibility of being what one is — we are at the same time riveted to ourselves, enclosed in a tight circle that smothers.'[80] There is now, furthermore, the realization that the existent is not the overseer of its own fate, but a creature trammeled by destiny.[81]

Levinas's focus on practical existence parallels the thought of Heidegger, particularly as it adumbrates those horizonal areas animated in regional ontologies.[82] These animated areas, however, are still haunted by the vestigial *there is* rumbling in the brute nothingness of anxiety. What is more, according to Levinas emphasis on these affectivities confirms that 'For Heidegger one does not reach nothingness through a series of theoretical steps, but, in anxiety, from a direct and irreducible access. Existence itself, as through the effect of an intentionality, is animated by a meaning, by the primordial ontological meaning of nothingness.'[83] Heidegger's primary concern is with the being of being, with the disclosure and withdrawal of existence, which in effect subtends the existent to this ontological grounding in *Dasein*.[84] For Heidegger 'man's understanding of being is not an isolated faculty, nor merely a part of himself, but determines through and through his whole way of being. Man's way to be is to understand.'[85]

Is this understanding registered from the ego's perspective, where everything is circuited theoretically through self? Or from Being's perspective, as existence discloses and withdraws? Or is being is as being does?[86] According to Jeffrey Bloechl, 'being appears in and through *the* ego, and the ego is singled out, most deeply, as that which and through being appears.'[87] For Levinas, this reversibility, 'enclosing the human spirit in the seamless garment of being as distinct from beings,' depicted a crisis in Western philosophy.[88] A he saw it, Western thought was rooted in ontology. Moreover, this grounding consigned one to an idealism to be passively accepted unless one awakened to a hermeneutic of escape — the serious game.

According to Levinas, one's existential condition, that of shameful nakedness, 'means that we cannot hide what we should like to hide. The necessity of fleeing, in order to hide oneself, is put in check by the impossibility of fleeing oneself. What appears in shame is thus precisely the fact of being riveted to oneself, the radical impossibility of fleeing oneself to hide from oneself.'[89] Certainly one can simply accept this situation. The *il y a* ineluctably rumbles from backstage one's every act of being; and the virulent neutrality of existence still circumscribes as it clings. Added to this, acceptance of being in a sense confirms the fact that being is an issue for itself, that it manifests itself through itself, that it throws itself perpetually into this exercise of being. 'For Levinas,' however, according to Manning, 'the central question is not, what does *Dasein* comprehend about its own being and being in general; rather, it is the more fundamental question concerning the emergence of being out of Being, "the meaning of the fact that in Being there are Beings."' [90] Neither acceptance nor comprehension, however, obviates 'a kind of dead weight in the depths of our being, whose satisfaction does not manage to rid us of it.'[91] Nausea, nakedness, shame, pleasure – each and all signify the circumscription of a corporeal self anchored in substance: a self-positing self persistent, concrete, and engaged.

Being projecting itself and retracting itself, the disclosure and withdrawal of existence, reflect what Colin Davis calls Heidegger's moments of lived time in an embodied situation: 'The *Da* (there) of *Dasein* (literally: being there) indicates *Dasein's* situatedness in time and space; and this situatedness is the inescapable condition which makes it possible for the truth of Being to be revealed. Being cannot be known outside the moment and place from which Dasein understands it.'[92] In addition to this, notes Peperzak, 'the structure of *Dasein* is care, characterized through "thrownness," "project," and "fallenness," and unified by "anxiety." Anxiety is not directed toward any object or particular being; it understands that the end of human existence is neither a goal nor a possible reality which has to be actualized. It is *nothing*.'[93] Being understanding itself: existence being an issue for existence: it appears that Heidegger has swapped Husserl's transcendental ego with Being, owing to the fact that Heidegger 'renews the question of Being and replaces consciousness, which is free and transcendental, with *Dasein*. . . . But Heidegger has knocked consciousness off its pedestal and made the *Da* of *Dasein* the very foundation and condition of its truth.'[94]

Heidegger certainly was a departure for Levinas. By not only focusing on the horizon- affectivities discovered in works of Husserl, but by allowing them precedence, Heidegger in essence performed his own unique reduction. Yet this merely confirmed the Parmenidean notion that being and thought are the same, since many of the operational functions of being mirrored the agential functions of consciousness. Levinas took issue with this monism, declaring in fact that the myriad differences that manifested in embodied existence were not subsumable into one theme or concept – an assertion leading Atterton to claim that 'The plurality of what exists, for Levinas, is not just an appearance, but rather part of the very nature of reality as such.'[95]

The Crossroads

For Levinas, even though Heidegger made allowances for engaging others with his notion of *Mitsein* (Being With), an allowance significant in its ontological concern, still this concession more or less presented others as modalities of being rather than as embodied encounters.[96] Thus Heidegger, in effect, by ontologizing the other's existence, betrays presence as intelligibility

— disclosing moreover being's circumscription, being trapped. In a conversation with Richard Kearney, Levinas discusses at length how this reduction of being into presence essentially subverts interhuman relationships:

> For me, Heidegger never really escaped from the Greek language of intelligibility and presence. Even though he spent much of his philosophical career struggling against certain metaphysical notions of presence . . . he ultimately seems to espouse another, more subtle and complex, notion of presence as the coming-into-presence of being. Thus, while Heidegger heralds the end of the metaphysics of presence, he continues to think of being as a coming-into presence that he denounces. This ambiguity also comes to the surface when Heidegger interprets our being-in-the-world as history. The ultimate and most authentic mission of existence or *Dasein* is to recollect and totalize its temporal dispersal into past, present, and future. Dasein is its history to the extent that it can interpret and narrate its existence as a finite and contemporaneous story, a totalizing copresence of past, present, and future. The interhuman relationship emerges with our history, with our being-in-the-world, as intelligibility and presence. The interhuman realm can thus be construed as a part of the disclosure of the world as presence. *But it can also be considered from another perspective—the ethical or biblical perspective that transcends the Greek language of intelligibility—as a theme of justice and concern for the other as other, as a theme of love and desire, which carries us beyond the infinite being of the world as presence.* . . . So I would maintain, against Heidegger, that philosophy can be ethical as well as ontological.[97]

In Levinas's view, Heidegger's ontology was 'an ontology of the Neutral, an ontology without morals.'[98] And despite his concern for what he considered moral misgivings, Levinas, according to Paul Ricoeur, 'never stopped explaining himself in terms of Heidegger. Because he [Heidegger] was the closest stranger. This [Heidegger's] was an ontology without ethics. And the problem, for Levinas, was to exit ontology and to make ethics the first philosophy.'[99] Nonetheless, by subsuming multiplicities under the concept of Being, Heidegger was operating philosophically from the Western tradition. This tradition, moreover, was chary of the interhuman — hence reluctant (more specifically, unable) to assume the ethical event into a totalizing third term.[100] Heidegger's ethical insensitivity only confirmed the fact that his ontology, radical though it was, was not radical enough to break away from the ontological reduction and its violation of others.[101]

Levinas, even as early as his 1935 essay *On Escape*, was loyal to an unorthodox aspiration. He had sensed the violence prevalent in the 'lower realities' of a philosophical zeitgeist he deemed somnambulant and bourgeois.[102] With uncanny prevision, he also alerts his readers to a revolution, one opposed to the numbing yet violent revelation of being and all its subversive gravitas. 'Such a revolt no longer has anything in common with what opposed the "I" to the "non-I."For the being of the "non-I" collided with our freedom, but in so doing it highlighted the exercise of that freedom.' Bringing our attention back to the serious game, Levinas next asserts that 'the being of the I, which war and war's aftermath have allowed us to know, leaves us with no further games. The need to be right, or justified, in this game can only be a need for escape.'[103]

Levinas was at a crossroads. Husserl's and Heidegger's influence on him was formidable; he always acknowledged their authority. Yet this influence failed to negate his belief that they never properly and sympathetically engaged the other. And here, in this early work *On Escape*, Levinas sketches out for himself and his reader a methodological itinerary, one both bold and merciful. Effectually, to escape being was to begin a journey whose destination *is* the other:

> The urge is creative but irresistible. The fulfillment of a destiny is the stigma of being: the destination is not wholly traced out, but its fulfillment is fatal, inevitable. One is at the crossroads, but one must choose. We have embarked. With the vital urge we are going toward the unknown, but we are going somewhere. . . . It is this category of getting out, assimilable neither to renovation nor to creation, that we must grasp in all its purity. It is an inimitable theme that invites us to get out of being . . . Thus, to the need for escape, being appears not only as an obstacle that free thought would have to surmount, not even as the rigidity that, by inviting us to routine, demands an effort toward originality; rather it appears as an imprisonment from which one must get out.[104]

Lasting Companion

In the preface to his first major work, *Totality and Infinity*, Levinas acknowledges a debt to Franz Rosenzweig, one whose work *The Star of Redemption* (1921) is 'too often present in this book to be cited.'[105] This quote may be applied to the thought of Levinas as a whole, for Rosenzweig's influence never diminished. And while Husserl and Heidegger may have helped Levinas develop a method, it was Rosenzweig that inspired him with a mission. Rosenzweig in fact reinvigorated Levinas's Judaic upbringing, and the thought espoused in *The Star of Redemption* invited Levinas back to these roots. This book marked a milestone for Levinas. Its impact is inestimable. For Levinas, 'Rosenzweig embodied a paradoxical destiny. Doubly an heir of the Enlightenment . . . he would develop a universal concept of the Jewish ethic, adapted to the times of the diaspora. His philosophy of anxiety, combined with the study of Jewish texts, revisited the essential question: What message does Israel have for humankind vis-à-vis Greek philosophy, particularly in light of this covenant, which the non-Jew does not know yet that he can no longer ignore?'[106]

A Hegel scholar, Rosenzweig uncovered a subversive totalitarianism in Hegel's system that alerted Levinas to similar strains he had detected in Heidegger. Significantly, Levinas not only inherited but implemented Rosenzweig's syncretism of Jewish and Christian thinking. Referring to Rosenzweig, Levinas tells us of something 'which is essential. The idea of reconciliation with Christianity. Not a synthesis but a symbiosis, or if you prefer, a privileged neighborliness, a shared life . . . . The truth of Judaism would be the one which is given to a people who are always already "near to" the Lord, but who do not see the world. Christianity would be the truth of the one who is on the road to the Eternal, traversing the world.'[107]

Recalling our theme of Levinas's mission to the Gentiles, noting also how this theme collates with what he called an authentic Eucharist, alerts one to an emphasis in Rosenzweig on mission. For Rosenzweig, mission was exclusively a Christian obligation, one whose task was to faithfully engage a pagan culture and spread the good word. As Cohen suggests, 'Whether Christianity be therefore understood as essentially different from Judaism or whether Christianity is simply missionizing Judaism, the Judaicization of the world, what is clear is that for Rosenzweig it is Christianity and not Judaism which has the task of overcoming paganism and spreading the good word.'[108] Moreover, Judaism was likened to a fire, with Christianity acting as its rays. Judaism, for Rosenzweig, was an inward, centripetal religion, while Christianity, like its rays, moved centrifugally outward. Rosenzweig asserts that the Christian 'is ever and only en route. His real concern is only that he is still and yet on the way, still and yet between departure and goal.'[109] Rosenzweig furthermore viewed time from the template of past-creation, present-redemption, and future-revelation, working these moments around the evening-morning-afternoon services of the Jewish Sabbath. Focusing on this series infused sacredness into history, a sacredness Rosenzweig modeled into the processional election of a people.[110] 'Sacred history is the progressive election of the nations. And this work of eternalization or election is performed, in Rosenzweig's view, by Christianity and by Christianity only.'[111]

Rosenzweig believed that time and history revealed the redemptive process of election, and that this election precipitated a redemption when all would become as Jews, not racially but spiritually.[112] 'The Jews then are waiting for the world to catch up. But the world does not catch up accidentally. Christianity is the sole agent or instrument of the eternalization, hence the redemption of the world, at which time both the Christian mission and Jewish exclusiveness will be superfluous and only truth will reign.'[113] In other words, the truth is for all people, but the spreading of truth is the Christian mission.

Levinas was tremendously moved by this universalizing call, one that reoriented his philosophy, providing religious underpinning to his ethical stance.[114] Most important, it provided a methodological vehicle from the 'us' to the 'others,' rupturing the isolation of being. For Levinas, Rosenzweig

> maintained that the Jew is close to the Lord, that the world is not yet close to the Lord, and that Christianity is the manner in which those who are not close to the Lord go across the world toward Him. The figure of Christ turned toward God appeals to all men; in Judaism there is already attainment, but not for everyone. Thus two different but indispensable moments. Whatever be the contestable parts of this argument, the striking event remains: for the first time in religious history, the announcement of a truth in the form of two truths, susceptible of encountering each other without coinciding. *There is us, but there are also the others.*[115]

There is a way and means of escape from being. And the way through — is the way to — the Other.[116] And the means is through responsibility and deposition, i. e., the sacrifice of self.[117] But before the self can be sacrificed, a Levinasian understanding of its creation is in order.

Notes

1. Robert John Sheffler Manning, Interpreting Otherwise than Heidegger: Emmanuel Levinas's Ethics as First Philosophy (Pittsburgh: Duquesne University Press, 1993). Manning notes that 'Levinas has always insisted, in fact, that his philosophy, from the earliest to the most recent, follows in the phenomenological tradition of his two great mentors, Husserl and Heidegger. Thus to understand Levinas's philosophy, it is necessary to understand its relationship to these two giants of early phenomenology,' 16. For more on Husserl's influence on Levinas, see also Jeffrey Bloechl, *Liturgy of the Neighbor: Emmanuel Levinas and the Religion of Responsibility* (Pittsburg: Duquesne University Press, 2000) 89-91; Richard A. Cohen, *Elevations: The Height of the Good in Rosenzweig and Levinas* (Chicago: The University of Chicago Press, 1994) 116f.; Richard Kearney, "Dialogue with Emmanuel Levinas,"in *Face to Face With Levinas* (Albany, New York: State University of New York Press, 1986) 14-17; Levinas, *Ethics and Infinity*, p. 30; Levinas, *Outside The Subject*, trans. Michael B. Smith (Stanford, California: Stanford University Press, 1993) 38f.; Brian Schroeder, *Altared Ground: Levinas, History, and Violence* (New York: Routledge, 1996) 91.

2. Robert John Sheffler Manning, *Interpreting Otherwise than Heidegger: Emmanuel Levinas's Ethics as First Philosophy* (Pittsburgh: Duquesne University Press, 1993). Manning notes that 'Levinas has always insisted, in fact, that his philosophy, from the earliest to the most recent, follows in the phenomenological tradition of his two great mentors, Husserl and Heidegger. Thus to understand Levinas's philosophy, it is necessary to understand its relationship to these two giants of early phenomenology,' 16. For more on Husserl's influence on Levinas, see also Jeffrey Bloechl, *Liturgy of the Neighbor: Emmanuel Levinas and the Religion of Responsibility* (Pittsburg: Duquesne University Press, 2000) 89-91; Richard A. Cohen, *Elevations: The Height of the Good in Rosenzweig and Levinas* (Chicago: The University of Chicago Press, 1994) 116f.; Richard Kearney, "Dialogue with Emmanuel Levinas,"in *Face to Face With Levinas* (Albany, New York: State University of New York Press, 1986) 14-17; Levinas, *Ethics and Infinity*, p. 30; Levinas, *Outside The Subject*, trans. Michael B. Smith (Stanford, California; Stanford University Press, 1993) 38f.; Brian Schroeder, *Altared Ground: Levinas, History, and Violence* (New York: Routledge, 1996) 91.

3. "Levinas and Judaism," *The Cambridge Companion to Levinas*, 36.
4. Ibid.
5. Basic Philosophical Writings, 10.
6. See Critchley, Introduction to *The Cambridge Companion to Levinas*, 6.
7. Ibid.
8. *Foundations of the Metaphysics of Morals*, trans. Lewis White Beck, critical essays ed. Robert Paul Wolff (New York: Bobbs-Merrill Co., 1969) 4. See also Sebastian Gardner, *Kant and the Critique of Pure Reason* (London: Routledge, 1999) 23.
9. *The Metaphysics of Morals*, trans. Mary Gregor (Cambridge: Cambridge University Press, 1991) 198. See also Allen W. Wood, *Kant* (Oxford: Blackwell, 2005) 81.
10. The Levinas Reader, 206.

11. Putnam, "Levinas and Judaism," 54f.
12. Forward to *The Theory of Intuition in Husserl's Phenomenology*, by Emmanuel Levinas (Evanston, Illinois: Northwestern University Press, 1973) xiii.
13. Interpreting Otherwise than Heidegger, 21, emphasis in text.
14. Levinas, "Hermeneutique et au delà," *De Dieu qui vient a l'idée* (Paris: Librairie Philosophique J. Vrin, 1986) 159f.; "Hermeneutics and Beyond," *Of God Who Comes To Mind*, trans. Bettina Bergo (Stanford, California: Stanford University Press, 1998), 100f. See also Glen Morrison, "Levinas' Philosophical Origins: Husserl, Heidegger and Rosenzweig," in *The Heythrop Journal* 46 no. 1 (2005): 42.
15. Edmund Husserl, Ideas Pertaining to a Pure Phenomenology and to a Phenomenological Philosophy, First Book, trans. F. Kersten (The Hague: Martinus Nijhoff, 1982) 18.
16. Levinas, *The Theory of Intuition in Husserl's Phenomenology*, 3. See also Levinas, *Humanism of the Other*, where it is noted that for anything 'to be given to consciousness, to glimmer for it, the given would have to be previously placed on an illuminated horizon, similar to the word that receives the gift of being understood from a context to which it refers. Signification would be the very illumination of this horizon. This notion of horizon, or world, conceived on the model of a context . . . is then the place where signification is situated,' 11.
17. See Levinas, *Discovering Existence With Husserl*, trans. Richard A. Cohen and Michael B. Smith (Evanston, Illinois: Northwestern University Press, 1998) 80; Leslie Macavoy, " The Other Side of Intentionality," in *Addressing Levinas*, eds. Eric Sean, Antje Kapust, and Kent Still (Evanston Illinois: Northwestern University Press, 2005) 112f; Manning, *Interpreting Otherwise Than Heidegger*, 25.
18. Introduction to *The Cambridge Companion To Levinas*, eds. Simon Critchely and Robert Bernasconi (Cambridge: Cambridge University Press, 2002), 7. Critchley adds that 'On this model the philosopher, unlike the natural scientist, does not claim to be providing us with new knowledge or fresh discoveries, but rather with what Wittgenstein calls *reminders* of what we already know but continually pass over in our day-to-day life. Philosophy reminds us of what is passed over in the naïveté of what passes for common sense,' ibid, emphasis in text. For another fine reading paralleling this Wittgensteinian link to Levinas, see Jean Greisch, "The Face and Reading: Immediacy and Mediation," trans. Simon Critchley, *Re-Reading Levinas*, 77.
19. Levinas, *Éthique et Infini*, 26f.; *Ethics and Infinity*, 31, emphasis in text.
20. *On Levinas*, 12. See also Stephen H. Watson, "Reason and the Face of the Other," *Journal of the American Academy of Religion* 54 no. 1 Spring (1986): 45.
21. See Levinas, Discovering Existence With Husserl, 74-83; Bob Plant, Wittgenstein and Levinas: Ethical and Religious Thought (London: Routledge, 2005) 46; Steven G. Smith, The Argument to the Other: Reason Beyond Reason in the Thought of Karl Barth and Emmanuel Levinas (Chico, California: Scholars Press, 1983) 92.
22. See Hent de Vries, *Philosophy and the Turn to Religion* (Baltimore: The Johns Hopkins University Press, 1999) 212.
23. Levinas, The Theory of Intuition in Husserl's Phenomenology, 147.
24. Ibid. See also Jeffrey Dudiak, The Intrigue of Ethics: A Reading of the idea of Discourse in the Thought of Emmanuel Levinas (New York: Fordham University Press, 2001), 226f.
25. See also Levinas, *En découvrant l'existence avec Husserl et Heidegger*, 139; *Discovering Existence With Husserl*, trans. Richard A. Cohen and Michael B. Smith (Evanston, Illinois: Northwestern University Press, 1998) 124.

26. Cf. Simon Critchley, Introduction to *The Cambridge Companion to Levinas*, where it is noted that the deep structures of intentional life are illumined through the phenomenological reduction, 7.
27. See Levinas, "Meaning and Sense," in *Basic Philosophical Writings*, 36f.
28. Emmanuel Levinas, "Signature," in Difficult Freedom: Essays on Judaism, trans. Sean Hand (Baltimore: The Johns Hopkins University Press, 1990) 291f., emphasis in text. In classic phenomenological description, Husserl addresses these horizons when he says that 'what is actually perceived, and what is more or less clearly copresent and determinate (to some extent at least), is partly pervaded, partly girt about with a *dimly apprehended depth or fringe of indeterminate reality*. I can perceive it with rays from the illuminating focus of attention with varying success. Determining representations, dim at first, then livelier, fetch me something out, a chain of such recollections takes shape, the circle of indeterminacy extends ever farther, and eventually so far that the connection with the actual field of perception as the immediate environment is established, *Ideas*, 102, emphasis in text.
29. It should be mentioned that these horizons became blurred at times for Husserl, as noted by Rudolph Bernet, when, referring to Husserl, he states that 'The interests, methods of approach, doctrines, and also the meaning of the words themselves have become so diverse that one eventually wonders what one is talking about,' "The Encounter With the Stranger: Two Interpretations of the Vulnerability of the Skin" in *The Face of the Other and the Trace of God*, ed. Jeffrey Bloechl (New York: Fordham University Press, 2000) 44.
30. Levinas, The Theory of Intuition in Husserl's Phenomenology, 3f.
31. Ibid., emphasis in the text. See also Levinas, "Signature," *Difficult Freedom*, 292.
32. Ibid., 121.
33. Maurice Natanson, *Edmund Husserl: Philosopher of Infinite Tasks* (Evanston, Illinois: Northwestern University Press, 1973), 24, emphasis in text.
34. Levinas, "Philosophy and Awakening," in *Discovering Existence With Husserl*, 178.
35. "Otherness as Attending to the Other," in *The Question of the Other: Essays in Contemporary Continental Philosophy* (Albany, New York: State University of New York Press, 1989) 125.
36. Levinas, "Philosophy and Awakening," in *Discovering Existence With Husserl*, 178.
37. This reduction to responsibility expressed through perennial revolution for Levinas entails converting the love of wisdom into the wisdom of love. For an excellent study reflective of this conversion, see Roger Burggraeve, *The Wisdom of Love in the Service of Love: Emmanuel Levinas on Justice, Peace, and Human Rights*, trans. Jeffrey Bloechl (Milwaukee: Marquette University Press, 2002).
38. Cf. Bernhard Waldenfels, "Response and Responsibility in Levinas," *Ethics as First Philosophy*, where these vague approximations are called 'empty intention(s),' 43.
39. Charting these reflections, for Levinas, required 'A radical reflection obstinate about itself, a *cogito* which seeks and describes itself without being duped by a spontaneity or ready-made presence, in a major distrust toward what is thrust naturally onto knowledge,' *Ethics and Infinity*, 30.
40. Levinas, De Dieu qui vient a l'idée, 49f.; Of God Who Comes To Mind, 25, emphasis in text.
41. Introduction to Discovering Existence with Husserl, xvii.
42. Levinas, *The Theory of Intuition in Husserl's Phenomenology*, 94. Levinas later feels that this narrowness militates against the metaphysical relation of otherness. He further describes this metaphysical relation in Husserl as disengaged from

intentionality and proximity, hence non-linkable with the subject/object schematic. See *Totalité et Infini*, 81; *Totality and Infinity*, 109.

43. Ibid., 156. Concerning being and theory, Levinas states that 'Being, which is without the density of existents, is the light in which existents become intelligible. To theory as comprehension of beings the general title ontology is appropriate,' *Totalité et Infini*, 13; *Totality and Infinity*, 42.

44. Ibid., 157.

45. See Richard A. Cohen, *Ethics, Exegesis, and Philosophy: Interpretation After Levinas* (Cambridge: Cambridge University Press, 2001) 117f.

46. "Levinas's Critique of Husserl, *The Cambridge Companion to Levinas*, 87.

47. Totalité et Infini, xvii ; Totality and Infinity, 28.

48. Simon Critchley, Introduction, *The Cambridge Companion To Levinas*, 7.

49. "An Ethical Transcendental Philosophy," *Face to Face with Levinas*, 105.

50. Levinas felt that for Husserl perception was characterized by the fact that it had a 'flesh and bones' object upon which to focus, thus bestowing upon it a privileged and primary intuitive act. According to Levinas, perception for Husserl was what gave us being, and by reflection on the act of perception one was able to seek the provenance of this notion of being. See *The Theory of Intuition in Husserl's Phenomenology*, 71. See also Claudia Welz, "God – A Phenomenon? Theology as Semiotic Phenomenology of the Invisible," *Studia Theologica* 62 (2008): 4-7.

51. See Barry Wood and David Woodruff Smith, introduction to *The Cambridge Companion to Husserl*, eds. Barry Wood and David Woodruff Smith (Cambridge: Cambridge University Press, 1995)11; Natanson, *Husserl*, pp. 197f; Klaus Held, " Husserl's Phenomenological Method," in *The New Husserl: A Critical Reader*, ed. Don Welton (Bloomington: Indiana University Press, 2003) 21f.

52. Levinas, The Theory of Intuition in Husserl's Phenomenology, 150f, emphasis in text.

53. Edmund Husserl, *Cartesian Meditations,* quoted in Atterton, *On Levinas*, 13.

54. See Jeffrey Dudiak, The Intrigue of Ethics: A Reading of the Idea of Discourse in the Thought of Emmanuel Levinas, 225.

55. See Levinas, "Ethics as First Philosophy," in *The Levinas Reader*, ed. Seán Hand (Oxford: Blackwell Publishers Ltd., 1989) 77.

56. Levinas, *En découvrant l'existence avec Husserl et Heidegger*, 49; *Discovering Existence with Husserl*, 84. See also Joanna Hodge, "Ethics and Time: Levinas between Kant and Husserl," *Diacritics* 32 no. 3/4 (2002) 118f.

57. See Levinas, "Transcendence and Height," in *Basic Philosophical Writings*, where it is noted that 'The ontological event accomplished by philosophy consists in suppressing or transmuting the alterity of all that is Other, in universalizing the immanence of the Same or of Freedom, in effacing the boundaries, and in expelling the violence of Being. The knowing I is the melting pot of such a transmutation,' 11.

58. *Totalité et Infini*, 15f ; Totality and Infinity, 45.

59. Levinas, *The Theory of Intuition in Husserl's Phenomenology*, 154, emphasis in the text. On Heidegger's influence on Levinas, see Levinas, *Ethics and Infinity*, 39-41; Levinas, *Proper Names*, trans. Michael B. Smith (Stanford, California: Stanford University Press, 1996) 3; Levinas, *Time And The Other*, trans. Richard A. Cohen (Pittsburg: Duquesne University Press, 1987) 44; Levinas, *Discovering Existence with Husserl*, trans. Richard A. Cohen and Michael B. Smith (Evanston, Illinois: Northwestern University Press, 1998) 118; Levinas, *Alterity and Transcendence*, trans. Michael B. Smith (New York: Columbia University Press, 1999) 74; Adriaan Peperzak, *To The Other: An Introduction to the Philosophy of Emmanuel Levinas* (West Lafayette,

Indiana, 1993) 11-14; Sonia Sikka, "Questioning the Sacred: Heidegger and Levinas on the Locus of Divinity," in *Modern Theology* 14, no. 3 (1998):305; Michael B. Smith, *Toward The Outside: Concepts And Themes In Emmanuel Levinas* (Pittsburg: Duquesne University Press, 2005) 62; Edith Wyschogrod, *Emmanuel Levinas: The Problem of Ethical Metaphysics* (New York: Fordham University Press, 2000) 13.

60. Levinas, *Éthique et Infini*, 23f. ; *Ethics and Infinity*, 28f.

61. *Interpreting Otherwise Than Heidegger*, 28. For more on Levinas and the question of being, see Levinas, "Is Ontology Fundamental," in *Emmanuel Levinas: Basic Philosophical Writings*, 2f.; John Llewelyn, "Levinas and Language," in *The Cambridge Companion to Levinas*, 121f; Adriaan Theodoor Peperzak, *Beyond: The Philosophy of Emmanuel Levinas* (Evanston, Illinois: Northwestern University Press, 1997) 10; David Wood, "Some Questions For My Levinasian Friends," in *Addressing Levinas*, 157.

62. In *Ethics and Infinity*, Levinas notes that 'I know that the homage I render to *Sein und Zeit* seems pale to the enthusiastic disciples of the great philosopher,' 41.

63. Review of *On Being With Others: Heidegger-Derrida-Wittgenstein* by Simon Glendinning. *Mind*, New Series 109, no. 434 (Apr., 2000), http://www.jstor.org.stable/2660149.html (accessed March 3, 2008).

64. According to George Drazenovich, '*Dasein* is a German term that is used extensively by Heidegger to explain the existence anything has. It refers to the way a particular thing has of existing. . . . It is a deliberate existential understanding as opposed to a theoretical way of understanding being,' "Toward a Levinasian Understanding of Christian Ethics: Emmanuel Levinas and the Phenomenology of the Other," *Cross Currents* 54, no. 4 (Winter 2005): 52.

65. Simon Critchley, introduction to "Is Ontology Fundamental," *Levinas: Basic Philosophical Writings*, 1.

66. Levinas, *Éthique et Infini*, 35 ; *Ethics and infinity*, 38f. See also Atterton, *On Levinas*, 15; Levinas, *Existence and Existents*, 4; Levinas, *Proper Names*, trans. Michael B. Smith (Stanford, California: Stanford University Press, 1996) 3; Levinas, "Philosophy, Justice, and Love," in *Entre Nous*, 116; Levinas, "Phenomenology," in *Discovering Existence with Husserl*, 43.

67. Levinas, The Theory of Intuition in Husserl's Phenomenology, 154.

68. "Levinas's Teleological Suspension of the Religious," *Ethics as First Philosophy*, 153.

69. See François Raffoul, "Being and the Other," in *Addressing Levinas*, eds. Eris Sean Nelson, Antje Kapust, and Kent Still (Evanston, Illinois: Northwestern University Press, 2005). Speaking of escape, Raffoul notes that 'One could in fact approach Levinas's thought as a whole from this effort to exit, or go beyond, and go toward an other that does not come back, and in that sense is Absolute,' 139.

70. Interpreting Otherwise Than Heidegger, 30.

71. Levinas, *On Escape*, 52, emphasis in text. For more on Heidegger's *ontological difference*, see Smith, *Toward the Outside*, 137; Manning, *Interpreting Otherwise*, 40; Hutchens, *Levinas: A Guide For the Perplexed*, 128; Richard A. Cohen, *Ethics, Exegesis, and Philosophy: Interpretation After Levinas* (Cambridge: Cambridge University Press, 2001) 123; Jean-Luc Marion, "A Note Concerning the Ontological Indifference," *Graduate Faculty Philosophy Journal* 20 no.1 (1998): 25f. For an interesting perspective in one of his later works (1978) on Heidegger's *ontological difference*, see "Transcendence and Evil," *Collected Philosophical Papers*, where Levinas says as follows: 'For the difference between being and beings does not presuppose anything common but the paper on which the words which designate them are written, or the air in which the sounds

which serves to pronounce them vibrate. *The difference between being and beings is difference itself,*' 177, emphasis added.

72. Levinas, in "Reflections on Phenomenological Technique," *Discovering Existence with Husserl,* comments that 'we are straightaway within being; we are ourselves part of its play; we are partners in the revelation. It remains only for us to describe these modes of revelation which are modes of existence,' 97.

73. See Levinas, "Apropos of Buber: Some Notes," in *Outside the Subject,* trans. Michael B. Smith (Stanford, California: Stanford University Press, 1993) 44. In ''Humanism and An-archy,' in *Humanism of the Other* (Chicago: University of Illinois Press, 2006) Levinas states that 'There where I could have remained a spectator, I am responsible . . . Nothing is theater anymore, the drama is no longer a game. Everything is serious,' 55.

74. Wyschogrod points out that these everyday concerns particular to Dasein, the quotidian rounds of humans being human, sometimes mute the transcendence of true authenticity. She thus finds the true task of ontology is that of uprooting Dasein from the trappings of everydayness: 'This enables Dasein to recollect itself, to assume itself; on the other hand Dasein may lose itself once more in the fallenness of inauthenticity. In choosing authenticity, Dasein is deliberately engaged, faithful to itself,' *The Problem of Ethical Metaphysics,* 11.

75. Antipodal conflict depicts the ego or I in works of Levinas. 'The I is the very crisis of the being of a being in the human,' "Philosophy and Transcendence," in Levinas, *Alterity and Transcencence,* trans. Michael B. Smith (New York: Columbia University Press, 1999) 28.

76. Manning, Interpreting *Otherwise Than Heidegger,* 32.

77. "Being and the Other," in *Addressing Levinas,* eds. Eris Sean Nelson, Antje Kapust, and Kent Still (Evanston, Illinois: Northwestern University Press, 2005) 139.

78. In *Totality and Infinity* Levinas makes mention of how the isolation of the same is a 'psychism' that constitutes an event in being. Unique to this pyschism is a paradox: namely, a chronological order distinct from logical order, one where progression in effect reflects what Levinas terms 'separation,' 54; *Totalité et Infini,* 24f. See also ''Enigma and Phenomena" in *Basic Philosophical Writings,* 69.

79. Levinas, De l'existence a l'existant, 30; Existence and Existents, 10.

80. *On Escape,* 66. See also Michael Brogan, "Nausea and the Experience of the Il Y A: Sartre and Levinas on Brute Existence,' *Philosophy Today* July (2001), http://www.highbeam.com/doc/1P3-75424066.html (accessed Oct. 23, 2007).

81. Ibid, 72. See also Levinas, "Transcendence and Height," in *Basic Philosophical Writings,* 21.

82. See Smith, *Toward the Outside,* 59f.

83. Levinas, Éthique et Infini, 37 ; Ethics and Infinity, 40f.

84. According to Paul Ricoeur, 'Being is clearly otherwise than entities. . . . Essence is the very fact that there is theme, ostension, *doxa or logos,* and thus truth,' "Otherwise: A Reading of Emmanuel Levinas's *Otherwise than Being or Beyond Essence,*" in *Yale French Studies: Encounters With Levinas* (New Haven, Connecticut: Yale University Press, 2004) 89.

85. Madga King, *A Guide to Heidegger's* Being and Time (Albany: State University of New York Press) 20.

86. Richard Polt insightfully notes that 'asking about Being is not like asking about a typewriter. . . . We are asking about a "thing" that is no thing at all,' *Heidegger: An Introduction* (Ithaca, New York: Cornell University Press, 1999) 28.

87. Liturgy of the Neighbor: Emmanuel Levinas and the Religion of Responsibility (Pittsburgh, Pennsylvania: Duquesne University Press, 2000) 107.

88. Ibid. See also Levinas, "Is Ontology Fundamental," in *Basic Philosophical Writings*, where the point is made that 'To comprehend our situation in reality is not to define it but to find ourselves in an affective disposition. To comprehend being is to exist. All this indicates, it would seem, a rupture with the theoretical structure of Western thought. To think is no longer to contemplate but to commit oneself, to be engulfed by that which one thinks, to be involved. This is the dramatic event of being-in-the-world,' 4.

89. Levinas, *On Escape*, 64.

90. Interpreting Otherwise Than Heidegger, 41; citation from Existence and Existents, 101.

91. Levinas, *On Escape*, 60.

92. *Levinas*, 15. See also Sonia Sikka, "Questioning the Sacred: Heidegger and Levinas on the Locus of Divinity" *Modern Theology* 14 no. 3 (1998): 305.

93. *Beyond*, 48.

94. Ibid., 16.

95. *On Levinas*, 6; See also Levinas, "Meaning and Sense," in *Basic Philosophical Writings*, 46.

96. 'Clearly, in Heidegger the way to authenticity is the way away from sociality, which is primarily a polluting and distorting influence, and toward solitude and invidualization.... This is why Levinas says in Heidegger authentic *Dasein* is informed primarily by solitude rather than by the social relation,' Manning, *Interpreting Otherwise Than Heidegger*, 51.

97. *Face to Face With Levinas*, 20f, emphasis added.

98. Levinas, Éthique et Infini, 94f. ; Ethics and infinity, 90.

99. Quoted in Salomon Malka, *Emmanuel Levinas: His Life and Legacy*, trans. Michael Kigel and Sonja M. Embree (Pittsburgh: Duquesne University Press, 2002) 198.

100. According to Levinas, 'A relation whose terms do not form a totality can hence be produced within the general economy of being only as proceeding from the I to the other, as a *face to face*, as delineating a distance in depth – that of conversation, of goodness, of Desire – irreducible to the distance the synthetic activity of the understanding establishes between the diverse terms, other with respect to one another, that lend themselves to its synoptic operation,' *Totalité et Infini*, 9; *Totality and Infinity*, 39, emphasis in text.

101. See Steven G. Smith, *The Argument To The Other: Reason Beyond Reason in the Thought of Karl Barth and Emmanuel Levinas* (Chico, California: Scholars Press, 1983). Smith notes that Heidegger's thought, despite its innovation, is still an ontologism reflective of 'ethical and political insensitivity,' 67.

102. Levinas, *On Escape*, 53.

103. Ibid.

104. Ibid., 54

105. Totalité et Infini, xvi; Totality and infinity, 28.

106. Malka, *Levinas*, 63. For more on Rosenzweig's influence on Levinas, see Roger Burggraeve, *The Wisdom Of Love In The Service Of Love: Emmanuel Levinas On Justice, Peace, And Human Rights*, trans. Jeffrey Bloechl (Milwaukee, Wis.: Marquette University Press, 2002) 35; Tina Chanter,"Levinas and Impossible Possibility: Thinking ethics with Rosenzweig and Heidegger in the wake of the Shoah," *Research in Phenomenology*, 1998, Vol. 28, 91; Cohen, *Elevations*, 162-172; Davis, *Levinas*, 100; Theodore De Boer, "An

Ethical Transcendental Philosophy," in *Face To Face With Levinas*, 83; Robert Gibbs, *Why Ethics? Signs of Responsibility* (Princeton, New Jersey: Princeton University Press, 2000) 227-240; Jean Greisch, "The Face And Reading: Immediacy and Mediation," trans. Simon Critchley, in *Re-Reading Levinas*, eds. Robert Bernasconi and Simon Critchley (Bloomington, Indiana: Indiana University Press) 69; Susan Handelman, "Facing the Other: Levinas, Perelman and Rosenzweig," *Religion and Literature*, 22, 2-3, 1990, 61f.; John Llewelyn, *Appositions of Jacques Derrida and Emmanuel Levinas* (Bloomington, Indiana: Indiana University Press, 2002) 94; Smith, *Toward the Outside*, 62.

107. Robbins, *Interviews With Levinas*, 95. Consonant with these impressions are the thoughts from *In the Time of the Nations*, trans. Michael B. Smith (Bloomington In.: Indiana University Press, 1994) 151f. : 'From these insights is derived in particular the astonishing idea of absolute truth splitting, by its very essence, into Christianity and Judaism – two adventures of the spirit that are both ... necessary to the veracity of the True.' See also Michael Mack, "Franz Rosenzweig's and Emmanuel Levinas's Critique of German Idealism's Pseudotheology," *Journal of Religion* 83 no. 1 (2003): 63.

108. *Elevations: The Height of the Good in Rosenzweig and Levinas* (Chicago: The University of Chicago Press, 1994) 21. See also Robert Gibbs, *Correlations in Rosenzweig and Levinas* (Princeton: Princeton University Press, 1992) 4.

109. Franz Rosenzweig, *The Star of Redemption*, trans. William W. Hallo (Boston: Beacon Press, 1972) 339.

110. Commenting on how these progressions constitute a 'Christian Chronology,' Rosenzweig mentions how 'All the time that succeeds, from Christ's earthy sojourn to his second coming, is now that sole great present, that epoch, that standstill, that suspension of the times, that interim over which time has lost its power. Time is now mere temporality. As such it can be surveyed in its entirety from any one of its points, for beginning and end are equidistant from each of its points. Time has become a single way, but a way whose beginning and end lie beyond time, and thus an eternal way,' *The Star of Redemption*, 338f.

111. Cohen, *Elevations*, 13.

112. For more on Rosenzweig's notion of universal redemption, see Splenger, "Christian, Muslim, Jew: Franz Rosenzweig and the Abrahamic Religions," *First Things* no 176 O (2007): 29-33; Paul Golomb, "A Matter of Time: The Jew, Christian, and Muslim in Conversation," *Cross Currents* 54 no 4 Wint (2005)18-24; Jeremy Worthen, "Beginning Without End: Christianity in Franz Rosenzweig's *Star of Redemption*," *Journal of Ecumenical Studies* 39 no 3-4 Sum-Fall (2002): 348-352.

113. Cohen, *Elevations*, 14. See also Bettina Bergo, "Is There a Correlation Between Rosenzweig and Levinas?" *Jewish Quarterly Review* 96, no. 3 (2006): 404f.

114. For a detailed analysis concerning Levinas's debt to Rosenzweig, see Levinas, "Between Two Worlds," *Difficult Freedom*, 181-201.

115. *Is It Righteous to Be?* 71, emphasis added.

116. Levinas, "Exercises on 'The Madness of the Day,'" in *Proper Names*, trans. Michael B. Smith (Stanford, California: Stanford University Press, 1996), gnomically encapsulates this proposal thusly: 'Relation to the other – a last way out,' 165.

117. As Levinas states in *Ethics and Infinity*, 'It is I who support the Other and am responsible for him. One thus sees that in the human subject, at the same time as a total subjection, my primogeniture manifests itself. My responsibility is untransferable, no one could replace me. In fact, it is a matter of saying the very identity of he human I starting from responsibility, that is, starting from this position

or deposition of the sovereign I is in self consciousness, a deposition which is precisely its responsibility for the Other,' pp. 100f; *Éthique et Infini*, 107f.

Chapter Two

Positioning

In *On Escape* Levinas set the task — getting out of being. He also issued a challenge, noting that 'Every civilization that accepts being — with the tragic despair it contains and the crimes it justifies — merits the name "barbarian."'[1] And the 1940's would witness Levinas's thought formulating around a counter-ontology that would reflect his hermeneutic of escape. *Existence and Existents* (1947) finds Levinas again attending to the relationship and distinction between beings and Being, the same distinction witnessed in Heidegger's *ontological difference*.[2] Beginning with the haunting and anonymous *il y a* discussed earlier, Levinas presents the emergence of human subjectivity contradistinctive the fluidity of Being.[3] Significant in this work, notes Robert Bernasconi, is Levinas's approaching 'the relation of beings to Being not as something given, but as an accomplishment.'[4] Levinas, moreover, likens this accomplishment to 'a process of auto-position in our existence, by which a domain of inwardness and privacy is established, by which a stance is first possible, by which substance takes form, by which the identity of an existent that is in itself is effected.'[5]

Due to the fact that existence and the existent exist in different ways, Levinas involves his discussion with various moods — states such as fatigue, indolence, and insomnia — in order implement a distinction. Llewelyn, calling this syndrome of moods 'ontological claustrophobia,' further notes that they facilitate Levinas's 'pointing to a powerlessness beyond the power of the self.'[6] Further, in order to introduce a distance between existence and the existent, Levinas hones in on these moods in order to animate various affectivities and tonalities normally unintelligible.[7] Ambient awareness of these tonalities alerts one to the present, where the relationship between the existent and existence, between beings and Being, is distinguished by the drag of indolence. Notable here is what is called the 'instant of the effort,' a creative lunge where 'effort lurches out of fatigue and falls back into fatigue.'[8] Calling this lunge and retraction 'the creative moment of force,' Levinas makes the assertion that 'Effort is not a cognition; it is an event,' emphasizing that 'it is by starting with the instant of effort and its internal dialectics that we shall perhaps be able to grasp the notion of activity and its role in human existence.'[9] In this laboring in and of the moment, time assumes a creative duration commensurate with the instantiating effort.[10]

Engaging the moment involves the existent in an ontological adventure, one where action and resistance are constitutive: 'To act is to take on the present.'[11] In this agency, according to Adriaan Peperzak, 'The past and the future are presented as secondary forms of the present; remembrance and expectation bring them back or reduce them to the presence of a thought that ties all faces of temporality together in a supratemporal, eternal, "Now."'[12] Consequential is the existent's positing itself, assuming form even amidst the fatigue prompted by the tarrying drag of existence. This drag produces a distancing in existence evidenced by the 'relationship between an existent and itself. It is the upsurge of an existent in existence. And conversely this almost self-contradictory moment of a present that tarries behind itself could not be anything but fatigue; Fatigue does not accompany it, it effects it; fatigue is this time-lag.'[13] Levinas now describes the creation of the subject, a monumental occurrence in his saga of escape:

> If the present is thus constituted by the taking charge of the present, if the time-lag of fatigue creates the interval in which the event of the present can occur, and if this event is equivalent to the upsurge of an *existent* for which *to be* means *to take up being*, the existence of an existent is by essence an activity. An existent must be in act, even when it is inactive. This activity of inactivity is not a paradox; it is the act of positing oneself on the ground, it is rest inasmuch as rest is not a pure negation but the very tension of a position, the bringing about of a *here*. The fundamental activity of rest, foundation, conditioning, thus appears to be the very relationship with being, the upsurge of an existent into existence, a hypostasis.[14]

Hypostasis is an essential event in Levinas, as it not only depicts the birth of subjectivity, but also depicts the drama of separation between the ego and the self.[15] In this drama, 'existing involves a relationship by which the existent makes a contract with existence. There is a duality in existence, an essential lack of simplicity. The ego has a self, in which it is not only reflected, but with which it is involved like a companion or partner; this relationship is what is called inwardness.'[16] Consciousness, the hypostasized corporal self, now becomes explicit to itself in inwardness, bathed in an intelligible medium of light.[17] Moreover, consciousness, participating in wakefulness, 'contains a shelter from that being with which, depersonalized, we make contact in insomnia, that being which is not to be lost or duped or forgotten, which is, if we may hazard the expression, completely sobered up.'[18] Being sobered up is a being awakened.[19]

The Present (The Exceptional Situation)

Levinas, in presenting these myriad moods and affectations, must employ descriptive analyses beyond the ken of phenomenology. Thus he implements a poetic language more attuned to a fluidity 'which eludes descriptive phenomenology. Here description would make use of terms while striving to go beyond their consistency; it stages *personages*. . . . A method is called for such that thought is invited to go beyond intuition.'[20] Staged personages aptly describe what figures in Levinas's style here, as form and content seem to blend with the dreamy occurrences of sleep, relaxation, and drowsiness.

Again we meet the *il y a* as attention, presupposing a free ego, manifests as vigilance. Claire Elise Katz believes that 'although consciousness participates in this vigilance, it cannot deliberately withdraw into sleep; insomnia prevents consciousness from escaping itself.'[21] Levinas sees this participation as a raw tearing, noting that 'we are, thus, introducing into the impersonal event of the *there is* not the notion of consciousness, but of wakefulness, in which consciousness participates. Consciousness is a part of wakefulness, which means that it has already torn into it.'[22] Paul Davis finds a strange medium as he examines 'the way in which Levinas would sometimes seem to subordinate the *il y a* to a certain linearity, thinking it between ontology and ethics. . . .'[23] Additionally, Davis concludes that the reduction of ontology in Levinas allows a more vivid expression of the ethical, particularly as experienced in the teleology of desire.[24]

Levinas now, contra-intuitively it would seem, distinguishes consciousness by contrasting the *there is* through its ability to sleep with the biblical story of Jonas. This analogy not only illustrates this relationship, but serves Levinas as a vehicle for presaging a seminal theme to be addressed later: the trace. Remember Jonas had attempted the impossible: to flee from god. Michael Smith provides the connections:

> As the elements are raging about him, he descends into the hull of the ship and goes to sleep. Sleep is thus a dimension of consciousness into which consciousness can disappear, and from which it can reemerge. There are many crossings between sleep and wakefulness, for there is a whole backdrop on unconsciousness, astir with whisperings, behind consciousness. Levinas compares the consciousness-unconsciousness manifold to the wink, which is made up of a looking and a not looking. (He also) uses a term not unrelated to the wink that will reappear in his later writings: the *scintillement* or *clignotement*, a twinkling, the pulsation of light that is also used to indicate the manifestation, in the modality of ambiguity, of the infinite or the transcendent in being . . . . Levinas is able to preserve the modality of ambiguity – the wavering per se – not as a deficient mode of certainty or a lack of clarity, but as an original structure of presentation: that of the infinite in the finite, later refered to as "the trace."'[25]

Again the lag, the interruption, establishes itself as the wink, looking and not looking, mirroring a present always trying to catch up with itself, or (like Jonas) always caught in retreat. In his study *By Way of Interruption*, Amit Pinchevski captures this dragging exasperation depicted by Levinas when he notes that 'there is always something that escapes presence, that is, the Other's alterity. Interruption thus signifies a certain absence, a withdrawal from presence.'[26]

Consciousness coming out of rest, de-positioning itself — then coming to itself — in effect suspends the subject while attenuating the subject.[27] This self destruction, witnessed as a disintegration of hypostasis, is positively pronounced as an overwhelming emotion.[28] Emotion in Levinas, what Bettina Bergo calls 'a sensuous understanding without comprehension,' thus anchors the subject while destabilizing the subject[29] — prompting a fundamental vertigo haunted by the abysmal, chaotic *there is*.[30] Oddly, then, this twinkling of consciousness, this surrendering to sleep followed by resurgence, implies a position preceding understanding, in effect modulating the emotional bearings of consciousness into states which assume stances through these positionings. Apropos this twinkling, Alphonso Lingis allows that 'from the earliest texts Levinas set out to show how consciousness does not go without unconsciousness.'[31] Notwithstanding this flickering, however, Levinas is firm in asserting that 'place . . . is a base. This is what makes the body the very event of consciousness. It is nowise a thing . . . it is a position. It is not situated in a space given beforehand; it is the irruption in anonymous being of localization itself.'[32]

Here are thematic sketches, adumbrations of themes, which will be developed more fully later in Levinas. Key features attributable to the notion of the present will transpose into constituents of being — particularly as the ontological adventure manifests in moments or modalities of what Levinas will later call essence.[33] Also, Levinas's notion of 'the return of the present to itself' will emerge in his motif of recurrence, along with the idea of the self 'riveted to itself,' demonstrating the polarity within the ego and the self.[34] For now, however, these modalities are contingent on the notion of the present, particularly as it is put forward in its evanescence. Again, the logic of interruption, the drag of duration, is agential in the event of being. Regarding this point, Wyschogrod says that 'Levinas argues from the premise that power belongs to potentiality and not to act,' leading her to assert that 'the event of existence must also differ from the realization of a previously existent goal.'[35] Levinas speaks to this event as follows:

> Its evanescence is the ransom paid for its subjectivity, that is, for the transmutation, within the pure event of being, of an event into a substantive – a hypostasis. Of itself time resists any hypostasis; the images of current and flux with which we explain it are applicable to beings in time, and not to time itself. Time does not flow like a river. But the present brings about the exceptional situation where we can give an instant a name, and conceive it as a substantive. . . . The present is a halt, not because it is arrested, but because it interrupts and links up again to the duration to which it comes, out of itself. Despite its evanescence in time, in which alone it has been envisaged, or rather because of that evanescence, it is the effectuation of a subject.[36]

Man Alone

Levinas at this early stage has established subjectivity, a key concept involved in responsibility. This involvement is not unusual, for, as notes Mark C. Taylor, 'The distinguishing characteristic of modern philosophy is its tendency to think Being in terms of subjectivity,' marking the subject as 'essentially *creative* or *constructive*.'[37] Levinas has also introduced constitutive modalities reflective of the contingencies of the present, plus established the dialectic between the ego and the self.[38] He has implemented a hermeneutic of interruption that retards time as it inflects consciousness. He has also, through his characterization of being, smudged the distinction between consciousness and unconsciousness by his methodological use of the *scintellement*, or wink, whose manifestation accentuates ambiguity.

These fundamental analyses all presuppose a created and creative subjectivity: a subjectivity that, according to Levinas, is both position and event.[39] Moreover, it is in the mercurial transition from event to entity that the "I" assumes status, one in fact closely related to the present, as both are constituted by the self-referential movement of recurrence: 'The "I" has to be grasped in its amphibiological mutation from an event into an "entity," and not in its objectivity. It consists in this *original* possession of being, in which the "I" nevertheless reverts ineluctably to itself.... The present and the "I" are the movement of self-reference which constitutes reality.'[40] This process, characterized by the *substancing* of events, and the *eventing* of substance, presents 'an instant (that is) like a breathlessness, a panting, an effort to be. The freedom of the present finds a limit in the responsibility for which it is the condition. This is the most profound paradox in the concept of freedom: its synthetic bond with its own negation. A free being alone is responsible, that is, already not free.'[41]

Here is one of the earliest mentionings in Levinas of the antipodal relation between freedom and responsibility. Didier Franck captures this moment well: 'Now, if the substantial subject is free, it is – in the self-reference of the present, prisoner of itself. At the instant of its initiation in Being, the subject is thus free and not free, taking charge and taken in charge.'[42] This is a fundamental junction. The subject exists in its taking a position, an effort consubstantiating it with the world and with light. This event is localized as the emergence of a self, where consciousness and position vie on the boundary of unconsciousness bordered by sleep.[43] And the *there is*, as always, participates anonymously and subversively, circumscribing the ego as it reverberates in the infinite chasm riveting existents to existence, beings to being.[44]

Hence freedom is contingency, conditioned from 'a moment of a deeper drama which does not play itself out between a subject and objects – things or events – but between the mind and the fact of the *there is*, which it takes up. *It is enacted in our perpetual birth*.'[45] In this perpetual birth, freedom blanches when faced with the brute fact of existence, from the ineluctable truth pinioning the ego to its own being – and this truth, according to Levinas, manifests as solitude steeped in injustice.[46] Here is the crude reality as Levinas now presents it: In a world corded of light, intentions, and desire — the ego cannot evade itself. In fact, it is stuck to itself. This fact defines its solitude.[47]

Again one comes to a crossroads in Levinas's thought. The ego, closed up in existence, finds its solitude categorical. Objects of light clothed in being, everything Levinas calls the understood universe, are essentially reducible to an ego that is alone. The only way out is the other. In a monumental passage, Levinas asserts that

> solitude is accursed not of itself, but by reason of its ontological significance as something definitive. Reaching the other is not something justified of itself; it is not a matter of shaking me out of my boredom. It is, on the ontological level, the event of the most radical breakup of the very categories of the ego, for it is for me to be somewhere else than my self; it is to be pardoned, to not be a definite existence. The relationship with the other is not to be conceived as a bond with another ego, not as a comprehension of the other which makes his alterity disappear, nor as a communion with him around some third term. ... Phenomenological description, which by definition cannot leave the sphere of light — that is, man alone shut up in his solitude, anxiety and death as an end, whatever analyses of the relationship with the other it may contribute, will not suffice. Qua phenomenology it remains within the world of light, the world of the solitary ego which has no relationship with the other qua other, for whom the other is another for me, an alter ego known by sympathy, that is, by a return to oneself.[48]

The relationship with the other occurs within the dialectic of time. And the radical ontological breakup of the categories of the ego is circumscribed by this dialectic.[49]

Towards Time

With the other comes time and the giving over to patience. Jill Robbins suggests that 'to be patient means to be given over to the future ... (a future) not to be confused with the time of personal immortality — to be patient is to go beyond the horizon of *my* time, beyond the being unto death. Yet the absolutely patient action is ethics itself.'[50] The solitary subject, burdened by the present, undone by the thought of freedom, discovers that time is not the vagary of motion, but is indeed constituted by the relationship with the other: 'Is not sociality something more than the source of our representation of time: is it not time itself?... The dialectic of time is the very dialectic of the relationship with the other, that is, a dialogue which in turn has to be studied in terms other than those of the dialectic of the solitary subject.'[51] This relationship is specifically reintroduced in a series of lectures presented by Levinas, published also in 1947. As maintained by Richard Cohen, *Time and the Other* 'begins with existence without existents, describes the origination of the distinct existent, the subject, then moves to the progressively more complex constitutive layers of subjectivity.'[52] Again Levinas begins with the *there is*, and again he ends with the enigma of the other.

In *Existence and Existents* Levinas presents instants in time as the subject's escape from the *il y a*, as an unavoidable burden of being chained to oneself, where the relationship between beings and being emerges in time as the weight of existence on the existent. In *Time and the Other* the instant arises again as the manifestation of the subject being out of phase with itself, of its attempt to rid itself of being anchored to itself. Levinas emphasizes that time must be addressed in its full dimensionality. For Rudolf Bernet, this emphasis 'invokes re-commencement, forgiveness, and hope in order to illustrate how the present, past, and future of my life come to me from the other. Only the "instant" linked to the unexpected upsurge of the other can change my life to the point of forcing or allowing me to re-commence from the beginning.'[53] Corroborating, Cohen allows that

> for Levinas, the classical conception cannot account for the "fact" – which is the core of Levinas's own theory of time – that the other person encountered face-to-face is not the subject's contemporary, that they do not meet one another "at the same time." The time of the Other and my time, or the times of mineness, ecstatic temporalities, do not occur at the same time. Veritable time, in Levinas's sense, is the effect or event of the disjointed conjunction of these two different times: the time of the Other disrupts or interrupts my temporality. It is this upset, this insertion of the Other's time into mine, that establishes the alterity of veritable time, which is neither the Other's time nor mine.[54]

Alterity is a term used by Levinas to denote otherness, and the disjointed conjunction between the other's time and the time of mineness Levinas will call diachrony. [55] By insisting on the dimensional otherness and noncoincidence of temporality, the alterity of the other person becomes cognate with the otherness of time, one not viewed 'as a degradation of eternity, but as the relationship to that which – of itself unassimilable, absolutely other – would not allow itself to be assimilated by experience; or to that which, of itself infinite – would not allow itself to be comprehended.'[56] Consequentially, diachrony serves to address another singular Levinasian theme, proximity, which depicts 'a relationship without terms, an awaiting without an awaited, an insatiable aspiration. It is distance that is also a proximity – which is not a coincidence or a lost union but signifies all the surplus or all the goodness of an original proximity.'[57] Implied in this original proximity, in time viewed as diachrony as one approaches the other, is God – for, according to Levinas, one approaches God through approaching the other.[58]

In *Time and the Other* Levinas works out the terms specifying what a relationship with the other would entail. Revisiting the *there is*, existents and existence, hypostasis, and solitude, Levinas later takes up everyday life in all its various modes and manifestations, noting, despite its being 'haunted by matter,' that 'everyday life is a preoccupation with salvation.'[59] For Levinas that salvation will come through the other. And it begins with the encounter Levinas calls the face-to-face. 'It is unquestionably *the face*,' notes Peter Atterton, 'that provides our everyday and most immediate access to the other.

The ethical relation is enacted face-to-face.' Atterton adds further that the term face does not only mean a person's countenance, i. e., an object of vision that can be captured in works of art or frozen in one's persona. 'The face rather is *personification* in that it presents – rather than represents – the Other in person. It is the very presence of that which does not present itself to knowledge and understanding in the manner of things.'[60]

Bob Plant thus allows that it is not wholly inaccurate to view Levinas's implementation of the face from a phenomenological perspective; sounding a note of caution, however, he notes that the prescriptive relationship is 'tense.' Plant adds that 'Levinas is uncomfortable speaking of a phenomenology of the face since phenomenology describes what appears, and the face is special insofar as it transcends an exact phenomenological description.'[61] Bernard Waldenfels accurately depicts the apparent ambiguity in the face in works of Levinas by stressing 'the nakedness of the face,' which means 'that the other's otherness eludes every qualification we may apply. . . . Its nakedness is not factual, so that it could be eliminated, but is due to an essential poverty which makes the poor and stranger equal to us.'[62]

Levinas's anchoring the face in intersubjective time attenuates some ambiguities. Noting that the face-to-face relation is a situation where the subject is assumed by the event of the other, Levinas manages to tie this event to the presence of the future in the instant, noting that 'the situation of the face-to-face would be the very accomplishment of time; the encroachment of the present on the future is not the feat of the subject alone, but the intersubjective relationship.'[63] One is introduced here to several key concepts and themes that will assume specific shape later in *Totality and Infinity*. The face-to-face relation is the fundamental event for Levinas, and it is through the intersubjective that one engages transcendence.[64] What is more, and this is crucial, the inner dialectic involved in the relationship with the other, which engages time, issues forth asymmetrically in what Levinas calls intersubjective space:

> But already, in the very heart of the relationship with the other that characterizes our social life, alterity appears as the nonreciprocal relationship – that is, as contrasting strongly with contemporaneousness. The Other as Other is not only an alter ego: the Other is what I myself am not. The Other is this, not because of the Other's character, or physiognomy, or psychology, but because of the Other's very alterity. The Other is the weak, the poor, "the widow and the orphan," whereas I am the rich or the powerful. It can be said that intersubjective space is not symmetrical.[65]

Here is essentially the core concept of what will later develop into our key theme of responsibility. The other's alterity, or the other's otherness, is not reducible to an "I," an ego, but is unique in its modality to the point of transcendence.[66] Moreover, in the intersubjective space where the interhuman event transpires, symmetry, the agency of totality, is overcome not by force, but by goodness.[67]

Provisionary Contextualization

Existence and Existents and *Time and the Other* present several motifs that become dominant themes in later Levinas. Summarizing these two works will help piece some of these themes together and will provide an introductory foundation for more specific analyses of the Other. Narrating philosophically the hypostatic creation of the subject out from the haunting *il y a* portrays what Levinas calls the moment of force, instantiating an effort commensurate with the internal dialectics assumed by the creative duration of time. Thus the present is an act consequential of the existent's self-positing, an event moreover prompting an interruption – a lunge and drag distancing existence from the existent – resulting not only in fatigue but ontological dephasing.[68] Roger Burggraeve views this dephasing as dramatized by an ego which 'is and remains itself by repeatedly establishing itself in its being, localizing itself physically, and ceaselessly identifying with itself as the origin and endpoint of its own act of being.'[69]

Hypostasis for Levinas not only depicts the birth of subjectivity but also dramatizes the dialectic between the ego and the self, one that is made explicit through the inwardness of consciousness. However, subjectivity is also disturbed by disparate affectations, some of which Levinas has employed in order to present not only the ways consciousness is always caught in the interruptions witnessed through the volatized hypostasis, but also the ways in which emotions serve to anchor the labile subject in this constant yet blinking event of localization. This interruption of consciousness also implies emotional bases that collapse the distinction between event and substance, hence suggesting positions preceding understanding, many that will be implicated in the 'extradition to the other' effected through responsibility.[70]

Levinas enlists the indeterminacy unique to the corporal self as a backdrop across which the flickerings of consciousness and unconsciousness – variegated through the myriad moods and activities such as insomnia, fatigue, and solitude – perform the drama of awakening from subjectivity into light, then falling back into indolence and sleep. Focusing on these affective interruptions, moreover, allows Levinas access to peripheral modes that further compass the inner dialectics of self-positioning. The ego and the self, gripped by the gravitas of being, riveted to existence, are engaged in a dilemma: Is the "I" free or is it responsible? This paradox is unending, as witnessed and enacted through what Levinas calls our perpetual birth. 'Perpetual birth' is called by John Llewelyn 'presencing,' a word akin to the word 'event' used by Levinas. According to Llewelyn, 'The uncommon sense of the instant as an active stance and presencing which Levinas describes as the perpetual birth of the I cannot but find itself gravitating toward the common sense of the instant as a chronological point.'[71] What is more, the interminability of this inner instant encloses the ego in a rending solitude.

The reduction of the ego to solitude renders it wrenchingly alone.[72] This aloneness is categorical and absolute in its incessancy. 'I am all alone. It is thus the being in me, the fact that I exist, my *existing*, that constitutes the absolutely intransitive element, something without intentionality or relationship. One can exchange everything between beings except existing. Inasmuch as I am, I am a monad.'[73]

According to Levinas, this monadic existence is accursed, portraying as it does being shut up in solitude, hoarded by anxiety and death.[74] The coming of the other not only precipitates the radical breakup of this categorical solitude: it also constitutes time. As B. C. Hutchens notes,

> time for a hypostasizing self just consists in what it regards time to be. Enter the other person, whose approach disturbs the synchronic time of the self. Suddenly, there is the face of the other person that is not an object like other objects. The apparition of the face of the other person is not merely a temporal event that one could predict. One neither anticipates its approach nor projects it as approaching. It is purely futural and, as such, ungraspable; indeed, it imposes upon the self, seizing it and divesting it of its temporal resources. . . . The approach of the other person represents the "masterful" self's contact with a second consciousness of time. For the self, the time of the other person is incommensurate with its own consciousness of time. There is no way that the self may reduce the other's experiential perspective on time to its own arrogation of time. Once diachrony is apparent to the self, there is a refusal of conjunction, an inability to bring the two times together into a single, objective time. The time of the other person is the "Other" of the time of the self.[75]

For Levinas, nothing within the needs and economy of being can account for the fact the one encounters the other asynchronously, begetting a dephased, veritable time of disjointed conjunctions (diachrony) marked by the other's interruption.[76] Moreover, the dimensional otherness prompted by this non-coincident temporality is analogous with the alterity of the other person.[77]

Through the face-to-face encounter, one inassimilable and incomprehensible, proximity — a concept Levinas utilizes to depict a relationship without terms, one implying an emotional distance or unquenchable aspiration — signifies an original goodness attributable to the other.[78] And in this dimension of encounter, in this intersubjective space, the other is inalienably other, what "I myself am not,' thus marking an alterity made both mysterious and noble by the likes of the widow, orphan, and stranger. It is the other, then, that breaks open the material existence where the ego and the self are reduced to an ontological event.

It is the other also that interrupts the freedom of the ego, one that is so seized by the conclusiveness of existence that 'to shatter the enchainment of matter is to shatter the finality of hypostasis.'[79] This shattering is the result of the radical instance, of an experience of relation, one not bounded in and by the determination of matter. 'Every single experience,' notes Peperzak, 'includes, besides an element of self-consciousness, also the acceptance of a surprising element that is irreducible to a spontaneous production by the ego itself. . . . Self-consciousness discovers itself as an original and irreducible relation to some "other" that it can neither absorb nor posit by its own, a priori capacities.'[80]

It has been necessary to present this particular stage of what Levinas calls the ontological adventure with specific focus on subjectivity and its coming to be. And it will be the subject's struggle with solitude and freedom, notable in its manifold and at times dialectical affectivities, which will mark the initial movement through desire towards a metaphysical adventure inflected towards the other. Through Levinas's thorny nomenclature marked by redundancy and tautology, the subject, or self, or ego qua "I," is still enchained to itself — and still haunted by a menacing anonymity rounded off to the neutral term being.[81] Having managed to escape from the trammels of his earlier influences, and having pronounced in *On Escape* the necessity of leaving being, one now at the terminus of his two early works of 1947 is still burdened, like Levinas's subject, by the economy of being. *Existence and Existents* along with *Time and the Other* leave one with a free and created subject involved in and involving time, and the hypostasized event, radically foundational, yet finite, with the introduction of the other, presages the transcendence and infinity that will arrive in the face of the other. For Levinas this arrival announces the ethical event. Thus now our analysis moves towards transcendence, towards infinity — towards the other.

Notes

1. Levinas, *On Escape*, 73.

2. See Smith, *Toward the Outside*, 137; Manning, *Interpreting Otherwise*, p. 40; Hutchens, *Levinas: A Guide For the Perplexed*, p. 128; Richard A. Cohen, *Ethics, Exegesis, and Philosophy: Interpretation After Levinas* (Cambridge: Cambridge University Press, 2001) 123, emphasis in text.

3. Hent de Vries, in *Minimal Theologies: Critique of Secular Reason in Adorno and Levinas* (Baltimore, Maryland: The Johns Hopkins University Press, 2005) states that 'In Levinas's view the *il y a* resides in the cleft between Being and nonbeing like an excluded middle,' 443.

4. Introduction to *Existence and Existents*, xi.

5. Levinas, *De l'existence a l'existant*, 83 *Existence and Existents*, 45. See also Wyschogrod, *Ethical Metaphysics*, 49.

6. *Emmanuel Levinas: The Genealogy of Ethics*, 19.

7. See Dudiak, *The Intrigue of Ethics*, 228f.

8. Ibid. 19. See also Katz, *Levinas, Judaism, and the Feminine*, 24.

9. Levinas, *De l'existence a l'existant*, 45; *Existence and Existents*, 20f.

10. For Levinas, pure time is experienced also as 'escaping *a limine* (from the threshold) by virtue of its lapse, all activity of representation.' It is also experienced 'as non-intervention, as being-without-insistence, as being-on tiptoe, as being without daring to be: instance of the instant without the insistence of the I, and already a lapse, that "leaves while entering,"' "Philosophy and Transcendence," in *Alterity and Transcendence*, 20.

11. Levinas, *De l'existence a l'existant*, 49; *Existence and Existents*, 23.

12. *To The Other: An Introduction to the Philosophy of Emmanuel Levinas,* 33.
13. Levinas, *De l'existence a l'existant,* 51 ; *Existence and Existents,* 24f.
14. Ibid., p. 25, 4. emphasis in text. In *Ethics and Infinity* Levinas 'spoke thus of the "hypostasis" of existents, that is, the passage going from *being* to a *something,* from the state of a verb to the state of a thing,' 51, emphasis in text.
15. For more on hypostasis in Levinas, see Roger Burggraeve *The Wisdom Of Love In The Service Of Love,* 47f; John Llewelyn, *The Genealogy of Ethics,* 27; Claire Katz, *Levinas, Judaism, and the Feminine,* 22f.; Richard Cohen, *Ethics, Exegesis, and Philosophy,* 176; Michael Purcell, *Levinas and Theology* (Cambridge: Cambridge University Press, 2006) 90f.
16. Levinas, *De l'existence a l'existant,* 43 ; *Existence and Existents,* 16.
17. Levinas felt that the event of hypostasis was constituted by light, knowing, and consciousness. See ibid., p. 44. See also Levinas, "Philosophy and the Idea of Infinity," in *Collected Philosophical Papers,* 52.
18. Ibid., 62f.; 33. Being sobered up will trope herein for a hermeneutic of responsibility.
19. See Levinas, "From Consciousness to Wakefulness," in *Discovering Existence with Husserl,* 166.
20. Levinas, *De l'existence a l'existant,* 63 ; *Existence and Existents* 34, emphasis in text.
21. *Levinas, Judaism, and the Feminine: The Silent Footsteps of Rebecca* (Bloomington, Ind.: Indiana University Press, 2003), 24.
22. Levinas, *De l'existence a l'existant,* 62 ; *Existence and Existents,* 33. This tearing in consciousness presages the fission or denucleation prevalent in Levinas's later thought. It will also prefigure the 'authentic Eucharist' witnessed in responsibility, one fulfilled through substitution, which will be dealt with extensively in chapter seven: 'It is a being torn up from oneself for another in the giving to the other the bread out of one's own mouth.... The identity of the subject is here brought out, not by a rest on itself, but by a restlessness that drives me outside of the nucleus of my substantiality,' *Otherwise Than Being Or Beyond Essence,* trans. Alphonso Lingis (Pittsburg, Pennsylvania: Duquesne University Press, 1998) 142.
23. "A Fine Fisk," *Re-Reading Levinas,* 214.
24. Ibid.
25. *Toward the Outside,* 194.
26. *By Way of Interruption*: *Levinas and the Ethics of Communication* Pittsburg, Pa.: Duquesne University Press, 2005) 96.
27. This troubling of consciousness, experienced as disintegration, hints at transcendence. In a later work Levinas defines consciousness as 'the presence of the subject to transcendent things,' "La Ruine de al Representation," *En découvrant l'existence avec Husserl et Heidegger,* 53;   "The Ruin of Representation," *Discovering Existence With Husserl,* 114.
28. See Andrew Tallon, "Nonintentional Affectivity," *Ethics as First Philosophy,* 110.
29. *Ethics and Politics,* 94.
30. Due to the fact that the *il y a* collapses the distinction between subject and object, Edith Wyschogrod has called it an 'ontological black hole,' "Derrida, Levinas, and Violence," in *Derrida and Destruction,* ed. Hugh J. Silverman (New York: Routledge, 1989)184.
31. Introduction to *Collected Philosophical Papers,* xx.
32. Levinas, *De l'existence a l'existant,* 122 ; *Existence and Existents,* 69.

33. For instance, in *Otherwise Than Being or Beyond Essence* Levinas notes that 'in this work the term *essence* designates being as differentiated from entities.' He also notes that this term designates 'the process or event of being,' 189.

34. Smith, *Toward the Outside*, 197. Also, Alphonso Lingis notes that 'the ego is not an atomic unity, but a unity for itself; it refers to itself . . . it is recurrence. It is being affected with oneself, being encumbered with oneself. The ego is a weight for itself; such is its constituent materiality,' Introduction to Emmanuel Levinas's *Collected Philosophical Papers*, xxi.

35. *The Problem of Ethical Metaphysics*, 14.

36. Levinas, *De l'existence a l'existant*, 125f. ; *Existence and Existents*, 71f. Later, in "Reflections on Phenomenological 'Technique,'" in *Discovering Existence with Husserl*, Levinas calls these situations intentions irreducible to knowledge, ones that 'can be posited as conditions of knowledge, without this positing taking on the appearance of an irrational decision,' 101.

37. *Alterity* (Chicago: The University of Chicago Press, 1987) 37f., emphasis in text.

38. Levinas, "Humanism and Anarchy," *Humanism of the Other*, 54f.

39. See Simon Citchley, Introduction, *The Cambridge Companion to Levinas*, 20f.

40. Levinas, *De l'existence a l'existant*, 136; *Existence and Existents*, 79, emphasis in text. Regarding inflection within consciousness Levinas, in "In Praise of Insomnia," in *God, Death, and Time*, trans. Bettina Bergo (Stanford, California: Stanford University Press, 2000), notes that "If the awakening that, within consciousness, is already paralyzed should be inflected toward a content that is assembled into presence, then awakening does not come down to the watching-over that is already a search for the identical, which absorbs us and in which we sleep," 209.

41. Ibid. In "The Temptation of Temptation," in *Nine Talmudic Readings*, trans. Annette Aronowicz (Bloomington: Indiana University Press, 1990), Levinas notes that 'To say that the person begins in freedom, that freedom is the first causality and that the first cause is nobody, is to close one's eyes to the secret of the ego,' 49; *Quatre Lectures Talmudiques* (Paris: Editions de Minuit, 1968), 107.

42. "The Body of Difference," *The Face of the Other and the Trace of God: Essays on the Philosophy of Emmanuel Levinas*, 24.

43. For more on the unconscious in works of Levinas and how it manifests through multiform affectivities, see Andrew Tallon, "Nonintentional Affectivity," *Ethics as First Philosophy*, 112f.

44. Much of Levinas's thought on the *there is* parallels that of Maurice Blanchot's. See Simon Critchley, "*Il y a* – A Dying Stronger Than Death," *Oxford Literary Review* 15, no 1-2 (1993): 110-113.

45. Levinas, *De l'existence a l'existant*, 143 ; *Existence and Existents*, 85, emphasis in text.

46. Andrius Valevicius, *From the Other to the Totally Other: The Religious Philosophy of Emmanuel Levinas* (New York: Peter Lang Publishing, Inc., 1988), corroborates this point when he notes that 'A life in freedom is a life of discovering oneself unjust. It is not a question of the structure of the free will spontaneously unfolding to grasp its happiness but rather an inversion wherein freedom beholds itself as unjust. As my demands increase so does the judgment which falls upon me, in other words, my responsibility; and the acuteness of these responsibilities increases the demands upon me. In such a movement my freedom does not have the last say in matters, I never rediscover my solitude, (and) moral consciousness is essentially insatiable, or in other words, always desire,' 38.

47. This incessant circuitry of self is notable through its lack of an ethical ethos.

48. Levinas, *De l'existence a l'existant*, 144f. ; *Existence and Existents*, 85f.
49. See Smith, *Toward the Outside: Concepts and Themes in Emmanuel Levinas*, 61f.
50. "Tracing Responsibility," *Ethics as First Philosophy*, 175, emphasis in text.
51. Levinas, *De l'existence a l'existant*, 160 ; *Existence and Existents*, 96.
52. Introduction to Emmanuel Levinas, *Time and the Other*, trans. Richard A. Cohen (Pittsburgh : Duquesne University Press, 1987) 1.
53. "Levinas's Critique of Husserl," *The Cambridge Companion to Levinas*, 94.
54. Introduction to *Time and the Other*, 12. For more on Levinas and time see Tina Chanter, "The Temporality of Saying: Politics Beyond the Ontological Difference," *Graduate Faculty Philosophical Journal* 20, 21, no 2—1 (1998) 507f.
55. Later Levinas will collate this conjunction with responsibility: 'The dia-chrony of a past that does not gather into re-presentation is at the bottom of the concreteness of the time that is the time of my responsibility for the Other,' "Diachrony and Representation," 112.
56. Levinas, *Time and the Other*, 32.
57. Ibid.
58. See Kearney, "Dialogue with Emmanuel Levinas," in *Face to Face with Levinas*, 23. Cf. Levinas, "The Thinking of Being," in *Of God Who Comes to Mind*, where Levinas is convinced that nearness to God is irreducible to knowledge. Levinas also thinks that this proximity adds meaning to duration, hence patience. In fact, this patience for Levinas is collateral with antecedent responsibility, 119.
59. Levinas, *Time and the Other*, 58.
60. *On Levinas*, 27, emphasis in text.
61. *Wittgenstein and Levinas*, 131.
62. 'Levinas and the Face of the Other," *The Cambridge Companion to Levinas*, 71.
63. Levinas, *Time and the Other*, 79.
64. In *Ethics, Exegesis and Philosophy*, Cohen notes that 'The transcending dimensions constitutive of time – the pastness of the past, the futurity of the future – would derive not from the subject alone, or from its historical context, but from the ethical transcendence of the inter-subjective relations,' 153.
65. Levinas, *Time and the Other*, 83f.
66. Later in *Time and the Other* Levinas investigates femininity as the fundamental modality of alterity, portraying sexuality and eroticism as the irreducible terms involved in this otherness. His more mature thought, however, goes back even further, to what he present as a 'nudity' expressed in the 'imperative demand' of the face-to-face relation. What is more, this imperative demand is formally presupposed in one's noninterchangeable obligation to the other. See "Being-for-the Other," in *Is It Righteous To Be?* 115.
67. Goodness in Levinas is addressed more specifically in chapter seven.
68. See Levinas, *De l'existence a l'existant*, 51; *Existence and Existents*, 24.
69. *The Wisdom of Love In The Service Of Love*, 47.
70. Levinas, "Truth of Disclosure and Truth of Testimony," in *Basic Philosophical Writings*, 103. See also Levinas, *Existence and Existents*, 69.
71. *Emmanuel Levinas: The Genealogy of Ethics*, 50.
72. Cf. Levinas, "Substitution," in *Basic Philosophical Writings*, where the reduction of the ego is commensurable to 'a return of the Ego to the passivity of the self, an anarchic passivity whose active source is not thematizable. Subjectivity in this sense is not a for-itself but an in-itself,' 88.

73. Levinas, *Time and the Other*, 42. Cf. Levinas, *Ethics and Infinity*, where 'one can exchange everything between beings, except existing. In this sense, to be is to be isolated by existing. I am a monad inasmuch as I am,' 59.

74. See Levinas, *De l'existence a l'existant*, 144; *Existence and Existents*, 86.

75. *Levinas: A Guide for the Perplexed*, 70.

76. For Levinas there is a tension as consciousness is present to itself and that keeps watch, noting how the same is out of phase with itself, a difference identity cannot comprehend. This out-of-phase nature registers for Levinas as insomnia, "From Consciousness to Wakefulness," *Of God Who Comes To Mind*, 25.

77. Consonant with this point, Levinas asserts that 'To be sure, need is also a dependence with regard to the other, but it is a dependence across time, a dependence that is not an instantaneous betraying of the same but a suspension or postponement of dependence, and thus the possibility to break, by labor and by economy, the very thrust of the alterity upon which need depends,' *Totalité et Infini*, 88; *Totality and Infinity*, 116.

78. Levinas describes proximity 'as irreducible to consciousness and thematization.' Thus proximity is a relationship irreducible to images, one moreover frustrating any logical schematic,' "Substitution," *Basic Philosophical Writings*, 80.

79. Levinas, *Time and the Other*, 57.

80. *To the Other*, 16.

81. Bernhard Waldenfels, in "Levinas and the Face of the Other," *The Cambridge Companion to Levinas*, comments that 'Levinas is like a wanderer who sketches his map not in advance but while marching ahead,' 73.

Chapter Three

Upon Transcendence

"Philosophy and the Idea of Infinity" is an exemplary essay for introducing one to the mature thought of Levinas. First published in 1957, this work anticipates much of what will later be developed in Levinas's masterpiece *Totality and Infinity*. Through its more extensive utilization of concepts analyzed in Levinas's earlier work, themes such as inwardness, solitude, and freedom, and the ways these intersect with our motif of responsibility, "Philosophy and the Idea of Infinity" acts as a hermeneutic bridge connecting the early and later thought of Levinas. Moreover, this essay's operative reduction of the ego to assimilative violence allows one a key perspective, at this particular stage, of the self's journey towards sacrificial substitution which will be addressed in the penultimate chapter of this thesis. This penultimate address will, in turn, offer critical insight into the last chapter's dovetailing of responsibility with Levinas's missional challenge to Christians.

"Every philosophy seeks truth."[1] Opening this essay with what seems such a trite truism seems risky, but Levinas embraces the risk. For immediately he implicates truth with experience, an experience however bespeaking of a distinct and inassimilable reality, one that moves us beyond our nature. Through this displacement, 'Truth would thus designate the outcome of a movement that leaves a world that is intimate and familiar, even if we have not explored it completely, and goes toward the stranger, toward a beyond.Truth would imply more than exteriority: transcendence.'[2] There is freshness in encountering this word exteriority after such obsessive exposition on inwardness. What is more, being addressed in a context other than the need to escape opens transcendence as well.[3]

In both cases, the face of the other is the initiating factor. In fact, Pierre Hayat discovers in the face a peculiar, inchoate inspiration stirring the subject towards responsibility:

> In order for a true transcendence to be possible, the other must concern the I, while at the same time remaining external to it. It is especially necessary that the other, by his very exteriority, his alterity, should cause the I to exit the self. Levinas wants to show that the other, by his face, attests to himself, simply, directly, without going through any mediation. That exceptional capacity of the face to testify to itself outside all objective context and independently of the intersubjective field is, of itself, a message addressed to the subject. By the non-ordinary manner in which it manifests itself, the face opposes violence with metaphysical resistance. In so doing, the face raises the subject to responsibility.[4]

Peperzak believes this exceptional capacity of the face to foil mediation is confluent with Levinas's notion of an exteriority dependent upon heteronymous distance, a distance that opens ideally to metaphysics and the divine. Contra most conceptions considering exteriority 'as a qualification of a reality that . . . can be assimilated and integrated in the form of a representation or concept,' Peperzak views Levinas's impression to suggest, 'on the contrary, the transcendent, which cannot be engulfed by consciousness.'[5]

Revisiting freedom, Levinas attributes autonomy, 'the *reduction of the other to the same*,' to man's ego – particularly as it is distinguished by its 'conquest of being by man over the course of history.'[6] Crucial here is Levinas's distinction between the ego and its assimilative properties; its reduction of myriad events to a quasi- history where Robert Bernasconi sees 'no separation from out of which a unity can be established, except a unity without rest or peace.'[7] Noteworthy as well is Levinas's neologism for the singularity of the ego – ipseity. Ipseity names what the ego performs. 'The identity of the ego, for and by whom the universe of beings opens and unfolds itself as a panoramic world, is not a static substance surrounded by things . . . but rather an active process by which its own being is changed as much as the world of things and events in which it is involved.'[8] This conformation accounts for the assimilation of all otherness that Levinas finds endemic to Western civilization, one where the world reflects the ego and vice versa. 'Thus Western thought very often seemed to exclude the transcendent, encompass every other in the same, and proclaim the philosophical birthright of autonomy.'[9]

Concerning the relationship between the other and the same, focus now falls on autonomy and heteronomy, as well as freedom's compliance with the former. According to Levinas,

> Autonomy, the philosophy which aims to ensure the freedom, or the identity, of beings, presupposes that freedom itself is sure of its right, is justified without recourse to anything further, is complacent in itself, like Narcissus. When, in the philosophical life that realizes this freedom, there arises a term foreign to the philosophical life, other – the land that supports us and

disappoints our efforts, the sky that elevates and ignores us, the forces of nature that aid and kill us, things that encumber us or serve us, men who love us and enslave us – it becomes an obstacle; it has to be surmounted and integrated into this life. But truth is just this victory and this integration.[10]

There is an assimilative violence in the autonomy of the self, particularly in the way it reduces all the elements of exteriority into synoptic truth.[11] Thus freedom in this sense numbs reality, denaturing it into a safe haven of the same where it obeys the law of the same – hence opening the self to heteronymous resistance. Jeffrey Bloechl notes that in such a situation, 'the ego cannot hope to succeed with that resistance because it pursues it in a manner reinscribed with the very sphere of violence it would like to escape.'[12] This reinscription, according to Brian Schroeder, betrays 'the self (as) a theoretical fiction; and to reduce the metaphysical terms of exteriority and interiority (other and the same) to a cognitive level is to commit the violence of the same.'[13] Schroeder also feels that the inability of the self to address radical otherness further exasperates this resistance, adding to the sphere of violence noted by Bloechl.

Autonomy and Heteronomy (The Wounding Stone)

Understanding autonomy and heteronomy in Levinas is vital for discerning the genealogy of responsibility in his work. Having established a posited ego, one whose freedom is foundational, Levinas asks the question: 'Autonomy or heteronomy?'[14] Autonomy and heteronomy, the same and other, have been a common theme in Western philosophy since Plato's dialogues.[15] Observing the West's predilection for privileging the same, a tendency where all otherness, all alterity, is incorporated into singleness – whether this be presented as freedom, vision, being, or power – convinced Levinas that an ontological sovereignty was operational.[16] This observation led Levinas to assert that 'Philosophy is atheism, or rather unreligion, negation of a God that reveals himself and puts truth into us. This is Socrates's teaching . . . every lesson introduced into the soul was already in it. The I's identification, its marvelous autarchy, is the natural crucible of this transmutation of the other into the same.'[17] Referencing the Platonic theory of knowledge as presented in Socrates's maieutics asserts the notion that the ego already knows that which it seeks to know, again promoting the primacy of the subject, again transmuting heteronomy into autonomy – the 'sin of the mind.'[18]

Levinas's problem lies in the difficulty of describing the relational dynamic of the same and the other without this description itself being homogenized into totality: 'This is more difficult than it might appear, since it is in the nature of the *relation* to bring the Other into the self's sphere of familiarity, thus making it intelligible from the perspective of the self and reducing its true otherness.'[19] Owing to the self's affirmation of its freedom, one whose agency is the business of integrating everything into knowledge, consciousness becomes a legislation of the same. And this legislation, moreover, becomes locked in an idealism where the ego structures its own reality according to its own logic, becoming what Levinas (co-opting Husserl's term) calls an egology.[20]

Understanding the same's tendency towards mediation is crucial to establishing separation between autonomy and heteronomy. This bent towards neutralism is in fact a fundamental stance the ego assumes as it domesticates reality. Reducing this bent to the ontology of power, states Hutchens, frees one 'to do what one likes, however violently, to oneself, other persons and one's total situation, because one is free from difference. The reduction of the other to the same emancipates the self from the need to admit difference.'[21] This reduction manifests as freedom, comprehension, and possession. It all begins in what Levinas calls the 'recourse to neuters' where otherness may be reduced to 'an abstract essence which is and is not. In it is dissolved the other's alterity.' Effecting poetic nuances in order to more fully color this philosophical naturalization, Levinas issues that

> the foreign being, instead of maintaining itself in the inexpugnable fortress of its singularity, instead of facing, becomes a theme and an object. It fits under a concept already, or dissolves into relation. It falls into the network of a priori ideas, which I bring to bear, so as to capture it. To know is to surprise in the individual confronted, in this wounding stone, this upward plunging pine, this roaring lion, that by which it is not this very individual, this foreigner, that by which it is already betrayed and by which it gives the free will, vibrant in all certainty, hold over it, is grasped and conceived, enters into a concept.[22]

This conceptualized roaring lion becomes for Levinas the reign of power, something one will encounter more forcefully in the preface to *Totality and Infinity*. For now, however, it is enough to recognize that the philosophy of the same wages war, one where 'Freedom is put into question by the other, and is revealed to be unjustified, only when it knows itself to be unjust,' — thus creating 'a new situation (where) consciousness's presence to itself acquires a different modality; its positions collapse.'[23]

The Neuter

Thus far the ontological adventure has included every other in the same.[24] Inasmuch as there was consciousness, there was legislation of heteronomy by autonomy, the law of the same (*auto nomos*). In order to contextualize philosophically his argument, Levinas, in a section of "Philosophy and the Idea of Infinity" entitled "Narcissism, or the Primacy of the Same," takes Heidegger's thought to task. Heidegger in *Being and Time* had called for a program intent on disestablishing the history of ontology, but Levinas detected in Heidegger's work a propensity towards the neuter, one which was radically reductive. This predilection, in fact, leads Peperzak to assert that 'Although Being is neither a universal nor a supreme foundational being, it illuminates and dominates thought as a Neutral which, nevertheless, does not abolish but affirms the central position of *Dasein*, which replaced the transcendental I of modern philosophy.'[25]

From a variant critical perspective, Jeffrey Dudiak calls this neutral third 'mediatory,' noting that it buffers the shock of differences and opens the way to Levinas's concept of totality.²⁶ According to Levinas, Heidegger had in effect replaced the Platonic preeminence of reason, where the ego simply recollects what it already knows, with the freedom of Being. Again being is an issue for itself; again one encounters the rule of the same. Lacking is charitable concern for the other. Addressing this issue, Levinas notes in an interview that

> Heidegger defines *Dasein* in almost Darwinian fashion as "a being that is concerned for its own being." In *Being and Time* he defines the main characteristic of *Dasein* as that of *mineness* – the way in which being becomes mine, imposes or imprints itself on me.... I become I only because I possess my own being as primary. For ethical thought, on the contrary, *the self*, as this primary of what is mine, is *hateful*. Ethics is not, for this reason, a depersonalizing exigency. I am defined as a subjectivity, as a singular person, as an "I," precisely because I am exposed to the other. It is my inescapable and incontrovertible answerability to the other that makes me an individual "I." So that I become a responsible or ethical "I" to the extent that I agree to depose or dethrone myself – to abdicate my position of centrality – in favor of the vulnerable other.²⁷

Fundamentally for Levinas Heidegger's was a philosophy that operated through the sovereignty of the same over the other – one effective through the reducible neuter.²⁸ Moreover, since Heidegger's notion of being was 'inseparable from the comprehension of being,' Levinas issued the critique that in fact 'Being is not a being. It is a neuter which orders thought and beings....'²⁹ And this neutral Being consequentially betrays an anonymity allowing reason prominence again. This reduction also compromises freedom; for the singularity, whether it assumes the name soul, ego, or consciousness, still mediates through its recourse to neuters.

One may sense by now in this proclivity to singularity an absence of alterity marked by neutrality and finitude. Missing is transcendence, infinity – the other. And, as Bettina Bergo notes, for Levinas this ontological monism 'only carries us back to a system of meanings which exclude the other from consideration because, as Heidegger argued, our existence is not defined by a potential openness to others but by a potential openness to being itself.'³⁰ This openness to being itself only closes one in the circuitry of the same, a circuitry that integrates and systematizes all otherness. Alterity is schematized. And this schema had become for Levinas a worldview clothed in 'universalization, the secret weapon of Western thought (that) turns out to be the source of all betrayals and overpowering of reality as it is ... and which is also the civilization of exploitation and imperialism.'³¹

At this stage the ontological adventure had begun to betray its violent freedom. And for Levinas this adventure, with Heidegger as a figurehead, had become a 'religion in reverse show(ing) in what intoxication the lucid sobriety of philosophers is steeped.'³² Its legacy moreover exhibited a tradition of pride and cruelty. Mercifully now Levinas shifts emphasis and direction, reversing terms and themes towards a tradition recognizing the other – but not before, in concluding this section, begging justice into the question: 'To conclude, the well-known thesis of Heideggerian philosophy—the preeminence of Being over beings, of ontology over metaphysics—ends up affirming a tradition in which the same dominates the other. . . . Does not justice consist in putting the obligation with regard to the other before obligation to oneself, in putting the other before the same?'[33]

Thinking Infinity

Part three of "Philosophy and the Idea of Infinity" is entitled "The Idea of Infinity." Announcing a reversal of terms, Levinas immediately affirms another tradition, one that 'does not read right in might and does not reduce *every other* to the same.'[34] Levinas's intent now appears to be that of translating the principle points of his Judaic faith, specifically its concern and obligation for the stranger, into a philosophical and "Greek" language, without seeming to proselytize. In order to fulfill that intent, he takes recourse to two formal philosophical structures, one found in Plato and the other Descartes. These two ideas, in fact, are so influential to Levinas's thinking that it is necessary to analyze them in detail.

Having found Western thought and practice 'marked by a striving for totalization, in which the universe is reduced to an originary and ultimate unity by way of panoramic overviews and dialectical syntheses,' Levinas now maintains that 'the human and the divine Other cannot be reduced to a totality of which they would only be elements.'[35] For Levinas, this irreducibility could be traced back to two basic premises found in Plato and Descartes.

Familiar with the incessant need to escape being that has threaded throughout Levinas's thought, one now finds him appropriating Plato's notion of the good beyond being and Descartes's idea of the infinite. In Plato's world of forms, the idea of the good was supreme, hence there was here a formal precedence antecedent and transcendent to being.[36] Levinas puts into effect this dimensional transcending of ontology through the face of the other by soliciting Plato – who dared to inquire, against good sense, 'Is not the idea of being younger than the idea of the infinite? Should we not concede that philosophy cannot confine itself to the primacy of ontology, as has been taught up to now. . . ?'[37] Establishing a formal model of the good breaking through the closed ambit of the ontological by enlisting the standard set by Plato himself freed Levinas to proceed more boldly with his projected metaphysical ethics.[38] Nonetheless, it should be noted that Plato's thought and Levinas's are sometimes at odds. As Wyschogrod comments, 'While Platonic metaphysics has correctly understood the nature of this problem (the idea of otherness), it was unable to develop a set of tactics for bypassing or solving it. The reason for this is that Plato's idea of the one is dominated by ontology. The one is inseparable from being.'[39]

It is Descartes's idea of the infinite, however, that finds wider circulation in Levinas's works. In "Philosophy and the Idea of Infinity" Levinas notes that 'In Descartes the I that thinks maintains a relationship with the infinite. This relationship is not that which connects a container to a content, since the I cannot contain the infinite, nor that which binds a content to a container, since the I is separated from the infinite.'[40] Levinas is here sketching a philosophical model analogous to the argument developed in the third of Descartes's *Meditations on First Philosophy*. Here, seeking clarity and distinction, Descartes implements his famous reduction upon the items of consciousness. These inventories, in turn, were compelled by an obsessive need for analytical surety. Operating on the premise that, if a firm foundation is to be established, certainty must be at a premium, Descartes developed a methodology of exaggerated or hyperbolic doubt. Nothing was exempt from this doubt.[41] It became the litmus test for every conceivable thing. 'Under this test,' comments Bernard Williams, 'the Doubt is extended, as well as to God and the past, to every judgment about publicly perceptible objects, including Descartes' own body: they are now, at this stage, collectively doubted.'[42] Descartes knew that philosophy required observation, and that observation depended on the senses. Yet the senses could be deceptive. And if the senses could deceive us some of the time, why not all of the time? More significantly, if a part was wrong, what about the whole?

Simply put, every idea Descartes came up with, other than that of God and himself, could have been produced by his own consciousness and sensorium. This led Descartes to a profound conclusion:

> Nor can it be supposed that several causes concerned in my production, and that from one I received the idea of one of the perfections I attribute to Deity, and from another the idea of some other, and thus that all those perfections are indeed found somewhere in the universe, but do not all exist together in a single being who is God; for, on the contrary, the unity, the simplicity or inseparability of all the properties of Deity, is one of the chief perfections I conceive him to possess; and the idea of this unity of all the perfections of Deity could certainly not be put into my mind by any cause from which I did not likewise receive the ideas of all the other perfections; for no power could enable me to embrace them in an inseparable unity, without at the same time giving me the knowledge of what they were (and their existence in a particular mode).[43]

This quote is germane for two reasons: one, it introduces an instrumental self, one involved in a 'production' -- the processes of which schematize God. Two, it introduces the notion of an inherent idea overflowing its possessor, the idea of infinity. Later, when Descartes speaks of this idea, he says that 'it is innate, in the same way as is the idea of myself.'[44] Not only is this a traditional idea of God found in metaphysics, but it also affirms the irreducible originality of this notion in Descartes by pointing out that it must have necessarily been put in him by a transcendent source — and thus not the result of negating finitude.[45]

All My Crimes

Descartes ends the third of his *Meditations* rhapsodically adoring God. As if surrendering to the incapacity of a theoretical access to divinity, and affirming at the same time another way, his probing analysis at least momentarily submits to adoration and gratitude:

> But before I examine this with more attention, and pass on to the consideration of other truths that may be evolved out of it, I think it proper to remain here for some time in the contemplation of God himself – that I may ponder at leisure his marvelous attributes – and behold, admire, and adore the beauty of this light so unspeakably great, as far, at least, as the strength of my mind, which is to some degree dazzled by the sight, will permit. For just as we learn by faith that the supreme felicity of the next life consists in the contemplation of the divine majesty alone, so even now we learn from experience that a like meditation, though incomparably less perfect, is the source of the highest satisfaction of which we are susceptible in this life.[46]

Significantly Levinas, as he addresses philosophically something that both engages and enraptures (i. e., the idea of infinity), finds himself bespeaking as well of the entrance of infinity as an epiphany.[47] Notwithstanding the similarities, the experience is more sobering than bedazzling, for, as notes Llewelyn, 'the other is the Other in the majesty Descartes attributes to the Infinite – though, it must be added at once, this majesty is attributed by Levinas to the Other's being the hungry stranger, the orphan, and the widow.'[48] What is more, there is a revelatory aspect of this idea being placed in us: 'In thinking infinity the I from the first *thinks more than it thinks*. Infinity does not enter into the *idea* of infinity, is not grasped; this idea is not a concept. The infinite is the radically, absolutely, other. . . . It has been *put* into us. It is not a reminiscence. It is experience in the sole radical sense of the term.'[49]

Interestingly one is back at experience. But it is now a proleptic experience that Jill Robbins calls 'an irreversible movement that goes out unto the other, a departure without return which he (Levinas) associates with the biblical Abraham. . . . The one-way movement is exemplified by *goodness* and *the work*, according to the particular inflection he gives these terms.'[50] Noting that Levinas began this essay stating that 'every philosophy seeks truth' and that 'truth implies experience,' – experience that will transport us beyond what constitutes and surrounds us – one could find enigmatic the question now posed by Levinas: 'How can such a structure be still philosophical? What is the relationship which, while remaining one of the more in the less, is not transformed into the relationship in which, according to the mystics, the butterfly drawn by the fire is consumed in the fire?'[51]

Essentially these are both one question. And they have one answer. In fact, there is always only one answer to the question of Levinas: the other. In section four, "The Idea of Infinity and the Face of Another," – one entwining philosophy, truth, experience, and infinity – Levinas offers up his eminent theme: 'Experience, the idea of infinity, occurs in the relationship with the other. The idea of infinity is the social relationship.'[52] Now Levinas's analysis is in concrete form, structuring the experience of truth and the truth of experience into a relation with the other:

> To be sure, the other is exposed to all my powers, succumbs to all my ruses, all my crimes. Or he resists me with all his force and all the unpredictable resources of his own freedom. I measure myself against him. But he can also – and here is where he presents me his face – oppose himself to me beyond all measure, with the total uncoveredness and nakedness of his defenseless eyes, the straightforwardness, the absolute frankness of his gaze. . . . (T)rue exteriority is in this gaze which forbids me my conquest. Not that conquest is beyond my too weak powers, but *I am no longer able to have power*: the structure of my freedom is completely reversed. Here is established a relationship not with a very great resistance, but with the absolutely other, with the resistance of what has no resistance, with ethical resistance. It opens the very dimension of infinity, of what puts a stop to the irresistible imperialism of the same and the I. We call a face the epiphany of what can thus present itself directly, and therefore also exteriorly, to an I.[53]

The face is an essential motif in Levinas, the locus where immanence is transcendent and transcendence is immanent. And while the face is a focus for Levinas, one should exercise caution in relying too much on visual synoptics. Indeed, as Bob Plant notes, 'Levinas emphasizes this because the visual metaphor harbors precisely those dangers he thinks should be guarded against; namely, the assimilation of what is "other" to epistemological categories.'[54]

From the Idea to the Presence of Infinity

It is not by accident that, in the crucial passage cited above, the face and the ethical are introduced together. And naturally there is resistance involved, particularly as exteriority prompts the social relationship. Exteriority threatens inwardness, and the face presents an object unlike others. First, the face 'is not equivalent to the distance between a subject and an object. An object is integrated into the identity of the same; the I makes of it its theme, and then its property, its booty, its prey or its victim.'[55] In an interview Levinas extended this point by noting that 'the face is not of the order of the seen, it is not an object, but it is he whose appearing preserves an exteriority which is also an appeal of an imperative given to your responsibility: to encounter the face is straightaway to hear a demand and an order.'[56]

Second, and more significant, is the fact that 'the epiphany of a face is wholly language.' [57] Unlike Descartes's bedazzled contemplation when meditating upon the idea of infinity placed in him by the divine, for Levinas the opening of the dimension of infinity is attributable to what is exterior to the I, and exteriority is epiphanized in the ethical resistance of the face.[58] This ethical resistance is a pure act defying totalization and, according to Atterton, is betrayed in philosophies that 'can always be qualified, retracted, and even contradicted if need be in order to make room for an altogether different conceptuality.'[59] What is more, 'Ethical resistance is the presence of infinity.'[60]

Pursuing the essay's logic, one may now assert 1) 'Every philosophy seeks truth'; 2) 'Truth implies experience'; 3) 'Experience, the idea of infinity, occurs in the relationship with the other. The idea of infinity is the social relationship'; and 4) 'Ethical resistance is the presence of infinity.' Intriguingly, one moves from the idea of infinity in experience, through the social relationship with the other, to the presence of infinity in ethical resistance. There is presence in moral resistance, one that awakens and sobers, one 'where our freedom renounces its imperialism proper to the ego, where it is found to be not only arbitrary, but unjust. But then the other is not simply another freedom; to give me knowledge of injustice, his gaze must come to me from a dimension of the ideal. The other must be closer to God than I.'[61]

Themes and motifs gather about the face of the other. Proximity now is tinged with divinity, and justice awakens in what heretofore has been an isolated self. The narcissistic self, in the relation with the face, finds its centripetal interests violent when confronted with the vulnerable and destitute other, and Plant feels the nearness of the other to God prompts Levinas to register the primordial heaviness of being as guilt.[62] Here one discovers experientially a more fundamental knowing, one contingent upon this nascent conscience inspired by the face of the other. Ethics then for Levinas is preoriginal, since according to Peperzak it is 'the revelation of a fact and the source of all obligations and prohibitions. . . . The ethical relation is not a "superstructure" but rather the foundation of all knowledge, and the analysis of this relation constitutes a "first philosophy."'[63]

Resistance

Again, "Philosophy and the Idea of Infinity" only adumbrates what will be analyzed later in *Totality and infinity*. But for now one is engaged fully in ethical resistance, a resistance incited by the other and made conscious through the epiphany of language. This resistance is the presence of infinity, one that calls our freedom into question. Preliminary to knowledge, the ethical relationship that objectifies this resistance, inundating as it does every conception of the same, breaks with cognition and is thus a pure experience devoid of the ontological trappings of truth earlier aligned with reality. And much of the epiphany of language involves the risk the self takes in trusting this purer experience, a trust moreover felt as a response to a command. As B. C. Hutchins notes, 'Although language is an exchange of ideas about the world, it nonetheless originates in the face-to-face relation. If the face of the other person were not original, that is, if it did not express a command that I must obey, then there could be no exchange of themes.'[64] And without an exchange of themes, there is only the self in isolation.

Here the risk of language exposes the self, awakening as it does a remote sense of responsibility reflecting an inchoate reaction to the command. According to Wyschogrod, 'When we look at the face of the Other we know that we are commanded to honor the alterity of the Other by recognizing an asymmetry between us.... We do not interpret what we feel as belonging to a teleological nexus, but as bearing a moral imperative.'[65] The self is thus knocked off balance, with its privileged status equivocated by its proximity to the other.[66] This deposition of the self through its exposure to the other consequentially imposes the notion that the self's true identity results from this vulnerability, not from any knowledge per se assumed by the subject.

Colin Davis corroborates, commenting that 'The subject is not described by Levinas in terms of consciousness, intentionality, interiority, self-possession, freedom, commitment or choice.... It exists in proximity to the Other, it approaches the Other, achieving the conditions of communication ... in vulnerability.'[67] But there is still this ethical resistance, one chastening the subject, one in fact purifying experience from its assimilation into cognitive sameness.

In the section of "Philosophy and the Idea of Infinity" entitled "The Idea of Infinity is a Desire," Levinas addresses this 'movement of the soul that is more cognitive than cognition.' Here Levinas asserts that 'The ethical relationship is not grafted on to an antecedent relationship of cognition.... The idea of infinity, in which being overflows the idea, in which the other overflows the same, breaks with the inward play of the soul and alone deserves the name experience, a relation with the exterior.'[68] After earlier asking how one might arrive at truth, Levinas now brings us to the analysis of a relationship even more basic than cognition and more fundamental than knowledge. And this relationship is the result of the engagement with the other, an encounter that impedes itself upon one, calling into question freedom and prompting an upsurge of diffused guilt irreducible to cognition. Remember: the other not only modulates freedom into another register, that of responsibility, but – being closer to God – brings one closer to ownership of one's injustices.[69] There is still, however, this resistance, one marked positively by a profound and unremitting compulsion. Needed is a proper definition for this ethical urge, one that will allow Levinas an interpretive vehicle to carry his analysis towards transcendence.

Desire

The hermeneutic vehicle Levinas designates to fill this ethical urge is Desire: 'Infinity is not the object of contemplation, that is, is not proportionate to the thought that thinks it. The idea of infinity is a thought which at every moment thinks more than it thinks. A thought that thinks more than it thinks is a desire. Desire "measures" the infinity of the infinite.'[70] For Levinas desire is unquenchable and hence irreducible to need. Commensurate with the overflowing endemic to the idea of infinity, desire, comments Peter Atterton, 'is distinguished from "need" (e.g., the need for food) precisely to the extent that it cannot in principle be satisfied. Essentially insatiable, Levinas likens it to a desire that nourishes itself, one might say, with its hunger. It is like the love Shakespeare writes about in his Sonnet 73: "Consumed with that which it was nourish'd by."'[71]

Apropos this feeding hunger, Drabinski notes that 'The Needed – the object of need – is, at least teleologically, reducible to the subject of Need. The lack in the subject that desires as Need determines what it desires with regard to its position of interest. Therefore Need does not seek the foreign; Need seeks only what might satisfy the void opened by lack.'[72] And since this desire is precognitive it transcends categories, operating affectively yet without this affect reaching fulfillment. The other incites this desire, but since the other – like the idea of infinity – overflows any concept aiming at its reduction, there is no objective adequation.[73] According to Levinas

> The term we have chosen to mark the propulsion, the inflation, of this going beyond is opposed to the affectivity of love and the indigence of need. Outside of the hunger one satisfies, the thirst one quenches and the senses one allays, exists the other, the absolutely other, desired beyond these satisfactions. . . . This desire without satisfaction hence takes cognizance of alterity of the other. It situates it in the dimension of height and of the ideal, which it opens up in being . . . The true desire is that which the desired does not satisfy, but hollows out. It is goodness. It does not refer to a lost fatherland of plentitude; it is not homesickness, it is not nostalgia. It is the lack in a being which *is* completely, and lacks nothing.[74]

Now, if the idea of infinity, as Levinas notes, has been 'put into us,' structuring a relationship where 'the more in the less' prompts an affectivity sensed as ethical resistance; and if this resistance is, moreover, transposed into a metaphysical Desire hungering for the other, then this Desire fits as well into a hermeneutic of escape, of perpetual leave-taking. Yet it is a leave-taking obliged to the face of the other.[75]

In the last section of this essay, "The Idea of Infinity and Conscience," Levinas addresses the question of how this escape can avoid being homogenized into totalization: 'Is not knowing a face *acquiring* a consciousness of it, and is not to acquire consciousness to adhere *freely*? Does not the idea of infinity, qua *idea*, inevitably refer back to the schema of the same encompassing the other? – Unless the idea of infinity means the collapse of the good conscience of the same.'[76] The face puts the self and all its pretentions to freedom in question, finding moreover the presumptive machinations of the will not only arbitrary but elementary. 'If the concept of freedom is the supreme concept, the Other will succumb to the philosophical domination of the same. . . . The I must be awakened by the presence, or rather by the word, of the face that uncovers the wickedness of egocentrism. An autonomous ego is not innocent; its free spontaneity is violence.'[77]

Again one is exhorted to awaken, to challenge the spontaneity of freedom that manifests in reason and theories sponsored in traditions of Western philosophy. For Claire Elise Katz, 'The ethical theories to which Levinas responds are at the level of ontology. He distinguishes his version of ethics from the ethical theories of others by his characterization of the relationship between ethics and ontology.'[78] As for Peperzak, awakening is facilitated by awareness, awareness that even with freedom – the epitome of being – the same still assimilates otherness. He notes further that 'Levinas discovers in freedom a much deeper meaning than the one it holds in philosophies that place it at the summit of all beings.'[79]

Being Measured

Only the face of the other can break the chain of freedom. According to Levinas, 'The other's face is the revelation not of the will, but its injustice. Consciousness of my injustice is produced when I incline myself not before facts, but before the other. In his face the other appears to me not as an obstacle, nor as a menace I evaluate, but what measures me.'[80] Being measured by the face of the other is being measured by infinity.[81] And from this measurement one realizes that spontaneous freedom is appropriative, a realization which discloses itself as shame. Llewelyn finds in this disclosure a 'sharpness of shame' and feels that in Levinas its existence may be defined thusly: 'one is ashamed of oneself because one is ashamed of one's self.'[82] Hence one encounters a solitude and inwardness traumatized through this shame, and freedom now discovers 'itself to be murderous and usurpatory in its very exercise.'[83] This discovery incites a hollowing out of inwardness heralding an ethical consciousness marked by 'the concrete form of a movement more fundamental than freedom, the idea of infinity.'[84]

Here ethical resistance – the presence of infinity – is now ethical consciousness, a consciousness made real in a freedom invested by the heteronymous other, an investiture aggravated and ennobled through responsibility. As Levinas notes,

> The will that is judged, in the meeting with the other, does not assume the judgment it welcomes. That would still be a return of the same deciding the other in the final analysis – heteronomy absorbed in autonomy. The structure of the free will becoming *goodness* is not like the glorious and self-sufficient spontaneity of the I and of happiness, which would be the ultimate movement of being; it is, as it were, its converse. The life of freedom discovering itself to be unjust, the life of freedom in heteronomy, consists in an infinite movement of freedom putting itself ever more into question. This is how the very depth of inwardness is hollowed out. The augmentation of exigency I have in regard to myself aggravates the judgment that is borne on me, that is, my responsibility. And the aggravation of my responsibility increases these exigencies. In this movement my freedom does not have the last word; I never find my solitude again – or, one might say, moral consciousness is essentially unsatisfied, or again, is always a desire.[85]

Aggravation and moral exigency experienced as Desire now move as goodness concretized through responsibility.

Freedom, however, the self's assertion, is implicated in the circuitry of certainty, one yielding to a situational proof underscored by a neutralized presupposition reduced to free will.[86] This is the result of a solitary subject whose self-circumscription is a last refuge. 'As a welcome of the real into my a priori ideas, an adhesion of my free will, the last gesture of cognition,' notes Levinas, 'is freedom. The face to face situation in which this freedom is put into question as unjust, in which it finds it has a master and a judge, is realized prior to certainly, but also prior to uncertainty.'[87] Davis considers this situation, while discoverable and encountered in a variety of empirical events, not formally empirical. 'This is because the encounter with the other lies at the origin of the separateness of the self; only by discovering the irreducibility of the alterity of the Other can I understand that I am neither solipsistically alone in the world nor part of a totality to which all others also belong. This encounter is, Levinas insists, ethical. It characterizes human relations at their most basic level.'[88]

The measuring up of oneself against the perfection inherent in the idea of infinity, as well as in the face of the other, prompts shame as the self discovers an existence invested by a moral exigency welcomed and judged by the other.[89] This shame, moreover, is but the result of freedom finding itself adjudicated and put into question, resulting in the hollowing out of inwardness.[90] And the hollowing out prompts a righteous aggravation, one ennobled by the disquietude of a moral consciousness invoking a reality overflowing a priori categories, and one also critiquing a solipsistic self trammeled by its own freedom. As notes Levinas, 'this situation is an experience in the strongest sense of the term: a contact with a reality that does not fit into any a priori idea, which overflows them. . . . No movement of freedom could appropriate a face to itself or seem to "constitute" it. The face has already been there when it was anticipated or constituted.'[91]

This fact of antecedence constitutes the face as a pure experience, one irreducible to concept or category – irreducible, in other words, to autonomy and totality. Thus the face displays a heightened ambiguity that according to Bernhard Waldenfels 'announces the corporeal absence of the other. . . . The human face is just the foyer of such bewilderment, lurking at the borderlands which separate the normal from the anomalous.'[92] This anomalous visage, prompting ethical resistance, now exaggerates the shame and disequilibrium characterizing the self.

Disalignment

Levinas has thus proposed a dimension more fundamentally transcendent than those captured by ontological certainties.[93] This dimension is marked by ethical resistance, a situation of justice which modulates into a moral exigency experienced as aggravation and unquenchable desire – shaming the consciousness of the self.[94] According to Levinas,

> the purely negative incomprehension of the other, which depends on our bad will, must be distinguished for the essential incomprehension of the infinite, which has a positive side, is conscience and desire. . . . The desire for infinity does not have the sentimental complacency of love, but the rigor of moral exigency. God commands only through men for whom one must act. Is not moral conscience the critique of and the principle of the presence of self to self? Then if the essence of philosophy consists in going back from all certainties toward a principle, if it lives from critique, the face of the other would be the starting point of philosophy. . . . This situation is the moral

conscience, the exposedness of my freedom to the judgment of the other. It is a disalignment which has authorized us to catch sight of the dimension of height and the ideal in the gaze of him to whom justice is due.[95]

From this ethical perspective regarding the other (from which all of Levinas's work may be viewed), the solipsism and autonomy disclosed by the subject – from the hypostatic event to self awareness – seems to be not so much flawed as necessary. Regarding this necessity, Peperzak believes that 'without autonomy and a certain egoism, the separation between the Same and the Other would be impossible: the two poles would inevitably fuse. However, the autonomy of the I must be submitted to the primordial relationship and discover its true significance by respecting the highness of the Other, which gives it its task.'[96]

Respecting the highness of the Other, though contra-conceptual, does nonetheless suggest that freedom has been rectified through the ego's turning from its injustice towards a devotion to the other.[97] Hence freedom now has both meaning and mission – for the ethical resistance that marks the presence of infinity is suddenly experienced as the face of the other, one through whom God commands. Consequentially, this being commanded both rectifies and delineates subjectivity. From Levinas's perspective,

> I am defined as a subjectivity, as a singular person, as an "I," precisely because I am exposed to the other. It is my inescapable and incontrovertible answerability to the other that makes me an individual "I." So that I become a responsible or ethical "I" to the extent that I agree to depose or dethrone myself – to abdicate my position of centrality – in favor of the vulnerable other.[98]

It appears the aggravation of responsibility precedes the freedom of consciousness.[99] This point will be made more explicit in the analysis of *Totality and Infinity*, but suffice it for now to state that 'one must say that the consciousness of the ego finds itself constituted as already related to the Other before any possibility of getting ahold of itself or of identifying itself with itself as consciousness.... The face (or the word, or the Other) is the most immediate revelation there is.'[100] Stated differently, for Levinas conscience is antecedent to consciousness – since it critiques the presence of self to self. Further, this critique serves to obviate any concept or perception of the ego, bringing one back again to the pure experience of a horizontal revelation prompted by the face of the other.

But most important, by dethroning the ego, by becoming a responsible "I," what began this essay as an experience of truth becomes an evocation of God; for as the self abdicates its centrality for the vulnerable other, it is responding as if to a command from God, prompting the presence of infinity. And this presence is in the face of the other, a face precedent to being, a face that traces ethical resistance into its own time and history. And this tracing of the face suggests for Bettina Bergo 'that there is a "level" – of "existence" – that precedes that of freedom, consciousness and beings. This level is irreducible to being because it is lost in efforts to thematize and describe it; so it stands metaphorically on the hither side of being. It stands paradoxically, for Levinas, both beyond being because it is never reducible to the to conceptualization *and* it shines through being.'[101] As a result, this visitation of the face constitutes what Levinas calls the 'epiphany of the other':[102]

> The other comes to us not only out of context but also without mediation; he signifies by himself. The cultural meaning which is revealed—and reveals—as it were *horizontally,* which is revealed from the historical world to which it belongs, and which, according to the phenomenological expression, reveals the horizons of this world – this mundane meaning is disturbed and jostled by another presence that is abstract (or, more exactly, absolute) and not integrated into the world. This presence consists in coming toward us, in *making an entry.* . . . The epiphany of the face is a *visitation.*[103]

At the beginning of "Philosophy and the Idea of Infinity" Levinas asks a question: 'Autonomy or heteronomy?'[104] At the end of the essay, asserting a new beginning, one where 'the face of the other would be the starting point of philosophy,' he answers his own question by stating that 'This is a thesis of heteronomy which breaks with a very venerable tradition.' [105] Breaking away from the tradition of autonomy, the law of the same, again involves escape – involves engaging one's self in a situation of moral conscience, involves exposing one's freedom to the judgment of the other. This engagement finds full treatment in Levinas's first major work, *Totality and Infinity.*

Notes

1. Levinas, "La philosophie et l'idée de l'Infini," *En découvrant l'existence avec Husserl et Heidegger,* 165 ; "Philosophy and the Idea of Infinity," in *Collected Philosophical Papers,* 47.
2. Ibid.
3. See Robert Gibbs, "Height and Nearness," *Ethics as First Philosophy,* 13. Gibbs asserts that owing to responsibility in Levinas, transcendence disrupts presence, commanding one to remain in the here and now.
4. Preface to Emmanuel Levinas, *Alterity and Transcendence,* xiii.
5. *To The Other,* 89.
6. Levinas, "La philosophie et l'idée de l'Infini," 166; "Philosophy and the Idea of Infinity," 48, emphasis in text.
7. "What is the Question to which 'Substitution' is the Answer," in *The Cambridge Companion to Levinas,* 242.
8. Peperzak, *To The Other,* 92.
9. Levinas, "La philosophie et l'idée de l'Infini," 166 ; "Philosophy and the Idea of Infinity," 48.
10. Ibid., 167 ; 49.
11. See Llewelyn, *Appositions of Jacques Derrida and Emmanuel Levinas,* 88.
12. *Liturgy of the Neighbor,* 38.
13. *Altared Ground : Levinas, History, and Violence,* 122.

14. Levinas, "La philosophie et l'idée de l'Infini," 166; "Philosophy and the Idea of Infinity," 48.
15. See Samuel Moyn, *Origins of the Other: Emmanuel Levinas Between Revelation and Ethics*, 5f.
16. In "Is Ontology Fundamental," Levinas basically asserts that the whole human being is contingent on ontology. He goes on to mention that both scientific life and the multivalent sensibilities circumscribed by affective life all involve the comprehension of being reduced to truth, *Basic Philosophical Writings*, 3.
17. Levinas, "La philosophie et l'idée de l'Infini," 167 ; "Philosophy and the Idea of Infinity," 49f.
18. Elsewhere Levinas calls this 'globalizing vision' the 'culmination of philosophy itself. One can see this nostalgia for totality everywhere in Western philosophy, where the spiritual and the reasonable always reside in knowledge. It is as if the totality had been lost, and this loss were the sin of the mind.' *Ethics and Infinity*, 76.
19. Davis, *Levinas: An Introduction*, 41 emphasis in text.
20. Levinas, "La philosophie et l'idée de l'Infini," 168 ; "Philosophy and the Idea of Infinity," 50.
21. *Levinas : A Guide for the Perplexed*, 41.
22. Levinas, "La philosophie et l'idée de l'Infini," 168 ; "Philosophy and the Idea of Infinity," 50.
23. Ibid. Elsewhere Levinas notes this tendency to violent reduction when he comments that it leads 'to full self-consciousness affirming itself as absolute being, and confirming itself as an I that, through all possible "differences," is identified as master of its own nature as well as of the universe and able to illuminate the dark recesses of resistance to its power,' "Ethics as First Philosophy," in *The Levinas Reader*, trans. Sean Hand (Oxford: Blackwell Publishers Ltd, 1989) 79.
24. Bernasconi and Critchley, in their introduction to *Re-Reading Levinas*, liken this reduction to 'the assimilation of otherness into Sameness, where the other is digested like food and drink,' xi.
25. *To the Other*, 53.
26. *The Intrigue of Ethics: A Reading of the Idea of Discourse in the Thought of Emmanuel Levinas* (New York: Fordham University Press, 2001) 14.
27. *Face To Face With Levinas*, 26f, emphasis in text.
28. In fairness to Heidegger, is should be mentioned that 'Levinas's ethical critique of Heidegger's ontology has to be evaluated in terms of Levinas's own philosophical project, in terms of his own counteroption to Heidegger's ontology that Levinas continually offers. Levinas's critique of Heidegger's ontology has to be understood in light of Levinas's own phenomenological analysis of being, which finds in being that which is beyond and more important than knowledge of being – the Good, the ethical relation between persons, or ethics itself. Most importantly, Levinas's criticisms of Heidegger's ontology on ethical grounds have to be evaluated in light of Levinas's own insistence that ethics is not a branch of philosophy, but first philosophy,' Manning, *Interpreting Otherwise Than Heidegger*, 91.
29. Levinas, "La philosophie et l'idée de l'Infini," 170 ; "Philosophy and the Idea of Infinity," 52.
30. Bergo, *Levinas: Between Ethics and Politics,* 47. See also Sonia Sikka, 'Questioning the Sacred: Heidegger and Levinas on the Locus of Divinity,' *Modern Theology*, 14, 3, 1998, 299-323.
31. Peperzak, *To The Other*, 98. For Levinas, some of Heidegger's followers, those whom he called the 'orthodox Heideggerians,' continued in this philosophical

naturalism. 'The orthodox Heideggerians admit of no other discriminating features between two thoughts than those involving the truth of being that governs them. . . .They have nothing but disdain for any reference to ethical certainties, which would indicate an inferior thinking, and insufficient thinking – opinion. The appeal to ethics runs contrary to the fundamental dogma of Heideggerian orthodoxy: priority of being in relation to beings,' "The Poet's Vision," in *Proper Names*, trans. Michael B. Smith (Stanford, California: Stanford University Press, 1996) 136f.

32. Levinas, "La philosophie et l'idée de l'Infini," 171 ; "Philosophy and the Idea of Infinity," 53.

33. Ibid.

34. Ibid., emphasis in text.

35. Peperzak, preface to *Basic Philosophical Writings*, x.

36. In the *Republic* 509b, Plato has Socrates pronounce the good above and beyond being, trans. Benjamin Jowett (New York: Barnes and Nobles Classics, 2004), 220.

37. Levinas, "Transcendence and Height," in *Basic Philosophical Writings*, 21. See also Mary-Ann Webb, "Eros and Ethics: Levinas's Reading of Plato's 'Good beyond Being,' *Studies in Christian Ethics*, 19, no. 2 (2006): 205-222.

38. See Levinas, "Dialogue with Emmanuel Levinas," in *Face to Face with Levinas*, 25.

39. *The Problem of Ethical Metaphysics*, 1.

40. Levinas, "La philosophie et l'idée de l'Infini," 171f. ; "Philosophy and the Idea of Infinity," 53f.

41. According to Jeffrey Dudiak, 'For Levinas, and according to Levinas for Descartes too, the halting of such recurrent doubt is only accomplished . . . when God (The Other in Cartesian terminology, according to Levinas) guarantees the *cogito* by providing it with a principle that comes to it from the outside – the idea of the infinite,' *The Intrigue of Ethics*, 156.

42. *Descartes: The Project of Pure Enquiry* (Middlesex, England: Penguin Books, 1978) 57.

43. Rene Descartes, *Meditations on First Philosophy*, III, in *The Rationalists*, trans. John Veitch (Garden City, New York: Dolphin Books, 1960) 141.

44. Descartes, 142; For more on Descartes and Levinas, see Keith Devlin, *Goodbye Descartes: The End Of Logic And The Search For A New Cosmology Of The Mind* (New York: John Wiley and Sons, 1997) 275; Roger Scruton, *A Short History of Modern Philosophy* (London: Routledge, 1995) 35; Bernard Williams, "Descartes," in *The Great Philosophers: An Introduction To Western Philosophy*, ed. Bryan Magee (Oxford: Oxford University Press, 1987) 85-88; Hent De Vries, *Minimal Theologies: Critiques of Secular Reason in Adorno and Levinas*, trans. Geoffrey Hale (Baltimore: The Johns Hopkins University Press, 2005) 75.

45. Cf. 'To be sure, is it not astonishing that in creating me, God should have endowed me with this idea, so that it would be like a mark of the craftsman impressed upon his work, although this mark need not be something distinct from the work itself,' Descartes, *Meditations on First Philosophy*, III, 40.

46. Ibid., 41.

47. Levinas, "La philosophie et l'idée de l'Infini," 173; "Philosophy and the Idea of Infinity," 55.

48. *Appositions of Jacques Derrida and Emmanuel Levinas*, 206.

49. Levinas, "La philosophie et l'idée de l'Infini," 172 ; "Philosophy and the Idea of Infinity," 54, emphasis in text.

50. "Tracing Responsibility," in *Ethics as First Philosophy*, 174, emphasis in text.

51. Levinas, "La philosophie et l'idée de l'Infini," 172; "Philosophy and the Idea of Infinity," 54.

52. Ibid. Levinas's grounding of experience in the idea of infinity prompts Robert Bernasconi to note that 'This notion of the infinite in the finite provides the basis for Levinas's attempt to find a way between transcendence and immanence. He turns aside from that version of the philosophy of transcendence which relies on mysticism at the expense of terrestrial existence, as much as from the philosophy of immanence which confines the source of meaning in this world. . . . That the infinite is in the finite means that the metaphysical relation is inscribed within the unfolding of terrestrial existence. . . . It is reflected *within* the totality and history, *within* experience,' "Levinas," in *Continental Philosophy 1: Philosophy and Non-Philosophy Since Merleau-Ponty*, ed. Hugh Silverman (New York: Routledge, 1988) 233f., emphasis in text.

53. Levinas, "La philosophie et l'idée de l'Infini," 173 ; "Philosophy and the Idea of Infinity," 55, emphasis in text.

54. *Wittgenstein and Levinas: Ethical and Religious Thought* (London: Routledge, 2005) 133.

55. Levinas, "La philosophie et l'idée de l'Infini," 173 ; "Philosophy and the Idea of Infinity," 55. This point is re-emphasized in *Totality and Infinity* where Levinas discusses the relations whose terms do not form a totality and thus are capable of being produced within the general economy of being through the face-to-face encounter. This encounter, moreover, is distinguished by both distance and depth – both finding meaning through the goodness rendered in irreducible desire, 39; *Totalité et Infini*, 9.

56. Levinas, "Interview with Francois Poirie," in *Is It Righteous To Be?* 48.

57. Levinas, "La philosophie et l'idée de l'Infini," 173 ; "Philosophy and the Idea of the Infinity," 55.

58. See Gibbs, *Correlations in Rosenzweig and Levinas*, 182f.

59. *On Levinas*, 54.

60. Levinas, "La philosophie et l'idée de l'Infini," 173 ; "Philosophy and the Idea of the Infinity," 55.

61. Ibid., 173f.; 55f.

62. *Wittgenstein and Levinas: Ethical and Religious Thought* (London: Routledge, 2005) 127.

63. *To The Other*, 65.

64. *Levinas: A Guide for the Perplexed*, 50f.

65. *The Problem of Ethical Metaphysics*, 224f.

66. In "Transcendence and Height," Levinas tells us that 'The putting in question of the I – which coincides with the nonallergic presence of the Other – does not consist simply in losing its natural foundation and confidence but in an elevation; consciousness finds in itself more than it can contain, the commitment is a promotion. And it is already in this sense that we propose to speak of a dimension of height that opens within being,' *Basic Philosophical Writings*, 18.

67. *Levinas: An introduction*, 78.

68. Levinas, "La philosophie et l'idée de l'Infini," 174 ; "Philosophy and the Idea of Infinity," 56. Cf. 'In thinking infinity the I from the first *thinks more than it thinks*,' 172; 54, emphasis in text.

69. Invoking justice will tie Levinas's motifs to Judaic law, clarifying his later emphasis on responsibility. Recurrent in his work is the frequent citation from Dostoyevsky's *Brothers Karamazov*: 'All of us are guilty of everything and responsible for everyone in the face of everything and I more than others.' Cf. Levinas in *Ethics and*

infinity, regarding Dostoyevsky's quote, noting that 'This is not owing to such or such guilt which is really mine, or to offences that I would have committed; but because I am responsible for a total responsibility, which answers for all the others and for all in the others, even for their responsibility. The I always has one responsibility *more* than all the others,' 99; *Éthique et Infini*, 105, emphasis in text.

70. Levinas, "La philosophie et l'idée de l'Infini," 174 ; "Philosophy and the Idea of the Infinity," 56.

71. *On Levinas*, 24.

72. *Sensibility and Singularity: The Problem of Phenomenology in Levinas* (Albany, New York: State University of New York Press, 2001) 111.

73. See Wyschogrod, *The Problem of Ethical Metaphysics*, 244.

74. Levinas, "La philosophie et l'idée de l'Infini," 174f.; "Philosophy and the Idea of Infinity," 56f.

75. See Amit Pinchevski, *By Way Of Interruption*, 76f.

76. Levinas, "La philosophie et l'idée de l'Infini," 175 ; "Philosophy and the Idea of Infinity," 57, emphasis in text. It should be noted that for the understanding of this last section, 'one must be aware of the fact that the French *conscience* can mean both "consciousness" and "conscience" (*conscience morale*),' Peperzak, *To The Other*, 115.

77. Peperzak, *To The Other*, 68.

78. *Levinas, Judaism, and the Feminine*, 14.

79. *To The Other*, 70.

80. Levinas, "La philosophie et l'idée de l'Infini," 175f. ; "Philosophy and the Idea of Infinity" 57f.

81. As earlier noted in reference to Levinas's alignment with the thought of Descartes, the idea of infinity has been put into one. Thus, being measured by the other is being measured by infinity, as these terms are cognate in Levinas. Moreover, this being measured only accentuates and exasperates one's imperfections. See Levinas, *Ethics and infinity*, 91f.

82. *Emmanuel Levinas: The Genealogy of Ethics*, 18.

83. Levinas, "La philosophie et l'idée de l'Infini," 176; "Philosophy and the Idea of Infinity," 58.

84. Ibid.

85. Ibid, emphasis in text.

86. See Burggraeve, *The Wisdom of Love*, 47f.

87. Levinas, "La philosophie et l'idée de l'Infini," 177; "Philosophy and the Idea of Infinity," 59. Cf. Davis, *Levinas*, where it is noted that 'The encounter is not an empirical event (thought it may be enacted in any number of empirical events); it is rather, in terms continually used by Levinas, original, essential, or fundamental' (48). Davis further comments that the encounter with the other is foundational to the separateness of the self and is thus fundamentally ethical. It is fundamentally ethical because it is antecedent and because it depicts human relations at their basic level.

88. *Levinas*, 48.

89. Cf. Levinas, "Subjectivity of Responsibility," in *God, Death, and Time*, where one finds that the ethical relationship does not so much disclose something given as expose one to another, an exposure Levinas feels is antecedent to any decision. This exposure, moreover, prompts a kind of violence, a trauma precipitated by the other's command to the same, a command discoverable in the urgency 'that calls for my help, to the point where I always come to late, for there is not time to wait for me,' 187.

90. This 'hollowing out' Levinas will later call *denucleation* and *fission*, as when he states in *Otherwise than Being* that 'the approach of the neighbor is a fission of the

subject beyond lungs, in the resistant nucleus of the ego, in the undividedness of its individuality. It is a fission of the self, or the self as fissibility, a passivity more passive still than the passivity of matter,' 180.

91. Levinas, "La philosophie et l'idée de l'Infini," 177; "Philosophy and the Idea of Infinity," 59.

92. "Levinas and the Face of the Other," *The Cambridge Companion to Levinas*, 63.

93. See Llewelyn, *Appositions*, 151.

94. This shame is inescapable. 'The unlimited and initial responsibility that justifies the concern for justice, for the self, and for philosophy can be forgotten. In this forgetfulness, consciousness is pure egoism. But the egoism is neither first nor last. The impossibility of escaping God – the adventure of Jonas – dwells in the depths of myself as a self, as an absolute passivity,' Levinas, "Substitution," in *Basic Philosophical Writings*, 95.

95. Levinas, "La philosophie et l'idée de l'Infini," 177; "Philosophy and the Idea of Infinity," 59.

96. Peperzak, *To The Other*, 70. See also Anthony J. Steinbock, "Face and Revelation," in *Addressing Levinas*, 131.

97. Levinas comments in "A Religion for Adults," *Difficult Freedom* that in order to know oneself one must be ever cognizant of the faults one has committed against the other. This cognizance makes one mindful that the other is situated in an ideal yet divine dimension of height allowing one to be in touch with God. What is more, for Levinas what unites self-consciousness and the consciousness of God is the moral relation, 17.

98. Levinas, "Dialogue with Emmanuel Levinas," in *Face to Face With Levinas*, 26f.

99. Bloechl asserts that for Levinas the responsibility that fully engages freedom antecedes an objective framework (*Liturgy of the Neighbor*, 32), while Chalier sees freedom in Levinas as an answer to a calling ("Levinas and the Hebraic Tradition," *Ethics as First Philosophy*, 7f.). Cohen collates freedom with 'an unmeasured and unmeasurable responsibility, one directed from and toward the *outside* of thought': in other words, from and toward the other (*Elevations*, 160, emphasis in text).

100. Peperzak, *To The Other*, 72.

101. *Levinas: Between Ethics and Politics*, 93, emphasis in text. Bergo adds: ' It (the face) arrests the free play of power and knowledge. It places a consciousness, an individual into question. Now if the face actually *did* this, if the face actively stopped me in my tracks, as if by design, then how could I ever refuse it? My obligation to the other would be absolute and so utterly independent of time, of history, that what Levinas calls eschatology would no longer be a position from which to judge the history of men, but would *be* history in its entirety,' ibid.

102. Levinas, "Meaning and Sense," in *Basic Philosophical Writings*, 53.

103. Ibid, emphasis in text.

104. Levinas, "La philosophie et l'idée de l'Infini," 166; "Philosophy and the Idea of Infinity." 48.

105. Ibid., 178; 59.

Chapter Four

Ethical Optics

Much of what has been issued forth regarding "Philosophy and the Idea of Infinity" finds full treatment in Levinas's first major book-length essay, *Totality and Infinity: An Essay on Exteriority* (1961). And since this work presents extensively themes sketched out thus far, a treatment of its contents is necessary. For the purpose of this study, most analysis herein will revolve around the preface, section 1, section 3, and the conclusion, as these are the loci where motifs in "Philosophy and the Idea of Infinity" most fully resonate. This chapter will also offer an excursus on the biblical patriarch Abraham, a paradigmatic figure able to exegete and model Levinas's ethical metaphysics.

Again one finds Levinas focusing on transcendence as it manifests in the face-to-face relationship, but here a more expansive collocation between this relationship and the ethical assumes prominence. Keeping in mind Levinas's conviction that the presence of infinity emerges in ethical resistance – where truth awakens as an experience of desire for the other – one engaging *Totality and Infinity* begins early to glimpse themes Levinas will thread more intricately into what he calls an 'eschatology of messianic peace.'[1] The main thrust at this stage of the analysis will be to present precisely the ways these themes are conjugate with responsibility in Levinas.

As if to provide a hermeneutical dynamic from which to launch his metaphysical ethics,[2] Levinas opens his preface with a question: 'Does not lucidity, the mind's openness upon the true, consist in catching sight of the permanent possibility of war? . . . War is not only one of the ordeals – the greatest – of which morality lives; it renders morality derisory.'[3] Cognizance of this possibility of war, along with awareness of how it is complicit with political subterfuge, prompts Levinas to assert that 'Everyone will agree that it is of the highest importance to know whether we are not duped by morality.'[4]

Some might consider harsh these polemic insertions of war and lucidity immediately into the text, particularly those unmindful of Levinas's earlier inquiry: autonomy or heteronomy?[5] For here it appears Levinas is intensifying his exposition concerning the relation between the same and the other, mindful that 'Such a relation is not possible unless its two terms are in a very strong sense of the word *exterior* to each other. Their separation from one another must resist all attempts at fusion or totalizing. They are not and cannot become two moments of one union.'[6] However, owing to the fact that struggle and escape have been a common theme for Levinas, beginning from the hypostasis of the subject from the *il y a* to its antagonistic engagement with freedom and justice, this brusque insertion in the preface of antipodal realities functions to concretize life, truth, and experience.[7] Moreover, readers accustomed to the internecine dramas enacted through usurpatory and assimilative egos earlier in Levinas certainly should not find too incongruent these conflicts assuming wider margin:

> In war reality rends the words and images that dissimulate it, to obtrude in its nudity and in its harshness. Harsh reality (this sounds like a pleonasm!), harsh object-lesson, at the very moment of its fulguration when the drapings of illusion burn war is produced as the pure experience of being. . . . Not only modern war but every war employs arms that turn against those who wield them. It establishes an order from which no one can keep his distance; nothing henceforth is exterior. War does not manifest exteriority and the other as other; it destroys the identity of the same.[8]

Hence the reality of being is not only harsh but shows its face in war: and one who fails to face this reality is already duped by morality. Around this motif ranges the essential problematic of *Totality and Infinity*, one constellated by what Peperzak calls 'a bewildering collection of topics, such as the place and function of politics, the relations between faith and thought, history and eschatology, totality and infinity, language and hypocrisy, theory and practice, methodology, ethics, and phenomenology.'[9] And strangely, yet provocatively, Levinas's evocation of a messianic eschatology adds suspense as well as tension to the already taut ethical resistance promulgated thus far.

Levinas, however, does not limit himself to the prototypical conflicts common to relations between the ethical and the political, but intrepidly moves into the more radical dimension where the ethical is originary – hence metaphysical. 'The thought of Emmanuel Levinas,' notes Wyschogrod, 'is no less than an attempt to accomplish a radical reversal of traditional procedures by grounding metaphysics in ethics rather than in constructing an ethic upon preestablished metaphysical foundations.'[10] In addition to this, by initiating a new paradigm whereby responsibility merges into the social arena via justice, Levinas remains true to his Judaic heritage championing charity and mercy – thus pairing metaphysics (the universal) and ethics (the particular.) This pairing prompts Bernasconi to comment that 'one can see what Levinas is attempting to do when he looks to Judaism to negotiate the relation between the particular and the universal. Judaism is a particularity that promotes universalism, conditions it.'[11]

Peace as Precedence

Levinas fixes the reality of war with the concept of totality, one he believes to dominate Western philosophy. This reality for Levinas collapses individuals into faceless 'bearers of forces that command them unbeknown to themselves. The meaning of individuals (invisible outside of this totality) is derived from the totality. The unicity of each present is incessantly sacrificed to a future appealed to to bring forth its objective meaning. For the objective meaning alone counts.'[12] This objective meaning for Levinas implicates the intrigues of history with what he calls natural opinion, again betraying forces complicit with moralities founded upon politics. Of course this is a politics founded upon sophism and nihilism. Cohen finds that for Levinas, however, this subversion could be obviated by a political emphasis deferential to the ethical, one 'where morality and justice do not contradict one another, where giving all to one deprives no one else.'[13]

Sensing the need for a different register, Levinas presents an eschatological vision commensurate with the aforementioned desire ingredient to the idea of infinity. It is essential to note at this stage the hermeneutical prolepsis implemented by Levinas, for just as our analysis keeps its course owing to the gravity of responsibility, themes and motifs keyed early in *Totality and Infinity* work within the circuitry of prophecy and eschatology – implicating God and philosophy. Consequently eschatology here mirrors desire, for it operates outside totality and beyond the pale of autonomy.[14] According to Levinas,

> Its real import lies elsewhere. It does not introduce a teleological system into the totality; it does not consist in teaching the orientation of history. Eschatology institutes a relation with being *beyond the totality*, or beyond history, and not with being beyond the past and the present.... This "beyond" the totality and objective experience is, however, not to be described in a purely negative fashion. It is reflected *within* the totality and history, *within* experience. The eschatological, as the "beyond" of history, draws beings out of the jurisdiction of history and the future; it arouses them in and calls them forth to their full responsibility.[15]

Much here warrants clarification. As in "Philosophy and the Idea of Infinity," the importance here of experience in the thought of Levinas assumes a prominent role. Significantly, what Levinas is seeking is an originary and primordial experience, one where – from a metaphysical perspective – vision and ethics are one.[16] What is more, through his inclusion of the politics of war into the realm of ethics, Levinas again implicates freedom into his argument as reason and justice militate against the subversive assimilations of institutionalization. This explains Levinas's radical search for 'another peace: a prepolitical one that does not result from the calculations of a rational or reasonable compromise, destroyed as soon as the balance of power is shaken, but rather – as an originary peace – one that precedes the emergence of any violence.'[17]

Prelapsarian yet proleptic, early in the preface Levinas offers an original peace reminiscent of a foregone paradise, one inassimilable in history and lost to memory. Hence this peace is eschatological and – owing to a biblical dialectic strained by king and prophet, one assumed in the opposition between politics and ethics – messianic.[18]

But assumption is not distinction. Something distinct is something totalized, something contextualized, and Levinas – in order to present his eschatological vision uncontaminated by autonomy – 'does not envisage the end of history within being understood as a totality, but institutes a relation with the infinity of being which exceeds the totality.'[19] Michael Smith believes Levinas implements this prophetic stance to contrast the ontology of war with messianic eschatology. However, according to Smith, 'the true significance of eschatology is elsewhere. . . . Levinas's use of prophetic eschatology refers to a contact with being beyond the totality.'[20] This relation is fundamental and, since inassimilable, cannot be integrated into synthetic regimes loyal to the same. Notes Peperzak:

> This relation cannot be absorbed or dialectically integrated by any whole, for it resists synthesis and transcends all possibilities of totalizing. It is, therefore, "beyond" or "before" or "transcendent with regard to" the dimensions of politics, economy, history, and ontology in its classical and modern synthetic or dialectical form. This relation is a not a moment of the universe; it is the original *relatedness to the infinite*. This reason of transcendence, with all its consequences for the issues of human existence and philosophy, is the theme or topic of *Totality and Infinity*. Against all the philosophies of "totality" . . . Levinas will show how a nontotalitarian transcendence is possible and how its recognition leads to a radical transformation of the very project of philosophy.[21]

One now must issue the question: How is this nontotalitarian transcendence possible? And how does the originary relation of transcendence relate the subjective ego to the infinite without subjectivity being overwhelmed? Again one finds the answer in the face-to-face relation, a relation where intentionality is superseded by the respect offered charitably to the other, a relation made concrete through hospitality and responsibility.

The Gleam of Exteriority

Mentioned above is Levinas's conviction that the 'beyond of totality' is 'reflected *within* totality and history, *within* experience.' Yet later he notes that 'The first "vision" of eschatology . . . reveals the possibility of a *signification without context*. The experience of morality does not proceed from this vision – it *consummates* this vision; ethics is an optics. But it is a vision without image, bereft of the synoptic and totalizing objectifying virtues of vision. . . .'[22] Begging the question, How can an experience occur yet have a signification without context? one must rigorously keep in mind that the focus here is transcendence as it comes to pass in the face-to-face relation. In fact, 'Levinas understands the task of ethics,' notes Bernasconi, 'to be that of disturbing my good conscience, not re-establishing it. This opens the way to an ethics based not on autonomy, but on heteronomy.'[23]

And since ethics must be rooted in a nonsynthesizable concreteness chary of integration into the logical and manipulative subterfuges of totality, only that grounded in eschatology could be impervious to what Levinas calls 'the natural locus of evidence,' — prompting his conviction that 'Of peace there can be only an eschatology.'[24]

Once more Levinas is twining philosophy with a justice circumscribed by Jewish law, casting the moral message of biblical prophets into a new paradigm where transcendence concretizes into a radical responsibility beholden to the face of the other.[25] Thus for Levinas, 'Without substituting eschatology for philosophy . . . we can proceed from the experience of totality back to a situation where totality breaks up, a situation that conditions the totality itself. Such a situation is the gleam of exteriority or of transcendence in the face of the other.'[26] For Jeffrey Bloechl, the exteriority of the face of the other in Levinas is absolute. This exteriority, he notes, frustrates one's concentration owing to its sheer foreignness. Notes Bloechl: 'The face marks my limits; it commands me and my truths before there is any question of appropriation. It does not enter my world, not even as absent. . . . I do not find the face that commands me, nor do I give it to myself. I experience it as an event announcing my having already been found.'[27]

Thus in quick, bold strokes Levinas prefaces *Totality and Infinity* by introducing war and peace into the crucible of intersubjectivity, precipitating an exteriority where the idea of infinity is now produced in the human arena — hence widening considerably and provocatively perspectives previously collapsed by monadic subjectivity. As when escaping the anonymous rumbling of the *there is* prompted a constraining through the solipsism of egology; and as when breaking away from the trammels of self precipitated a reflexive ethical resistance; now a more harsh reality presents itself — one stressed by war yet called to an eschatological and messianic peace by the naked face of the stranger.[28] Yet again, negligence would prevail if one did not ask: how does transcendence work its way into this war? and how can the face-to-face relation constitute a 'signification without context'? Anticipating this query, Levinas insinuates this 'vision without image' into his ethical optics, assuring one that

> If, as this book will show, ethical relations are to lead transcendence to its term, this is because the essential of ethics is in its *transcendent intention*. . . . Already *of itself* ethics is an "optics." It is not limited to preparing for the theoretical exercise of thought, which would monopolize transcendence. The traditional opposition between theory and practice will disappear before the metaphysical transcendence by which a relation with the absolute other, or truth, is established, and of which ethics is the royal road. . . . It will appear in the eyes of the reader, so naturally indifferent to the vicissitudes of this chase, as a thicket of difficulties where nothing guarantees the presence of game.[29]

Towards a Yonder

Just as Levinas opened "Philosophy and the Idea of Infinity" with "Autonomy and Heteronomy," he opens *Totality and Infinity* with "The Same and the Other." Here however the treatment is fuller and more provocative. Immediately one engages transcendence as the reader is invited to turn 'toward the "elsewhere" and the "otherwise" and the "other" . . . toward a yonder.'[30] This yonder, elsewhere, or other is approachable only through an unprecedented metaphysical desire, one bent by a longing commensurable to the insatiable yet sublime hunger that 'is like goodness – the Desired does not fulfill it, but deepens it.'[31] This deepening, in fact, prompts Michael Purcell to claim that for Levinas 'Desire is otherwise; . . . it is excess which provokes and sustains desire. Desire is provoked by the utter surplus of the other person.'[32]

Mindful of Levinas's assertion that his eschatological vision is not only imageless but also reflects a signification without context, one is now alerted to the fact that desire is metaphysical because it 'implies relations with what is not given, of which there is no idea.'[33] Hermeneutic in scope, this situation sans signification allows Levinas ingress through desire into an exteriority where remoteness is irreducible to ideas yet 'has a meaning. It is understood as the alterity of the Other and of the Most-High. The very dimension of height is opened by metaphysical Desire. That this height is no longer the heavens but the Invisible is the very elevation of height and its nobility. To die for the invisible – this is metaphysics.'[34]

Notably Levinas has involved here the other, God, desire, and sacrifice – cardinal points adumbrating responsibility. What is more, since desire in Levinas lacks the structure of intentionality – and since desire and the desired are non-correlate, defying adequacy – that which distances them is distinguishable by an absolute separation irreducible to synthesis, fusion, or autonomy.[35] This distance for Levinas marks a metaphysical dimension where desire for the other, annunciating transcendence, perforates totality:

> This absolute exteriority of the metaphysical term, the irreducibility of movement to an inward play, to a simple presence of self to self, is, if not demonstrated, claimed by the word transcendent. . . . Thus the metaphysician and the other cannot be *totalized*. The metaphysician is absolutely separated. The radical separation between the same and the other means precisely that it is impossible to place oneself outside of the correlation between the same and the other so as to record the correspondence or the non-correspondence of this going with this return. Otherwise the same and the other would be reunited under one gaze, and the absolute distance that separates them filled in.[36]

From a critical perspective, Jeffrey L. Kosky suggests that 'such respectful separation is, according to Levinas, the distance in and through which the absolutely other appears. Not defined by its opposite, the absolutely other is distant without this distance depending on its relation to another term.'[37]

Hence it is with this radical separation and inadequation in mind that one must exegete Levinas's eschatological vision without image. And this vision can only be fulfilled owing to a subjectivity's willingness to sacrifice its interests to and for the other through a radical hospitality objectifying the above-mentioned *way of existing* – thus empirically implementing Levinas's ethical optics. This way of existing correlates with the motif of escape; furthermore, in light of Levinas's pronouncement that 'This book will present subjectivity as welcoming the other, as hospitality; in it the idea of infinity is consummated,'[38] it certainly appears that hospitality hermeneutically links the metaphysician to the other, marking the distance of transcendence by concretizing responsibility.[39]

But what about concretizing the metaphysician? At this point, as B. C. Hutchens offers, 'It would be tempting to be scathingly critical of Levinasian "ethical responsibility" : *it consists in nothing but an empty caricature of a self responding without comprehension to an equally empty command that it could not know how to obey issuing from another person incoherently described.* If one were unimpressed by Levinas, or even hostile to his way of thinking, this would be a devastating criticism.'[40] Hence logistically this analysis betrays dissemblance is it fails to provide a paradigmatic figure portraying one who implements Levinas's ethical optics, who displays this radical hospitality – all the while sojourning 'toward a yonder.' Of consequence Levinas himself calls on one biblical patriarch to model and establish a precedent for his ethical metaphysics.

A Pending Presence

Remembering Levinas's contention that 'the Other's hunger – be it of the flesh, or of bread – is sacred,'[41] reconfirms a central tenet of Levinas's ethical thought: one called to the other's hunger is elected to serve the other. 'To recognize the Other is to recognize a hunger. To recognize the Other is to give. But it is to give to the master, to the lord, to him whom one approaches as "You" in a dimension of height.'[42] Moreover, mindfulness of the fact that Levinas regarded this election as a 'particularism that conditions universality' – and that this election for Levinas was 'the revelation of morality which . . . is a nobility based not on royalties or a birthright conferred by a divine caprice, but on the position of each human . . . perceiving that I am not *the equal* of the Other' – facilitates a closer understanding of 'this state of mind that we normally call Jewish messianism.'[43] So doing, one also becomes aware of the fact that 'The role played by ethics in the religious relation allows us to understand the meaning of Jewish universalism.'[44] Furthermore, understanding the part performed by responsibility in this relation adds emphasis to Levinas's mission to the Gentiles.

Actually, in line with these roles and ways they thread with Levinas's mission, Llewelyn comments that Jewish particularism is 'consistent with Israel having been chosen historically to preach universalism and to be an example to light the way for the Gentiles.' Realizing responsibility complements this election, Llewellyn adds: 'but the lesson it teaches on Levinas's interpretation is that this historical particularism reflects the ethical particularism of each . . . because I demand more of myself than of others.'[45]

All said, it still merits attention that in order to implement a particularism so foundational, one upon which hinges Levinas's ethical messianism, a figure for this particularism is needed. And just as significant, also needed is an exemplar who fashions through desire for the other a relationship with a surplus exterior to totality, a relationship at once transcendent yet reflected within experience – hence prefiguring the eschatological *beyond* of history commensurable 'with a surplus always exterior to the totality.'[46]

For Levinas Abraham provides this locus, one where the drama of subjectivity assumes narrative dimensions through the unfolding of responsibility. According to Jill Robbins, Abraham is 'paradigmatic' for Levinas, a figure prompting one towards the gift of 'radical generosity' experienced in 'the cyclical movement of warm thanks, recognition, and gratitude.'[47] For Jeffrey Dudiak, Levinas's use of Abraham elicits a proper image for 'the sojourn of the psyche into being,' one where the adventure does not circle back but continues perpetually onward.[48] Moreover, Levinas notes that, owing to the fact that 'the proximity of God is experienced in Judaism through memory,' and that Abraham's prevalence in this memory is foundational to what he calls 'Holy History,' one is able through sensibility to mark the passage of time 'to the point of resonating with, and telling itself in, the actuality of every lived present.'[49] As significant, for Levinas this resonance involves 'A consciousness that is immediately narration, an interiority in which some story stirs, giving the present its meaning. Consciousness is not, in this case, just the actualizing of the new, but also the narration of the past by which consciousness is sustained and ordered.'[50]

Noteworthy here is the implication that consciousness presupposes an antecedent Holy History that is constituent of a narrative irreducible to natural history, one sensitive to the stirrings of interiority.[51] According to Levinas, 'Interiority is the very possibility of a birth and a death that do not derive their meaning from history. Interiority institutes an order different from historical time in which totality is constituted, an order where everything is *pending*, where what is no longer possible historically remains always possible.'[52] In other words, an interiority which breaks away from the trammels of self – that breaks the circle of homecoming foundational to subjectivity—becomes constellated in another order, one no longer susceptible to the gravity of totality, and one forwarding towards the horizonal dimensions of the other.

Rise and Go

How does responsibility for Levinas assume flesh and blood in the person of Abraham? He often referred to this patriarch in order to root his ethical metaphysics in an empirical dimension. Moreover, since Abraham is considered the biblical father of nations, by extension he must also be responsible for nations -- and his leave- taking and sojourning towards and for the other are prototypical of one exemplifying responsibility and faith.⁵³ Catherine Chalier notes Abraham's presence as well:

> The figure of Abraham, contrasted with that of Ulysses, is often found in Levinas's work. While the latter dreams at the end of his heroic adventures, of coming back home, to celebrate his reunion with his people and perhaps to forget the time of his long separation from his native land, the former must rise and go without looking back, without hope of coming back. He also knows that this going away involves all his descendents, since he forbids his servant to bring his son back to his land. . . . (T)his commandment uproots Abraham from his native realm. It forbids him to believe that he can find himself by cultivating a nostalgia for his past. Abraham discovers his integrity as a man called to be a blessing to all families of the earth, only on condition that he loses himself, that is, only on condition that he gets rid of all that which, by keeping him prisoner of the past – words, images, possessions – would make impossible for him the going forward to the Promised Land. It is a land to which he none the less proceeds, day after day, for his entire humanity lies in his answer to the call he heard. But it is a land which he has no certainty of entering and settling.⁵⁴

Abraham's blessing is contingent on his obedience, on his being uprooted and on his breaking the circuits of violence original to a self-inflected subjectivity. Brian Schroeder's study of history and violence in Levinas bases its thesis on the notion that 'much of the force of Levinasian ethics revolves around the premise that violence first arises conceptually. . . . By extension, violence also arises in the will to comprehend the Absolute as ground, to name the Infinite. In this regard, Levinas remains fundamentally Jewish.'⁵⁵ The images, words, and possessions subverting Abraham's exodus to the Promised Land are analogous to the synoptic violence of totality and war underscored by Levinas.⁵⁶ Again exile assumes dimensions of escape; and the passion of a self at war encapsulates a story writ large in Holy History, one where Israel is aligned with eschatological messianism: 'What a paradox Holy History is . . . an eschatology through the Passion of Israel among the nations. Passion of Humanity bleeding through the wounds of Israel.'⁵⁷ This is a passion played out in the figure of Abraham, one 'where what is no longer possible historically remains always possible.'⁵⁸ And, crucially, it is a passion where God and the stranger are indissolubly the other.

For reference, Levinas notes Genesis 18. In this passage, Abraham recognizes the sacredness of the other's hunger, and his decision to serve the stranger becomes an election honoring the master and God.⁵⁹ The passage depicts a scene: it was warm, with the heat penetrating even the shade under the oaken sanctuary of Marme where Abraham had pitched his tent. Seizing a moment for rest, he dozed at the entrance of his tent as Sarah moved about inside. Awakened, Abraham detected in the near haze the figures of strangers.

> When he saw them, he ran from the tent entrance to meet them, and bowed down to the ground. He said, "My lord, if I find favor with you, do not pass by

your servant. Let a little water be brought, and wash your feet, and rest yourselves under the tree. Let me bring a little bread, that you may refresh yourselves, and after that you may pass on – since you have come to your servant. . . ." Abraham ran to the herd, and took a calf, tender and good, and gave it to the servant, who hastened to prepare it. Then he took curds and milk and the calf that he had prepared, and set it before them; and he stood by them under the tree while they ate. [60]

Here the Old Testament motif regarding radical hospitality assumes an ethical refrain concerning those destitute and abandoned. Significantly, an imperial voice often breaks into biblical narratives enough to let all know that God wants us to be mindful of strangers. Exodus 23:9 says 'You shall not oppress a resident alien; you know the heart of an alien, for you were aliens in the land of Egypt.' Leviticus 19:34 says that 'you shall love the alien as yourself,' while Numbers 15: 15 stresses that 'you and the alien shall be alike before the Lord.' Psalm 146:7 assures happiness for one 'who keeps faith forever; who executes justice for the oppressed; who gives food to the hungry.' But here with Abraham there is a theophanic and covenantal horizon within the seemingly ordinary, ordinary at least until men become angels – who become God. Not only is the relation between the three strangers and the Lord blurred; the narrative never clearly delineates the trio, shifting deftly between speaking of them as a group to the Lord alone.[61] In fact, the text is anticipatory as *they* say 'Do as you have said' (v. 5); later *they* ask 'Where is your wife Sarah?' (v. 9). However, sodality becomes unanimity when 'The Lord' asks Abraham 'is anything too wonderful for the Lord?'(v. 13f.) Stranger angels here speak as the Lord, but not before Abraham 'ran from the tent to meet them, and bowed low to the ground' (v. 2).

A Vigilant Crisis

Genuflecting to the other – offering water, bread, and rest. Sacrificing the best for the least, bidding mercies tender and good, hastening to prepare, setting it before them – and standing by vigilantly while the strangers feast: These are genuine acts of worship, devotion that in 'this text involves not only human hospitality, but also hospitality toward God. One could speak in terms of Matthew 25; acting on behalf of one of "the least of these" constitutes an act on behalf of God. Hospitality toward God is not simply a spiritual matter, but a response of the whole self in the midst of the quite mundane affairs of everyday life. Although we are not always able to identify the presence of God in the midst of life, God assumes flesh and blood in the neighbor.'[62] Implementing an ethical optics, Abraham in this passage literally sees God in the stranger, confirming Levinas's assertion that 'The dimension of the divine opens forth from the human face. . . . His very epiphany consists in soliciting us by his destitution in the face of the Stranger, the widow, and the orphan.'[63] What is more, Rabi Jonathan Sacks tells us

> *God cares about the stranger, and so must we.* Abraham invites three strangers into his tent and discovers that they are angels. Jacob wrestles with an unnamed

adversary alone at night and thereafter says, "I have seen God face to face." Welcoming the stranger, said the sages, is even greater than "receiving the divine presence." . . . The human other is a trace of the Divine. As an ancient Jewish teaching puts it: When a human makes many coins in the same mint, they all come out the same. God makes every person in the same image – His image – and each is different. The challenge to the religious imagination is to see God's image in one who is not in our image.[64]

The call of the stranger now assumes an ethico-theophanic dimension, straining towards an awareness Levinas likens to insomnia. Abraham's awakening beneath the oaks to the approach of the stranger – and his radical response – summon him to a crisis, one vigilant and obedient to the other.

Abraham's vigilance models in effect a liturgy to the other.[65] By inspiring a leave-taking motif implemented polemically against a Greek ethos heralding return, this patriarch exemplifies the exilic and sojourning self in Levinas's ethical thought.[66] In fact, Levinas cautions against contextualized significations and frequently references the biblical Abraham contra the mythical Ulysses in order that the circuit of homecoming might emphatically be broken. This referencing Levinas calls work: '*A work conceived radically is a movement of the same unto the other which never returns to the same.* To the myth of Ulysses returning to Ithaca, we wish to oppose the story of Abraham who leaves his fatherland forever for a yet unknown land, and forbids his servant to even bring back his son to the point of departure.'[67] In his essay "Meaning and Sense" Levinas is corroborative:

> But a departure with no return, which, however, does not go forth into the void, would also lose its absolute *orientation* if it sought recompense in the immediacy of its triumph, if it awaited the triumph of its cause impatiently. The one-way movement of "unique sense" would be reversed and become a reciprocity. . . . As an absolute orientation toward the Other, as sense, a work is possible only in patience, which, pushed to the limit, means the Agent to renounce being the contemporary of its outcome, to act without entering the Promised Land.[68]

The functional thesis incumbent in this leave-taking methodology eschews contextualization, emphasizing an enacted responsibility to the point of hermeneutical hyperbole. Levinas calls this performative responsibility a 'liturgy,' mentioning that 'it is not to be ranked alongside "works" and ethics.[69] It is ethics itself.'[70] Thus: if one is to implement Levinas's ethics, an ethics that is an optics (yet without image), one that breaks from contextualization through a methodology of responsibility analogous to Abraham, and one that 'is not only gratuitous but requires on the part of him who exercise(s) it a putting out of funds at a loss'[71] – and if this exercise at a loss is as Levinas calls it a liturgy, which for him is ethics itself – then those affected are called to a responsibility to the other so extreme as to be liturgical, so vigilant as to be ethical.

A Hyperbolic Hermeneutic

Rising from slumber, leaving the comforts of one's post, preparing and extending a ritualized hospitality — all indicate a giving at a loss, a surrendering asymptotic to sacrifice. Levinas's move to the stranger, moreover, is predicated by what Samuel Moyn calls 'making the move from abstract existence to concrete, particular existence . . . one founded on a transcendence internalized to the asymmetrical relationship to the other person.'[72] Rather than focusing on the economy of being, Levinas submits that 'Asymmetrical intersubjectivity is the locus of transcendence,' arguing further that 'the subject, while preserving itself, has the possibility of not returning to itself.'[73] Again alluding to Abraham, Levinas is staging an exodus away from ontological security.

Paired with transcendence, however, indeed inseparably linked, is the responsible self — dispatched to radical ethical service where obligation and transcendence weave into one revelatory strain.[74] This obligation is rooted in the ethical superiority of the other person, one inscribed in a liturgical emphasis grounding communion with connection. Yet it is connection where loss of self is gain, where one's own humanity is offered mercifully for the humanism of the other. To be sure, 'a humanism of the other is the heart of Levinas's philosophy.' As Cohen comments, based on an 'inexorable imperative of the other,' Levinas's humanism honors

> the superlative moral priority of the other person. . . . Of course, transcendence and responsibility are inseparable moments of concrete ethical encounter, the face-to-face of the self and other. The "otherness" of the other person arises precisely as the moral imperative that pierces the self with moral obligation, with service to the other. Indeed, the true self-hood of the self occurs precisely in and as this service. One is not called on to "love thy neighbor *as* oneself," according to the biblical precept, as if self-love preceded other-love and were the measure of other-love. Rather, the proper formulation of Levinas's thought is more extreme, an infinite demand never satisfied even in its fulfillment: to "love thy neighbor *is* oneself." The moral self is the self-emptying, the "fission," the "denucleation," of selfhood in and as responsibility for the other — up to the ultimate self-sacrifice, to die for the other's welfare.[75]

More detailed analysis of self-fissuring and denucleation will be presented later — at this stage simply its accent is warranted; for it is in *emphasis*, in an extreme (at times hyperbolic) exaggeration in regards to the other, that a hermeneutic in Levinas takes shape.

What Levinas does is take an ineluctable event, the encounter with a stranger, and weaves it into an ethical metaphysics honoring his Talmudic as well as phenomenological heritage.[76] But where Levinas's approach becomes foundational is in the face-to-face relation, where what he calls original relation assumes concreteness through excessive obligation to the other. Simply put: strangers happen. Whether woven into narratives where their presence is theophanic or stitched into episodes where they lay bleeding by the side of the road, strangers call us out of our reverie.[77] And the call is linguistic, invitational, and involving.

One does not truly respond to the other reflectively, but existentially – relationally – with an emphasis Levinas will deem invocative.[78] What is more, insofar as this relation is ethical, it must be articulated through moral expression, one that joins up both self-consciousness and consciousness of God.

Ethics is not 'the corollary of the vision of God, it is that very vision. Ethics is an optic, such that everything I know of God and everything I can hear of His word and reasonably say to Him must find ethical expression.'[79] This expression, however, will be met by forces of totalization and war: whether manifested as consumerism or solipsism, the machinations of totality never rest from their wares, churning into dogma insoluble mixes of ideology and individualism.[80] And systems never sleep. According to Wyschogrod,

> Overwhelmed by complexity, contemporary man turns from technology with its attendant institutions backed by formidable systems of information to seek the meaning of his existence. According to Levinas, these intricate structures are integrated into a totality that imposes its own purposes upon individual life. The totality in its turn is a vastly ramified extension of self. Man has sown his dragon's teeth.[81]

These intrigues of totality involve subtexts subversive to relations intent upon communion and relationship.[82] Moreover, reciprocal relations are susceptible to systemic homogenization. Generality, quid pro quo, mutual relations – any rounding off of the embodied self to the nearest whole diminishes the humanism of the other.[83] These generalizations warrant a weakness – and the problem is one of separation.

When processed into bearers of general characteristics, individuals lose touch with the fact that commonality can at times diminish traits unique and unassimilated. As Levinas notes, 'The alterity of the Other does not depend on any quality that would distinguish him from me, for a distinction of this nature would precisely imply between us that community of genus which already nullifies alterity . . . . The Other remains infinitely transcendent, infinitely foreign.'[84] For Levinas, what makes this expression of the other defy categorization is the nonreciprocal nature of the relation, the height and grandeur assumed by the other.[85]

Hearing Is Heeding

The eminent status granted the other prompts Levinas to wrestle with concepts analogous to the terms employed. Grappling with the radical exteriority created when the lines between the divine and disenfranchised stranger are blurred fuses primary religious concern with sleeve-rolled ethical injunctions. In fact, some see this unmitigated deference to the least and lost as a ceremonial enacting of the divine afflatus itself. Ted Jennings, citing Psalm 82 along with Exodus 3:1-17, discloses how when the psalmist glimpses 'the becoming God of God,' he also serves notice to 'the powerful but false gods of the earth.' Moreover, Jennings notes the psalmist's calling 'out to God to do that which the vision has anticipated: become the Lord of all the earth, the Lord of all the nations. And how is it that God may and must do this? Precisely as this claim of justice for the violated and humiliated.'[86] Jennings later refers to the famous theophany of God to Moses at the burning bush, one traditionally referenced anticipating ontological exposition: in other words, how is God's *I Am* collateral with *being itself*?

Sweeping around conventional commentary, and inspired by Levinas's ethical exigency, Jennings finds the words from the flaming bush God's response, reaction and preemption. Precluding obsession with God's being, Jennings allows that

> That which is not noted in the usage of this passage as a springboard into reflection upon the being of God, upon God as being or being itself, is precisely that *the being of God is this hearing and heeding of the afflicted*. It is not that God exists in some general sense, and then through anthropomorphic slippage from being and essence to existence and accident, comes to hear the heed and cry of this people. Rather it is in and through both the hearing and the heeding of the cry of the violated and humiliated that this One is, that the being of this One comes to be, that act and being, being as act, irrupts into history.[87]

After erasing in a sense any distinction between God's being and God's caring, Jennings moves next to aligning this disclosure with the core metaphysical ethics of Levinas.[88] He notes that 'Levinas is aware that to speak of the transcendent is to speak of another who cannot be captured in the system of representations by which we constitute the world as the home of consciousness. Rather transcendence points to the coming of an other who intersects, interrupts, and brings into question the totalitarian project of consciousness and culture.'[89]

In this interruption, at this intersection, Levinas erects a milestone to the other. What is more, Levinas also exposes fissures in the fabric of totality, breakages where only the relation to the other, 'situated in the world established by language – by transcendence' -- allows a disengagement from the genera implicated by homogenization.[90] By letting the other be other, Levinas assumes a nonviolent stance upright and straightforward, one not complicit with internecine totalitarianisms reflected in Western ontology. Again, this ethical stance instantiates a hermeneutical insomnia where vigilance allays the extenuation provoked when the humanism of the other is violated. Assuming this stance, for Levinas, is allowing oneself to be persuaded by a vulnerability channeled as desire for discourse with those once called the stranger, the widow, and the orphan. In essence, this vulnerability qua desire cannot be reduced to a relation of comprehension but can only be offered as responsibility for the other.

With Levinas, the smudging of boundaries separating transcendence from immanence opens vistas extending from the hospitable to the numinous.[91] There is also for him a bracketing of the stranger that allows an ethical exegesis of each encounter, one he reduces to a phenomenology of the face.[92] The other is graspingly, gloriously present. And there is, moreover, an obsessive vigilance for the welfare of the stranger:

> In ethics, the other's right to exist has primacy over my own, a primacy epitomized in the ethical edict: you shall not kill, you shall not jeopardize the life of the other. The ethical rapport with the face is asymmetrical in that it subordinates my existence to the other. There is a Jewish proverb which says that "the other's material needs are my spiritual needs"; it is this disproportion, or asymmetry, that characterizes the ethical refusal of the first truth of ontology – the struggle to *be*. . . . I have described ethical responsibility as *insomnia* or *wakefulness* precisely because it is a perpetual duty of vigilance and effort that can never slumber.[93]

The Curvature of Ethical Space

These addresses to the other anticipate much of what will later become foundational in Levinas's liturgy to the stranger. One recognizes in this conversation the primacy of the ethical event and its emphasis on a non-reciprocity reducible to our theme of responsibility. Further suggested are affective displacements of the cognitive, as enthusiasm and contact fuse with the ethical intention subordinated to the other's material needs. This fusing of the ethical and the affective incites a conversion, a reversal of nature beholden to the glory of the face. And there is defiance in this conversion, one that militates against the narcissism of a self turned inward – one that, as sacrifice, 'turns our nature inside out.'[94]

Much of this linguistic torsion insinuates itself into Levinas's notion of expression, grafting what is asymmetrical into a hermeneutic contravening logic. Here Levinas situates one in a subjective field deforming vision, a locus subordinate to the command and authority of the 'curvature of space.' Enigmatically, he states that 'This "curvature of space" expresses the relation between human beings. That the Other is placed higher than me would be a pure and simple error if the welcome I make him consisted in "perceiving" a nature.'[95] For Levinas perceiving in this sense would be an act of violence subverting the asymmetrical height incumbent of the other – betraying, in fact, the reality that 'Man as Other comes to us from the outside, a separated – or holy—face. His exteriority, that is, his appeal to me, is his truth. . . . This surplus of truth over being and over its idea, which we suggest by the metaphor of the "curvature of space," signifies the divine intention of all truth. This "curvature of space" is, perhaps, the very presence of God.'[96]

Levinas is provocatively asserting his conviction that there is a metaphysical inflection enacted through responsibility that is analogous to the fissional dynamics inherent in his notion of the idea of infinity.[97] He also invites critical response concerning this assertion, prompting John Caputo to designate this inflection in Levinas an 'undeconstructed transcendental move (that) engages in a kind of totalizing – of maximizing – of otherness.' Caputo finds this maximization 'extreme – *ad infinitum* – and beyond any limits.'[98]

The inclusion of the curvature of space into intersubjective dialogue, further, betrays a fideism regarding the other refractory to ontological assumptions and ramped towards an excess which is more intentional than representational. Hence one senses it being a statement of faith rather than reasonable assertion when Levinas claims that 'The idea of the infinite is not an intentionality for which the Infinite would be the object. Intentionality is a movement of the mind adjusted to being. . . . The idea of the infinite consists in grasping the ungraspable while nevertheless guaranteeing its status as ungraspable.'[99]

In any event, being unable to grasp, rather than exhibiting a defect, serves to further emphasize for Levinas the horizontal scaffolding circumscribing intentionality. Registering this scaffolding is not an intellectual endeavor, but an ethical inventory, one bent towards and obliged to the other: 'Ethical testimony is a revelation which is not knowledge. Must one still say that in this mode one only "testifies" to the Infinite, to God. . . ? What may pass for a "fault" of the infinite is to the contrary a positive characteristic of it — its very infinity.'[100]

From a cultural stance rooted in ideology, or from an ontological stance rooted in being, arguing this infinite responsibility for the other is a futile endeavor.[101] But viewed through the lens of ethics (Remember Levinas's credo: 'ethics is an optics'), responsibility becomes a phenomenology tendered toward the other.[102] And, aligned with the proposal that the offering of the self to the stranger tropes as liturgical, the assumption of this ethical optics further merges responsibility and intention into an enacted sacrificial drama where to engage the other is to give one's self as bread: 'It is the passivity of being-for-another, which is possible only in the form of giving the very bread I eat. But for this one has to first enjoy one's bread, not in order to have the merit of giving it, but in order to give it with one's heart, to give oneself in giving it.'[103]

Thus from a position issuing non-representational sensations as foundational, Levinas here is introducing the phenomenological assumption that consciousness is a specific tendency that can only be particularized as 'consciousness of . . .' – and that (further) this 'consciousness of . . .' is collateral with the knowing subject's intentionality. This tendency, according to Bergo, inflects consciousness through the interruption of transcendence, one 'without a thematizable return,' and one 'irrecoverable to thought.'[104] Levinas believes that this inclination can be shown to demonstrate that signification is sensibility, extrapolating from what he calls manifestation of being a more affective access to being. These tendencies toward accessing, notes Bergo, provide for Levinas a pattern of wearing away inveterate dispositions through 'a particular dephasing, a loosening up or unclamping of identity: the same prevented from coinciding with itself, at odds, torn up from its rest, between sleep and insomnia, panting, shivering.'[105]

Positioning oneself between sleep and insomnia for Levinas is a hermeneutical stratagem, one indicative of an interpretive vigilance intent on revealing what Theodore De Boer calls 'the horizons within which every object of thought is implanted and that are unsuspected by the naïve, direct gaze of that thought.'[106] What is more, here interpretive vigilance militates against epistemologies grounded in ontology, striking at the root and 'looking for a source beyond the source. When knowledge becomes critical, when it is unsettled, it moves back to what precedes its origin.'[107] Diachronic, antecedent to cognition, this source beyond the source is illuminated in those peripheral zones where affectivity takes on ethical status – one motivated by an obligation for the stranger. Indeed, according to Levinas, even prior to freedom there is an ethical exigency whose root is responsibility.[108] Situating responsibility at this root provides an Archimedean point Levinas will call separation.

Implementing separation interpretively establishes a categorical antecedent regarding responsibility. This employment, what Levinas calls a 'feat of radical separation,' opens space through a 'revolution in being.'[109] Articulating separation as 'not reflected in thought, but produced by it,' Levinas goes on to state that in separation 'the *After* or the *Effect* conditions the *Before* or the *Cause*.' Nominated 'the posteriority of the anterior,' Levinas takes a logically absurd ontological position and, through inflection, establishes a gap or interval where he may put into service his hyperbolic hospitality for the other.[110] Llewelyn sees this service as reflective of a relation that provides room for an individual subject to fully welcome the other into not only the economy of the self, but one's home. This welcoming, notes Llewelyn, is salvific:

> If the other were only my other dialectically opposed to, so posed by myself, this relationship would be an internal relation with myself and therefore logically already in my home, within the economy of the self, constitutive of myself according to a universal logical law and needed for the fulfillment of my identity, in order that its finitude be made good. The other would have revealed itself as a mediator of my being saved through the "production" of my separateness as part of the economy of a systematic whole. But it is my separateness that must be saved . . . if space is to be left for me to relate concretely to the singular other who faces. He or she is effaced as soon as the invisible ethical dimension of the face is made visible by being represented as a case falling under logical law. Thus represented, apparently non-apparent ethical exteriority shows itself as only a logical part of an economy of interiority.[111]

Here I Am (The Human Adventure)

Through ingenious surrender, Levinas has for strategic purposes set up base far off from safe haven. Separated from the neutrality of homogenization, Levinas's move to the periphery allows him a participial locus, one where 'Being is exteriority, and exteriority is produced in its truth in a subjective field.'[112] Through this production, Levinas (by collating topography and ontology) anticipates the distinction he will delineate through separation. Thus with Levinas one is again outside familiar confines with the other, putting to question the genera of the world.[113] This station outside camp

Levinas calls home. One welcomes the other into the home by showing an extreme hospitality to the face, thus grounding ethical truth in proximity. According to Cohen, 'Truth thus emerges in an excessive proximity, a proximity to the otherness of the other closer than being, yet one wherein the other's alterity remains absolute. Truth is produced in an excessive nearness and distance whose claim is nothing other than the call of a moral force. Thus an always utterly unique relation – the face-to-face relation – becomes the source of universality.'[114] The face for Levinas, according to Wyschogrod, is the 'disincarnate presence of the other. It prevents totalization and the triumph of totality. It is the source of revelation of the other who cannot be encompassed in cognition. It calls separated being . . . (and) the self into question.'[115]

Engaging the face from the home outside camp, offering radical generosity to the stranger, instantiates a metaphysical discourse where separation provides a dialectical correlation necessary for the transcendent event Levinas calls hospitality. Because of this event of hospitality, notes Bernasconi, 'my home is no longer the site of inwardness . . . it has become the site of contestation.'[116] This contestation reflects a self torn toward the other. Again topography and ontology modulate into an agential register where the other is both key and scale.[117] Significantly, the face for Levinas heightens at this site of contestation where the metaphysical becomes empirically concrete. Hospitality catalyzes this event:

> The "vision" of the face as face is a certain mode of sojourning in a home, or – to speak in a less singular fashion – a certain form of economic life. No human or interhuman relationship can be enacted outside economy; no face can be approached with empty hand and closed home. Recollection in a home open to the Other – hospitality – is the concrete and initial fact of human recollection and separation; it coincides with the Desire for the Other absolutely transcendent. . . . But the separated being can close itself up in its egoism, that is, in the very accomplishment of its isolation. And this possibility of forgetting the transcendence of the other – of banishing with impunity all hospitality (that is, all language) from one's home, banishing the transcendental relation that alone permits the I to shut itself up in itself – evinces the absolute truth, the radicalism, of separation.[118]

Asymmetry accentuates a subjectivity beholden and wholly obligated to the other. Dudiak in fact thinks that 'if this relation is to be produced *as ethical*, it must be produced as an asymmetrical relation, must be produced as *my* ethical responsibility for the other, as my unilateral responsibility to the other.'[119] Derrida tends to frame this asymmetry in a theologically determined space;[120] Kosky agrees, noting that 'its asymmetry is meaningful, or means the peace that Levinas wants it to mean, only if one presupposes that the other is not another like me but an other determined as God or resembling God.'[121]

In fact, there is in Levinas a constant weaving of thematic threads and shuttling of motifs in attempt to emphasize the asymmetrical lowliness of subjectivity when viewed in both the physical and metaphysical light of the other. In this light, moreover, there is an interconnection bracketed which frustrates any naïve sense of freedom that attempts to monopolize the transcendence of the face.[122]

In essence, subjectivity – when sacrificed to the stranger – offers itself to 'the face, whose ethical epiphany consists in soliciting a response' to the 'transcendence of the other that accounts for freedom.' In effect, 'the force of the other is already and henceforth moral.'[123] It is through endeavoring to register this force that the notion of the 'curvature of space' begins to assume more than metaphorical significance. In fact, Michael Smith maintains that it is within this metaphysical relation that the idea of infinity betrays a spatial import, one embedded in the labile and polyvalent nuances of the face. The face 'is dwarfed by a "proximity" (whose) approach to the other . . . is infinite in the sense that the closer we are the farther we are, and the more responsible we are the more inadequate, the more "accused" or "persecuted" by the other.' Further, there is a 'positive sense given to this accusation, or this existence in the accusative case, and this persecution. *The same must be awakened or troubled by the other.*'[124]

All of Levinas's writings are punctuated with the choral 'here I am' performed as both testimony and prophecy.[125] Existence in the accusative sense provides Levinas with an anachronistic assumption indicating the awakened self's obsessive vigilance towards the other. As notes Burggraeve, 'Through its commanding character, the Other stands over me as "law" bearing down on me from a height which is ethical. As such, the Other is not my equal but rather my "superior": not only my Teacher . . . but also my "Lord and master," who from an ethical height inspires in me awe. . . .'[126] Signaling not only presence but willingness, one finds in this heightened awe the idea of the infinite embedded in a desire for offering, this need to give one's self. And this performative testimony manifestly assumes prophetic dimensions through its complete kenosis, through its comprehensive surrendering to and being ordained by the other.[127] This accusative existence, moreover, when couched in words of obedience and submission, when stated baldly in the simple 'here I am,' announces that the infinite has come to pass.

Again, here an enacted drama depicts the permeable boundaries separating transcendence from immanence, smudged delineations where 'the other within the same, worrying me as responsibility, as the summons of me by the other, constrains an irreplaceable subject to substitution.'[128] For Levinas, the saying of 'here I am' gives words to the performance of obligation, breathes into discourse a witness to the glory of the infinite.[129] Here 'language, a sign given to the other, is sincerity or veracity, according to which glory is glorified. The Infinite thus has glory only through subjectivity, through the human adventure of the approach of the other, through substitution for the other, through expiation of the other.'[130] Thus saying and doing, participial agency, meet in Levinas's accentuation of 'here I am.' Provoked by the exigency of the other, geared to the prophecy and testimony obeisant to the infinite irreducible to objectification, the movement now modulates for Levinas into an ethical message:

The infinite thus has glory only through subjectivity, through the human adventure of the approach of the other, through substitution for the other, through the expiation of the other. The ethical is the field wherein the very paradox of an Infinite in relation to the finite is significant, without faltering in this relation. . . . In the responsibility for the other, we are at the heart of the ambiguity of inspiration, . . . the diachronic ambivalence that make(s) ethics possible.[131]

The Gravitas of Self

Recapitulating: in order to sacrifice, the self needs a home. Noting that 'separation is produced positively in localization,' and that 'to be separated is to dwell somewhere,' Levinas has the self carve out a space from whence to await and serve the other.[132] This space is filled by subjectivity, for Levinas a pacific regime incarnating responsibility. Subjectivity can and may be sacrificed.

By presenting the subject saying 'here I am' as pure witnessing to the Infinite, Levinas also proposes that this testimony assumes ethical traction in and through an excessive obligation to the other. In the service of humanity, the self is – like Abraham – an exile warped and woofed in covenantal responsibility.[133]

Responsibility for Levinas is incited by the face of the other presented as a master commanding from on high. Mysteriously the master in *Totality and Infinity* intersects every event as and with the other. Again there is an epistemological inflection, another curvature that enters into a new register. Within this novel space, 'the relation with the Other breaks the ceiling of the totality. It is fundamentally pacific.' Crucially, here in relation 'I must encounter the indiscrete face of the Other that calls me into question. The Other – the absolutely other – paralyzes possession, which he contests by the epiphany of his face. He can contest my possession only because he approaches me not from the outside but from above.'[134] From a non-localized place of height and grandeur, the other as master now challenges the self's estate. Epistemology suddenly encounters the exigency of ethics: 'I must know how *to give* what I possess.'[135]

This constraint prompts vigilance. According to Levinas, 'it is because it suspects that it is dreaming itself that it awakens.' The self dreaming itself is one oblivious to the other who is master – and only an inversion amounting to 'knowing oneself as a theme attended to by the Other' is worthy to be submitted 'to an exigency, to a morality' where the 'welcoming of the Other is ipso facto the consciousness of my own injustice – the shame that freedom feels for itself.'[136] Consciousness of shame inverts freedom into responsibility. Experienced as the intuition of a command, the engagement with the other reduces into a discursive relation where language becomes justice. In this relation 'the epiphany of the face qua face opens humanity. The face in its nakedness as a face presents to me the destitution of the poor one and the stranger' whom 'the Other already serves. He comes to join me. But he joins me to himself for service; he commands me as a Master.'[137] Here is the convergence of the other — the master — with the widow, orphan and stranger. From the hollowed out space of subjectivity, an Abrahamic self, commanded toward vigilant awakening, says again 'here I am.'[138]

From Abraham to the Master; from the widow to the orphan to the stranger; from one to the other: a pacific regime of subjectivity, an exegesis of exodus, an exposition of exile. The exorbitant hospitality Abraham offers to three strangers modulates into the adoration of worship. The sacrifice of self, precipitated through volitional shame, engenders a different freedom which translates into responsibility. And last: the stranger, the orphan, the widow — viewed through the lens of an ethical optics — are now seen as a Master who too says 'here I am.'

Notes

1. Levinas, *Totalité et Infini*, x ; *Totality and Infintiy*, 22.
2. Edith Wyschogrod was the first to designate Levinas's work as an ethical metaphysics, a nomenclature now respected by most commentators, *Emmanuel Levinas: The Problem of Ethical Metaphysics*.
3. Levinas, *Totalité et Infini*, ix ; *Totality and Infintiy*, 21.
4. Ibid.
5. Levinas, "La philosophie et l'idée de l'Infini," 166; "Philosophy and the Idea of Infinity," 48. Walter Brueggemann makes a current and critical assessment of autonomy in "From Anxiety and Greed to Milk and Honey," where he notes that 'A sense of the isolated, self-sufficient economic individual is deeply rooted in modern rationality and comes to full expression in U. S. "individualism" that resists communitarian connectedness and imagines the individual person to be the primary unit of social reality. Such an individual is completely autonomous, owes no one anything, is accountable to no one, and can rely on no one except himself or herself. Such a self . . . is without restraint and is self-authorized to enact Promethean energy to organize life around one's own needs, issues, and purposes.' Significantly, Brueggemann then lines out how Biblical faith 'vetoes' autonomy, an insight analogous to Levinas's implementation of responsibility through hospitality. For instance, Brueggemann asserts that Biblical faith 'is an invitation away from autonomy to covenantal existence that binds the self to the holy, faithful God and to neighbors who are members in a common economy.' Biblical faith is also 'an invitation away from greed to the neighborly practice of generosity,' *Sojourners*, 23, no. 2 (2009): 21f.
6. Peperzak, *To The Other*, 120.
7. See Levinas, "The Ego and Totality," *Collected Philosophical Papers*, 40.
8. Levinas, *Totalité et Infini*, ixf. ; *Totality and Infintiy*, 21. According to John Llewelyn, war for Levinas means an allergy exemplified by a resistance of energies and counter-energies in opposition to powers of totality and homogeneity. This resistance assumes shape in ethical resistance, prompted by the weakness of the other. Llewelyn goes on to note that 'paradoxically, it is the vulnerability of the other, the nakedness of the face, which wounds me,' *Appositions of Jacques Derrida and Emmanuel Levinas*, 7f.
9. *To The Other*, 121f.
10. *The Problem of Ethical Metaphysics*, xxx.
11. "Only the Persecuted. . ." in *Ethics as First Philosophy*, 83.

12. Levinas, *Totalité et Infini*, x; *Totality and Infinity*, 21f.
13. *Ethics, Exegesis, and Philosophy*, 10.
14. See Colin Davis, *On Levinas*, 100.
15. Levinas, *Totalité et Infini*, xf; *Totality and Infinity*, 22f, emphasis in text.
16. In all fairness, it should be noted here that, according to Michael B. Smith, 'This metaphysical arrangement represents an interesting stage in Levinas's progression toward "the one," more fully elaborated and modified in *Otherwise than Being*.... One senses in all this that Levinas is not committed to any of these metaphysical schemata irrevocably, but that his is a guided intuition of what needs to be accommodated in such a schemata,' *Toward the Outside*, 212.
17. Peperzak, *To The Other*, 127. Concerning this preoriginal notion of peace, Levinas, in his preface to the German edition of *Totality and Infinity*, notes that this peace may not be enough to uncover all things nor confirm them in themselves as they appear originally, as they, in other words, 'appear as coming to hand and are taken and understood.' Being taken and understood naturally included being possessed, exchanged, and argued about. Here Levinas asserts the problem of peace and reason 'in terms of a different and no doubt older conjunction,' *Entre Nous: Thinking-of-the-Other*, 198.
18. See Gibbs, *Correlations in Rosenzweig and Levinas*, 152f.
19. Levinas, *Totalité et Infini*, xi ; *Totality and Infinity*, 23.
20. *Toward the Outside*, 211.
21. *To The Other*, 129, emphasis in text. See also Robert Gibbs, *Why Ethics: Signs of Responsibility*, 34.
22. Levinas, *Totalité et Infini*, xif; *Totality and Infinity*, 23, emphasis in text.
23. "The Ethics of Suspicion," *Research in Phenomenology* 20 (1990): 6.
24. Levinas, *Totalité et Infini*, xif; *Totality and Infinity*, 23. See also Roger Burggraeve, *The Wisdom of Love in the Service of Love*, where it is noted, in response to the idea that Levinas involved ethics in a socio-political order, 'Still, this political messianism cannot be given the last word, but must be transcended by the messianism of the uniquely responsible ego,' 159.
25. See Atterton, 29f.
26. Levinas, *Totalité et Infini*, xiii ; *Totality and Infintiy*, 24.
27. *Liturgy of the Neighbor*, 37.
28. Elsewhere Levinas speaks of a human nakedness reducible to strangeness and solitude, one that cries out its misery with a grieving heart. This nakedness, according to Levinas, calls upon one from its weakness and defenselessness as from a strange and imperative authority he names 'the word of God and the verb of the human Face, *Entre Nous*, 198f., emphasis in text. Cf. Waldenfels, "Levinas and the Face of the Other," *Cambridge Companion to Levinas*, where the face of the other and God's voice re-emphasize the asymmetry of the ethical event. Notes Waldenfels: 'The face of the other who commands justice for others, dwells itself on this side of right and wrong, good and evil,' 69f.
29. Levinas, *Totalité et Infini*, xviii ; *Totality and Infinity*, 29, emphasis in text.
30. Ibid., 3; 33.
31. Ibid., 4; 34.
32. *Levinas and Theology*, 123.
33. Levinas, *Totalité et Infini*, 4 ; *Totality and Infintiy*, 34.
34. Ibid.
35. Cf. *To The Other*, p. 135, where human existence is presented as a two-dimensional reality, one reality distinguished by the egocentric self and the other by a

transcendence reflective of the other. In this dimension of transcendence alterity and the impossibility of totalization assign Levinas the difficult task of describing this enterprise without gathering it into the homogeneity and sameness against which he militates. According to Peperzak, Levinas must be sure not to reduce otherness, separation, and transcendence to any unity.

36. Levinas, *Totalité et Infini*, 5f. ; *Totality and Infintiy, 35*, emphasis in text.
37. *Levinas: The Philosophy of Religion*, 7.
38. Levinas, *Totalité et Infini*, xv ; *Totality and Infintiy*, 27.
39. Jacques Derrida has poignantly asked: 'Has anyone ever noticed? Although the word is neither frequently used nor emphasized within it, *Totality and Infinity* bequeaths to us an immense treatise *of hospitality*,' *Adieu: To Emmanuel Levinas*, trans. Pascale-Anne Brault and Michael Naas (Stanford, California: Stanford University Press, 1999) 21, emphasis in text.
40. *Levinas: A Guide for the Perplexed*, 54, emphasis in text.
41. Levinas, *Difficult Freedom*, xiv.
42. Levinas, *Totalité et Infini*, 48 ; *Totality and Infinity*, 75.
43. Ibid., emphasis in text.
44. Levinas, *Difficult Freedom*, 21.
45. *Appositions of Jacques Derrida and Emmanuel Levinas*, 139.
46. Cf. Levinas, *Totalité et Infini*, xf ; *Totality and Infinity*, 22f. Brian Schroeder comments that 'Prophecy is a modality of eschatological expression because prophecy . . . accompanies revelation whereby the self is called to responsibility for the spontaneous capriciousness of its own freedom and for the freedom of the Other. Ethical signification is revealed in the vulnerable face of the Other as the call to respond . . . to the Invisible, to *Adonai* – "Here I am,"' *Altered Ground: Levinas, History, and Violence*, 144. See also Jacques Derrida, "At This Very Moment in This Work Here I Am," *Re-Reading Levinas*, 25.
47. "Tracing Responsibility," *Ethics as First Philosophy*, 174.
48. *The Intrigue of Ethics*, 10f.
49. Levinas, *In The Time of Nations*, trans. Michael B. Smith (Bloomington, Indiana: Indiana University Press, 1994) 77.
50. Ibid., 77f. Cf. Charles E. Scott, "A People's Witness beyond Politics," *Ethics as First Philosophy*, 27.
51. Cf. Levinas addressing what he calls a 'revolution in being' precipitated by 'The posteriority of the anterior – an inversion logically absurd,' but one nonetheless distinguished by the fact that 'in it the *After* or the *Effect* conditions the *Before* or the *Cause*.' This phenomenon, where 'Even its cause, older than itself, is still to come,' is conditioned 'only by memory or by thought,' Levinas, *Totalité et Infini*, 25; *Totality and Infinity*, 54, emphasis in text.
52. Levinas, *Totalité et Infini*, 26 ; *Totality and Infinity*, 55, emphasis in text. See also Brian Schroeder, *Altared Ground: Levinas, History, and Violence*, 151 n. 13.
53. According to Jeffrey Bloechl, 'By faith he [Abraham] loved God, expected the impossible, and also struggled with God. This faith had already led him into exile from the land of his forefathers, and now was about to be put to the test. This faith . . . is to be contrasted with reflection, in which one measures, compares and anticipates. Faith opens beyond these things, beyond the possible measured by its calculus. For Abraham to love God in faith was to have followed his call out into the desert, trusting in a promise without any further assurances. For him to expect the impossible in faith was to have trusted that one day "in his seed all generations of the earth will be blessed,"' *Liturgy of the Neighbor,* 159f. For a trenchant Christian

perspective of how this faith 'always already' operates through Abraham, see Wolfhart Pannenberg, *Systematic Theology*, v. III, trans. Geoffrey W. Bromiley (Edinburgh: T&T Clark, 1998) 65.

54. Catherine Chalier, "Levinas and the Talmud," *The Cambridge Companion to Levinas*, 106. The biblical passages herein relevant to Abraham are Genesis 12: 1-4; Genesis 18: 1-14; Genesis 22: 1.

55. *Altared Ground: Levinas, History, and Violence*, 19.

56. See Levinas, *Totalité et Infini*, xf., 196f., 200 ; *Totality and Infinity*, 22f., 222f., 225.

57. Levinas, *In the Time of Nations*, 88.

58. Levinas, *Totalité et Infini*, 26 ; *Totality and Infinity*, 55.

59. Consider Levinas's query: 'What else could descent from Abraham mean? Let us recall the biblical and Talmudic tradition relating to Abraham. Father of believers? Certainly. But above all the one who knew how to receive and feed men: the one whose tent is wide open on all sides. Through all these openings he looked out for passersby in order to receive them,' *Nine Talmudic Readings*, 99; *Du Sacré Au Saint* (Paris: Editions de Minuit, 1977) 19.

60. Gen. 18:2-8; See also Levinas, *In the Time of Nations*, 124.

61. Apropos of these personal encounters, Walter Brueggemann mentions that 'In addition to the great public ways of direct relationship in theophany, it is evident in Israel's testimony that Yahweh on occasion deals directly with individual persons. Much of this evidence is unreflective and almost incidental.... Yahweh's way with Abraham is direct and immediate, a means whereby the power and summons of promise are irreversibly embedded in the life of Israel,' *Theology of the Old Testament: Testimony, Dispute, Advocacy* (Minneapolis: Fortress Press, 1997), 570.

62. Terrence E. Fretheim, "The Book of Genesis: Introduction, Commentary, and Reflections" in *The New Interpreter's Bible*, v. 1 (Nashville: Abingdon Press, 1994) 464; further emphasizing this point, Andrius Valevicius mentions that 'The relation with God begins in the relation with other men . . . The phenomena of the other opens up the way to the holiness of God,' *From the Other to the Totally Other: The Religious Philosophy of Emmanuel Levinas* (New York: Peter Lang, 1988) 5.

63. Levinas, *Totalité et Infini*, 50 ; *Totality and Infinity*, 78.

64. *The Dignity of Difference*, 60, emphasis in text; see also Michael Scott Horton, "Meeting a Stranger: A Covenantal Epistemology" *Westminster Theological Journal* 66, no. 2 (Fall 2004): 338.

65. See Levinas, "La trace de l'autre," *En découvrant l'existence avec Husserl et Heidegger*, 190; "The Trace of the Other," *Deconstruction in Context*, ed, Mark C. Taylor (Chicago: The University of Chicago Press, 1986) 348f. See also Bloechl, *Liturgy of the Neighbor*, 259-261; Catherine Chalier, "Levinas and the Talmud," *The Cambridge Companion to Levinas*," 107; Levinas, *Difficult Freedom*, 16; Levinas, "Meaning and Sense," in *Basic Philosophical Writings*, 49.

66. Levinas believes that 'Philosophical knowledge is a priori: it searches for the adequate idea and ensures autonomy. In every new development it recognizes familiar structures and greets old acquaintances. It is an odyssey where all adventures are only the accidents of a return to self,' "Transcendence and Height," *Basic Philosophical Writings*," 14.

67. "La trace de l'autre," 190; "The Trace of the Other," 348, emphasis in text. See also Miroslav Volf, *Exclusion and Embrace: A Theological Exploration of Identity, Otherness, and Reconciliation* (Nashville, Tennessee: Abingdon Press, 1996) 38f.

68. Levinas, "Meaning and Sense," *Basic Philosophical Writings*, 49f, emphasis in text.

69. For more on this performative aspect in Levinas, see Llewelyn, *Appositions of Jacques Derrida and Emmanuel Levinas,* 176f.

70. Levinas, "Meaning and Sense," *Basic Philosophical Writings,* 49.

71. Ibid; Significant is Levinas' assertion that "The Greek word *leitourgia* means public service performed by private citizens at their own expense," 176, note 52.

72. *Origins of the Other: Emmanuel Levinas Between Revelation and Ethics* (Ithaca, New York: Cornell University Press, 2005) 207.

73. De l'existence a l' existant, 165; *Existence and Existents,* 100 ; See also Atterton, *On Levinas,* 5 ; Smith, *Toward the Outside,* 58 ; William Schweiker, "Disputes and Trajectories in Responsibility Ethics," *Religious Studies Review* 27, no. 1 (January 2001): 18-20.

74. See Jean-Luc Marion, "From the Other to the Individual," *Transcendence: Philosophy, Literature, and Theology Approach the Beyond,* ed. Regina Schwartz (New York: Routledge, 2004), 53.

75. Richard Cohen, intro. to *Emmanuel Levinas: Humanism of the Other,* trans. Nidra Poller (Chicago, Illinois: University of Illinois Press, 2006) xxvif, emphasis in text.

76. See Levinas, *Éthique et Infini,* 25-27 ; *Ethics and Infinity,* 30-32; see also "Enigma et phénomène," *En découvrant l'existence avec Husserl et Heidegger,* 212;"Enigma and Phenomenon," *Basic Philosophical Writings,* 72; *Humanism of the Other,* 72.

77. See Luke 10: 30-37.

78. Cf. *Basic Philosophical Writings,* 7, where it is noted that 'this tie to the other, which does not reduce itself to the representation of the Other, but rather to his invocation, where invocation is not preceded by comprehension, we call *religion.* The essence of discourse is prayer.'

79. Levinas, *Difficult Freedom,* 17.

80. According to Levinas, 'The myth of a legislative consciousness of things, where difference and identity are reconciled, is the great myth of philosophy. It rests upon the totalitarianism or imperialism of the same,' "Transcendence and Height," *Basic Philosophical Writings,* 14.

81. *The Problem of Ethical Metaphysics,* 1; See also Atterton, *On Levinas,* 81; Bauman, *Postmodern Ethics,* 220f. ; Levinas, "Meaning and Sense," *Collected Philosophical Papers,* 90; Peperzak, *To The Other,* 191.

82. See Davis, *Levinas: An Introduction,* 107; Levinas, "Meaning and Sense," *Collected Philosophical Papers,* 107.

83. See Levinas, *Humanism of the Other, passim.*

84. *Totalité et Infini,* 168; *Totality and Infinity,* 194; See also George Drazenovilch, "Toward a Levinasian Understanding of Christian Ethics: Emmanuel Levinas and the Phenomenology of the Other," *Cross Currents* 54, no. 4 (Wint 2005): 38 ; Lenka Karfikova, "God of Philosophers :The Idea of God in A. N. Whitehead and E. Levinas," *Communio viatorum* 48,no. 2 (2006): 119.

85. In "Transcendence and Height," Levinas states that 'it is in terms of the relation with the Other that I speak of God,' *Basic Philosophical Writings,* 29.

86. "Transcendence, Justice, and Mercy," in *Rethinking Wesley's Theology for Contemporary Methodism,* ed. Randy Maddox (Nashville, Tennessee: Kingswood Books, 1998) 70.

87. Ibid., emphasis in text.

88. Philippe Nemo, referring to Levinas, regards him as one 'who has centered all (his) work on metaphysics as ethics,' *Ethics and Infinity,* 31.

89. Jennings, "Transcendence, Justice, and Mercy," 72.

90. *Totalité et Infini*, 42; *Totality and Infinity*, 70; See also "God and Philosophy," *Collected Philosophical Papers*, 116 ; Bernet, "Levinas' Critique of Husserl," *The Cambridge Companion to Levinas*, 92 ; Peperzak, *To The Other*, 43f.

91. See Hent De Vries, *Minimal Theologies: Critiques of Secular Reason in Adorno and Levinas* (Baltimore: The Johns Hopkins University Press, 2005) 42.

92. See Colin Davis, *Levinas*, 46; Fabio Ciaramelli, "Levinas's Ethical Discourse Between Individuation and Universality," *Re-Reading Levinas*, 100; Robert Gibbs, *Correlations In Rosenzweig and Levinas*, 232.

93. Levinas, "Dialogue with Emmanuel Levinas," *Face to Face With Levinas*, 26f, emphasis in text.

94. Ibid.

95. *Totalité et Infini*, 267 ; *Totality and Infinity*, 291. See also Roger Burggraeve, who suggests that 'the double negation of the fundamental word of the face implies a duty to respect and promote the Other in his irreducible otherness – to do him justice in both his strength (irreducible unicity) and weakness (alienation-as-misery). This duty is manifest in the radical asymmetry of the ego and the Other. Levinas refers to this as the "curvature of intersubjective space,"' *The Wisdom of Love in the Service of Love: Emmanuel Levinas on Justice, Peace, and Human Rights*, 96.

96. Ibid.

97. See Dudiak, *The Intrigue of Ethics*, 246f.; Michael Smith, *Toward the Outside*, 10; Andrew Tallon, "Nonintentional Affectivity," *Ethics as First Philosophy*, 108.

98. *Against Ethics*, 84.

99. "Transcendence and Height," in *Basic Philosophical Writings*, 19.

100. Levinas, *Éthique et Infini*, 114 ; *Ethics and Infinity*, 108, emphasis in text.

101. For an argument 'against cultures as internally consistent wholes,' see Kathryn Tanner, *Theories of Culture: A New Agenda for Theology* (Minneapolis: Fortress Press, 1997) 42-44.

102. See Robert Gibbs, *Correlations in Rosenzweig and Levinas*, 9.

103. Levinas, *Autrement qu'être ou au-delà de l'essence* (The Hague : Martinus Nijhoff, 1974) 116 ; *Otherwise than Being or Beyond Essence*, trans. Alphonso Lingis (Pittsburgh, Pa.: Duquesne University Press, 1998) 72.

104. *Levinas: Between Ethics and Politics*, 97.

105. Ibid, 68f.

106. "An Ethical Transcendent Philosophy," *Face to Face With Levinas*, 106f.

107. Ibid.

108. See Robert Gibbs, *Correlations in Rosenzweig and Levinas*, 182.

109. *Totalité et Infini*, 24f ; *Totality and infinity*, 54. See also Regina M. Schwartz, who notes that 'Levinas has seen a revolutionary aspect of revelation, and by turning away from the understanding of the subject as solipsistic and instead constituting it by its responsibility for another, by justice, Levinas has not only delineated an understanding of the subject that is preeminently social, but also political (despite the frequent charge that his ethics lacks a politics),' "Revelation and Revolution," *Cross Currents* 56 no. 3 (Autumn 2006): 380.

110. Ibid., emphasis in text. According to Bernhard Waldenfels, 'Levinas draws the unusual conclusion that responsibility for the other precedes not only the dialogical exchange of question and answer but also every free initiative or involvement of myself, "Response and Responsibility," *Ethics as First Philosophy*, 45.

111. *The Genealogy of Ethics*, 69.

112. *Totalité et Infini*, 275; *Totality and Infinity*, 299.

113. See Jan De Greef, "Skepticism and Reason," *Face to Face with Levinas*, 162f.

114. *Elevations: The Height of the Good in Rosenzweig and Levinas,* 241

115. *Ethical Metaphysics,* 244.

116. "Only the Persecuted," *Ethics as First Philosophy,* 79.

117. See Cohen, *Elevations: The Height of the Good in Rosenzweig and Levinas,* 134; Jacques Derrida, "At this very Moment in this Work here I am," *Re-Reading Levinas,* pp. 27f.; Bob Plant, *Wittgenstein and Levinas,* 10; Adriaan Peperzak, *To The Other,* 63f.

118. *Totalité et Infini,* 147 ; *Totality and Infinity,* 172.

119. *The Intrigue of Ethics : A Reading of the Idea of Discourse in the Thought of Emmanuel Levinas,* 110, emphasis in text.

120. See Jacques Derrida, "Violence and Metaphysics," *Writing and Difference,* trans. Alan Bass (Chicago : University of Chicago Press, 1978) 102.

121. *Levinas and the Philosophy of Religion,* 30.

122. This frustration may be attributed to the enigmatic quality of what Bernard Waldenfels calls the 'fugitive face.' Complete surrender to this face in works of Levinas 'has the effect that the exteriority of the other penetrates the interiority of the self, generating certain whirls which are verbally reflected in an endless series of self-referential, paradoxical and hyperbolic expressions -- as if everything has been infected by a virus of otherness,' "Levinas and the Face of the Other," *The Cambridge Companion to Levinas,* 72f.

123. *Totalité et Infini,* 194 ; *Totality and Infinity,* 225.

124. *Toward the Outside,* 36; emphasis mine.

125. As has been emphasized throughout this analysis, to say 'here I am' is to say 'I am responsible.' Peperzak even believes that Levinas demonstrates that responsibility does not stem from any willful decision. In fact, he feels that (for Levinas) before one even thinks or chooses, one is responsible -- noting that 'my responsibility for the Others has begun before I became aware of my own being,' *Beyond: The Philosophy of Emmanuel Levinas,* 67f.

126. *The Wisdom of Love in the Service of Love,* 97.

127. See Brian Schroeder, *Altared Ground: Levinas, History, and Violence,* 18.

128. Levinas, "Truth of Disclosure and Truth of Testimony," *Basic Philosophical Writings,* 102.

129. According to John Llewelyn, 'Levinas is therefore speaking of a *Shema* that, however much inspired by the "Hear, O Israel," equates Israel with every me and makes each me the one that responds "Here, send me." My oneness is a oneness beyond number. It is the uniqueness of being elect,' *Appositions of Jacques Derrida and Emmanuel Levinas,* 136.

130. Levinas, "Truth of Disclosure and Truth of Testimony," *Basic Philosophical Writings,* 104.

131. Ibid., 104f.

132. *Totalité et Infini,* 142; *Totality and Infinity,* 168.

133. Levinas, "Truth of Disclosure and Truth of Testimony," Basic Philosophical Writings, 106. See also Robert Gibbs, *Correlations in Rosenzweig and Levinas,* 182.

134. *Totalité et Infini,* 145f. ; *Totality and Infinity,* 171.

135. Ibid., emphasis in text. Arne Johan Vetlesen offers a trenchant perspective when he notes that the other's coming is ambiguous, arriving 'as a master commanding me and as a being that is utterly defenseless, venerable, nude,' *Perception, Empathy, and Judgment: An Inquiry into the Preconditions of Moral Performance,* 203. Vetlesen errs, however, in tying too closely Levinas' face-to-face encounter with Sarte's analysis of 'the look.' There is a rapacity in Sarte's look incongruent with Levinas' face of the other, 202. For a more accurate exposition of Levinas and Sarte, see

Christina Howells, "Sarte and Levinas," *The Provocation of Levinas*, eds. Robert Bernasconi and David Wood (London: Routledge, 1988) 92f.

136. *Totalité et Infini*, 58f ; *Totality and Infinity*, 86 ; Hans Jonas states that 'morality is selfless' in *The Imperative of Responsibility*, 85.

137. Ibid 188; 213; Regarding Levinas' conviction that 'language is justice,' one may also reference the notion that the 'determination by situation and context, which fills out what is said to a totality of meaning and makes what is said really said, pertains not to the speaker but to what is spoken,' Hans-Georg Gadamer, *Truth and Method*, trans. Joel Weinsheimer and Donald G. Marshall (New York: Continuum, 1989) 489.

138. According to Jan De Greef, 'The question can certainly be a demand put to the Other. But the first question, evoking the "Here I am," is produced as my being put into question by the other and not my putting of the other into question. . . . The "Here I am" is already the response to the initial question "Where are you?" that calls man to the responsibility of justification,' "Skepticism and Reason," *Face to Face with Levinas*, 166.

Chapter Five

From Stranger to Neighbor

Abraham was presented in the previous chapter as a model for one concretizing the metaphysician through the implementation of Levinas's ethical optics.[1] He furthermore operates as a paradigm for one implementing antecedent responsibility, in effect personifying the responsibility keynoted in this analysis. Essential now is a more detailed investigation of other concepts and motifs found in Levinas, particularly the ways they are made evident through the responsibility herein presented as constitutive of Levinas's mission to the Gentiles. Thus far one has viewed transcendence as a coming about through the face-to-face relationship, a relationship Levinas presents as being ironically both experiential and non-contextual. This irony behaves hermeneutically for Levinas: for since there is no real formal bridge connecting what is pragmatic and reasonable in his ethical eschatology, but only the witness provoked by the face-to-face relationship, it is only through the paradigm of responsibility that transcendence comes to pass in each human engagement.[2]

Metaphysics for Levinas, like desire and the idea of infinity, becomes localized through language. This localization occurs because

> the absolutely other is the Other. He and I do not form a number. The collectivity in which I say "you" or "we" is not plural of the 'I.' I, you – these are not individuals of a common concept. Neither possession nor the unity of number nor the unity of concepts link me to the Stranger, the Stranger who disturbs the being at home with oneself. But the Stranger also means the free one. Over him I have no *power*. ... But I, who have no concept in common with the Stranger, am, like him, without genus. We are the same and the other. The conjunction *and* here designates neither addition nor power of one term over the other. We shall try to show that the relation *between* the same and the other—upon which we seem to impose such extraordinary conditions – is language.[3]

Levinas here joins discourse with desire and finds a more primordial connection with the other than that reduced to synthetic agencies.[4] In other words, language mirrors Levinas's vision without image, one that 'designates a relation with a reality infinitely distant from my own reality, yet without this distance destroying this relation and without this relation destroying this distance, as would happen with relations within the same. . . . We have called this relation metaphysical.'[5]

Charting this metaphysical relation is essential, for – according to Hent De Vries – metaphysics in Levinas is found within the 'reference to the truly other . . . (as it) announces itself in ethics.' De Vries further maintains that it is only in this metaphysical dimension that 'the Infinite leaves its trace' by troubling 'the relationship between religious inspiration and philosophical conceptuality or argumentation.'[6] This troubling, furthermore, leads Edith Wyschogrod to maintain that 'this can only be done by the Other. In fact, Levinas defines ethics as the putting into question of the same by the Other; the strangeness of the Other puts everything that we are into question. This putting into question undermines ontology: that is, metaphysics takes precedence over ontology.'[7]

Like the other, desire cannot be integrated into a functioning element of an autonomous economy, but operates rather as a non-schematized exteriority. 'Insofar as all visible realities can be mastered by putting them before me, by presenting them through reflection, the desired is invisible, irrepresentable, and nonconceptual. . . . *Desire does not have the structure of intentionality.*'[8] Since it is irreducible to a role in the drama of a self-enclosed subjectivity, the Other is an alien to the ego – a stranger to the self. Moreover Being, in its impersonal and singular perseverance, in its menacing neutrality, betrays the greed and violence contra-poised to the height and nobility of the Other.[9] According to Levinas, the resistance occasioned by this dimensional agitation effects a critique and apology – neither collapsible into an ontology, yet both challenging the economy of the same. Levinas – in a passage where spiraling, redundant hyperbole discloses its crucial import – frames this resistance ethically:[10]

> A calling into question of the same – which cannot occur within the egoist spontaneity of the same – is brought about by the other. We name this calling into question of my spontaneity by the presence of the Other ethics. The strangeness of the Other, his irreducibility to the I, to my thoughts and my possessions, is precisely accomplished as a calling into question of my spontaneity, as ethics. Metaphysics, transcendence, the welcoming of the other by the same, of the Other by me, is concretely produced as the calling into question of the same by the other, that is, as ethics that accomplishes the critical essence of knowledge. And as critique precedes dogmatism, metaphysics precedes ontology.[11]

Levinas is not normally inclined to such tautology.[12] In this instance, however, the redundancy is hermeneutical: for just as precedence is established historically with Abraham, here it is established metaphysically as ethics.

Concrete Moral Experience

Language implies separation.[13] And since ontology in Levinas's thought has been relegated subsequent status, attention to discourse and how it weaves through the constellated relationships between I's and others should clarify the constitutive particulars of the primordial metaphysical event accomplished through ethics. Ironically, the fundamental feat of separation so foundational in Levinas transpires owing to the other's inassimilable nature, one contrary to the ego's predilection towards mastery and possession. Regarding this feat, Gibbs allows that 'Ethics requires separation for the sake of the other person. So long as the other person is not separated, my here dominates the other person, permitting no ethical relations. Levinas identifies the separation in question here, the fundamental condition of ethics, as height. Separation becomes height in order to indicate the lack of reciprocity between us.'[14]

The other, moreover, due to its nonconformity to the patterns of phenomena networked throughout reality, cannot be assumed by history.[15] In view of this non-localized dimension threading between a philosophy of transcendence and a philosophy of immanence, Levinas

> propose(s) to describe, within the unfolding of terrestrial existence, of economic existence, a relationship with the other that . . . is not a totalization of history but the idea of infinity. Such a relationship is metaphysics itself. History would not be the privileged plane where Being disengaged from the particularism of points of view is manifested. . . . When man truly approaches the Other he is uprooted from history.[16]

Speaking with the other implicates separation without degrading into the political and dialectical wiles of autonomy – the law of self. So doing, discourse obviates the synoptic thesis and antithesis so prevalent in systems of totality, systems reducible to symmetry and categories of correlation. However, the 'separation of the I that is not the reciprocal of the transcendence of the other . . . imposes itself upon meditation in the name of a concrete moral experience: what I permit myself to demand of myself is not comparable with what I have the right to demand of the Other. This moral experience, so commonplace, indicates a metaphysical asymmetry.'[17] Hence for Levinas the presence of the Other contravenes the selfish and monopolizing will of the ego, submitting its freedom to the higher and more noble constraints reflective of metaphysical ethics.

The Breach that Leads to God

For Levinas freedom does not have the final say.[18] Nor is it the dominion of truth. In fact, for Levinas 'the locus of truth is society. The *moral* relation with the Master who judges me subtends the freedom of my adherence to the true. Thus language commences. . . . My freedom is thus challenged by a Master who can invest it.'[19] Interiority now is a provocation geared toward the revelation couched in language, one keyed to the transcendent as experienced through the encountered stranger. According to Levinas, it is through this verbal offertory to the other that God assumes the shape of justice:

> God rises to his supreme and ultimate presence as correlative to the justice rendered unto men. . . . The work of justice – the uprightness of the face to face – is necessary in order that the breach that leads to God be produced – and "vision" here coincides with this work of justice. Hence metaphysics is enacted where the social relation is enacted – in our relationship with men. The Other is the very locus of metaphysical truth, and is indispensable for my relation with God. He does not play the role of mediator. The Other is not the incarnation of God, but precisely by his face, in which he is disincarnate, is the manifestation of the height in which God is revealed.[20]

Levinas's metaphysics is actually performed in ethical relations, and this relation is distinguished by a separation maintained owing to the transcendence endemic to the idea of infinity. For some, however, this inordinate emphasis on ethical transcendence attenuates any substantive ethical initiatives, prompting B. C. Hutchins to comment that 'accepting these nebulous concepts might be impossible for the moral philosopher.'[21] But for Levinas this issue presses upon theology, as discourse prompted by this relation, irreducible to a system, constellates with what he calls religion: 'Religion, where relationship subsists between the same and the other despite the impossibility of the Whole – the idea of infinity – is the ultimate structure.'[22] And since, according to Levinas, 'the face to face remains an ultimate situation,' structure and event converge through the encounter with the stranger, a 'direct and full face welcome of the other by me' ennobled through discourse.[23]

This welcoming for Levinas betrays itself in ethical resistance, a resistance calling into question notions of freedom and consciousness.[24] Tracing back from this spontaneity, Levinas discovers the pre-originality of a foundationally critical exigency, one again he likens to an awakening, yet one again eluding thematization.[25] Significantly this awakening discloses the knowledge of freedom as created – hence subsequent – and the origin prior to origin as determined by the other, thus revealing that 'The welcoming of the Other is ipso facto the consciousness of my own injustice – the shame that freedom feels for itself.'[26] This shame, in fact, prompts Bob Plant to assert that 'Levinas's ethics is haunted by a very particular notion of guilt [which] maintains that simply in virtue of my being-in-the-world I live at the expense of another. Concerning the other our accounts are never settled. . . .'[27]

Awakening marks the beginning of an existence conditioned by the exigency of responsibility.[28] Submitting oneself to this constraint is tantamount to yielding to a morality where the other becomes the standard by which one is measured. Levinas marks this point by noting that 'the dimension of *height* in which the Other is placed is as it were the primary curvature of being from which the privilege of the Other results, the gradient of transcendence.'[29]

The Trace

Responsibility for Levinas answers to a face.[30] This face, according to Schroeder, masks an 'epiphanic appearance of the absolutely other as the Other,' corroborating Wyschogrod's notion that 'it (the face) is the source of revelation of the other who cannot be encompassed in cognition.'[31] The presence of a face 'signifies an irrecusable order, a command, which calls a halt to the availability of consciousness. Consciousness is put into question by the face.'[32] According to Levinas, this being commanded by and put to question by the face arrests the self, awakening it to vulnerability.

> The putting into question of the self is precisely the welcome of the absolutely other. The epiphany of the absolutely other is a face in which the other calls to me and signifies an order to me by its nudity, its denuding. Its presence is a summation to respond. The I does not simply become conscious of this necessity to answer, as if it were a matter of an obligation or a duty which it would have to decide of. To be an I then signifies not to be able to slip away from responsibility. . . . *The attitude irreducible to a category* is not to be able to slip away from responsibility, not to have a hiding place in inwardness in which one can return to oneself, to go forward without regard for oneself. There is continual increase of demands put on one: the more I face my responsibilities the more I am responsible.[33]

And the way one faces one's responsibilities is through obliging the face.[34]

Levinas believes that 'a face enters our world from an absolutely alien sphere – that is, precisely out of an absoluteness, which in fact is the name for fundamental strangeness. The signification of a face in its abstractness is, in the literal sense of the term, extra-ordinary.'[35] Begging the obvious, Levinas asks how such a production is possible – then submits an answer: the trace. Through the trace Levinas implicates ethics with a shared horizon where God and the other are indissoluble.[36] Moreover, the idea of the trace allows Levinas a way to graph the disturbance created by the face as it enters concrete reality.

The trace also infuses a semblance of signification for Levinas, a way of charting the *beyond* and *elsewhere* that occupy much of his writings.[37] The problem, however, is the propinquity between the other and the absent. The other comes from elsewhere, yet its provenance smudges the boundaries between being and revelation, dissolving and disrupting correlations between signs and the signified.[38] Waldenfel follows Levinas's graph, tracing the trace to the face: 'Being present only as remnant of somebody who has passed, thus referring to an immemorial past, the trace of the other marks and even constitutes the other's face.'[39]

Hence the trace is a disturbance, a calling, and an invitation to exodus.[40] Irreducible to a sign, yet able, just as tracks lead to prey, to point towards what has left them behind, the trace nonetheless is distinguished owing to the fact that 'the track or trail is emblazoned in the order of being and becomes part of that order, but the trace "means" while retaining its transcendence. It means without intending to be a sign, without meaning to mean. It means beyond any project that has the trace for its intention.'[41] Significantly, this *meaning beyond* assumes a polyvalence in Levinas too rarified for the agencies of consciousness and intentionality. What is more, these regional scaffoldings peripheral to the agential legislation of consciousness are 'like the prey that flees the noise of the hunter across a field covered in snow, thereby leaving the very traces that will be its ruin. We are thus responsible beyond our intentions. It is impossible for the regard that directs the act to avoid the nonintended action that comes with it.'[42]

The trace also inflects memory and time, since to be present or remembered is tantamount to being totalized, subsumed in autonomy.[43] Thus subsumed, one again would be implicated in the saga of an ego subject to the constitutions and temporalizations geared to economies of a self turned inward. According to Levinas,

> A trace is the insertion of space in time, the point at which the world inclines toward a past and a time. . . . But it is in the trace of the other that a face shines; what is presented there is absolving itself from my life and visits me as already absolute. Someone has already passed. His trace does not *signify* his past, as it does not *signify* his labor or his enjoyment of the world; it is a disturbance imprinting itself (we are tempted to say *engraving* itself) with an unexceptional gravity.[44]

Cognizance of Levinas's assertion that (1) we are responsible beyond our intentions, particularly in regards to his fundamental contention that (2) the face commands, and (3) the face, through the trace, both shines and disturbs, alerts one to an inquiry: Who is this third person outside the distinction between entities and being, and what does He have to do with the trace?[45] The answer again is the other.[46]

God is the Other

It is important to note that for Levinas cause and effect are not registered in the usual and putative dominion of things, and that his ethical optics implicates a vision irreducible to image and hence non-contextualized.[47] Similarly the trace cannot be circumscribed by the history of things, particularly the ways these things are restricted by human agency and causal efficacy. The trace then localizes the absence earlier noted as the breach that betrays God. And the face witnesses to this betrayal, concretizing responsibility beyond intentionality through involvement with that in which objectivity participates – the other.[48]

According to Levinas, 'The revealed god of our Judeo-Christian spirituality maintains all infinity of his absence, which is in the personal order itself. He shows himself only by his trace, as is said in Exodus 33. To go toward Him is not to follow this trace which is not a sign; it is to go toward the others who stand in the trace of illeity.'[49] Again, God is in the gap; and the face, the disincarnate presence of the other, mirrors the visitation and transcendence inflected by the disturbance of what Levinas calls the 'unexceptional gravity' of the trace.[50] Significantly, John Drabinski finds this trace 'absolute in its unencompassability and therefore to be understood on the model of modification, transformation, or alteration. This description brings the "gap" or "irreversible lapse" that marks the relation of the Same to the Other into relief.'[51]

One now engages a decisive register in Levinas's thought. In line with vigilance and escape and in response to solipsistic interiority, the self's adventure is now called to a higher expression: sacrificial goodness.[52] Levinas contends that through submitting to exterior being one enters into the forthrightness of the face- to- face, an existence ennobled by responsibility and obligation.[53] This existence 'places the center of gravitation of a being outside of that being. The surpassing of phenomenal or inward existence does not consist in receiving the recognition of the other, but in offering him one's being. To be in oneself is to express oneself, that is, to already serve the Other. The ground of expression is goodness.'[54]

Hence discourse, modulated into an expression of goodness, becomes a ritual of sacrifice – one functioning through service and responsibility to the other. And in point of fact, crucially, according to Levinas, 'God is the other.'[55] And ethics is where the face meets the trace. It is 'a comportment in which the other, who is strange and indifferent to you, who belongs neither to the order of your interest nor to your affections, at the same time matters to you. . . . Here it is precisely the strangeness of the other and, if one can say so, his "stranger-ness" which links you to him ethically.'[56] How do God and the other meet in the trace of the face? Again, through responsibility: 'the face is not of the order of the seen, it is not an object, but it is he whose appearing preserves an exteriority which is also an appeal or an imperative given to your responsibility: To encounter a face is straightaway to hear a demand and an order . . . you hear the word of God.'[57]

The Shock of the Divine

Thus God, the other, the face and the trace merge in responsibility.[58] In a fashion, even the *Imago Dei* finds its way into this quotient, since for Levinas 'the face is in the image of God.'[59] Furthermore Levinas himself, as earlier noted, references Exodus 33, where the passing of God's glory is shown only through God's trace. Ethically this situation incites the realization that God can only be traced by approaching the other, by implementing a discourse whose expression calibrates with responsibility – and whose mode, notwithstanding the equivocacy, honors the moment.[60] When one sacrifices one's self through responsibility to the other, God breaks through. As notes Burggraeve:

> According to Levinas, an uncontaminated God, in whose image and likeness we ourselves are created, allows itself to be heard in the "otherwise than being" of responsibility-to-and-for-the-Other. The situation where God breaks in on us is, for Levinas, not the miracle or mystery of nature (it is not creation, but ethics which comes first). The "shock of the divine" happens primarily in the shattering of the immanent order of being which I can encompass in

individual comprehension and make my own in individual capacity. This breakthrough happens in the face. If God is infinitely Other, he can have left in the Face of the Other person only a trace of his irrecoverable past, never again to be retrieved. . . . Hence is responsibility the intrigue of God's passing, or more strongly, His very life.[61]

Radical humility can only be effectuated when acceptance is the basis of a foundational ethical relation, one where justice is proclaimed through responsibility, and one where the call of the face awakens both concrete and incarnate care.[62]

And yet the face's defiance of the powers of possession, its allergic reaction to one's grasp, precipitates 'the relation with infinity, the idea of infinity in us, conditions it positively. Infinity presents itself as a face in the ethical resistance that paralyses my powers and from the depths of defenceless eyes rises firm in its nudity and destitution. The comprehension of this destitution and this hunger establishes the proximity of the other.'[63] Significantly, infinity here is deformalized through the comprehension of the other's dereliction, situating the sense of meaning in ethics, a work for which there is no compensation. Yet there is also elevation: moral height. 'Stripped of its form, the face is chilled to the bone in its nakedness. It is a desolation. The nakedness of the face is destitution and already supplication in the rectitude that sights me. But this supplication is an obligation. Humility unites with elevation. And announces thereby the ethical dimension of visitation.'[64]

Hence the subject, disabused of its selfishness, comes to the realization that 'Man as Other comes to us from the outside, a separated — or holy— face.'[65] And through welcoming the holy yet derelict face, obligation

modulates into hospitality, for — as Levinas asserts — 'The subject is a host.'[66] Again one must reference Abraham, the consummate host, guilelessly and gratuitously offering charity to strangers. So doing, the boundary between immanence and transcendence is rendered transparent through the giving of self and substance.[67] Moreover, according to Levinas, through hospitality transcendence and immanence intersect in a vision of the face where home and heart converge.[68] This convergence prompts recollection, a separation issuing from an economy coincident with desire:

> But the transcendence of the face is not enacted outside of the world, as though the economy by which separation is produced remained beneath a sort of beatific contemplation of the Other (which would thereby turn into idolatry that brews in all contemplation). The "vision" of the face as face is a certain mode of sojourning in a home, or – to speak in a less singular fashion – as a certain form of economic life. No human or interhuman relationship can be enacted outside of economy; no face can be approached with empty hands and closed home. Recollection in a home open to the Other – hospitality – is the concrete and initial face of human recollection and separation; it coincides with the Desire for the other absolutely transcendent. The chosen home is the very opposite of a root. It indicates a disengagement, a wandering which has made it possible, which is not a *less* with respect to installation, but the surplus of the relationship with the Other, metaphysics.[69]

Thus in Levinas the other comes to one from the outside as a holy and separate face. The transcendence of the face, however, is not enacted outside the world, but in a concrete yet wandering home recollected through hospitality.[70] What is more, God is in the trace of the other.[71] Disclosed in these perspectives are views both phenomenal and enigmatic.

A Glimpse of Faith (This Beggar's Solicitation)

"Phenomenon and Enigma" (1965) provides a critical bridge connecting Levinas's middle and later works. In this essay Levinas asks the question: 'Does not the invisibility of God belong to another game, to an approach which does not polarize into a subject-object correlation but is deployed as a drama with several personages?'[72] Afterward, as if answering with a question, one reads 'Could faith be described then as a glimpse into a time whose moments are no longer related to the present as their term or their source? This would produce a diachrony which maddens the subject but channels transcendence.'[73] It would also, according to Michael Smith, present 'a temporality no longer connected to the present. It might be termed an essentialist view of time, in which the pastness of the past is not to be confused with a former state of the world. It is to this sort of temporality that Levinas refers when he speaks of the deformalization of time. It is the interpretation of time as meaning.'[74]

There is another immediate inquiry: 'Is transcendence a thought that ventures beyond or an approach beyond thought which speech ventures to utter and whose trace and modality it retains?'[75] The reader at this point would be justified in asking Levinas: 'by madden, do you mean anger or confuse?' And in response Levinas would be equally justified in responding: 'Neither. It is meant to disturb.' As point of fact, Levinas would add that

> Everything depends on the possibility of vibrating with a meaning that is not synchronized with the speech that captures it and cannot be fitted into its order; everything depends on the possibility of a signification that would signify in an irreducible disturbance. If a formal description of such a disturbance could be attempted, it would have us speak of a time, a plot, and norms that are not reducible to the understanding of being, which is allegedly the alpha and the omega of philosophy. How could such a disturbance occur? If the Other is presented to the Same, the co-presence of the Other and the Same in a phenomenon forthwith constitutes an order. The discordance that may be produced within this order proposes itself as an invitation to the search for a new order in which this first discord would be resolved: the discordance becomes a problem. The science of yesterday, before the new facts of today, thus makes its way toward the science of tomorrow.[76]

Interestingly the saga of subjectivity now finds itself called to a supra-narrative whose plot and time honor the vibrancy of a third direction, one allied with a disturbance irreducible to transcendence-immanence polarities.[77] This disturbance in plot and time occasions Levinas to create a nomenclature reaching for a hermeneutical equivalence of this disturbance, one referencing the dimension and depth of 'an irreversible, immemorial, unrepresentable past.'[78] What is more, according to Cohen, ethics is implicated in this narrative, and the disturbances caused by these infra-vibrancies further disrupt the sovereignty of the self. How? 'Time and ethics effect a "curvature." Time, which is at once the structure of intersubjectivity, language, and ethics, effects the very singularization of the first person, wherein subjectivity, as we have seen, is elected to goodness, indebted to the infinite demands of the other, a donation, an inexhaustible reserve, even if what is given are only words of comfort or a silent presence.'[79] Cohen is suggesting, in other words, that ethics transposes disturbance into a singular goodness, a transposition owing to the other.

Mindful of Levinas's aforementioned spiraling style, here one is reintroduced to the trace as the verbal medium enlisted to convolve the immemorial past with this irreducible disturbance. Again, Levinas asks and answers: 'What is this original trace, this primordial desolation? It is the nakedness of a face that faces, expressing itself, interrupting order.... In this defeatism, this dereliction, ... this beggar's solicitation, expression no longer participates in the order from which it tears itself but thus faces and confronts in a face, approaches and disturbs absolutely.'[80]

Analytically, one here would be well served by transposing the earlier discussed ethical resistance into what now appears as disturbance. As if smudging the prints left on his earlier works, Levinas assures us a trace can become a sign, but one harbored in a face signifying vacancy: 'The gaping open of emptiness is not only the sign of an absence. A mark traced on sand is not a part of the path, but the very emptiness of a passage. And what has withdrawn is not evoked, does not return to presence, not even to an indicated presence.'[81]

Insinuating an element of recollection into this dereliction and disturbance, Levinas weaves together the stranger and neighbor, allowing expression and proximity to establish an ethical conjuncture and simultaneity reconnecting the absolute past to the present. At this juncture, according to Bloechl, 'Everything I do occurs within the horizon or a relation with what has already withdrawn from the act I undertake. For Levinas to be is to respond.... The other person is, in short, already there, even before I relate to myself.'[82] Accordingly, disturbance rendered to the other prompts an ethical offering to the other, one given subtle significance through asymmetrical obligation.[83] Notes Levinas: 'Disturbance is a movement that does not propose any stable order in conflict or in accord with a given order.... It enters in so subtle a way that unless we retain it, it has already withdrawn.'[84] This subtle retention prompted through proximity provokes an ethical intentionality witnessed through responsibility.[85]

Enigma: A Stranger is Needed

A movement carrying away the signification it delivered constitutes for Levinas a new modality, one captured by the word *enigma*.[86] Contrasted with phenomenon, Levinas uses the term enigma as a navigational apparatus allowing the incognito other safe passage through disturbance, a way — in other words — for the other to appear without this appearance being folded into totality.[87] He notes that 'the enigma does not come from afar to obscure a phenomenal manifestation (but) extends as far as the phenomenon that bears the trace of the *saying* which has already withdrawn from the *said*. All the moments of historical time are fissile; the enchainment of the Story is exposed to interruption.'[88] According to Levinas, the enigma operates by collapsing the disturbances of phenomena into a face ('The human face is the face of the world itself'), by linking significations occluded by traces just 'as the perfect crime artist inserts the traces of his violence in the natural folds of Order. Phenomena open to disturbance, a disturbance letting itself be brought back to order: such is the ambiguity of an Enigma.'[89]

Levinas now dovetails subjectivity with the enigma in a seam so delicate as to suggest dissimulation. So doing provokes the ethical exigency indistinguishable from the responsibility emphasized throughout this analysis. Indeed, by deploying subjectivity into this 'drama with several personages,' Levinas weaves us back into the saga of a self exiled, a self sacrificed to the other—disclosing along the way the steady strain and hammering in the war for eschatological peace. This disclosure prompts what Levinas deems an extravagant movement, one allied with the preoriginary responsibility woven in the idea of infinity:

> But the Enigma concerns so particularly subjectivity, which alone can retain its insinuation, this insinuation is so quickly belied when one seeks to communicate it, that this exclusivity takes on the sense of an assignation first raising up such a being as subjectivity. Summoned to appear, called to an inalienable responsibility – whereas the disclosure of Being occurs in the knowledge and sight of universality – subjectivity is enigma's partner, partner of the transcendence that disturbs being. . . . This extravagant movement of going beyond being or transcendence toward an immemorial antiquity we call the idea of infinity.[90]

Notwithstanding the enigmatic language utilized in order to analyze the enigma, of essence is Levinas's threading responsibility, subjectivity, and transcendence into an expression of goodness calling one to a movement beyond being. Modeling humility, a subjectivity transcending yet yielding to being prompts what Levinas calls the 'breaking up the *undephasable simultaneity* of phenomena. The God "remaining with the contrite and humble" (Isaiah 57:15), on the margin, a persecuted truth, is not only a religious consolation, but the original form of transcendence.'[91] Again one witnesses Levinas universalizing the self in crisis, finding in this disturbance an ethical resistance operating as a 'node of intrigue, . . . a new modality which is expressed by that "if one likes" and that "perhaps," which one must not reduce to the possibility, reality, and necessity of formal logic. . . .'[92]

Language lost in a synchronism fallen out of tune, discourse unaccustomed to the ineluctably inexpressible – what is this disarticulating moment Levinas calls disturbance? One knows (1): 'disturbance is not the breakup of a category too narrow for the order, which this breakup would then let shine forth in the setting of a broader category.'[93] Thus disturbance is non-categorical. One knows (2): 'Nor is it the shock of a provisional incomprehension which will soon become understanding. It is not as something irrational or absurd that disturbance disturbs.'[94] Disturbance, thus, exceeds reason – yet is rational.[95] And one knows (3): 'The disturbance that is not the surprise of the absurd is possible only as the entry into a given order of another order which does not accommodate itself with the first.'[96] Thus now one is operating in a dimension radicalizing the mutual exclusivities of transcendence and immanence. Woven into what Levinas calls *'the unbreakable plot,'* these three keys fit together opening one door: 'And yet disturbance is possible only through an intervention. A stranger is needed, one who has come, to be sure, but left *before* having come, absolute in his manifestation.'[97] What is more, this intervention, this ethical exigency where a naked face interrupts order, re-contextualizes the stranger: 'Across the unbreakable chain of significations, standing out against the historical conjuncture, was there not an expression, a face facing and interpellating, coming from the depths, cutting the threads of the context? Did not a neighbor approach?'[98] Pointedly, expression here carves out a depth and dimension in an immemorial past, one where relationships untrammeled by memory and time converge through proximity – hermeneutically translating the stranger into a neighbor – grounding existence in ethics.[99]

Proximity

Robert Bernasconi observes the significance of "Enigma and Phenomena" in Levinas's oeuvre, noting that it

> marks an important stage in the transition from *Totality and Infinity* to *Otherwise than Being*. Levinas draws attention to one of the changes himself. In a note he observes that he has overcome his previous reluctance to use the term *neighbor*. Previously the focus had fallen on the stranger. *Stranger* suggested itself to Levinas as a term for the Other for whom I am responsible, not least because it suggested the alterity of the Other as someone to whom I was not already in debt or with whom I was not communally bound. The introduction of the word *neighbor* alongside the word *stranger* would be relatively unimportant did it not bring with it the notion of proximity.[100]

Proximity is a central motif in Levinas. As Smith notes, 'proximity is the field that Levinas opens between the same (or the subject) and the other, in which the "intrigue of the infinite" unfolds. It evokes a spatiality of a rather abstract nature since it is the distance between the poles of a relation.'[101] Through proximity, disturbance and ethical resistance modulate into ethical intentionality. This modulation occurs as a result of collapsing one's relationship with the other into that with God. Simply, but not easily, this reduction necessitates openly and honestly embracing enigma. 'To endure the contradiction between the existence included in the essence of God and the scandalous absence of this God is to suffer an initiation trial into religious life which separates philosophers from believers. That is, unless the obstinate absence of God were one of those paradoxes that call to the highways.'[102]

The above statement fundamentally encapsulates the third direction in the new order charted out by Levinas.[103] And while more specific detail will be offered later through analysis of "God and Philosophy," attention now must be paid to this mystifying pronouncement of an obstinate yet absent God. First: the statement, while enigmatic, is unambiguous. God's apparent absence, *Deus absconditus*, is interpreted as a potential call the highways.[104] Second: Whom does one meet on the highways? Mostly the other. Where is God for Levinas? God is in the trace of the other. Third: what is proximity? It is the shock of the divine, where distance becomes devotion. How does this transpire? By the stranger becoming a neighbor. And how does the stranger become neighbor? Through an ordination witnessed through responsibility:

> Responsibility in fact is not a simple attribute of subjectivity, as if the latter already existed in itself; it is, once again, initially for another. The proximity of the Other is presented as the fact that the Other is not simply close to me in space, or close like a parent, but he approaches me essentially insofar as I feel myself – insofar as I am – responsible for him. . . . The tie with the Other is knotted only as responsibility, this moreover, whether accepted of refused, whether knowing or not knowing how to assume it, whether able or unable to do something concrete for the Other. To say: here I am. To do something for the Other. . . . The face orders and ordains me. Its signification is an order signified. To be precise, if the face signifies an order in my regard, this is not in the manner in which an ordinary sign signifies its signified; this order is the very signifyingness of the face.[105]

It would appear that responsibility transforms disturbance into devotion, one made concrete through a willingness to sacrifice for the other.[106] This willingness – this intervention of meaning through the enigma – this vigilance that 'hearkens to those footsteps that depart, is transcendence itself, the proximity of the Other as Other.'[107]

One would be remiss not to include here John D. Zizioulas's critique that 'Levinas seeks to avoid using comprehension as a means of establishing otherness by insisting that the other does not affect us in terms of a concept or theme, but in and through the concrete situation of speaking or calling or listening to the Other. . . .'[108] Notwithstanding Zizioulas's contention that Levinas, more than any other philosopher, brings us closer to the Greek patristic view of otherness, there still lingers the problem of how Levinas's thought actually liberates beings from the totalitarianism of Being. For Zizioulas, this problem 'raises the question of the *eschatology of otherness* in Levinas's thought.'[109] In other words, Zizioulas believes that for Levinas the ultimate goal is not the other but the desire of the other – a contention reducibly charging Levinas with a transcendence run amuck. Levinas's motif of proximity, however, particularly the way it is threaded through the idea of infinity towards responsibility, does concretize a situation where the other is both present and waiting, hence qualifying it as both concept and theme.

Granted: this qualification comes through transcendence, yet rests on the concrete other. As Bloechl comments, 'Levinas's turn to eschatology can come as no surprise' when it is 'understood as the necessarily finite expression of a desire beyond all limits. . . . In it, in the present moment, one catches sight of human life tentered between a thirst older and more enduring than all beginnings, and the withdrawal of any satisfaction into a future more remote than any projection or anticipation.'[110] Thus for Levinas the situation vis-à-vis the other comprises a both/and rather than either/or hermeneutic, one both concrete and conceptual – and one, despite Zizioulas's objections, comprehensive.[111]

The Truth of Transcendence

Proximity is a prelude to a requisition. It is a call, an assignation.[112] Alphonso Lingis comments that Levinas continually works out this calling through 'the example of the neighbor whose proximity, whose nearness, consists in his touching us, affecting us, while remaining uncomprehended, unassimilable, by us.'[113] What is more, according to Levinas 'this assignation – categorical in its straightforwardness but already discrete, as though no one assigned and no one checked – summons one to moral responsibility. Morality is the Enigma's way.'[114] It is not by accident that the last two sections of "Enigma and Phenomenon" are entitled respectively "Ethics" and "Beyond Being." Anticipating his later magnum opus *Otherwise than Being*, and true to his steady keynoting of the royal road of ethics, these two sections presage much of Levinas's later works. Substantive here is Levinas's weaving together the idea of infinity and our theme of responsibility, as he asks and answers the question: 'How is a response made?'

> To the idea of the Infinite only an extravagant response is possible. There has to be a "thought" that understands more that it understands, more than its capacity, of which it cannot be contemporary, a "thought" which, in this sense, could go beyond its death. To understand more than one understands, to think more than one thinks, to think of what withdraws from thought, is to desire, with a desire that, unlike need, is renewed and becomes ardent the more it is nourished with the Desirable. To go beyond one's death is to sacrifice oneself. The response to the Enigma's summons is the generosity of sacrifice outside the known or the unknown, without calculation, for going on to infinity.[115]

A central concern of "Philosophy and the Idea of Infinity" has been recalibrated: responsibility is now commensurate with Desire, and going beyond being becomes coordinate with sacrifice, a sacrifice transcending death.[116] Critchley, expanding upon this idea of sacrifice, observes that 'to die for the Other is always secondary within the logic of fundamental ontology;

it would always be but a sacrifice. Now, for Levinas, it is precisely the ethical relation, understood as the priority that the Other has over me that is primary; the fact that I would be prepared to sacrifice myself for the Other, to substitute myself and die in the Other's place.'[117]

Remembering the saga of the self, one distinguishable by solipsism and sovereignty, adds clarity to Levinas's statement here that 'the unwonted intrigue which solicits the I and comes to a head beyond cognition and disclosure in Enigma is ethics. The relationship with the infinite is not a cognition but an approach, a neighboring with what signifies itself without revealing itself. . . .'[118] More important, one now finds Levinas adding characters to the unbreakable plot, gracing ambiguity with a precision granting infinite desire freedom to modulate into morality. In a decisive passage, one learns that

> Desire, or the response to an Enigma or morality, is an intrigue with three personages: the I approaches the Infinite by going generously toward the You, who is still my contemporary, but, in the trace of Illeity, presents himself out of a depth of the past, faces, and approaches me. I approach the infinite insofar as I forget myself for my neighbor who looks at me; I forget myself only in breaking the undephasable simultaneity of representation, in existing beyond my death. I approach the infinite by sacrificing myself. Sacrifice is the norm and the criterion of the approach. And the truth of transcendence consists in the concording of speech with acts.[119]

By demonstratively presenting desire as the response to an enigma, collapsing this enigma into morality, and bracketing these with speech acts, Levinas has woven into his intrigue a hermeneutic that can be presented as follows: 'All speaking is an enigma.'[120] Like the self isolated yet desiring escape, and like father Abraham relentlessly taking leave: one is incessantly and obsessively approaching the other — saying 'Here I am.'[121] This is the other that calls. And, as Mark Taylor reminds us, 'this is the Other that approaches Abraham from behind and whispers in his ear.'[122]

Notes

1. See Levinas, *Totalité et Infini*, 5f.; *Totality and Infinity*, 35f. See also Regina M Schwartz, "Revelation and Revolution," *Cross Currents* 56 no. 3 (Autumn, 2006): 381.

2. Levinas believes that the perseverance of being, the effort to be, is ruptured by the effort effected through responsibility to the one who is separated as a stranger. He also believes that this responsibility is incumbent immediately upon the other's approach. Levinas further speaks of this solicitude for the other as a religious moment, one rooted in the saying of a simple 'hello,' *Is It Righteous to Be*, 59.

3. Levinas, *Totalité et Infini*, 9; *Totality and Infinity*, 39, emphasis in text.

4. Steven G. Smith corroborates this point when he states that 'the Other is prior to my freedom,' For Smith, the synthetic agencies are those circumscribed by theoretical, practical, and axiological constitutions of consciousness, *The Argument to the Other*, 76.

5. Levinas, *Totalité et Infini*, 11 ; *Totality and Infintiy*, 41f.
6. *Minimal Theologies: Critiques of Secular Reason in Adorno and Levinas* (Baltimore: The Johns Hopkins University Press, 2005) 350f. See also Claire Elise Katz, "Raising Cain: The Problem of Evil and the Question of Responsibility, *Cross Currents* 55 no 2 (Summer, 2005): 217f.
7. *The Problem of Ethical Metaphysics*, 103.
8. Peperzak, *To The Other*, 134, emphasis in text.
9. See Richard J. Bernstein, "Evil and Theodicy," *Cambridge Companion to Levinas*, 263f.
10. Regarding Levinas's byzantine style, Peperzak argues that 'There seems to be no systematic scheme but rather a system of fragments that have been rearranged after their writing. And yet, the fragments form a coherent text not broken by abrupt disruptions or startling turns. One of the difficulties is, however, that they move rather quickly from one topic to another in order to show a certain coherence between them and to convince the reader that the traditional views must be rethought in their entirety. Levinas's meditations perform a spiraling thought... (and) by following that movement, the reader is confronted with constellations rather than with single phenomena; many repetitions, which most often are also further developments of insights expressed before, make a patient reader acquainted with a surprising but revealing approach and challenge,' *To The Other*, 142.
11. Levinas, *Totalité et Infini*, 13 ; *Totality and Infinity*, 43.
12. See Jean-François Lyotard, "Levinas's Logic," *Face to Face with Levinas*, 118f.
13. See Jeffrey Dudiak, *The Intrigue of Ethics*, where it is noted that the separation of the other from the same is a result of 'ethical refusal,' a movement ingredient in an ethical relation leading up to where 'the face speaks.' Regarding this ethical moment, Dudiak comments that 'in the encounter with the face, we are already in the realm of language,' 109.
14. "Jewish Dimensions of Radical Ethics," *Ethics as First Philosophy*, 14f. For more on separation in Levinas, see Meredith Gunning, *About Face*, 277f.
15. For more on history in Levinas, and the way responsibility enters a historical world aestheticized as a salvation drama, see Rebecca Comay, "Facies Hippocratica," *Ethics as First Philosophy*, 232.
16. Levinas, *Totalité et Infini*, 23; *Totality and Infinity*, 52, emphasis added. See also Wyschogrod, *Ethical Metaphysics*, where it is noted that the creation of totality is the function of history. She further maintains that history chronicles the non-living, but that the living individual exhibits a fate both private and non-totalized. Hence she asserts that 'separated being exists as interiority. It inaugurates a dimension in which everything that has been closed to history remains open. The destiny of the individual is distinct from historical destiny,' 85.
17. Ibid., 24 ; 53.
18. In "Levinas and the Hebraic Tradition," *Ethics as First Philosophy*, Catherine Chalier argues that in Levinas's thought responsibility takes precedence over freedom. Interestingly, she also notes how 'in Hebrew, "responsibility" (*ahariout*) and "other" (*aher*) are closely linked. Both words share the same link,' 8.
19. Levinas, *Totalité et Infini*, 74f. ; *Totality and Infinity*, 101, emphasis in text. For an interesting Christian parallel to this assertion by Levinas, see H. Richard Niebuhr, *Christ and Culture* (Harper Torchbooks: New York, 1956). Niebuhr contends that 'We make our free decisions not only in such dependence on origins beyond our control, but also in dependence on consequences that are not in our power,' 250.

20. Levinas, *Totalité et Infini*, 52f.; *Totality and Infinity*, 78f. Elsewhere Levinas contends God comes to one's mind antecedent to any musings on first causes; that, in fact, it is the nudity of the face that takes priority, one that implores one to oblige the neighbor: 'For me, theology begins in the face of the neighbor. The divinity of God is played out in the human. God descends in the "face" of the other,' *Is It Righteous to Be?*, 236.

21. *Levinas: A Guide for the Perplexed*, 157.

22. Levinas, *Totalité et Infini*, 52f. ; *Totality and Infinity*, 80.

23. Ibid. This 'full face welcome of the other by me' puts to task one's spontaneity and freedom, initiating the call to responsibility manifesting a higher freedom. Michael B. Smith is of the opinion that, for Levinas, this sense of freedom releases one from self-tyranny as well as calls one towards a higher vocation, namely, the call and command of the other. Smith further asserts that one's response to this call is what 'makes us most distinctly ourselves,' "Levinas: A Transdisciplinary Thinker," *Addressing Levinas*, 67.

24. For another view where freedom is questioned in regards to man's volition, see Karl Barth, "The Gift of Freedom," *The Humanity of God* (Atlanta: John Knox Press, 1960). Here Barth asserts that man's freedom is contingent upon God's grace: 'In His free grace, God is for man in every respect; He surrounds man from all sides. He is man's Lord who is before him, above him, after him, and thence also with him in history, the locus of man's existence,' 72.

25. This awakening is incited by diachrony and can be detected in the synthesizing ability of the 'I' – as witnessed in non-ending and exigent responsibility. See Gunning, 214.

26. Levinas, *Totalité et Infini*, 58 ; *Totality and Infinity*, 86.

27. *Wittgenstein and Levinas: Ethical and Religious Thought* (London: Routledge, 2005), 7.

28. See James Hatley, "Beyond Outrage," *Addressing Levinas*, 44.

29. *Totalité et Infini*, 194 ; *Totality and Infinity*, 225.

30. See Rudolf Bernet, "The Encounter with the Stranger," *The Face of the Other and the Trace of God*, 53.

31. *Altared Ground*, 134; *The Problem of Ethical Metaphysics*, 244.

32. Levinas, "La trace de l'autre," 195; "The Trace of the Other," 353.

33. Ibid., 353f., emphasis in text. For Levinas, 'Face and discourse are tied. The face speaks. It speaks, it is in this that it renders possible and begins all discourse. I have refused the notion of vision to describe the authentic relationship with the Other; it is discourse, and, more exactly, response or responsibility, which is authentic relationship.... Now, in the face such a I describe its approach, is produced the same exceeding of the act by that to which it leads. In the access to the face there is certainly an access to the idea of God,' *Éthique et Infini*, 91, 96; *Ethics and Infinity*, 87f., 92.

34. See Colin Davis, *Levinas*, 133.

35. "La trace de l'autre," 195; "The Trace of the Other," 352. Cf. Hent De Vries, *Minimal Theologies: Critiques of Secular Reason in Adorno and Levinas*, 373.

36. See David Michael Levin, "Tracework: Myself and Others in the Moral Phenomenology of Merleau-Ponty and Levinas," *International Journal of Philosophical Studies* 6 no. 3 (1998): 347f.

37. See Robert Gibbs, "Jewish Dimensions of Radical Ethics," *Ethics as First Philosophy*, where it is noted that the trace of God, as the infinite, orders one to draw near to the other person. Gibbs calls the force of this order a 'shift into a theological gear' for Levinas, 17.

38. Cf. Levinas "Signification and Sense," *Humanism of the Other*, 32. See also Bettina Bergo, *Levinas Between Ethics and Politics*, 161.

39. "Levinas and the Face of the Other." *The Cambridge Companion to Levinas*, 77.

40. Regarding this call, John Olthuis, *Knowing Other-wise*, p. 143, takes issue with Levinas, contending that one's calling to the other in effect empowers the other and totalizes the other. Notes Olthus: 'It is Levinas's view of power as inherently power-over that I see as highly problematic. Accepting that domination is indigenous to power and at the same time decrying such power-egoism leaves Levinas only one alternative: the ethical priority of the other.' As has been presented, one would think Levinas would agree that the other has ethical priority. In fact, the ethical priority of the other prompts the exigent responsibility analyzed herein.

41. Edith Wyschogrod, *The Problem of Ethical Metaphysics*, 160. Drabinski corroborates Wyschogrod here, noting in effect that the trace neither indicates, reveals, nor dissimulates. In concert with Levinas, Drabinski goes on to mention that the trace exhibits a third way, one suggestive of a 'radical absence,' *Sensibility and Singularity: The Problem of Phenomenology in Levinas*, 158f.

42. Levinas, "Is Ontology Fundamental," *Basic Philosophical Writings*, 4.

43. See Amit Pinchevski, *By Way of Interruption: Levinas and the Ethics of Communication*, 86.

44. Levinas, "La trace de l'autre," 195 ; "The Trace of the Other," pp. 358f, emphasis in text. See also Graham Ward, "The Revelation of the Holy Other as the Wholly Other," *Modern Theology* 14, no. 2 (1993): 161f.

45. This third person He, introduced by Levinas in "The Trace of the Other" through the concept *illeity*, allows an ingress of God without employing negative theology. 'Derived from the pronoun *il*, illeity entails the refusal of any direct, personal, or intimate relationship with God. Levinas rejects Buber's I-Thou relationship because it implies too much familiarity with the Other, who should be addressed with the more formal *vous*; but this *vous* is in turn too familiar, too direct an address for God. God is glimpsed only in the third person, neither a presence nor an absence, but a trace, infinitely close and absolutely absent. Illeity is alterity at the furthest remove; and to be in the image of God is to stand in the trace of Illeity. God is not the supreme Other, but rather the absent condition, or the incondition as Levinas frequently writes, of the encounter with the Other,' Colin Davis, *Levinas*, 99.

46. The answer is the other specifically owing to the asymmetrical nature of the relation. As John Llewelyn notes, 'each other is a You related to me dissymmetrically because I am more responsible than each and every other to the point of being responsible even for their responsibilities,' *Appositions*, 135.

47. Cf. Levinas, *Totalité et Infini*, xif. ; *Totality and Infinity* 23.

48. Edward Farley calls the face the 'origin of obligation.' What is more, he sees the face as exhibiting an inherent vulnerability, one that seizes and holds us: 'Before the vulnerable face we are close to the being of obligation, the very thing that brings it into being,' *Deep Symbols: Their Postmodern Effacement and Reclamation* (Valley Forge, Penn.: Trinity Press International, 1996) 50f.

49. Levinas, "La trace de l'autre," 202; "The Trace of the Other," 359.

50. Ibid.

51. *Sensibility and Singularity*, 162f.

52. For more on gratuitous sacrifice and giving in Levinas, especially as it is emphasized in ethical situations interwoven both formally and concretely, see Robert Bernasconi, "What is the Question to which 'Substitution' is the Answer," *Cambridge*

Companion to Levinas, 248f. Sacrificial goodness finds its ultimate expression in substitution, the theme of Chapter 7 in this analysis.

53. See also Peter Atterton, *On Levinas,* 29f.

54. Levinas, *Totalité et Infini,* 158 ; *Totality and Infinity,* 183.

55. Ibid., 186; 211. Levinas makes this assertion within the context of Descartes' 'non-constitution of infinity' as referential to its mutation into an object of being. It is also contextualized with Levinas's contention that 'the infinite cannot be thematized' and is thus 'a relation with a total alterity irreducible to interiority.' Thus it is the other's and God's irreducibility that prompts the above copula.

56. Levinas, "Is It Righteous To Be?" 48.

57. Ibid. According to Jeffrey L. Kosky, '... if it belongs most essentially to the face of God to disappear in what shows or presents it, then it would not appear in the discourse of the very metaphysics which thinks it. In fact, biblically, the God who is absent from images and idols on earth is present to his people Israel in the commands and imperatives which make up his law.... Thus, in describing the imperative issuing from the face of the other, ethical metaphysics would be a profoundly theological discourse, to the degree that it responds to a command issued from the essentially hidden face of God,' *Levinas and the Philosophy of Religion,* 35f.

58. Responsibility is at the heart of this cross and is the lynchpin of this thesis. One might dare to say that what is Levinasian herein is reducible to responsibility. And as we shall witness in chapter seven, responsibility finds its logical terminus in the other – as experienced through substitution.

59. Edith Wyschogrod, *The Problem of Ethical Metaphysics,* p. 163. See also George Drazenovich, "Towards a Levinasian Understanding of Christian Ethics: Emmanuel Levinas and the Phenomenology of the Other," *Cross Currents* 54 no. 4 (2005): 42.

60. Cf. Valevicius: 'The ethics of Levinas is an excessive ethics; excessive alterity, excessive passivity, excessive responsibility. The problem with Levinas's asymmetrical relation to the Other ... is that the Other is like a God to me,' *From the Other to the Totally Other: The Religious Philosophy of Emmanuel Levinas,* 89.

61. *The Wisdom of Love in the Service of Love,* 117-121. See also John Llewelyn, *Emmanuel Levinas: The Genealogy of Ethics,* 138f.

62. Levinas considers this incarnate care as reflecting the impossibility of looking back and escaping responsibility. He feels moreover that it offers no hiding place for the self. In fact, regarding the self Levinas views responsibility as a power rendered powerless by what he calls a 'primordial rectitude,' one witnessed through 'a sense of being.' See "Signification and Sense," *Humanism of the Other,* 34.

63. Levinas, *Totalité et Infini,* 174 ; *Totality and Infinity* pp. 199f. See also Jill Robbins, "Visage, Figure: Reading Levinas's *Totality and Infinity, Yale French Studies* 0 no. 79 (1991) 143.

64. Levinas, "Signification and Sense," *Humanism of the Other,* 32. See also Richard A. Cohen, "Absolute Positivity and Ultrapositivity," *The Question of the Other,* 39.

65. Levinas, *Totalité et Infini,* 267 ; *Totality and Infinity,* 291.

66. Ibid., 276; 299.

67. Apropos this assertion, Pannenberg notes that 'if Christian love is essentially a participation in God's love for the world, then we have to ask whether we can distinguish at all between love of God and love of neighbor,' *Systematic Theology,* v. III, 187.

68. See Roger Burggraeve, "The Bible Gives to Thought: Levinas on the Possibility and Proper Nature of Biblical Thinking," *The Face of the Other and the Trace of God,* 171.

69. Ibid., 147 ; 172, emphasis in text. Levinas's intermingling of transcendence and immanence can both illumine and obfuscate. Two seminal essays are suggested for the reader wanting a detailed analysis of both perspectives. Theodore De Boer notes that 'there are a number of passages in the writings of Levinas in which we find him coming out in favor of a phenomenological and transcendental method.' De Boer further 'endeavor(s) to demonstrate that Levinas integrates phenomenological ontology into dialogical thinking,' stating that 'Only the philosophy of the other, only "metaphysics," is able to provide a foundation for this ontology.' Later De Boer comments that 'In Levinas, however, this transcendental condition is an ethical experience enacted in discourse,' an assertion followed by his belief that 'Levinas's philosophy of language reveals a metaphysical depth-dimension of language,' "An Ethical Transcendental Philosophy," *Face to Face With Levinas,* 83-110. Robert Bernasconi – in response to the Levinasian question: 'what status is to be accorded the face-to-face relation?' – notes that 'Here interpretations diverge. Some interpreters understand it as a concrete experience that we can recognize in our lives. Other commentators have understood the face-to-face relation to be the condition for the possibility of ethics and indeed of all economic existence and knowledge. If the first interpretation arises from what might be called an empirical reading, the second might be referred to as the transcendental reading.' Later Bernasconi observes that 'Levinas may on occasion call the face abstract, but he does so only in the sense that it is a disturbance which breaks with cultural meaning and calls into question the horizons of the world. The face is also the most concrete in that the face cannot be approached with empty hand but only from within society,' "Rereading Totality and Infinity," *The Question of the Other,* 23-34.

70. See Chris Harris, "Toward an Understanding of Home: Levinas and the New Testament," *Religious Education* 90 no. 3 (Summer/Fall 1995) 434.

71. See Luce Irigary, "Questions to Emmanuel Levinas on the Divinity of Love," *Re-Reading Levinas,* trans. Margaret Whitford, for a fascinating look at the other and God in works of Levinas from a feminist perspective, 114-117.

72. "Énigme et phénomène," *En découvrant l'existence avec Husserl et Heidegger,* 210 ; ''Enigma and Phenomenon," *Collected Philosophical Papers,* 67.

73. Ibid.

74. *Toward the Outside,* 61f.

75. Ibid. Two comments regarding this 'approach beyond' may be significant. One, Levinas in a footnote to the above question adds that 'It has to be said that this transcendence consist in going beyond being, which here means that the aim aims at what refuses the correlation which every aim as such established and which consequently is nowise represented, not even conceptually. The primordial feeling, precisely in its ambiguity, is this desire for Infinity, the relationship with the Absolute which does not become correlative with it, and consequently in a sense leaves the subject in immanence.' (178, note 6). This primordial feeling Levinas likens to Jean Wahl's notion of 'the greatest transcendence, that which consists in transcending transcendence, that is, relapsing into immanence' (ibid). The second comment apropos of this 'beyond' has to with Levinas hinting at 'the possibility of the third direction or radical *irrectitude* that escapes the bipolar game of immanence and transcendence proper to being, where immanence always wins out over transcendence,' "Signification and Sense," *Humanism of the Other,* 40, emphasis in text.

76. ''Énigme et phénomène," 210 ; ''Phenomenon and Enigma," 67.

77. This disturbance is allied with the diachrony within the consciousness of time, where it is experienced as an extreme passivity. John Drabinski views this passivity as a

locus where the face assumes an obligation demonstrating how disturbance functions in the ethical relation, *Sensibility and Singularity*, 166.

78. "Énigme et phénomène," 207 ; "Phenomenon and Enigma," 65.

79. *Elevations: The Height of the Good in Rosenzweig and Levinas*, 15.

80. "Énigme et phénomène," 207f. ; "Phenomenon and Enigma," 65f. See Levinas, "Ethics as First Philosophy," *The Levinas Reader*, for another sample of Levinas's serpentine style. Here he notes that 'in its expression, in its mortality, the face before me summons me, calls for me, begs for me, as if the invisible death that must be faced by the Other, pure otherness, separated, in some way, from any whole, were my business.... The Other becomes my neighbor precisely through the way the face summons me, calls for me, begs for me, and in so doing recalls my responsibility, and calls me into question,' 83.

81. Ibid., 211; 70.

82. *Liturgy of the Neighbor*, 3.

83. See John D. Caputo, *Against Ethics: Contributions to a Poetics of Obligation with Constant Reference to Deconstruction*, 120.

84. "Énigme et phénomène," 208 ; "Phenomenon and Enigma," 66.

85. See Amit Pinchevski, *By Way of Interruption: Levinas and the Ethics of Communication*, 9.

86. In works of Levinas the term *enigma* polemically engages phenomena, withdrawing when the phenomenon appears. Ingredient to language, transparent to transcendence, it 'joins the long list of other terms in Levinas's writing which represent the disruption of totality,' Davis, *Levinas*, 90.

87. Cf. Peperzak, *To The Other*, where it is noted how Levinas in all his works attempts to present the human other as radically different from all other beings. Peperzak further mentions that, due to the phenomenal being restricted by what he calls egological understanding, the other is irreducible to such a totality. Hence, this alterity 'is not a phenomenon but rather an "enigma" not to be defined in phenomenological terms. If visibility, in a broad and metaphorical sense, is a feature of every being that can become a phenomenon, Levinas may even call the other "invisible," 21f.

88. "Énigme et phénomène," 211 ; "Phenomenon and Enigma," 69, emphasis in text.

89. Ibid.

90. Ibid., 214; 72.

91. Ibid., 214; 71, emphasis in text. Levinas, in "A Religion for Adults," *Difficult Freedom*, tells us that 'The fact that the relationship with the Divine crosses the relationship with men and coincides with social justice is therefore what epitomizes the entire spirit of the Jewish Bible. Moses and the prophets preoccupied themselves not with the immortality of the soul but with the poor, the widow, the orphan, and the stranger. The relationship with man in which contact with the Divine is established is not a kind of *spiritual friendship* but the sort that is manifested, tested, and accomplished in a just economy and for which each man is responsible,' 19f., emphasis in text.

92. Ibid.

93. Ibid. For more on how this disturbance 'unsettles (or un-saddles) me in a way that fundamentally alters me,' see Rudi Visker, *Truth and Singularity*, 254

94. Ibid., 215; 72.

95. See Gibbs, *Correlations in Rosenzweig and Levinas*, 207.

96. "Énigme et phénomène," 215 ; "Phenomenon and Enigma," 72. This disturbance is non-philosophical and hence interruptive. It is interruptive because it is ethical, and problematizes issues of justice. Hence it is prophetic. See Robert Bernasconi, "Levinas," *Philosophy and Non-Philosophy Since Merleau-Ponty*, 257f.

97. Ibid., 214; 71f, emphasis in text. In "Humanism and An-archy" Levinas links inwardness with this deformation of time. '*Inwardness is the fact that in being the beginning is preceded.* But what precedes does not present itself to the free gaze that would assume it, does not become present or a representation. Something has already come to pass "over the head" of the present, has not crossed the cordon of consciousness and does not let itself be recuperated, something that precedes the beginning and the principle, that is an-archically *despite* being, reverses or precedes being,' *Collected Philosophical Papers*, 133, emphasis in text.

98. Ibid., 211f.; 69. See also Mark Taylor, Introduction to *Deconstruction in Context: Literature and Philosophy*, 25.

99. Cf. "Philosophy and Transcendence," *Alterity and Transcendence,"* where Levinas extrapolates upon a past irreducible to the present, one moreover signifying a preoriginary ethical responsibility for the other. Simply by emphasizing the "here I am," Levinas suppresses identity while highlighting a pristine past where ethics is obligation. This obligation for the other, for Levinas, is what 'regards me' by being 'my business,' 32.

100. Introduction to "Enigma and Phenomenon," *Basic Philosophical Writings*, 65, emphasis in text. Cf. Charles E. Scott, "A People's Witness beyond Politics," *Ethics as First Philosophy*, 26f.

101. *Toward the Outside*, 91.

102. "Énigme et phénomène," 204; "Phenomenon and Enigma," 62.

103. By 'the third' one does not mean to indicate simply an empirical fact reducible to comparison. For Levinas it is a structure contingent upon the proximity of the neighbor, one where the invisible as well as visible other represent all persons. As Perperzak notes, 'The visage of the other is incomparable and identical with every other visage. The third, who shows him/herself in the visage of my neighbor, is the origin of appearance and, thus, of the realm of phenomena and phenomenology. The relation to the third, through which the realm of the Said is recovered and justified, rectifies the asymmetry of immediate and intimate relations,' *To The Other*, 230.

104. Regarding this covertness of God in relation to Levinas's ethical metaphysics, Jeffrey Kosky comments that 'if it belongs most essentially to the face of God to disappear in what shows or presents itself, then it would not appear in the discourse of the very metaphysics which thinks it. In fact, biblically, the God who is absent from images and idols on earth is present to his people Israel in the commands and imperatives which make up his law. Out of the hiddenness of God in the burning bush issues the law and the commandments that make it up so that closeness or proximity to God is not articulated in spatial terms as nearness to the center marked by a temple or other image that presents God but in terms of threats and promises and obedience. Thus, in describing the imperative issuing from the face of the Other, ethical metaphysics would be a profoundly theological discourse, to the degree that it responds to a command issued from the essentially hidden face of God,' *Levinas and the Philosophy of Religion*, 35f.

105. Levinas, *Éthique et Infini*, 103f.; *Ethics and Infinity*, 97f., emphasis in text. See also James H. Olthuis, "Face-to-Face: Ethical Asymmetry or the Symmetry of Mutuality," *Knowing Other-wise: Philosophy at the Threshold of Spirituality*, ed. James H Olthius (New York: Fordham University Press, 1997) 136f.

106. This devotion is irreducible to metaphors apposite vision, as it tends to be more aligned with the hunger and reaching consequential of Desire and the idea of infinity. It really presents itself, according to Levinas, as a relationship of pure patience, one marked by a diachrony not only prior to consciousness but older than consciousness. Levinas attempts to limn this pre-consciousness by noting that it displays 'an intentionality, a thematization, and the impatience of a *grasping*,' Foreword to *Of God Who Comes To Mind*, xiii, emphasis in text.

107. "Énigme et phénomène," 213 ; "Phenomenon and Enigma," 70.

108. *Communion & Otherness*, ed. Paul McPartlan (London: T & T Clark, 2006) 49.

109. Ibid., 50, emphasis in text.

110. *Liturgy of the Neighbor*, 142f.

111. For more on how desire manifests itself in works of Levinas, and ways this desire is reflected in the transcendent/concrete dialectic, see Peperzak, "Presentation," *Re-Reading Levinas*, 53f.

112. See Bernhard Waldenfels, "Levinas and the Face of the Other," *The Cambridge Companion to Levinas*, 74f.

113. "The Sensuality and the Sensitivity," *Face to Face with Levinas*, 228.

114. "Énigme et phénomène," 215; "Phenomenon and Enigma," 72.

115. Ibid., 215f.; 72.

116. Cf. 'The distance that separates happiness from desire separates politics from religion. Politics tends toward reciprocal recognition, that is, toward equality; it insures happiness. And political law concludes and sanctions the struggle for recognition. Religion is Desire and not struggle for recognition. It is the surplus possible in a society of equals, that of glorious humility, responsibility, and sacrifice, which are the condition for equality itself,' Levinas, *Totalité et Infini*, 35; *Totality and Infinity*, 64.

117. *The Ethics of Deconstruction*, 224.

118. "Énigme et phénomène," 216 ; "Phenomenon and Enigma," 73.

119. Ibid., 215; 72. Concerning illeity, Colin Davis remarks that 'Derived from the pronoun *il*, illeity entails the refusal of any direct, personal or intimate relationship with God.... God is glimpsed only in the third person, neither a presence nor an absence, but a trace, infinitely close and absolutely distant. Illeity is alterity at the furthest remove; and to be in the image of God is to stand in the trace of this Illeity. God is not the supreme Other, but rather the absent condition, or the incondition as Levinas frequently writes, of the encounter with the Other,' *Levinas*, 99.

120. Ibid., 212; 69. This 'speaking' or ethical language for Levinas contrasts with knowledge, and acquires its meaning in its approach to the neighbor. 'Language, contact, is the obsession of an "I" beset by the others. Obsession is responsibility. But the responsibility characteristic of obsession does not derive from a freedom, for otherwise obsession would be only a becoming conscious.... Responsibility as an obsession is proximity; like kinship, it is a bond prior to every chosen bond. Language is fraternity, and thus a responsibility for the other, and hence a responsibility for what I have not committed, for the pain and fault of others,' Levinas, "Language and Proximity,' *Collected Philosophical Papers*, 123.

121. Meredith Gunning calls this isolated self seeking escape a 'Self-generating separated subjectivity.' She further contends that 'Levinas maintains that the Other disturbs the self-presence of the ego, such that the inner life of the self cannot be viewed as a center which was forged solely through and for its own aggrandizement. The interiority of subjectivity itself, while segregated from exterior forces, is not cut off entirely from the influence by the Other. The widow, orphan, and stranger can

trigger what Levinas dubs Desire – a non-needy yearning which incites the self to live for the Other. With Desire, he can explain how a seemingly separate being can become genuinely and intensively oriented toward other human beings in a non-egoistic sense. Thus, there is a strongly resounding overture which is but a muted chord in his earlier writings – namely that to live to and for the Other in responsibility is the true pulse of the self,' "About Face: Altered States of Subjectivity in Levinas," PhD diss., Fordham University, 2006, 46f.

122. *Alterity*, 213.

Chapter Six

This Strange Mission

Just as "Philosophy and the Idea of Infinity" critically bridges Levinas's early thought with his first major work *Totality and Infinity*, the essay "God and Philosophy" (1975) provides the same linkage to his later magnum opus *Otherwise than Being or Beyond Essence*. This essay, moreover, provides 'a far-ranging work that perhaps more than any other single essay serves as a summary of Levinas's mature thought. Levinas sets out to show not only that the intelligibility of transcendence lies outside ontological structures but also that it bears an ethical sense or direction.'[1] Focusing upon this ethical sense or direction, particularly as it finds meaning in responsibility, will add clarity to our thesis: namely, that Levinas's mission to the Gentiles is warped and woofed in a preoriginary obligation to and for the other. Just as important, this essay's unabashed inclusion of God in philosophical discourse confirms Theo de Boer's contention that 'Levinas is one of the few French philosophers whose work sometimes features God,' and that the goal of his work is 'to understand a god that is uncontaminated by Being.'[2]

Some however, most prominently Dominique Janicaud, view this inclusion of God into philosophical conversation as a betrayal of phenomenological protocol, calling it a 'theological swerve' that can 'make itself negative and thus exacerbate our ontological anxiety.'[3] In any event, Levinas addresses this anxiety, noting that 'Philosophical discourse must therefore be able to embrace God — of whom the Bible speaks — if, that is, this God has meaning. But once thought, this God is immediately situated within the "gesture of being."'[4]

Significantly, Gary A. Phillips sights this *tête-à-tête* in works of Levinas as a prime reason 'Levinas frequently returns to Abraham and his words "Here I am" throughout his philosophical writings to signal the erosive power of biblical witness. The biblical text ruptures being by directing us beyond system and thought to transcendence.' For Phillips, who reads Levinas from a postmodern perspective, this dialogue only prompts more questions: 'Will the Bible continue to interrupt totalities? How will the Bible and those who read it be interrupted by the faces of our neighbors?'[5]

"God and Philosophy" is also significant in that it allows a hermeneutical look into the trauma of awakening, one that reveals the intrigue of subjectivity as a desire that transposes responsibility for the other into a sobering so provocative that it bypasses intentionality for a rootedness in ethical holiness. In fact, within "God and Philosophy" one engages all the central themes of Levinas, yet on a higher level, one whose spiraling thought lifts and weaves earlier motifs into fuller, richer textures. Yet it is the insistence upon ethical exigencies and the demands they make upon subjectivity that grounds this essay as it does this thesis.

Levinas begins by establishing the eminence of philosophical discourse, as well as its comprehensive structure, in Western thought.[6] He asserts that 'The dignity of being the ultimate and royal discourse belongs to Western philosophy because of the strict coinciding of thought, in which philosophy resides, and the idea of reality in which this thought thinks.'[7] This synchrony of thought is tantamount to the synoptic maneuvers indigenous to being, and one would be correct in assuming that the emphasis of this coinciding for Levinas is not a coincidence. Indeed, he notes that 'For thought, this coinciding means not having to think beyond what belongs to "being's move," or at least not beyond what modifies a previous belongingness to "being's move," such as formal or ideal notions. For the being of reality, this coinciding means: to illuminate thought and the conceived by showing itself.'[8]

Yet what happens when meanings inherent in philosophy and theology clash, when immanence and transcendence vie for ascendancy? While God is reserved the place of eminence through dimensionalities of height and depth, are the criteria of ontological analogies any less significant by being placed proximal of this eminence? In response, Levinas stresses precedence over significance:

> The problem that is posed, consequently, and which shall be our own, consists in asking ourselves whether meaning is equivalent to the *esse* of being; that is, whether the meaning which, in philosophy, is meaning is not already a restriction of meaning; whether it is not already a derivation or a drift from meaning; whether the meaning equivalent to essence – to the gesture of being, to being qua being – is not already approached in the presence which is the time of the same.... Our question is whether, beyond being, a meaning might not show itself whose priority, translated into ontological language, will be called *prior* to being.... To ask oneself, as we are attempting to do here, whether God cannot be uttered in a reasonable discourse that would be neither ontology nor faith, is implicitly to doubt the formal opposition, established by Yehuda Halevy and taken up by Pascal, between, on the one hand, the God of Abraham, Isaac, and Jacob, invoked without philosophy in faith, and on the other the god of the philosophers. It is to doubt that this opposition constitutes an alternative.[9]

Rephrased and reinitiated, Levinas is posing again the struggle between the same and the other, between totality and infinity – one suggestive of a diachrony breaking apart the coincidence of meaning, essence, and presence.[10] This fissuring of presence allows Levinas a breach where a meaning beyond being can, through the trace, prioritize the passage of the divine, one antecedent and anarchic, hence one accordant with a third direction irreducible to theology and philosophy.[11]

This third way is geared in responsibility. In fact, responsibility is reflexive of the command, the ordination, coming from the face of the other. And in this response presence is hollowed out by the exigency of encounter, one whose 'absolute foreignness,' comments Bloechl, 'shakes my powers of comprehension, frustrating them and instructing me as to limitations I had not realized. Hence is the face a "trauma."'[12] According to Levinas, this trauma reflects 'the refusal of conjunction, the non-totalizable and infinite. But in the responsibility for the Other, for another freedom, the negativity of the anarchy, of this refusal of the present, of appearing, or the immemorial, commands me and ordains me to the Other, to the first one on the scene, and makes me approach him, makes me his neighbor.'[13] But that which signals this responsibility – which breaks the current of totality – also betrays the diachronous breach opening to infinity. Thus despite Jacques Rolland's criticism of responsibility as a disindividuation involving 'the loss of the ethical in its own right,' the fact remains that there must be something categorical that prompts severance from the gesture of being, from the knowledge, thought, and experience coterminous with philosophical and theological agendas.[14] Stated differently, something is needed to disrupt consciousness through consciousness: supra-consciousness. True to form, Levinas re-inventories an earlier motif, reclaiming a theme both categorical and hermeneutic: insomnia.

Sobering Up

Insomnia for Levinas adds purpose to disturbance; in that sense it is disturbance qualified. Coring out consciousness with its incessant demand, uncontained in its container as is the idea of infinity, insomnia assumes a formalism in Levinas through its reduction of essence.[15] Levinas likens this delimiting to a sobering up from being, and this sobering can be directly allied with awakening.[16] Tellingly, this awakening acts as inspiration for Levinas, channeling disturbance into the generosity and obedience ingredient to responsibility. This creative insomnia is attributable to the fact that the other awakens the same from within, unceasingly, coring out the unity of presence in the psychic life of consciousness, modifying the present.[17] Regarding the logic of this process, Levinas notes:

> It is as a modality or a modification of *insomnia* that consciousness is consciousness of, an assembling in being or in presence that – up to a certain depth of vigilance, where vigilance must clothe itself in justice – has import for

insomnia. Far from being defined as a simple negation of the natural phenomenon of sleep, insomnia – as wakefulness or vigilance – comes out of the logic of categories, prior to all anthropological attention and dullness .... This awakening is like a demand that no obedience equals, and no obedience puts to sleep: a "more" in the "less." Or, to utilize an antiquated language, there lies the spirituality of the soul which is ceaselessly awakened from its state of soul, in which the staying awake itself already closes up on itself or goes to sleep, resting within its state's boundaries. This is the passivity of Inspiration, or the subjectivity sobered up from its being.[18]

No longer content charting the haunting and rumblings of a self isolated in the *il y a*, Levinas now calls one as from a waking dream, one where consciousness—paralyzed by presence—is in need of recovery from the severe tension where the 'I think' reverberates *ad nauseam*.[19] This extreme consciousness, however, is not extreme enough, and is consigned to an existence dulled by 'anthropological attention.' Of significance here is Levinas's connecting spirituality with subjectivity, all under the rubric of inspiration. What is more, inspiration in Levinas allows a hyper-affectivity – one not folded in the manifestation of immanence and consciousness – another modality untrammeled by teleology. Stated differently, Levinas transposes inspiration into another key: transcendence. Regina Schwartz considers this key change reflective of the irreducibility of the other, an irreducibility moreover 'carrying the ethical consequence of responsibility.'[20] Jean Greisch, on the other hand, feels this transposition owes more to Levinas's 'discovery of a "signification without context" which . . . compels a complete rethinking of the relation between transcendence and intelligibility.'[21] For present purposes, however, Jeffrey Kosky's argument that transcendence in Levinas is best engaged by an 'affected subject' opting towards 'an interpretive choice' is granted privilege, since it brings our argument back to the face-to-face relation.[22]

For Levinas the face-to-face relation prompts transcendence, which is registered more emotionally than cognitively. As Andrew Tallon notes,

> a response is not an operation in the sense of cognitional and volitional operations. We must distinguish between operations — such as looking, seeing, thinking, forming concepts, judging, deciding – and responses. . . . The essence of affective intentionality is that the term of intention is not a concept or an act of will but a being-affected, in the first passive moment, and an affective response, in the second, spontaneous active moment. My response, then, while produced by me, depends on the other to whom it is a response and who has affected me in such a way as to engender this response.[23]

This response thus reflects the endemic structure of the elected self whose anarchic responsivity owes its occurrence to the other – not to any inherent capacity. Affectivity (or sensibility) involves the full and creative life of human existence before it is reduced to knowledge. Hence transcendence cannot be manipulated or conceptualized, but experienced expressively through engaging the other. Understanding Levinas requires understanding his notion of affectivity. As noted, these tonal sensibilities channel responsibility for Levinas, so much so that Leora Batnitzky finds them teleological hazards, particularly owing to their being 'based on his [Levinas's] arguments about sensibility as a kind of intentionality beyond instinct and beneath reason.' However, after noting the cognitive reverberation that occurs when 'I sense myself in sensibility,' Batnitzki does offer that it is 'by way of sensibility that the other comes to me' – in effect validating a major Levinasian motif while criticizing Levinas.[24]

Two views of affectivity diverge in "God and Philosophy." One states that 'the interpretation of affectivity, as a modification of representation or as founded upon a representation, succeeds to the degree to which affectivity is taken at the level of a tendency....'[25] Demonstrative of a sensibility geared to consciousness, one where presence, representation, and thematization take precedence, this is a model elucidatory of autonomy. However, according to Levinas 'This does not exclude the possibility that, on a path other than that of the tendency going toward its end, there breaks forth an affectivity that cuts through the shape and designs of consciousness and steps out of immanence; an affectivity that is transcendence. We shall attempt, precisely, to express the "elsewhere" of this affectivity.'[26]

Meaning Elsewhere

According to Levinas the ways of knowledge are inseparable from the unity of presence, from the 'I think' original to knowledge. Reduced to simultaneity, presence is the 'gesture of being,' the gathering and totalizing process common to temporality and experience. Most experience can be collapsed into meanings and thematizations, hence knowledge. However, Levinas – through his steady emphasis on awakening and diachrony, along with his insistence on a third direction – has channeled disturbance into positive ethical resistance clarified through responsibility. Now, along with constituting it as both responsible and transcendent, Levinas also reminds one that the subject is irreducible to systems, structures, or situations – hence founded and justified by standards inassimilable to any other than those grounded in the ethical. And it is to this ethical standard, raised through affectivity, that Levinas's attention now turns.

Interestingly, Levinas moves again to the ethical by hermeneutical default, as both God and philosophy – transcendence and immanence – are prone to the thematizations connatural with knowledge:

> A religious thought that appeals to religious experiences, allegedly independent of philosophy insofar as it is founded upon experience, already refers to the "I think" and is entirely connected to philosophy. The "narrative" of the religious experience does not shake philosophy and, consequently, could not break the presence and immanence of which philosophy is the emphatic accomplishment. It is possible that the word "God" may have come to philosophy from a religious discourse. But philosophy – even if it refuses it – understands this discourse as that of propositions bearing on a theme; that is, as having a meaning that refers to a disclosure, to a manifestation of presence. From the outset, then, the religious being interprets what he lives

through as experience. In spite of himself, he already interprets God, of whom he claims to have an experience, in terms of being, presence, and immanence.[27]

Speaking otherwise than being and presence — offering something contrary to that issued through manifestation — Levinas now focuses on breaking up the sovereignty of the 'I think' operative through knowledge.[28] And this breaking up begins in consciousness. 'It is not the proofs of God's existence that matter to us here but the breakup of consciousness, which is not a repression into the unconscious but a sobering up or an awakening, jolting the "dogmatic slumber" which sleeps at the bottom of every consciousness resting on its object.'[29]

Levinas reemploys here a major motif, the idea of infinity, as signifying the noncontained — with one formidable change: infinity has been paired with God. Obviating intentionality through its capacity of overflowing essentially every object of consciousness, the idea of God initiates the breakup necessary for the awakening to a different modality, one preliminary to Levinas's ethical metaphysics: 'We will say this: the idea of God causes the breakup of the thinking that — as investment, as synopsis, and synthesis — merely encloses in a presence, re-presents, brings back to present, or lets be. . . . The idea of God is God in me, but it is already God breaking up consciousness that aims at ideas, already differing from all content.'[30] This implementation of the idea of God is dual-purposed for Levinas. One, it presages and enables emphasis on the passivity resulting from the idea of God being placed into one's consciousness, a placing whose trauma incites the breaking up requisite for awakening. Apposite this is the philosophical precedence this notion merits through its kinship with Descartes's placing of the infinite previously discussed.[31] Two, the implementation of the idea of God adequately destabilizes consciousness, effectively breaking up the synthesis of the 'I think' — hence opening a diachronic dimension where affectivity can assume meaning.[32]

Levinas insists that the idea of infinity — or God — placed in one warrants a passivity so extreme as to question its reduction to consciousness.[33] This is a strategic inquiry — one foreshadowing a signifying otherwise, and one essential to our theme — as it involves the modulation of desire into responsibility for the other. It also allows Levinas a vehicle for linking awakening to a signification antecedent to presence, hence bridging it to the trace: 'The placing in us of an unencompassable idea overturns this presence to self which is consciousness; it thus forces through the barrier and the checkpoint, it confounds the obligation to accept all that enters from without. It is thus an idea signifying with a significance prior to presence . . . [and] accessible only in its trace.'[34] Situating this passivity in a provenance prior to demonstration confirms for Levinas that there is a signifying prior to the presence that assumes meaning in manifestation. More important, this antecedence or diachrony models for Levinas a situation where the trauma of awakening sobers one to a dimension other than those offered in exhibition. This is the dimension of the ethical — where doing is giving and subjectivity is sacrifice.[35]

Most Ardent, Noble, Ancient Flame

Levinas likens passivity to a realm encompassing the differential between the infinite and finite, noting that this difference is, in his words, a nonindifference, one that destabilizes the destiny of consciousness.[36] According to Levinas, this nonindifference is 'The secret of subjectivity. . . . The Infinite affects thought by simultaneously devastating it and calling it; through a "putting it in its place," the Infinite puts thought in place. It wakes thought up.'[37] Thought awakened, moreover, is thought no longer constrained by thought. It is thought 'which is hatched in the idea of the infinite – in the monstrosity of the Infinite *put* in me – an idea which in its passivity over and beyond all receptivity is no longer an idea.'[38] This thought beyond thought, this meta-thought, signals for Levinas a meaning through the trauma of awakening that can only be registered affectively. The passage in "God and Philosophy" where Levinas parses this affectivity is the heartbeat of the essay. Notably, it comes from a section entitled "Divine Comedy":

> The *in* of the infinite designates the depth of the affection by which subjectivity is affected through this "placing" of the infinite within it, without prehension or comprehension. A depth of undergoing that no capacity comprehends, and where no foundation supports it any longer, this depth in which every process of investment fails, and where the bolts that close the rear doors of interiority burst. Here is a placing without recollection, devastating its site like a devouring fire, bringing down the site in the etymological sense of the term "catastrophe." A dazzling where the eye holds more than it can hold; an ignition of the skin that touches and does not touch that which, beyond the graspable, burns. A passivity, or passion, in which Desire is recognized, in which the *"more in the less"* awakens with its most ardent, most noble, and most ancient flame, a thought destined to think more than it thinks. . . . This is a Desire for what is beyond satisfaction, and which does not identify, as need does, a term or an end. A desire without end, from beyond Being: dis-inter*estedness*, transcendence – desire for the Good.[39]

The fragmentary nature of the last sentence in the above passage models Levinas's theme: it is trying to say more than semantics or punctuation allow, lending credence to B. C. Hutchens's critical observation that 'Levinas's textual strategy is obliquitous,' and that his 'meanings are so protean that one is rarely certain what one has learned.'[40] It would appear that nonindifference now is commensurable with the idea of infinity, which is commensurable with the idea of God, which is commensurable with transcendence, which is commensurable with Desire, which is interminable – yet reaches for the good. Of consequence, however, is Levinas's collating passivity with desire, which as a dazzling disturbance shatters the container of thought, hence bursting interiority. This rupturing of subjectivity allows sensibility a channel inassimilable by consciousness yet resonant with the diachrony of the trace. What is more, as if sensing an interpretive emergency, Levinas – counter-intuitively it would appear – anchors his essay in love.[41]

Adding substance to what seems washed in commensurables, Levinas now alerts one to the notion that 'Love is possible only through the idea of the

Infinite, through the Infinite placed in me, by the "more" that ravages and wakes up the "less," turning away from teleology . . . .'[42] In other words, love mirrors the derelection of desire as it lives off the indigence upon which it feeds, thus tracking the trace of immanence and transcendence. Moreover, love is as the idea of infinity, posing as passion and passivity where desire is both dazzling and disturbing. This radical affectation registers the unfulfilled hollowing-out Levinas calls a divine comedy, one that – begging the obvious – seems bereft of both divinity and laughter. Needed is a love beyond eros, one grounded in responsibility witnessing to a goodness beyond being – one non-synthesized yet sensitive to a more distant beloved.[43]

Near Yet Different

According to Levinas, 'love is possible only through the idea of the infinite.'[44] For David Bentley Hart, however, who admits no sympathy for Levinas's thought, this infatuation with and adoration of the infinite 'indicates a kind of purely ethical sublime' that invites one 'to follow the call of the ethical into the darkness of an infinite obligation whose only visible aspect is the contextless, unlocalizable, inescapable face of the other.'[45] Ironically Hart's description, notwithstanding its intention, accurately depicts love in works of Levinas as witnessed through desire. Ennobling yet derelict, and – like Abraham – exiled yet elected, love for Levinas instills a commandment into subjectivity, one both awakening and holy, and one made sensible in desire. Irony, however, yields to *ad hominem* bombast as Hart later takes personal offence at Levinas's model of *eros* as caress in *Totality and Infinity*, noting 'even the meager warmth afforded by these feeble heliotropisms soon dissipates from the gelid pages of Levinas's texts.' Hart then adds another thrust: 'I confess that, with the exception of the obviously barbarous ideologies of this past century, I know of no modern philosophy of "values" more morally hideous than that of Levinas.'[46]

But back to love: 'affected by the Infinite, Desire cannot proceed to an end which it would be equal to; in Desire the approach distances, and enjoyment is but the increase of hunger.'[47] It is vital to this endeavor, however, that the desirable remain separated, that exodus not become homecoming. Thus in bold strokes Levinas adjoins God and desire; and this coupling, irreducible to the sovereignty of totality, renders it holy – hence proper to sacrifice:

> In order that disinter*estedness* be possible in the Desire for the Infinite – in order that the Desire beyond being, or transcendence, might not be an absorption into immanence, which would make its return—the Desirable, or God, must remain separated in the Desire; as desirable – near yet different – Holy. . . . (It is) love without Eros. Transcendence is ethics, and subjectivity, which is not, in the last analysis, the "I think" (which it is at first) or the unity of "transcendental apperception," is, as a responsibility for the other, a subjection to the other.[48]

It is not by accident that Levinas introduces the holy into the saga of subjectivity. In fact, according to Richard A. Cohen, 'Levinas does not deny the idea of election, but in his hands it becomes the individual's election to moral agency.... Holiness is precisely and concretely love for the neighbor, food for the hungry, shelter for the unsheltered, a kind word, a door held open, an "after you." The material needs of the other are my spiritual needs – such is holiness.'[49] Only the holy, moreover, can differentiate desire from the desirable, and separation in this sense behaves as ethical exigency, one where disturbance is transposed into devotion through the medium of responsibility. Elegantly phrased as 'the nobility of pure enduring,' Levinas now presents a crucial copula: transcendence is ethics.

But how does desire escape desire? Simply – but again not easily – through goodness, the supreme rectitude. The 'I' in its passivity, presented now as responsibility for and subjection to the other – glorified through election – suddenly through accusation becomes a hostage for the other. This is a harsh transition, yet one intrinsic to the self-fissuring Levinas calls enucleation: 'The hostage for another, the I obeys a commandment before having heard it; it is faithful to an engagement that it never made, and to a past that was never present. This is wakefulness – or the opening of the self – absolutely exposed, and sobered up from the ecstasy of intentionality.'[50] In truth, Levinas's metaphysical ethics may be formulaically asserted as that which transforms the ecstasy of intentionality into sacrifice through responsibility.[51] What is more, Levinas has 'designated this way for the Infinite, or for God, to refer, from the heart of its very desirability, to the nondesirable proximity of others, by the term "illeity"; this is an extra-ordinary turning around of the desirability of the Desirable ... a turning around by which the Desirable escapes the Desire.[52]

Close inspection reveals an important transaction here: noted earlier was Levinas's collation of the Desirable and God, as well as its tendency toward absorption in immanence, an appropriation mooted by the proximal yet different separation through holiness. Attention to this proximity, for Levinas, prompts an awakening – one relevant to our theme of responsibility. This awakening traumatizes the ego suffused in its own sovereignty, hence breaking the circuits of and enucleating the self. *Vis-à-vis* this vigilance, Drabinski tells us that 'my traumatic awakening initiates an account of what comes to be called ethical subjectivity.'[53] Yet this ethical subjectivity, according to Davis, becomes agitated owing to a 'self constantly caught unawares by the world and by itself, forever finding itself to be unlike what it believed it was.'[54]

Some, like Rudi Visker, at this point -- not without exasperation -- ask Levinas: "But how can a trauma, something which escapes my freedom, thus something of which I am not the subject but to which I am subjected – how can this liberate me?"[55] In fact, Visker views this impasse as indicative of Levinas's philosophy being 'no longer comprehensible.' Yet this deficiency is reducible to an asymmetry 'too asymmetric' – thus resulting in a blurred distinction between the 'otherness of God and that of the other person.'[56] The result of this blurring for Visker is the collapsing of ethics into religion. Critical here, however, is the manner by which Levinas inflects this trauma and dissimilitude into what he calls the nondesirable *par excellence*, or the other. This inflection exhibits a sobering of intentionality so profound as to render an exceptional reversal called 'illeity' whereupon the boundaries between God and the other are blurred. Stated differently: the other breaks the shell, opens the self, and charges it to sacrifice. This commanding precipitates the nobility of election, one so severely responsible that it modulates into a hostage situation.[57] This situation too harbors an enigma. For the movement towards the other, as reflected in *Totality and Infinity*, defines the subject as a host; yet later, as we shall see in *Otherwise than Being*, the subject is a hostage. So while the approach suggests hospitality, Michael Smith says that 'the condition is that of a hostage. . . . The ego is hostage in that it empties itself of its being.'[58] This emptying, again, is reminiscent of the escape from self addressed previously, and will reappear as election in Levinas.

In Spite of Myself

According to Levinas, the election made noble by illeity is conjugal to the awakening rendered through substitution, an awakening, moreover, made concrete through responsibility for the neighbor. This responsibility is owing to a separation in desire, one experienced as a command obliging one to the dereliction of the other. Honoring this obligation bequeaths an endurance to love, destabilizing the self to the point to where even the 'I think' becomes hostage to ethical exigency. This is a non-moment non-totalized, diachronic, and transcending being. What is more, this transcendence – as Levinas has noted – is the enduring goodness and pure election otherwise known as ethics.

> To be good is a deficit, a wasting away and a foolishness in being; to be good is excellence and elevation beyond being. Ethics is not a moment in being; it is otherwise and better than being, the very possibility of the beyond. In this ethical reversal, in this reference of the Desirable to the Nondesirable, in this strange mission that orders the approach to the other, God is drawn out of objectivity, presence, and being. He is neither an object nor an interlocutor. His absolute remoteness, his transcendence, turns into my responsibility . . . for the other.[59]

The neighbor traumatizes one in a time unassembled by presence. And this subjection, more undergone than undergoing, now consists 'in being struck by the "in" of infinity which devastates presence and awakens subjectivity to the proximity of the other. The noncontained, which breaks the container or the forms of consciousness, thus *transcends* the essence or the "move" of knowable being which carries on its being in presence.'[60] Ironically, or – to use a Levinasian term – enigmatically, being broken here is broken being, a state distinguishable by a transcendent non-temporality assuming an affective stance that is modeled through responsibility for and obeisance to the neighbor. This obligation, moreover, is an election – a chosenness commensurable with the response to a command, one that destabilizes temporality.⁶¹ According to Levinas, 'A difference gapes open between me and the other that no unity of transcendental apperception can undo. My responsibility for the other is precisely the nonindifference of this difference – the proximity of the other. . . . The proximity of a neighbor remains a diachronic break, a resistance of time to the synthesis of simultaneity.'⁶²

Amit Pinchevski's recent study orientated towards communication theory in Levinasian ethics focuses on this diachronic gap. Noting that fissuring 'occurs in the puncturing of the Saying in the Said, in the constant tension between the potential of language to thematize and its primary modality as a response-ability toward the other,' Pinchevski comes to the conclusion that 'interruption is thus immanent in communication.'⁶³ Pinchevski, however, at times confuses the potential of language and communication itself, stretching the canvass to accommodate a scene that never unfolds in Levinas. For example, when he notes that 'communication understood as a form of interruption . . . upholds the very possibility of being response-able to and for the other,' she totalizes the process – hence circumscribing interruption with what Levinas denominates the same.⁶⁴

Truer to heteronomy, Zygmunt Bauman views the stretching of interruption and diachrony not as canvassing but as the fulfillment of self-fissuring. Highlighting as well Levinasian vigilance and awakening, Bauman asserts that 'Awakening to being for the Other is the awakening of the self, which is the *birth* of the self.' Bauman, moreover, notes that 'it is through stretching myself *towards* the Other that I have become the unique, the only, the irreplaceable self that I am.'⁶⁵

Hence rather than communication, the 'now' in Levinas is an ethical moment irreducible to time and consciousness; and responsibility, antecedent to freedom, de-conditions and destabilizes the "I think" to the point of self-fissuring. Simply stated, knowledge – along with all the other accouterments of consciousness – is appropriate to presence, but not transcendence, which for Levinas is coordinate to ethics. Whether nominated desire, the idea of infinity, the noncontained, or God – there is a move which breaks and traumatizes. This trauma or provocation, moreover, through its destabilization, prompts an onrush of disturbance which, when met responsibly, is converted into the ethical owing to the proximity of the now neighbor. Charting our motif of escape, one may say this movement began in self-absorption. 'It ends up in substitution for the other, in the condition – or the unconditionality – of being a hostage. Such responsibility does not give one time, a present for recollection or coming back to oneself; it makes one always late. Before the neighbor I am summoned and do not just appear; from the first I am answering an assignation.'⁶⁶ John Llewelyn views answering this assignation as responding to the other that 'commands me to command, but that the superiority of the other in this relationship consists in the other's face being the face of the poor, the stranger, the widow and the orphan.'⁶⁷

According to Levinas, this exigent assignation is non-interchangeable and forbids any replacement. In point of fact, the only inescapable reality for

Levinas is the face of a neighbor, to whom and for whom one is pledged. And the cry of this neighbor 'has to be heard like cries not voiced or thematized, already addressed to God.'[68] What is more, 'My responsibility in spite of myself—which is the way the other's charge falls upon me or disturbs me, that is, is close to me – is the hearing or understanding of this cry. It is awakening. The proximity of a neighbor is my responsibility for him; to approach is to be one's brother's keeper; to be one's brother's keeper is to be a hostage.'[69]

The Glory of a Long Desire

One now approaches another vital crossroads in Levinas. The subject, self-encapsulated in early Levinas – yet driven by the haunting of the *there is* to beard autonomy and dare escape – at this point in later Levinas finds itself literally torn to give itself up.[70] Again allowing Abraham to model the self's sojourn, Levinas, in illustrating the notion of subjectivity being consumed for the other, now anchors the essay with the patriarch's words: 'I am ashes and dust.'[71] Critically, the subject at this juncture, rather than being self-consumed, is immolated for the other in the crucible of responsibility. And the ego now finds itself consigned to the fire of crisis, one Levinas likens to the consummation of a holocaust.[72]

Peperzak had noted earlier that disinterestedness in Levinas assumes a meaning beyond meaning in the passivity of being-for-the-other, a meta-meaning made concrete through peace and patience. But it is peace and patience caught fire, and whose flames flag glory: 'What is the meaning of this assignation in which the nucleus of the subject is uprooted, undone. . . . What do these atomic metaphors mean, if not an I torn from the concept of the ego . . . and thus left to an unmeasured responsibility, because it increases in the measure – or in the immeasurableness—that a response is made, increasing gloriously?'[73]

This iterating response made increasing glorious through responsibility leads one to another major motif in Levinas: recurrence. Having found a necessary need of a medium conveying the exposedness of self-consciousness without generically involving it in the plot or gesture of being, Levinas asserts that 'The recurrence in awakening is something one can describe as a shudder of incarnation through which *giving* takes on meaning, as the primordial dative of the *for another*, in which a subject becomes a heart, a sensibility, and hands which give.'[74] Dudiak sees this primordial generosity as 'constituted in terms of the gift that one potential interlocutor would make to the other,' arguing further that 'the one called to offer that gift, in the uncertainty of a risk, is *me*.'[75] He also considers this offering a gesture of peace that exposes one's desire as sacrificial, a sacrifice made real through responsibility.

In *Rethinking God as Gift*, Robyn Horner considers Levinas's subject qua heart as indicative of ambiguity in the gift, asking 'how can a gift be obligatory, or reciprocal? How can hospitality be something that is owed?' Extrapolating upon Levinas's recurrent reference to the gift of the heart offered as one's own mouthful of bread, Horner says that 'crucial to Levinas's understanding is that my being called to excess involves no reciprocity.'[76] Levinas's hermeneutic of giving thus reflects, in Horner's view, the asymmetrical nature operative in one's relation to the other.

It is not by accident that awakening through recurrence prompts a radical emphasis where giving assumes meaning, an intentionality that for Levinas exponentially modulates through responsibility. [77] Significantly, this emphasis on emptying conjectures towards a kenotic attitude drawn by the holy:

> This is the subject, irreplaceable for the responsibility there assigned to him, and who therein discovers a new identity. But insofar as it tears me from the concept of the Ego, the fission of the subject is a growth of obligation in proportion to my obedience to it; it is the augmentation of culpability with the augmentation of holiness, an increase of distance in proportion to my approach. There is no rest here for the self in the shelter of its form, in the shelter of its concept of ego! . . . (A)s a responsible I, I never finish emptying myself of myself. An infinite increase in one's exhaustion, wherein the subject does not simply become aware of this expenditure, but is its site and its event, and, if we may say this, its goodness. *The glory of a long desire!* The subject as hostage has been neither the experience nor the proof of the Infinite . . . he is awakened, that is, exposed to the other without restraint and without reserve.[78]

Extradition from interiority banishes the ego from home and the possibility of homecoming: an exile again assumes the features of Abraham.[79] Moreover, it would appear that the severe fission experienced by the ego releases a primordial energy, one that — when channeled through responsibility — becomes resonate with the holy. Becoming attuned to this resonance is accordant with keying in to goodness, a traveling and travail Levinas likens to glory.[80]

Levinas emphasizes the fact that his hermeneutic of giving assumes existential and ethical status concretely through sacrificial responsibility — that responsibility is the affective medium of both this devotion and donation: 'Responsibility for the other — for his distress and freedom — does not derive from any commitment, project or antecedent disclosure, in which the subject would be posited for itself before being-in-debt. Here passivity is extreme in the measure that the devotion for the other is not shut up in itself like a state of soul, but is itself from the start given over to the other.'[81] Giving over to the other awakens one to the exigency whose modality is glory, an honoring of the command issued from the dereliction of the neighbor's face as well as responsibility for that face.[82] Hence the subject is both host and hostage — both site and event — witnessing to the infinite other. But how does one witness to this surplus of goodness? And how can one find expression for this augmentation of holiness?

The Saying

There is a surplus precipitated by the breaking up of inwardness, one also destabilizing and de-positioning the subject whose fissuring modulates into substitution and expiation for the other. Designating the term sincerity to denote this revelation without reserve, Levinas now reduces the extravagant surplus to a pure witnessing to the infinite, a reduction he calls the *saying*. While Atterton feels that language in Levinas is irreducible to a functional tool conveying information, he is also quick to note that the ethical in Levinas is signified in the sincerity of pure saying: 'Levinas distinguishes between language in its expressive or ethical function, called "saying," and language in its theoretical or ontological function, the "said."'[83] However, this is 'a saying without words, but not with empty hands. If silence speaks, it is not through the hyperbolic passivity of giving, which is prior to all willing and thematization. Saying bears witness to the other of the Infinite which rends me, which in the Saying awakens me.'[84]

Wyschogrod believes that saying in Levinas must offer itself discursively, yet prior to thematization or what can be captured in the said. She also feels that 'Saying points to the glory of the infinite, the glory that resists entrapment in immanence and leaves the subject no place to hide.' Also collating this raw exposure to the other as a trauma, Wyschogrod describes the self's reflexive exiling of the subject from itself as self-presence. As a result of this exile, 'glory is the outcome of the trauma, the willingness of the subject to substitute the self for another.'[85] Thus the enucleated subject now finds expression through centrifugal exposure, an idiom whose testimony, prior to all experience, is made significant through responsibility. Channeling this wide band of sincerity and solicitude into a passivity obeisant to the proximity of the neighbor means for Levinas that 'the Infinite concerns me and encircles me, speaking to me through my own mouth. And there is no pure witnessing except of the Infinite.'[86]

True to form, Levinas widens the spiral again – this time, however, with a deft alacrity conjoining substitution with ethics. Noting his earlier assertion that transcendence is ethics, as well as his emphasis on eschatological messianism, Levinas now – by collapsing motifs – proposes that ethics is not only disinterestedness, but behaves as well 'as substitution for the other, as donation without reserve, break(ing) up the unity of transcendental apperception, which is the condition of all being and experience.'[87] What is more, mindful that this shattering of transcendental apperception is tantamount to the enucleation of the subject, one now finds a clearing for ethics through which infinity moves and becomes a solicitation to a stranger.

Stated differently, infinity now is proximity, one charged by and with the gravity of the neighbor. This charge, furthermore, in the crucible of subjectivity, transmutes into a command that one enigmatically yet significantly gives oneself.[88] Responding to this order for Levinas means surrendering to the saying of prophecy:

One might give the name "inspiration" to this intrigue of infinity in which I make myself the author of what I hear. Inspiration constitutes, on the hither side of the unity of apperception, the very psyche of the soul. It is inspiration or prophetism in which I am the interpreter of what I utter. . . . Prophetism as pure witnessing, pure because prior to all disclosure; this is a subjection to an order prior to the understanding of the order. It is an anachronism that, according to the recoverable time of reminiscence, is not less paradoxical than a prediction of the future. It is in prophetism that the Infinite passes – and awakens – and, as transcendence refusing objectification and dialogue, signifies in an ethical way. The infinite *signifies* in the sense in which one says, *to signify an order*; it orders.[89]

Through prophetic signification, Levinas has now reduced transcendence to a moral idiom cognate with the good beyond being, again transposing disturbance into ethical resistance, a resistance moreover betrayed in the saying dramatically reflective of the exposure to the other. As Critchley notes, 'The saying is my exposure – corporeal, sensible – to the Other, my inability to refuse the Other's approach. It is the performative stating, proposing, or expressive position of myself facing the Other.'[90] Bettina Bergo concurs with Critchley, noting that 'Saying expresses the meaning of the self as extreme vulnerability,' an openness she believes Levinas 'likens to being interrupted within oneself.'[91] In addition, according to Levinas this reduction of exposure to expression minimizes signification into 'the-one-for-the-other. However, significance becomes visibility, immanence, and ontology to the degree to which the terms are united into a whole, in which their very history is systematized, in order to be clarified.'[92] Thus one witnesses again how the breach of infinity can either prompt sacrifice for a neighbor or facilitate a blending into fugues of homogeneity.[93]

In essence Levinas is returning to his seminal theme, one disabusing transcendence, and hence God, from ontological totalization. And he is issuing as well a call for all to bear testimony to a meaning that 'draws its force from elsewhere. It begins in a cry of ethical revolt, a bearing witness to responsibility. . . . This is a meaning borne witness to in interjections and cries, before disclosing itself in propositions; a meaning signifying like a command, like an order that signifies.'[94] Hence what constitutes the ethical moment for Levinas assumes meaning paradoxically through the response to a primordial command, a testimony carried in the cry of a stranger-turned-neighbor ennobled by proximity. This obedience is antecedent and anarchic to consciousness, thus irreducible to systemizing and totalizing themes that congregate in what Levinas deems the Said. This irreducibility is affirmed by Hutchens, who states that what we mean when we express ourselves in dialogue 'is not always captured by the themes by which our interlocutors understand us. Thus, every utterance in dialogue consists of an expressive act of saying something meaningful ("saying") and a theme which is expressed and understood (the "said"). The two are distinct and mutually irreducible.'[95] Moreover responsibility, both site and event of this ethical moment, signals an agential awakening, one that for Levinas constitutes glory.[96]

God: The First Stranger

By way of summation: The Infinite has again come to pass, and its passage awakens one to prophesy, to witness to a glory long and desirous, and to testify to a transcendence that signifies by commanding one to the dereliction of a stranger. Enigmatically and anachronistically irreducible to the dialogue of objectification, the self, having broken its conceptual shelter, is now both host and hostage, a modality behaving ethically through the saying. Llewelyn feels that this saying is a 'word of welcome that would be the first always already spoken word of allegiance which makes the stranger a neighbor.'[97] "God and Philosophy" began by posing a problem, one inciting the inquiry as to whether there might not be meaning beyond being that slips through the nets of theology and philosophy, a meaning moreover silently vibrant in ontology yet prior to being. In other words, Levinas's inquiry issues a challenge, one which involves the consideration of a diachronic fissuring of consciousness that shatters presence and meaning.

Insinuated in this fissured energy is a third way, one where responsibility is both central and circumferential, and one whose permeable boundaries obviate any distinctions between God and the stranger. In essence, for Levinas this transparency, through proximity, renders the face of the first stranger on the scene a neighbor, one who ordains with a disturbance coring out consciousness.[98] This coring out, while aligned to insomnia, nonetheless defies logic and categories — a defiance Levinas finds tangential to the vigilant awakening to the face of the other. 'The face of the other,' notes Bloechl,

> seems to awaken me from a solitude that had turned a blind eye not merely to the proximate other, but also, in him and with him, all the others. I am awakened, in other words, directly from naïve egocentrism into a community. As responsible, I am not merely this one-for-that-single-other, but also a one-for-that-other-other, which is to say involved in something more than the asymmetry of the face-to-face. This ... is also the domain of consciousness, of reflection and decision, not to mention, of course, language. And with these resources, one is not only inclined but well able to turn his or her attention to the human condition. Thus, it is finally here that what has been conceptualized as *illeity* receives a name in everyday life. According to Levinas, there is only one word for my ground of all grounds, my having been ordered to the other prior to any principal. It is "Thanks to God," he says, "that I am another for the others." [99]

Suggestive of God and the idea of infinity, being ceaselessly awakened occasions itself non-teleologically as an affectivity whose transcendence is made concrete through ethics.[100]

Charting subjectivity through this enigmatic narrative involves allowing the unsuspected dialectics vacillating within presence their due portion, one that is assembled in what Levinas calls 'the Said.' However, the space between lines in Levinas, the gap in totality, is the demesne of God and the other, one whose meaning is not open to disclosures of being, but is pledged to an otherwise than being.[101] The key to owning this pledge is grounded in subjectivity, a grounding that both disturbs and devastates. Claire Elise Katz says that this disturbance and devastation indicate the flight from existence subjectivity feels while being thrown towards the other. Katz further asserts that subjectivity's disequilibrium is rooted in the feminine: 'My claim is that the relation to the feminine, conceived as radical alterity, is the means by which subjectivity is first constituted'[102]

British Feminist Luce Irigaray pairs Katz's take on alterity in Levinasian studies with what she calls 'the fecundity of a love whose most elemental gesture, or deed, remains the caress.'[103] For Irigary this caress precedes orality, essentially staking claim on the preoriginal disturbance grounded in subjectivity. This disequilibrium, moreover, registers under the name sobriety, an affectivity-in-depth that both burns and desires in what Levinas calls a Divine Comedy. The burning and desiring is satiated on insatiability, is drawn as in exile towards an interminable destination, and is experienced only through what Levinas mysteriously calls disinterestedness. Disinterestedness, since it is both ordained and destroyed by an unquenchable desire – one channeling holiness through responsibility – harbors what Levinas considers a monstrosity: the infinite placed in one, an affectivity so provocative as to be a passivity.[104] And passivity overflows freedom, emptying into the Good:[105]

> It is by the Good that the obligation to responsibility – irrevocable, irreversible, unimpugnable but not going back to choice – is not a violence that would collide with a choice; it situates an "interiority" preceding freedom and non-freedom, outside axiological bipolarity, an obedience to a unique value without anti-value, that is inescapable but that, "related" to the subject, is neither chosen nor non-chosen, and where the subject is elected, and keeps the trace of the election. A value never offered as a theme, not present, not represented and that, so as not to be thematized, not begin, is more antique than the principle and, in an immemorial past without present, by the ambiguity and the antiquity of the trace, non-absent. A value that, by abuse of language, is named. A value that is named God. Thematization would turn the pre-original passivity of the elected submitting to election into choice made by the subject, and would turn subjectivity – or subjection—into usurpation. Pure passivity preceding freedom is responsibility. But the responsibility that owes nothing to my freedom is my responsibility for the freedom of others. There where I could have remained spectator, I am responsible, that is to say again, speaking. Nothing is theater anymore, the drama is no longer a game. Everything is serious.[106]

Everything is serious because the ego now is no longer its own. The self once sovereign is now the self sacrificed, the self fissured, the self broken – and the self seized by the good. According to Levinas, 'there is no enslavement more complete than this seizure by the good, this election. But the enslaving character of responsibility that overflows choice – of obedience prior to the presentation or representation of the commandment that obliges to responsibility – is cancelled by the bounty of the Good that commands.'[107] Thus the good for Levinas is this irrefutable responsibility that is the infrastructure of his ethical hermeneutics. Meaning *is* responsibility:

responsibility *is* ethics. The twain shall and do meet. The precipitancy of goodness, according to Levinas, precludes the delicacy of decision, thus enabling and ennobling election: 'Here the impossibility of choice is not the result of violence – fatalism or determinism – it is the umimpugnable election by the Good that, for the elected, is always already accomplished. Election by the Good that is, precisely, not *action*; it is non-violence itself.'[108]

Another essential point maintained in "God and Philosophy" is Levinas's contention that disinterestedness, due to its governance by the desire for the Infinite, cannot be absorbed by immanence – and is thus non-totalizable. This irreducibility is attributable to the near yet different nature of the desirable, or God, from the desire – a separation Levinas regards as holy. Awakening or sobering to the call of holiness, one issued from the nearest stranger-turned-neighbor, incites an exigency so severe as to prompt substitution.[109] What is more, this substitution is tantamount to the enucleation of the self, a moment for Levinas indistinguishable from love and election. Gibbs views this moment as signifying uniqueness, a 'uniqueness of the elected one or of the one required who is not an elector, passivity which is not converted into spontaneity. Uniqueness not assumed, not subsumed, traumatic, election in persecution.'[110] This election is the heart of responsibility, one where even consciousness itself is subjection to the other. And subjection to the other, or responsibility, denotes transcendence, a site and event made concrete through ethics – which for Levinas is the very possibility of the beyond.[111]

Perhaps what is most significant in "God and Philosophy," however, is Levinas's crucial ethical reversal wherein the desirable and non-desirable, through proximal inflection, exchange roles – an inversion drawing God out of transcendence and into responsibility for the other. Foreshadowing much of what one encounters in *Otherwise than Being*, Levinas here asserts that God is not simply reflected in the first other encountered, a theme prevalent it all his works, but that God is also other than the other with an alterity antecedent to intentionality – hence other otherwise. Moreover, this alterity precedes the ethical relation with the other, prompting a de-formalism so severe as to blur the distinction between God and the stranger, veiling the modulations wherein God approaches as the neighbor for whom one sacrifices and substitutes oneself.[112] This moment, irreducible to consciousness, is experienced as an affective awakening that, while transcending presence, is nonetheless enigmatically temporalized through responsibility. Significantly, this responsibility is an election, one made glorious through its journeying to the other.[113]

Substitution, this perpetual pilgrimage through responsibility to the neighbor, renders the subject both host and hostage, one incessantly soliciting—hence witnessing – to what Levinas calls the glory of a long desire, a desire made holy through testimony. In this testimony, in this Saying, desire like infinity exponentially feeds on its own hunger, inducing an enucleation of subjectivity whose energy and surplus become an avenue of awakening. It is on this avenue of awakening, one that now moves through

Otherwise than Being, that Levinas's mission to the Gentiles assumes a greater depth and dimension, a depth and dimension whose ways and means are grounded in responsibility.

Notes

1. Robert Bernasconi, Introduction to "God and Philosophy," *Basic Philosophical Writings*, 129.
2. "Theology and the Philosophy of Religion According to Levinas," *Ethics as First Philosophy*, 161.
3. "The Theological Turn of French Phenomenology," *Phenomenology and the "Theological Turn,"* (New York: Fordham Press, 2000) 28. Ironically, Janicaud's essay presents his thesis with an almost religious fervor, his main argument essentially insisting that this theological swerve 'impose(s) itself by a *captatio benevolentiae* of phenomenology,' ibid.
4. Levinas, "Dieu et la Philosophie," *De Dieu qui vient a idée* (Paris: Librairie Philosophique J. Vrin, 1986), 94; "God and Philosophy," *Of God Who Comes To Mind*, 56.
5. "Levinas," *Handbook of Postmodern Biblical Interpretation*, ed. A. K. M. Adam (St. Louis, Mo.: Chalice Press, 2000) 159.
6. For Levinas, 'Philosophy is primarily a question of language, and it is by identifying the subtextual language of particular discourses that we can decide whether they are philosophical or not. Philosophy employs a series of terms and concepts – such as *morphe* (form), *ouisa* (substance), *nous* (reason), *logos* (thought) or *telos* (goal), etc. – that constitute a specifically Greek lexicon of intelligibility.... According to the Greek model, intelligibility is what can be rendered present, what can be represented in some eternal here and now, exposed and disclosed in pure light.... The Greek notion of being is essentially this presence,' "Dialogue with Emmanuel Levinas," *Face to Face with Levinas*, 18f.
7. Levinas, "Dieu et la Philosophie," 94; "God and Philosophy," 55. Cf. Regina Schwartz, Introduction, *Transcendence: Philosophy, Literature, and Theology Approach the Beyond*, ix.
8. Ibid. Elsewhere Levinas has compared this coinciding to 'An analysis in which the meaning of the meaningful would be equivalent to its aptness to the present and representation, to the simultaneity of the manifold entering into and unfolding within a theme; or, more radically yet, its aptness to *presence*, i.e., to being (taken in its verbal sense). As if, in the notion of presence—or in the notion of being expressed by presence – a privileged mode of time were fused with the birth of knowledge itself, in representation, thematization, and intentionality,' "Philosophy and Transcendence," *Alterity and Transcendence*, 12f.
9. Ibid., 96f.; 57, emphasis in text. Interestingly, Levinas begins *Otherwise than Being* by similarly delving into the essence of meaning: 'If transcendence has meaning, it can only signify the fact that the *event of being*, the esse, the *essence*, passes over to what is other than being,' 3, emphasis in text.
10. Western philosophy since Plato has entertained dialogue between the Same and the Other. According to Davis, 'The privileged term, Levinas argues, has always been the Same, which is conceived as incorporating, actually or potentially, that which lies outside it. . . . The characteristic gesture of philosophy is to acknowledge the Other in order to incorporate it within the expanding circles of the Same. The totality of being is flawless and all-encompassing; because it incorporates alterity within the

empire of the sameness, the Other is only other in a restricted sense,' *Levinas: An Introduction*, 40; Cf. Wyschogrod, who allows that the Same admits 'the possibility of suspending the otherness of the world by sojourning in it,' furthering that 'the reduction of the Other to the Same occurs in a concrete relationship to the world and is not merely formal,' *The Problem of Ethical Metaphysics*, 245. For Levinas, it is in this concrete relationship that essence is fissured and meaning assumes an ethical shape, *Otherwise than Being*, 148. See also the subsection entitled "The Same and the Other" in the introduction of this analysis for more on Descartes and the *cogito*.

11. Anarchy in Levinas needs clarification. 'The realm of the otherwise than being is distinguished by being **anarchic,** i.e. without *arche* – arche understood as beginning, rule, or principle. It is "a past that never was present." It is the locus (although locus here is used improperly, as neither time nor place pertain properly to this realm, and even the term realm must be taken figuratively) of God, the Infinity, and subjectivity,' Michael Smith, *Toward the Outside*, 12. As will be developed, anarchy is closely aligned with responsibility. In fact, according to Bernhard Waldenfels, 'This responsibility, beyond any initiative, refers to an "anarchist" pre-beginning, more beginning than any beginning I make; it refers to a prepast, more past than any past I remember.... I always come too late to assume my responsibility; so the response of my responsibility precedes every answer given by myself,' "Response and Responsibility," *Ethics as First Philosophy*, 45.

12. *Liturgy of the Neighbor*, 37.

13. Levinas, "Essence and Disinterest," *Basic Philosophical Writings*, 118.

14. "Getting out of Being by a New Path," p. 23. Cf. Fabio Ciaramelli, "Levinas's Ethical Discourse between Individuation and Universality," *Re-Reading Levinas*, 99.

15. See Edith Wyschogrod, "God and 'Being's Move' in the Philosophy of Emmanuel Levinas," *The Journal of Religion* 62, no. 2 (April 1982): 153.

16. Elsewhere Levinas refers to this sobering as 'An insomnia or severing that is not the finitude of a being incapable of rejoining itself and "remaining at rest" in the form of a state of mind, but transcendence rending or inspiring the immanence that, initially, envelops it, as if there could be an idea of the Infinite, that is, as if God could fit inside me. A waking without intentionality, but only awakened unceasingly from its very state of waking, sobering out of its identity into what is deeper than itself.... It resembles the freedom that bursts forth in the proximity of the neighbor, in responsibility for the other person, in which, however, as uniqueness of the noninterchangeable, as condition or uncondition of a hostage, I am unique and chosen,' "De la Conscience a la Veille," *De Dieu qui vient a idée*, 51f.; "From Consciousness to Wakefulness," *Discovering Existence with Husserl*, 162f.

17. This modifying of the present is as a cacophony in a symphony, breaking as it does the process that 'unfolds through consciousness like a "held note" in its forever, in its identity as the same, in the simultaneity of it moments.' This observation prompts Levinas to note that "Philosophy is not only knowledge of immanence, it is immanence itself,' "Dieu et la Philosophie," 100f.; "God and Philosophy," 60f.

18. Levinas, "Dieu et la Philosophie," 99 ; "God and Philosophy," 59, emphasis in text.

19. This state endemic to 'being' and 'the same' Levinas circumscribes under the philosophy of knowledge. It is a state from which we must recover through a sobering up – a process Levinas call a 'permanent revolution.' 'One must change levels. But it is not a matter of adding an inner experience to outer experience. We must return from the world to life, which has already been betrayed by knowledge. The latter delights in its theme and is absorbed in the object to the point of losing its soul and its name and of becoming mute and anonymous. By a movement against nature – because against

the world – we must return to a psychism other than that of the knowledge of the world.' In light of this movement Levinas asks: 'Must the liveliness of life be interpreted on the basis of consciousness?' "Philosophy and Awakening," *Discovering Existence with Husserl*, 174f.

20. *Transcendence: Philosophy, Literature, and Theology Approach the Beyond*, vii.
21. "The Face and Reading," *Re-Reading Levinas*, 68.
22. *Levinas and the Philosophy of Religion*, 103f.
23. "Nonintentional Affectivity," *Ethics as First Philosophy*, 110.
24. "Encountering the Modern Subject in Levinas," *Yale French Studies: Encounters with Levinas*, ed. Thomas Trezise (New Haven, Connecticut: Yale University Press, 2004), 20.
25. Levinas, "Dieu et la Philosophie," 101 ; "God and Philosophy," 61.
26. Ibid. Cf. 'What is termed an affective state does not have the dull monotony of a state, but is a vibrant exaltation in which dawns the self. For the I is not the support of enjoyment. The "intentional" structure here is wholly different; the I is the very contraction of sentiment, the pole of the spiral whose coiling and involution is drawn by enjoyment: the focus of the curve is part of the curve,' Levinas, *Totalité et Infini*, 91; *Totality and Infinity*, 118. See also John E. Drabinski, *Sense and Sensibility*, where it is noted that 'Levinas seeks in sensibility what is anterior to the work of the constituting subject on the world. The self-constituting signification *kath auto* is altered in sensibility from the constituted content to constituting structural item. This gives the anteriority of the sensible a transcendental role,' 108.
27. Ibid., 101f.; 61f. Simon Critchley remarks that 'Levinas's extensive writings on Judaic topics and the prominence of God and religion in his philosophical works have sometimes led to characterizations of Levinas's thought as a masked theology rather than as phenomenologically rooted in philosophy.... Levinas, however, without ever denying his roots, always insists on the philosophical character of his work. He invites all readers of his texts to validate the truth of his arguments on the basis of their own experiences and thought. But philosophy, as a language that strives for universality, does not exclude the explicit and implicit thoughts of particular traditions and spiritualities,' Preface to *Basic Philosophical Writings*, xii.
28. For more of the critical history behind this *cogito*, see Atterton, *On Levinas*, 9; Dudiak, *The Intrigue of Ethics*, 77; Horner, *Rethinking God as Gift*, 34; Taylor, *Alterity*, xxii. See also the subsection entitled "Thinking Infinity" in Chapter Three of this analysis for more on Descartes and the *cogito*.
29. Levinas, "Dieu et la Philosophie," 101 ; "God and Philosophy," Ibid., 61.
30. Ibid., 103; 63.
31. Some, like Peter Atterton, have noted Levinas's selective and atypical employment of Descartes. 'Descartes supplies Levinas with a model of philosophy as "critique" understood "as a tracing back to what precedes freedom," but nothing more. Levinas rejects Cartesian "subject-object" dualism, the project of setting philosophy on mathematical-like foundations, and the ontological argument for the existence of God,' *On Levinas*, 26.
32. Alphonso Lingis notes that 'Levinas contrasts presence, achieved in representation, and proximity, effected in sensibility. Cognition represents, it renders present across a distance.... (S)ensibility, affectivity, is the capacity to be affected by things, not only to receive their effects in oneself as signs of their exterior layouts, but to be afflicted by them, susceptible, exposed not only to their sense but to their force, capable of being pained by them. Exposure to exterior beings, exposure to alterity, sensibility has the structure of being-for-another. By virtue of this structure our existence is a sign, its positions and moves significant. Levinas understands the sense,

the meaning that forms in sensibility out of this vulnerability, this being-for-another, and not out of a synopsizing activity that would assemble and relate data,' Introduction, *Collected Philosophical Papers*, xx.

33. See Edward Farley, *Deep Symbols: Their Postmodern Effacement and Reclamation*, 21.

34. Levinas, "Dieu et la Philosophie," 107 ; "God and Philosophy," 64.

35. See Claire Elise Katz, *Levinas, Judaism, and the Feminine*, 3.

36. One might even say that for Levinas this destabilizing is original to the self. Cf. "Essence and Disinterestedness," where he indicates that the ego 'is outside of the community of genus and form and does not find any rest in itself, either; it is troubled and does not coincide with itself. The outside of itself, the difference from oneself, is nonindifference itself and the extraordinary recurrence of the pronominal or the reflexive, the *self* – which no longer surprises us because it enters into the current flow of language in which things show *themselves*, suitcases fold and ideas are understood. A unicity without place, without the ideal identity a being derives from the kerygma that indentifies the innumerable aspects of its manifestation, without the identity of the ego that coincides with itself, a unicity withdrawing from essence – such is man,' *Basic Philosophical Writings*, 114f., emphasis in text.

37. Levinas, "Dieu et la Philosophie," 109 ; "God and Philosophy," 66.

38. Ibid., emphasis in text.

39. Ibid., 110; 66f., emphasis in text. See also Samuel Moyn, who informs one that 'As Levinas's rhetoric suggests, the distinction between interiority and exteriority charts that between enjoyment and desire. In contrast to objects whose nature is finite, and that are there to be appetitively enjoyed, other subjects, whose nature is infinite, can only be desired with unfulfillable longing. "No journey, no change of climate or of scenery could satisfy the desire bent toward it," Levinas argued. "The metaphysical desire tends toward something else entirely, toward the absolutely other."' Moyn registers as well the ambiguity and hyperbolic rhetoric proper to Levinas: 'It is one thing to state a contrast between exteriority and interiority and between desire and enjoyment, but it is another to explain this contrast. And Levinas often seemed self-contradictory in his description of the new category, as if he may not have been certain how radically he wanted to describe the other. Levinas is famous for passages indulging in the rhetoric of exorbitancy familiar from invocations of the infinite in theological sources,' *Origins of the Other*, 252.

40. *Levinas: A Guide for the Perplexed*, 4. Hutchins further comments that that 'some critics, including several Continental philosophers notorious for their own abstruse prose, grumble about Levinas's lack of lucidity and conceptual exiguity,' ibid., 5.

41. Roger Burggraeve's important study, *The Wisdom of Love in the Service of Love: Emmanuel Levinas on Justice, Peace, and Human Rights*, highlights how, for Levinas, 'the wisdom of love is prior to the love of wisdom.' He further notes that 'the priority of the Other and of the wisdom of love is not an a priori for all thinking . . . but an insight that announces itself in the name of experience and reflection,' 187f.

42. Levinas, "Dieu et la Philosophie," 111; "God and Philosophy," 67.

43. Cf. 'Love aims at the Other; it aims at him in his frailty. Frailty does not here figure the inferior degree of any attribute, the relative deficiency of a determination common to me and the other. Prior to the manifestation of attributes, it qualifies alterity itself. To love is to fear for another, to come to the assistance of his frailty. In this frailty as in the dawn rises the Loved, who is the Beloved,' Levinas, *Totalité et Infini*, 233; *Totality and Infinity*, 256. See also "The Ego and the Totality," where Levinas says that 'To love is to exist as though the lover and the beloved were alone in the world. The intersubjective relationship of love is not the beginning, but the negation of

society.... Love is the ego satisfied by the you, apprehending in the other the justification of its being,' *Collected Philosophical Papers,* 31. See also John Llewelyn, *Emmanuel Levinas: The Genealogy of Ethics,* 148.

44. "Dieu et la Philosophie," 104; "God and Philosophy," 68.

45. *The Beauty of the Infinite: The Aesthetics of Christian Truth* (Wm. B. Eerdmans Publishing Co.: Grand Rapids, Mi., 2003) 14f.

46. Ibid., 80f. Hart is obviously brilliant. He does not need to dull his brilliance, however, with sharpshooting diatribes. It comes off brattish. In a later footnote he narrows his scope on John Caputo, calling *The Prayers and Tears of Jacques Derrida* 'a poor book in many ways,' 89n. 95.

47. Levinas, "Dieu et la Philosophie," 112 ; "God and Philosophy," 68.

48. Ibid., emphasis in text. Substitution will be more thoroughly dealt with subsequently. For now, suffice it to say that 'Substitution for another means, in the ultimate shelter of myself, not to feel myself innocent, even for the harm another does. I would go much further. "Ultimate shelter" is not a sufficient formula. It can make us believe that the I has a capsule. In order to explain the notion of substitution, it is necessary that I say more, that I use hyperbole: the individuation of the I, that by which the I is not simply an identical being, or some sort of substance, but rather that by which it is ipseity; that by which it is unique without drawing its uniqueness from any exclusive quality, all this is the fact of being designated, or assigned, or elected to substitute itself without being able to slip away. But to this unavoidable summons, to the "I" in general, to the concept, he who responds in the first person is torn loose: it is I, or even straightaway in the accusative, "here I am," Levinas, "Questions et Responses," *De Dieu qui vient a idée,* 144; "Questions and Answers," *Of God Who Comes To Mind,* 91.

49. *Elevations,* 130.

50. Levinas, "Dieu et la Philosophie," 113; "God and Philosophy," 68f.

51. Mark C. Taylor calls this predilection to sacrifice a consenting to an assignment. 'In this assignation, responsibility is antecedent to freedom. The subject's responsibility is manifested in its response-ability, i. e., in the self's ability to respond to the call of the Other.' Moreover, according to Taylor, the model of Abraham emphasizes our 'return to the altar of sacrifice where the encounter with alterity is enacted.... Levinas maintains that those who follow Abraham are called upon to make an "expenditure without return." ... The practice of such extraordinary generosity requires the most radical sacrifice of all – the sacrifice of one's very own self.... Since the subject's desire is always the desire of an Other, it can never be satisfied. The voice that approaches through the neighbor is the discourse of the Other, which "tears" the self from itself. This wound that never heals renders desire infinite. Through the infinity of desire, the Infinite draws near. The interplay of presence and absence in the desire of the Other marks the proximity of the infinite as an infinite proximity obsessing the subject,' *Alterity (*Chicago: The University of Chicago Press, 1987), 213f.

52. Levinas, "Dieu et la Philosophie," 113; "God and Philosophy," 69. See also Edith Wyschogrod, *The Problem of Ethical Metaphysics,* 162f.

53. *Sense and Sensibility: The Problem of Phenomenology in Levinas,* 8.

54. *Levinas,* 42.

55. "The Price of Being Dispossessed: Levinas's God and Freud's Trauma," *The Face of the Other and the Trace of God: Essays on the Philosophy of Emmanuel Levinas,* 253.

56. Ibid., 254.

57. According to Robert Gibbs, through this election 'The very intentionality of consciousness is reversed: the other has intentions for me, and I find myself accused by an other, by the intentionality of someone else, and so the self is extroverted.... I

must now welcome the other, giving the other the very home, food, clothing, etc., that were for my own enjoyment. I suffer to relieve the other's suffering, and in so doing become myself in a way that is impossible through my own enjoyable life. I become myself – I become free in responsibility – only when I answer for the other. I am hostage for the other, says Levinas at his hyperbolic best. Thus I am not my own master, but am substitute for this other. I must take the other's place, and no one may relieve me of my burden to take that place. I am uniquely responsible. No one can take my place – the place before the other – the hostage for the other.' *Correlations in Rosenzweig and Levinas*, 182.

58. *Toward the Outside: Concepts and Themes in Emmanuel Levinas*, 231.

59. Levinas, "Dieu et la Philosophie," 114f.; "God and Philoshpy," 69f. See also Richard A. Cohen, who notes that 'dis-inter*estedness*' is only thus ennobled owing to self-sacrifice. 'Indifference comes first: the indifference of the self satisfied with itself, content with its enjoyments, wrapped up in its concerns and interests.... Autoaffectation, freedom, egology, self-reference, come first.' However, 'The I's concern for the alterity of the Other comes in a *non*-indifference, rather than in a primary concern, because precisely a natural and original indifference to the alterity of the other must be disrupted,' *Elevations*, 164f., emphasis in text.

60. Ibid., 115; 70, emphasis in text.

61. This election which retards time is, for Levinas, the uniqueness of the self. 'I have called this uniqueness of the I in responsibility its chosenness. To a great extent, this makes reference to the chosenness at issue in the Bible. It is thought as the ultimate secret of my subjectivity. I am I, not as master who takes in and dominates the world, but as called, in an indeclinable manner, in the impossibility of *refusing* this chosenness (to refuse it would be to accomplish evil). Freedom is here a necessity, but this necessity is also a freedom,' *Is It Righteous To Be?* 66, emphasis in text.

62. Levinas, "Dieu et la Philosophie," 115 ; "God and Philosophy," 70. See also Peperzak, *Beyond*, where it is noted that 'Proximity, the relation of my being close to the Other through the exposition of my sensibility, is radically different; it cannot be thought in the categories of ontology. Saying and sensibility, exposition and vulnerability are ... names for that without which ontology and categories would be impossible. *And here Levinas clearly states that ontology and proximity – or Being and otherwise than Being – are necessarily connected to one another....* The ultimate meaning of Being cannot be found in its own dimension; the interest that essence holds for us owes its ultimate significance to the disinterested being-for-the-Other of responsibility, patience, and peace,' 113, emphasis in text.

63. *By Way of Interruption: Levinas and the Ethics of Communication* (Duquesne University Press: Pittsburg, Pa.: 2005) 11.

64. Ibid., 12f.

65. *Postmodern Ethics*, (Blackwell: Oxford, 1993) 77, emphasis in text.

66. Levinas, "Dieu et la Philosophie," 117; "God and Philosophy," 71. Ibid.

67. "Levinas and Language," *The Cambridge Companion to Levinas*, 130.

68. Levinas, "Dieu et la Philosophie," 118; "God and Philosophy," 72.

69. Ibid. Meredith Gunning points out that 'ethical terms like hostage, persecution and obsession all connote that the self's psyche is nonvoluntarily a "one – for –the other," or, to wield Levinas's phrase, they reinforce the theme that the self sacrifices for the other "despite oneself." Also, the Other has become the undesirable par excellence as opposed to eliciting desire,' "About Face," 8.

70. See Bob Plant, *Wittgenstein and Levinas: Ethical and Religious Thought*, 181.

71. Levinas, "Dieu et la Philosophie," 119 ; "God and Philosophy," 72. See Genesis 18: 27.

72. This is a universal conflagration and destiny, as, according to Levinas, we all carry 'the reflection of the flames of the Holocaust where the hopes created by the State of Israel are more and more deafened by the cries of its detractors – in these essential hours, for men who have lost all links which count socially with the Jewish people and its culture, these vestiges fill up with an overflowing meaning, one that is felt as the irresistible call to solidarity and to responsibilities, but also as election. All of this bears witness, simultaneously, to the exceptional depth in which, in human consciousness, holy History is played out, this "Divine Comedy," this Passion of Israel and the incomparable strength of rituals which, in the material of the world, are is inscription, commandment and memory,' "Demanding Judaism," *Beyond the Verse: Talmudic Lectures and Readings*, 8.

73. Levinas, "Dieu et la Philosophie," 119 ; "God and Philosophy," 72.

74. Ibid., 120; 73, emphasis in text. According to Levinas 'Sensibility is thus not simply an amorphous content, a fact in the sense employed in empiricist psychology. It is "intentional" in that it *situates* all content, and is situated not in relation to objects but in relation *to itself*. It is the *zero point* of situation, the origin of the fact of being situated itself. Prepredicative or lived relations are established as initial attitudes taken from this zero point. The sensible is a modification of the *Urimpression*, which is the *here* and *now* par excellence,' "Réflexions sur la 'technique' phénomènologique," *En découvrant l'existence avec Husserl et Heidegger*, 119; "Reflections on Phenomenological 'Technique,'" *Discovering Existence With Husserl*, 99, emphasis in text.

75. *The Intrigue of Ethics*, 150, emphasis in text.

76. *Rethinking God as Gift: Marion, Derrida, and the Limits of Phenomenology*, 11f.

77. In "Truth of Disclosure and Truth of Testimony," Levinas informs us that recurrence is not reflection on oneself. 'It is just the opposite of the return to the self, of self-consciousness. Recurrence is sincerity, effusion of the self, "extradition" of the self to the neighbor. One might, at the limit, pronounce the word *prayer* here – testimony, kerygma, confession, humility; but what is essential therefore lies – what a disappointment for those friends of the truth that thematizes being and for those of the subject that effaces itself before being! – in the fact that the responses are only heard in the demands, that the "provocation" that comes from God is in my invocation, that gratitude is already gratitude for the state of gratitude,' *Basic Philosophical Writings*, 106. See also Jeffrey Dudiak, *The intrigue of Ethics*, 296f.

78. Levinas, "Dieu et la Philosophie," 120 ; "God and Philosophy," 73, emphasis in text. Cf. Levinas, "Transcendence to the Point of Absence," where it is noted that 'The desired one thus remains transcendent to desire. It is in this reversal of terms that transcendence, or the dis-inter-estedness of desire, comes to pass. But how? Through the transcendence of infinity, which the word "Good" expresses. In order that disinterestedness be possible in desire, in order that the desire beyond being not be an absorption, the desirable (or God) must remain separated within desire: near, yet different – which is, moreover, the very meaning of the word "holy." Self in the accusative, under accusation by another, albeit without fault, faithful to an engagement that it never contracted, to a past that has never been present. As such the "me" is a wakefulness or an opening of a self absolutely exposed and sobered from the ecstasy of intentionality,' *God, Death, and Time*, trans. Bettina Bergo (Stanford, Ca.: Stanford University Press, 2000) 222f.

79. Catherine Chalier notes that 'In several of his lessons, Levinas thus insists on the thought of an infinite responsibility proper to the human psyche – responsible despite itself for the fate of the world – by shedding light upon it by means of the story of Abraham and, correlatively, by shedding light on this story by means of his thought,' "Levinas and the Talmud," *The Cambridge Companion to Levinas*, 109.

80. See Edith Wyschogrod, *Saints and Postmodernism: Revisioning Moral Philosophy* (Chicago: The University of Chicago Press, 1990) 99.

81. Levinas, "Dieu et la Philosophie," 121 ; "God and Philosophy," 74. Cf. Richard A. Cohen, *Elevations,* where it is noted that 'The material instant lies at the base, as it were, of the superlative passivity, the extremity of inwardness, demanded of a subject in response to the extremity of the transcendence of the other person,' 139.

82. Andrew Tallon asks one to 'Please note that this model [of responsibility] is not presented as a simple-minded psychologistic reduction; it is not an attempt to explain away responsibility as "nothing but" this or that. Quite the contrary, Levinas is showing us the radical truth of an ultimately untranscendable structure writ in the bone and sinew of human existence,' "Nonintentional Affectivity," *Ethics as First Philosophy,* 115. See also Brian Schroeder, *Altared Ground: Levinas, History, and Violence,* 100f.

83. *On Levinas,* 55.

84. Levinas, "Dieu et la Philosophie," 121 ; "God and Philosophy," 74.

85. *The Problem of Ethical Metaphysics,* xvif.

86. Levinas, "Dieu et la Philosophie," 121 ; "God and Philosophy," 74.

87. Ibid., 123; 75.

88. This command, according to John Llewelyn, is for Levinas tantamount to obedience. Llewelyn further thinks that in response to this command the identity of the subject in Levinas is deconstructed, altering the direction of intentionality, *Appositions of Jacques Derrida and Emmanuel Levinas,* 178.

89. Levinas, "Dieu et la Philosophie," 124 ; "God and Philosophy," 76, emphasis in text. Cf. Levinas, *Ethics and Infinity,* where 'Prophetism is in fact the fundamental mode of revelation – on condition one understands prophetism in a very much larger sense than that admitted by the gift, the talent or the special vocation of those whom one calls the prophets. I think prophetism as a moment of the human condition itself. For every man, assuming responsibility for the Other is a way of testifying to the glory of the Infinite, and of being inspired. There is prophetism and inspiration in the man who answers for the Other, paradoxically, even before knowing what is concretely required of himself. This responsibility prior to God's law is revelation. There is a text of the prophet Amos that says: "God has spoken, who would not prophesy?" where prophecy seems posited as the fundamental fact of man's humanity,' 113f.

90. *The Ethics of Deconstruction,* 7.

91. *Levinas Between Ethics and Politics: For the Beauty that Adorns the Earth,* 153f.

92. Levinas, "Dieu et la Philosophie," 124; "God and Philosophy," 76. Cf. Robert Manning, *Interpreting Otherwise than Heidegger,* 84.

93. See Hent De Vries, *Philosophy and the Turn to Religion,* 26; Visker, *Truth and Singularity,* 127.

94. Levinas, "Dieu et la Philosophie," 125 ; "God and Philosophy," 77. Cf. Levinas, "Freedom and Command," *Collected Philosophical Papers,* where it is said that 'We have sought to set forth exteriority, the other, as that which is nowise tyrannical and makes freedom possible, opposes us because it turns itself toward us. This exteriority is beyond the violence of brutality, but also that of incantation, ecstasy and love. One could call this situation religion, the situation where outside of all dogmas, all speculation about the divine or – God forbid – about the sacred and its violences, one speaks to the other. We have taken the position that commanding is speech, or that the true speech, speech in its essence, is commanding,' 23. See also Michael B. Smith, *Toward the Outside,* 31.

95. *Levinas: A Guide for the Perplexed,* 56f.

96. See John Caputo, *Against Ethics,* 124.

97. *Appositions of Jacques Derrida and Emmanuel Levinas*, 107. Jacques Derrida, in his important essay on Levinas entitled "Violence and Metaphysics," claims that 'By definition, if the other is the other, and if all speech is for the other, no logos as absolute knowledge can comprehend dialogue and the trajectory toward the other. This incomprehensibility, this rupture of logos is not the beginning of irrationalism but the wound or inspiration which opens speech and then makes possible every logos or every rationalism,' *Writing and Difference*, trans. Alan Bass (Chicago: The University of Chicago Press, 1978) 98.

98. See Brian Schroeder, *Altared Ground: Levinas, History, and Violence*, 49.

99. *Liturgy of the Neighbor*, 250f.

100. See Jan De Greef, "Skepticism and Reason," *Face to Face with Levinas*, 171.

101. See Levinas, "The Prohibition against Representation," *Alterity and Transcendence*, 129.

102. *Levinas, Judaism, and the Feminine*, 23.

103. "The Fecundity of the Caress," *Face to Face with Levinas*, 232.

104. Provocative passivity suggests 'a new concept of passivity, a passivity more radical than that of effect in a causal series, *beneath* consciousness and knowledge, but also *beneath* the inertia of things reposing on itself as substances and opposing their nature, material cause, to all activity; it would mean a passivity referred to the *wrong side* of being, prior to the ontological plane where being is posed as *nature*, referred to the anteriority of creation, not yet having an outside, to meta-physical anteriority. As if beyond the *ambit* of a melody a higher or lower register resonated and mixed with the chords that are heard, but with a sonority that no voice can sing and no instrument can produce,' Levinas, "Humanism and Anarchy," *Humanism of the Other*, 50, emphasis in text. See also Richard A. Cohen, *Elevations*, 163f.

105. See Bettino Bergo, *Levinas: Between Ethics and Politics*, 167.

106. Levinas, "Humanism and Anarchy," *Humanism of the Other*, 54f.

107. Ibid., 53. See also Roger Burggraeve, *The Wisdom of Love in the Service of Love*, 107.

108. Ibid., emphasis in text. Cf. "Essence and Disinterestedness," *Basic Philosophical Writings*, where Levinas notes that 'Arising at the apex of essence, goodness is *other* than being; it no longer keeps accounts....The ever possible sliding between subjectivity and being, of which subjectivity would be but a mode, the equivalence of the two languages, stops here. Goodness gives to subjectivity its irreducible signification,' 124, emphasis in text.

109. See Alvin Dueck and David Goodman, "Expiation, Substitution, and Surrender: Levinasian Implications for Psychotherapy," *Pastoral Psychology* 55 no. 5 (May, 2007): 601f.

110. *Why Ethics: Signs of Responsibilities*, 59.

111. See Brian Schroeder, *Altared Ground: Levinas, History, and Violence*, 102f.

112. For Levinas God is not separable from preoriginary responsibility. Thus God escapes objectification but is still proximal through illeity. Moreover, this proximity modulates into a command, one whose response is offered through Saying. See Levinas, *Dieu, la mort et le temps* (Paris, B. Grasset, 1993), 49; *God, Death, and Time*, 203.

113. Levinas elsewhere compares this call to awakening to being subpoenaed, noting that 'in the responsibility for others – the subject, the self – I am summoned to appear rather than simply appearing, replying to a subpoena that cannot be declined and seizes me precisely in my non-interchangeable identity by calling to me,' "The Name of God According to a Few Talmudic Texts," *L'Au-Delà du Verset*, 156; *Beyond the Verse: Talmudic Readings and Lectures*, 127.

Chapter Seven

Waging Peace

In *Otherwise than Being or Beyond Essence* Levinas presents responsibility as a dispossession of self so profound and provocative as to be a sacrifice and substitution for the other. Significantly, this responsibility is irreducible to idioms of ontology – exchanges, in other words, contingent upon the currency of being. Yet language presupposes an ontological medium circumscribed by essence and presence.[1] Thus Levinas again implements a vernacular reliant upon affective matrices – descriptions depictive of the horizonal scaffoldings suggestive more of moods than meaning.[2] Levinas utilizes these moods, or tonal affectivities, in *Otherwise than Being* to sketch rather than define the multifarious dimensions of interiority provoked through encounters with the other, disturbances which modulate into such movements as expiation, persecution, exile, and obsession.

It is owing to this excessive reaching for what exceeds conceptual or categorical grasp – i.e., non-philosophical experiences – that Levinas again charts a third way, this time one threading below or beyond what is reducible to theory or practice or collapsible into ontological totalizations.[3] What is more, saying in *Otherwise than Being* operates not unlike a Eucharist as responsibility assumes the shape of bread offered to the stranger. Regarding Levinas, according to Michael Purcell, 'one can express the structure of subjectivity eucharistically. Eucharistic responsibility is a responsibility which intends justice.'[4] Some, however, like Rudi Visker, question the limits of this intentional justice and consider this radical predilection towards responsibility 'an absurdity within the order of being.'[5] Visker takes issue with this hyperbolic obligation, wondering why one should be reproached 'for not having intervened in things gone wrong which we had nothing to do with, and which we did not even know about while they happened.'[6] Levinas's essential motif of substitution, addressed in this chapter, tackles this exigency head on.

By way of balance and bookend to *Otherwise than Being*, *Totality and Infinity* presented Levinas's metaphysical ethics as a call to the other, one intensified through the constraints piqued through proximity. Obligations and responsibilities to and for the other gravitate towards expositions conditional to morality and justice. And as Cohen notes,

> The primary labor of *Totality and Infinity* is to establish and elaborate the otherness of the other person as moral "height and destitution." Transcendence is found in the "face" of the other, the other person's imperative height whose first command is "thou shall not murder," unsettling, disrupting, inverting the more or less sophisticated economy of immanence, sensibility, labor, knowledge and reason. Only an excessive metaphysical desire, a desire for goodness – obligations, responsibilities, the call to justice – can do justice to the radical otherness of the other person. *Otherwise than Being* elaborates this ethics of alterity like ethics itself, by turning back to the moral sensibility of the subject awakened by the other, to its unique temporal and moral de-phasing, a fissured self, traumatized, held hostage by the other. . . . I am my brother's keeper, all the way. The alterity of the other is no less radical in *Otherwise than Being* than in *Totality and Infinity*, but Levinas's focus is now on the asymmetrical repercussion, the shock, the implosion of that alterity on a subjectivity subject precisely as moral subjection to and for the other.[7]

In *Otherwise than Being*, however, Levinas stresses responsibility to the point of substitution, an emphasis enacted hermeneutically.[8] This emphasis, furthermore, will essentially extend responsibility as articulation, an extension grounded and steeped in testimonial sacrifice. In this sense, according to Steven G. Smith, *Otherwise than Being* addresses this exaggerated obligation 'by showing performatively what it is that language can do other than represent objects or paradoxically nonobjects like "the other." The problematic of totality and the infinite is now stated as the problematic of *le Dit* (the "Said," the structurally coherent text created by language) and *le Dire* ("Saying," the primordially generous, nonthematic upsurge of communication).'[9] It is to this primordial upsurge of communication that we now turn.

All My Inwardness

For Levinas transcendence is possible only by passing over to what is otherwise than being: 'To be or not to be is not the question where transcendence is concerned. The statement of being's *other*, of otherwise than being, claims to state a difference over and beyond that which separates being from nothingness – the very difference of the *beyond*, the difference of transcendence.'[10] Pronouncing that difference implies reutilizing the saying and the said, motifs analogous to those operating in *Totality and Infinity* under the terms the Other and the Same.[11] Stating this difference also entails discerning in subjectivity a more radical perspective where transcendence is discovered in that creative lacuna between being and its otherwise, that ponderous breach punctuating works of Levinas. It is in this gap that the diachronic expression called saying interrupts being, an act owing to a performative responsibility that for Levinas is ethics itself.[12] This performative responsibility, moreover, involves a disinterestedness Levinas likens to 'a good violence.'

> It is necessary. The responsibility for another is precisely a saying prior to anything said. The surprising saying which is responsibility for another is against "the winds and tides" of being, is an interruption of essence, a disinterestedness imposed with a good violence. But one has to say that the gratuity nonetheless required of substitution, that miracle of ethics before the light, this astonishing saying, comes to light through the very gravity of the questions that assail it. It must spread out and assemble itself into essence, posit itself, be hypostasized, become an eon in consciousness and knowledge, let itself be seen, undergo the ascendancy of being. Ethics itself, in its saying which is responsibility, requires this hold.[13]

Hence responsibility becomes ethics for Levinas, and the saying implicates this responsibility with a transcendent primacy unoriginal to the said.[14] Also, since 'Proximity is quite distinct from every other relationship, and has to be conceived as a responsibility for the other,' it soon becomes apparent that there is a recurrence here expanding reference to the ethical event, furthering the significance of saying.[15]

This point is corroborated by Fabio Ciaramelli, who notes that *Otherwise than Being*'s distinction between the Saying and the Said shows that, 'despite the unfailing significance of the speaking subject's "position," insofar as it is said, the uniqueness of the first person becomes universal and thus requires a further reduction. We must remember that ethical language does not reach any definitive formulation. It calls, rather, for an endless thinking back from the Said to the Saying.'[16] And because the saying takes place in a pre-original time, one anarchic to the temporality and presence indigenous to ontology, the ethical event 'is bound to an irrecuperable, unrepresentable past, temporalizing according to a time with separate epochs, in a diachrony. An analysis that starts with proximity, irreducible to consciousness of, and desirable, if possible, as an inversion of its intentionality, will recognize this responsibility to be a substitution.'[17] Recognizing responsibility as a substitution brings us to the crux of *Otherwise than Being or Beyond Essence*. It also brings us to the event *par excellence* in Levinas's mission to the Gentiles.

As has been argued, escaping the self predominates Levinas's thinking. It has also been maintained that this exilic motif is constantly militated against by the neutralizing and assumptive properties of being – the persistence of being being persistent.[18] Thus it is not unusual that Levinas reconfigures notions of war in *Otherwise than Being* collaterally with his earlier ones in *Totality and Infinity*: 'The essence thus works as an invincible persistence in essence, filling up every interval of nothingness which would interrupt its exercise. . . . War is the deed or the drama of the essence's interest. They all clash, despite the differences of the regions to which the terms in conflict may belong. Essence thus is the extreme synchronism of war.'[19] Obviously one must ask if there is not a way out of this violent circle, this being at war. And anticipated also would be the inquiry: where is the peace? messianic, eschatological, or otherwise. Enigmatically, of course, Levinas would have us know that peace is the trauma of responsibility that comes pre-originally and diachronically through substitution, through ordination, and through goodness:[20]

> Diachrony is the refusal of conjunction, the non-totalizable, and in this sense, the infinite. But in the responsibility for the Other, for another freedom, the negativity of this anarchy, this refusal of the present, of appearing, of the immemorial, commands me and ordains me to the other, to the first one on the scene, and makes me approach him, makes me his neighbor. . . . All the negative attributes which state what is beyond the essence become positive in responsibility, a response answering to the non-thematizable provocation and thus a non-vocation, a trauma. This response answers, before any understanding, for a debt contracted before any freedom and before any consciousness of any present, but it does answer, as though the invisible that bypasses the present left a trace by the very fact of bypassing the present. That trace lights up as the face of a neighbor.'[21]

Ordained to sacrifice for the other, subjectivity is called now to an extreme patience and passivity, one passing as peace to the neighbor, or – as Anthony J. Steinbock calls it – 'an invitation to glory.'[22]

The Violent Election

According to Levinas signification antecedes being.[23] This assertion implies that the meaningful exceeds what is comprehendible. In fact, through ordination to the face, one is elected to a superlative humility, one whose supererogation, like the desire of infinity, is uncontained and uncontainable. And since signification for Levinas is irreducible to context, as such it occurs in a diachronic time not only a-thematic but contra-reason: 'The response of the responsible one does not thematize the diachronical as though it were retained, remembered or historically reconstructed. It cannot thematize or comprehend. Not out of weakness; to what could not be contained there corresponds no capacity.'[24] Now the good – like God, the other, and the idea of infinity – assumes for Levinas the role of the non-contained. And responsibility traces the gravity of the good.[25] Unending, un-begun, irrepresentable, immemorial – the good ordains one to responsibility:

> The non-present here is invisible, separated (or sacred) and thus non-origin, an-archical. The Good cannot become present or enter into a representation. The present is a beginning in my freedom, whereas the Good is not presented to freedom; it has chosen me before I have chosen it. No one is good voluntarily. We can see the formal structure of nonfreedom in a subjectivity which does not have time to choose the Good and thus is penetrated with its rays unbeknownst to itself. But subjectivity sees this nonfreedom redeemed,

exceptionally, by the goodness of the Good. The exception is unique. And if no one is good voluntarily, no one is enslaved to the Good.[26]

The phenomenology of responsibility for Levinas thus involves a uniquely obliged self whose commitment is not only graced by the good but transcends time and volition. What is more, being elected by the good for Levinas so inspires the self that sacrifice – i. e., complete, kenotic subjection to and substitution for the other – becomes its *modus operandi*: all the way to the point of expiation. Jeffrey Kosky says that for Levinas 'the self is an expiation, a martyr, and even a sacrifice, insofar as it sacrifices all concern for itself in responsibility for every other . . . . Expiation befalls me from the other; and in its befalling me, I am myself – as if I, the I, were a hostage. I am myself in my being sacrificed for others without this happening on my own initiative.'[27] This forgoing of self through responsibility for the other, moreover, bequeaths an exceptional passivity through the goodness of the good, authenticating the self's election.[28]

Strangely, due to its anarchic predilection towards substitution, the self's election renders it hostage to the good: 'The self, a hostage, is already substituted for the others. . . . The ego is not an entity "capable" of expiating for the others: it is this original expiation. This expiation is involuntary, for it is prior to the will's initiative. It is as though the unity and uniqueness of the ego were already the hold on itself of the gravity of the other.'[29] And significantly, the gravity of the other and the gravity of goodness merge here, the confluence saturating the self with a transcendence irreducible to ontological totalizations and syntheses. 'In this sense the self is goodness. It is with subjectivity understood as self, with the exciding and dispossession, the contraction, in which the ego does not appear, but immolates itself, that the relationship with the other can be communication and transcendence.'[30] And for Levinas, this communication and transcendence constitute the ethical.[31]

A Divine Discomfort

Election is confirmed by the traumatic obsession the self feels for the neighbor. In an articulate affectivity called saying, the subject obliges itself to an antecedent responsibility and surrenders as a hostage to the good. As Gibbs sees it, 'I become myself – I become free in responsibility – only when I answer for the other. I am hostage for the other, says Levinas at his hyperbolic best. Thus I am not my own master, but am substitute for the other.'[32] Accordingly, election for Levinas is the annunciation of this articulate affectivity. It is a heavy and non-transferable assignment:

> To support the universe is a crushing charge, but a divine discomfort. Has not the Good chosen the subject with an election recognizable in the responsibility of being hostage, to which the subject is destined, which he cannot evade without denying himself and by virtue of which he is unique? This antecedence of responsibility to freedom would signify the Goodness of the Good: the necessity that the Good choose me first before I can be in a position to choose, that is, welcome its choice. That is my pre-originary

> *susceptiveness*. It is a passivity prior to all receptivity, it is transcendent. It is an antecedence prior to all representable antecedence: immemorial. The Good is before being.... The Good assigns the subject, according to a susception that cannot be assumed, to approach the other, the neighbor.[33]

Since subjectivity cannot be contextualized within the framework of ontology, its agency – in fact, what constitutes one's humanity – is the 'for-the-other' put on view by a self, an exhibition translatable only through the idiom of ethics. And as this exhibition founded in agential responsibility shatters the order of being, it reduces all signification to the sobering exigencies inherent in a patience and suffering ontologically impossible yet ethically real.[34]

These exigencies are ethically real despite the fact their origins are undetectable. And they are akin to the tonal affectivities operative in horizonal zones whose movements are more adumbrated than delineated. As such, 'The ethical does not belong to any world or universe. It does not have a beginning but comes from nowhere, from a non-space and non-time before time. It does not differ from human subjectivity but constitutes its core, though it does not constitute a quiet essence or the busy dynamism of a "nature."'[35] Notably, the enucleation of this constitutive core of subjectivity occurs in a non-space and non-time through an 'undergoing by sensibility beyond its capacity to undergo. This describes the suffering and vulnerability of the sensible as *the other in me*. The other is in me in the midst of my very identification. The self-accusation of remorse gnaws away at the closed and firm core of consciousness, opening it, fissioning it.'[36]

Hence one now finds the self, what Levinas calls the subjection of subjectivity, pregnant with the other – a maternity modulating into a persecution qua patience made sensible through substitution. 'Maternity,' comments John Llewelyn, 'is carrying par excellence, the carrying of responsibility, vulnerability and suffering that is pre-natal not just in the biological sense, but in the philosophical sense in which the ethical is prior to the natural, to *phusis*, to being. For the very selfhood of the self even in its corporeal sensibility is "the flesh made word...."'[37] And this modality accommodates sensibility through a passivity that, being pre-original, betrays itself through sacrifice.[38]

A Sacrifice Without Reserve (Redeeming Violence)

An Abrahamic, hospitable self is a self sacrificed for the other. Indeed, hospitality hyperbolized can only find logical surrender through substitution.[39] And the agent for hyperbolized hospitality is responsibility. Epigramed by Levinas with the words of poet Paul Celen, chapter four of *Othewise than Being*, entitled "Substitution," begins with the words 'I am you when I am I.'[40] But these words were foreshadowed much earlier with Levinas's depiction of ethics as the breakup of essence, a breakup effected through sensibility. In fact, threaded throughout this analysis thus far is a saga depicting the exodus of a self made vulnerable through sacrifice.

Pointedly, the coming apart of identity, this self-fissuring prompted through sacrifice, the—for all practical purposes – weakening of being, fortifies responsibility.[41] In a very real way, in the realm of being beyond essence, vulnerability and dereliction are braced by the violent election to the good:

> Responsibility goes beyond being. In sincerity, in frankness, in the veracity of the saying, in the uncoveredness of suffering, being is altered. But this saying remains, in its activity, a passivity, more passive than all passivity, for it is a sacrifice without reserve, without holding back, and in this [sense] non-voluntary – the sacrifice of a hostage designated who has not chosen himself to be hostage, but possibly elected by the Good, in an involuntary election not assumed by the elected one. For the Good cannot enter into a present nor be put into a representation. But being Good it redeems the violence of its alterity, even if the subject has to suffer through the augmentation of this ever more demanding violence.[42]

From an early foreshadowing, sacrifice moves into the heart of Otherwise than Being and centers in "Substitution." In this seminal chapter subjectivity, the protagonist in the saga of self, owing to the trauma of an ethical election, transforms from a *me-for-myself* into a *one-for-the-other*. This transformation reflects the sacrifice effected through substitutionary responsibility. What is more, like Levinasian election, responsibility here is insinuated through a pre-original and provocative obligation. As notes Jeffrey Bloechl, 'The enormous sacrifice depicted in being one-for-the-other is not in the first place *willed* – but imposed. All willing . . . is circumscribed in an ethical relation older than any act or even its motivation. Responsibility is literally and profoundly preordained.'[43]

Since the ethical relation assumes any synoptic ontological event constitutive of knowledge and volition, ethics is pure and simply first; and since substitution prompted by responsibility is the event *par excellence* in Levinas, the for-the-other basic to this substitution is the keystone for Levinas. Thus one is affected by a preordained responsibility so radical as to be a sacrifice; an election to the good so severe as to be violence and trauma; and an ego so impinged upon by the neighbor as to be a hostage. And again the way depends upon the other. For Levinas, 'it is as if the other established a relationship whose whole intensity consists in not presupposing the idea of community. (This is) a responsibility stemming from a time before my freedom . . . a responsibility for my neighbor, for the other man, for the stranger or sojourner, to which nothing in the rigorously ontological order binds me. . . .'[44]

Some see Levinas's idea of substitutionary responsibility as antidotal to a subversive idolatry symptomatic of a civilization in the grips of egoistic dynamics. According to David Ford, 'There are allergic relations between people – we see others as threats to our freedom and the normal state of life as war or compromises between people and groups in tension rather than seeing human subjectivity as welcoming the other in hospitality and peace.'[45] By comparing Levinas's thought with that of Christian theologian Eberhard

Jüngel, particularly the ways the former's hyperbolic responsibility collates with the latter's Christocentricism, Ford has found Levinas's notion of substitution – and its cognates obsession, expiation, sacrifice, and kenosis – crucial in plumbing depths where 'the radical passivity of Levinas has an analogy in Jungel's notion of faith as "pure passivity" which is the subjective counterpart of the "new creation" of justification.'[46]

What is more, Ford torques this analogy in order to present 'what must seem impossible: to retain what I see as the heart of both extremes. In other words, I want to argue for a substitutionary self, defined by radical responsibility, and also for Jesus Christ dying for all.'[47] By so arguing, Ford issues an inquiry: 'Is it possible to envisage a Levinasian Christian theology?' Again paring Levinas with Jüngel, he answers that

> each has a substitutionary self in the pivotal position of his thought: Jüngel's is Jesus Christ while Levinas's is each responsible "I." They converge in their resistance to the dynamics of idolatry, but are also in obvious tension. My constructive proposal, mediated by Bonheoffer, is to affirm, in non-competitive relationship, both the substitutionary self in radical responsibility and the substitutionary life, death, and resurrection of Jesus Christ.[48]

As if sensing the radical implications of his argument, Ford offers a footnote allowing that 'Here my concern is not to argue against Levinas's Jewish witness so much as for the view that his philosophical position does not necessarily deny the Christian witness.'[49] Levinas would be inclined to see this position ontologically biased, hence totalized.[50] However, as presented in the next chapter, Levinasian pre-original responsibility does offer a unique perspective as well as distinct challenge to the Christian witness herein inscribed as his mission to the Gentiles.

The Elected Self

For Levinas only a substitution for the other irreducible to stratagems of belief allows one to escape circumscribed and totalized relations.[51] Only an 'I' hostage to and responsible for the other can artlessly say 'Here I am.' At the crux of the chapter entitled "Substitution," which is the heartbeat of *Otherwise than Being*, Levinas issues forth a calling to a restive freedom different from ones betraying synthesis, systemization, and solipsism.

> The word I means *here I am*, answering for everything and for everyone. Responsibility for the others has not been a return to oneself, but an exasperated contracting, which the limits of identity cannot retain. Recurrence becomes identity in breaking up the limits of identity, breaking up the *principle* of being in me, the intolerable rest in itself characteristic of definition. The self is on the hither side of rest. . . . It is to hold on to oneself while gnawing away at oneself. Responsibility in obsession is a responsibility of the ego for what the ego has not wished, that is, for the others. . . . What can it be but a substitution of me for the others? Through substitution for others, the oneself escapes relations. Here the overdetermination of the ontological categories is visible, which transforms them into ethical terms.[52]

Several key points demand attention. First, continuing the hermeneutical polemic indicative of Abraham and Ulysses, one is informed again that Abraham's call 'here I am' still proposes an exilic wandering where the self is not collapsible into ontological hegemonies. Indeed, there is here an exasperated restlessness illimitable and inimitable, prompting Bernasconi to comment that 'Unlike consciousness which loses itself to find itself, the Levinasian self is unable to take a distance from itself. It is unable to depart from itself so as to return, once having recognized itself in its past.'[53] Second, there is the issue of what constitutes the selfhood of the self, a return to the self more originary than self-consciousness per se, and an identity founded upon responsibility for the other. Characterized by an agitated gnawing named recurrence, this reiterating obsession with the neighbor is 'a materiality such that irritability, susceptibility or exposedness to wounds and outrage characterize its passivity, more passive than the passivity of effects. Maternity in the complete being "for the other" which characterizes it, which is the very signifyingness of signification, is the ultimate sense of this vulnerability.'[54] Hence recurrence for Levinas marks this anarchical obsession and trauma experienced by a subjectivity not only responsible for everyone — but finding its completion through a substitution experienced 'only as a persecution, but a persecution that turns into an expiation. Without persecution the ego raises its head and covers over the self.'[55]

A third point apropos of substitution concerns the self's election to what Levinas calls a different freedom — one irreducible to any initiatives besides those grounded in the ethical. This ethical grounding presumes an awakening to a wounded restiveness desirous of others. Moreover, it exhibits 'a pure self, in the accusative, responsible before there is freedom. Strictly speaking, the other is the end; I am a hostage, a responsibility and a substitution supporting the world in a passivity of assignation, even in an accusing persecution, which is undeclinable.'[56] In his essays on Judaism compiled in *Difficult Freedom*, Levinas proposes that ethical relations are tantamount to religious relations: in fact, both integrate freedom into desire for transcendence 'by experiencing the presence of God through one's relation to man [where] the Other is not a new edition of myself; in its Otherness it is situated in a dimension of height, in the ideal, the Divine, and through my relation to the Other, I am in touch with God.'[57]

Thus a wounding and indeclinable persecution occurs through a different freedom where the self touches God through the other. Levinas calls this contiguity a 'royal awakening' where 'the ritual gesture demands a courage that is calmer, nobler and greater than that of a warrior.'[58] This same courage was exhibited by Moses and the prophets who 'preoccupied themselves not with the immortality of the soul but with the poor, the widow, the orphan and the stranger. The relationship with man in which contact with the Divine is established is not a kind of *spiritual friendship* but the sort that is manifested, tested and accomplished in a just economy for which each man is responsible.'[59] Thus freedom for Levinas is exactly this election to responsibility for the other, an awakening to the fact that 'there is no moral awareness that is not an awareness of this exceptional position, an awareness of being chosen.'[60] Additionally this awareness, notes Cohen, inaugurates 'the individual's election to a moral agency. The irreplaceable self, the self confronted by the other, put into question by the other, made responsible for others, is the elected self.'[61]

The Restlessness of Peace

By presenting the subject as hostage, Levinas obviates the interminable parsing concerning freedom of the will. As Drabinski notes, 'Difference and separation put freedom in question at a structural moment genetically prior to the boundaries within which freedom is exercised.'[62] In fact, according to Levinas, pre-originary responsibility actually qualifies freedom: 'This liberation is not an action, a commencement, nor any vicissitude of essence and of ontology, where the equality with oneself would be established in the form of self-consciousness. [As] an anarchic liberation, it emerges, without being assumed, without turning into a beginning, in inequality with oneself.' [63] Understanding this inequality and diachrony latent in responsibility is essential for grasping how substitution is undergone rather than assumed. Freedom cannot be predicated upon thought, belief, or knowledge – as these would simply reflect the persistence of being rounded off to the nearest ontological whole. Thus freedom, according to Levinas, is either the simple and cheap freedom compromised by essence and knowledge, or else it is the difficult freedom made real though the ethical exigencies ennobled through anarchic responsibility:[64]

> Essence, in its seriousness as *persistence in essence*, fills every interval of nothingness that would interrupt it. It is strict book-keeping where nothing is lost nor created. Freedom is compromised in this balance of accounts in an order where responsibilities correspond exactly to liberties taken, where they compensate for them, where time relaxes and then is tightened again after having allowed a decision in the interval opened up. Freedom in the genuine sense can be only a contestation of this book-keeping by a gratuity. This gratuity could be the absolute *distraction* of a play without consequences, without traces or memories, of a pure pardon. Or, it could be responsibility for another and expiation.'[65]

Significantly the subject – as saying, as responsible, as accused, as irreplaceable, as asymmetrical, as obsession, as hostage, as passivity, as persecution, as substitution – is transcendent. For Levinas this means that, although it 'intervenes to hasten the assembling, to confer more chances to the packing in, to unite the elements into a present, to re-present them,' subjectivity nonetheless – while *of* being – is not *in* being.[66] This is so because the 'matrix of every thematizable relation, the-one-for-the-other, signification, sense or intelligibility, does not rest in being. Its restlessness must not be put in terms of rest.'[67] Hence subjectivity cannot be reduced to a commitment, since any commitment would presuppose an assumptive consciousness contingent upon the politics of logic. Rudi Visker captures the seeming absurdity of this position *vis-à-vis* logic when he notes that 'somehow, both saying and responsibility never quite "take place." They are *literally* misplaced, out of joint, pointing to an anachronism which cannot be resolved, synchronized, serialized, or situated, for example, in the chain of cause and effect, without nullifying the "plot" or "intrigue" in which they show up.'[68]

The root of the issue may be presented thusly: 'Any radical non-assemblable diachrony would be excluded from meaning. . . . The conjuncture in which a man is responsible for other men, the ethical relationship, which is habitually considered as belonging to a derivative or founded order, has been throughout this work approached as irreducible. It is structured as the one-for-the-other.'[69] In other words, according to Levinas, anything other than the ethical relationship is subsumed by an autonomy ingredient in the economy of the self, in an *as-for-me*. But the responsible self, subject to the other, breaks the story line of totality, structuring sensibility on proximity to the neighbor.[70] Further, this sensibility assumes signification prior to any commitment and is thus contingent upon the assignation of the subject to the other. Hence there is this infinite approach non-quantifiable by any cognates of essence yet evidenced in the goodness made glorious through what Levinas calls the exceptional plot of substitution: 'The I approached in responsibility is for-the-other. . . . (It) is consumed and delivered over, dislocates itself, loses its place, is exiled, relegates itself into itself, but as though its very skin were still a way to shelter itself in being, exposed to wounds and outrage, to the point of substituting for the other, holding on to itself only as it were in the trace of its exile.'[71] Substitution for the other is thus the logical extension of the exilic ego previously analyzed, fulfilling the asymmetrical craving of the Abrahamic self.[72]

Notably one's exilic trace leads to ground zero of substitution, a disinterestedness modulated into an inwardness where 'Peace with the other is first of all my business. The non-indifference, the saying, the responsibility, the approach, is the disengaging of the unique one responsible, me. The way I appear is a summons. . . . The "never enough" of proximity, the restlessness of this peace, is the acute uniqueness of subjectivity.'[73] Moreover, for Levinas signification as passivity acts as a vehicle carrying this anarchic peace – antecedent to the ontological hegemony of presence – into an arena of inspiration and witness.[74]

Being Torn

In the chapter entitled "Subjectivity and Infinity" of *Otherwise than Being* Levinas conjoins responsibility with what he calls the glory of the infinite. Incited by the obsessive restlessness straining the core of subjectivity, and reaching for a trope commensurable with the extreme exposedness implicit in saying, Levinas presents his ethical testimony as a provocation so severe as to be scandalous. Indeed, it is noted that this restlessness is betrayed by a saying unrestricted to thematization, one distinguished by a responsibility likened to 'a cellular irritability; it is the impossibility of being silent, the scandal of sincerity.'[75] This testimony offers a life uncontaminated by the alloying of essence, one made manifest in 'a being torn up from oneself for another in the giving to the other of the bread out of one's own mouth. . . . The identity of the subject is here brought out, not by a rest on itself, but by a restlessness that drives me outside of the nucleus of my substantiality.'[76]

This is the crisis of enucleation or self- fissuring, the provocation operative in a responsibility destined towards substitution. It reflects the burst of interiority through sacrificial giving to the other and is signaled through proximity. According to Levinas, the

> love of self is an egoism which founds a being and constitutes the first ontological experience. That experience calls for the opening of and veritable departure from self. The human will pass by another decisive stage in which the subject, despite its satisfaction, fails to suffice unto itself. Every departure from self represents the fissure that is installed within the same in relation to the other. Desire metamorphosed into an attitude of openness to exteriority, openness that is a call and a response to the other: the proximity of the other is the origin of every putting into question of the self.[77]

Levinas implements the metaphor of giving bread from one's own mouth often and in various transpositions throughout *Otherwise than Being*.[78] Alongside corroborating his assertion in *Totality and Infinity* that one cannot approach the other with empty hands, here the trope functions as a carrier of the substitutionary motif enlisted earlier, as when one reads that 'Being torn from oneself for another in giving to the other the bread from one's mouth is being able to give up one's soul for another. The animation of a body by a soul only articulates the-one-for-the-other in subjectivity.'[79]

Here sincerity as hospitality reflects the radical exponentials in a Eucharistic drama. According to Michael Purcell, 'Responsibility, as "for-the-other," has the same "for-structure" of the Eucharist. . . . Eucharist, as responsibility, is also a work of justice, even to the point of being subjected to death "for-the-other."'[80] There is a performative enacting here of an invisible gratuity where saying is made manifest through giving. We learn that 'sincerity is not an attribute of saying; it is saying that realizes sincerity. It is inseparable from giving, for it opens reserves from which the hand that gives draws without being able to dissimulate anything.'[81] Now subjectivity, enucleated and fissured by the hollowed-out ego, and summoned to carry the bread of peace to the other-turned-neighbor, opens itself to the glory of the infinite.

For Levinas, it is through sincerity that the saying of the ethical and the modality of the prophetic meet in responsibility. Where they meet signifies a glory traced in the face of the other:

> Does not the sense of sincerity refer to the glory of infinity, which calls for sincerity as for saying? ... Glory is but the other face of the passivity of the subject. Substituting itself for the other, a responsibility ordered to the first one on the scene, a responsibility for the neighbor, inspired by the other, I, the same, am torn up from my beginning in myself, my equality with myself. The

glory of the infinite is glorified in this responsibility.... The glory of the infinite is the anarchic identity of the subject flushed out without being able to slip away. It is the ego led to sincerity, making signs to the other, for whom and before whom I am responsible, of this very giving of signs, that it, of this responsibility: "Here I am."[82]

Being accused and susceptible, the saying of 'here I am' prompts a recurrence in subjectivity Levinas likens to persecution and martyrdom. Indeed, 'the ego stripped by the trauma of persecution of its scornful and imperialistic subjectivity, is reduced to the "here I am." . . . There is witness, a unique structure, an exception to the rule of being, irreducible to representation, only of the infinite.'[83]

Through witnessing, prophecy and the ethical converge in the saying of 'Here I am.' What is more, 'Glorification is saying, that is, a sign, given to the other, peace announced to the other, responsibility for the other, to the point of substitution.' [84] This annunciation of peace for Levinas is the transcendental base for ethical experience, reconciling autonomy and heteronomy, traumatizing subjectivity with a goodness irreducible to thematization yet witnessed in the giving of signs to the other. This giving 'signifies out of responsibility for the other, out of the-one-for-the-other, a subject supporting everything, subject to everything that is, suffering for everyone, but charged with everything, without having to decide for this taking charge, which is gloriously amplified in the measure that it is imposed.'[85]

Thanks to God

With subtlety and fine nuance Levinas inflects the maternity of heterogeneity into prophetic witness by asserting that 'Prophecy would be the very psyche of the soul: the other in the same, and all of man's spirituality would thus be prophetic.'[86] This prophecy bespeaks of the vigilance highlighted earlier. And this inflection, moreover, according to De Boer, is significant: 'Very specific experiences are at stake here: the being shaken out of its enchainment with being, the awakening of consciousness. It [Levinas's] is a philosophy of religion in the time of the suspicion of ideologies. This suspicion has its origin in a cry of protest against injustice, in prophecy.'[87] Here is a formidable transaction, one positioning the eschatological messianism in *Totality and Infinity* alongside the enigmatic and pre-original responsibility threaded throughout *Otherwise than Being*.

Patterning prophecy and infinity for Levinas is elemental to his ethical optics. The signification without context – vision sans image – so prevalent in *Totality and Infinity* now translates into an inspirational and provocative saying – and again responsibility is both medium and message: 'In the responsibility for the other we are at the heart of the ambiguity of inspiration. The unheard-of saying is enigmatically in the anarchic response, in my responsibility for the other. The trace of infinity is this ambiguity in the subject . . . a diachronic ambivalence which makes ethics possible.'[88]

Tracing infinity through the subject allows what Levinas calls the plot of ethics to be glorified through the witness of saying, or what figures as the anachronism of prophecy. And again the witness can be collapsed into the 'here I am' that choruses throughout works of Levinas. And true to diachrony, this witnessing occurs anarchically, anticipating presence yet still signifying in the name of God. Thus it lives in the antecedent saying experienced as the gift of gratitude:

> "Here I am," just that! The word God is still absent from the phrase in which God is for the first time involved in words. . . . To bear witness to God is precisely not to state this extraordinary word, as though glory would be lodged in a theme and be posited as a thesis, or become being's essence. As a sign given to the other of this very signification, the "here I am" signifies me in the name of God, at the service of men that look at me, without having anything to identify myself with, but the sound of my voice or the figure of my gesture – the saying itself. Witness is humility and admission; it is made before all theology; it is kerygma and prayer, glorification and recognition. . . (it) is the fact that the return is sketched out in the going, the appeal is understood in the response, the "provocation" coming from God is in my invocation, gratitude is already gratitude for this state of gratitude, which is at the same time or in turn a gift and a gratitude. The transcendence of the revelation lies in the fact that the "epiphany" comes in the saying of him that received it.[89]

Here God couches in the witnessing and revelation prompted by a prophecy irreducible to epistemic agency, yet inscribed in what Levinas calls the wandering cause of the trace. Prophecy in fact becomes modal in later Levinas, assuming a rhythmic consistency lock-stepped with the saying of the infinite through a sort of poetic knowing.[90] And the self in all its exilic grandeur makes transparent a transcendence illimitable and unconditioned by the gatherings of consciousness. As Jeffrey Kosky notes, 'As the responsible self, the prophet who witnesses God has no business of its own, no project for its own sake, no involvement in the world, according to which it would disclose God.'[91] Therefore this witness merges with the prophetic eschatology and messianism of earlier Levinas as it resonates with an antecedent peace uncontaminated by totalization.[92] And this peace is made real in ethical responsibility: 'here I am, under your eyes, at your service, your obedient servant. In the name of God . . . it is the "here I am" said to a neighbor to whom I am given over, by which I announce peace, that is, my responsibility for the other.'[93]

Thus peace and goodness preside in that infinite moment unassembled and immemorial, beyond the scope of ontological categories, yet plenary in the saying of 'here I am.' This is a negative instant that 'finds its positive form in proximity, responsibility, and substitution. . . . The refusal of presence is converted into my presence as present, that is, as a hostage delivered as a gift to the other. In proximity . . . the Infinite speaks through the witness I bear.'[94] Upon this witness hinges responsibility, revelation, and prophecy – all opening upon a peace irreducible to essence yet real in the dereliction of the other's face. Here the plot of ethics becomes a peace whose transcending presence passes understanding. Also passing is God, who again fills the gaps with agapic justice:

> It is only thanks to God that as a subject incomparable with the other, I am approached as an other by the others, that is, "for myself." "Thanks to God" I am another for the others. God is not involved as an alleged interlocutor: the reciprocal relationship binds me to the other man in the trace of transcendence, in illeity. The passing of God, of whom I can speak only by reference to this aid or this grace, is precisely the reverting of the incomparable subject into a member of society. . . .The equality of all is borne by my inequality, the surplus of my duties over my rights. The forgetting of self moves justice.[95]

This reverting of the subject into a member of society is owing to the third party Levinas introduces, an insertion providing a distanciation reducible to justice.[96] In fact, according to Michael Smith, for Levinas 'even the homogeneity of space is to be reduced to the notion of justice.'[97] Frank M. Yamada concurs, noting that 'the presence of *le tiers* (the third party) means that ethics must always touch the sociopolitical ground. Discussion about ethics must move beyond the realm of speculation to the realm of politics and social action.'[98]

One thus begins another octave, one synchronized and systematized by consciousness and intelligibility, but one now infused with a peace-bound responsibility. Essence again assumes time and place. That is why 'justice is necessary, that is, comparison, coexistence, contemporaneousness, assembling, order, thematization, the visibility of faces, and thus intentionality and the intellect, the intelligibility of a system, and thus a copresence on an footing as before a court of justice. Essence as synchrony is togetherness in a place.'[99] What is more, the restless self – whose exodus from selfishness towards selflessness has been charted thus far – now rests in the other, the stranger, the neighbor.

And the connection breaks and spirals upward as the subject as hostage – elected by the good, exposed in the passivity of saying – sacrifices itself again without reserve. This is the ethical revolution that has always already occurred – and always already occurs – in the expiation of substitution where the subject's sincerity and vulnerability go beyond being towards the otherwise than being.[100] It is sensibility made susceptible, the enucleation of self writ large in the shattering of essence. And it is the exile of an ego portrayed historically and paradigmatically in the figure of Abraham perpetually waging peace.

Notes

1. Cf. "*Totality and Infinity*": Preface to the German Edition," *Entre Nous*, where Levinas notes that '*Otherwise than Being or Beyond Essence* already avoids the ontological – or more exactly, *eidetic* – language which *Totality and Infinity* incessantly resorts to in

order to keep its analyses, which challenge the *conatus essendi* [persistence] of being, from being considered as dependent upon the empiricism of psychology,' 198.

2. See Llewelyn, *Appositions of Jacque Derrida and Emmanuel Levinas*, 175f.

3. See Robert Bernasconi, "Only the Persecuted...," *Ethics as First Philosophy*, where one finds that 'An experience is nonphilosophical for Levinas ... if it is not one of those experiences on which philosophy as constituted by the tradition has been based, such as *theoria* or *poiesis*,' 84.

4. *Levinas and Theology*, 157.

5. "The Question of God," *The Face of the Other and the Trace of God*, 254f.

6. Ibid.

7. Foreword to *Otherwise than Being or Beyond Essence*, xii.

8. See Jeffrey Dudiak, *The Intrigue of Ethics*, 111.

9. "Reason as One for Another," *Face to Face with Levinas*, 61.

10. Levinas, *Autrement qu'être ou au-delà de l'essence* (The Hague : Martinus Nijhoff, 1974) 14 ; *Otherwise than Being or Beyond Essence*, trans. Alphonso Lingis (Pittsburgh, Pa.: Duquesne University Press, 1998) 3, emphasis in text. See also Bernasconi, who notes that 'Responsibility for the other is the concretization of the structure designated by the verb "not to be." That is to say, responsibility answers to the fundamental problem of finding a way out that breaks open the principle of being in me and thus the limits of identity. It is in responsibility that the self is freed from itself, and indeed from every Other, so as to become substitutions for others,' "No Exit: Levinas' Aporetic Account of Transcendence," *Research in Phenomenology* 35 (2005): 114.

11. Cf. Peperzak's assertion that 'The Saying and the Said are not homogenous: yet there must be a way in which their difference holds them together. Similarly, in *Totality and Infinity*, the Other and the Same are related, despite their separation,' "The Anarchy of Transcendence," *Beyond: The Philosophy of Emmanuel Levinas*, 82. See also Michael B. Smith, *Toward the Outside*, 46f.

12. Cf. Levinas's assertion that ethical witnessing is a revelation which is not so much knowledge as engagement, *Éthique et Infini*, 114 ; *Ethics and Infinity*, 108.

13. Levinas, *Autrement qu'être ou au-delà de l'essence*, 75 ; *Otherwise than Being or Beyond Essence*, pp. 43f. See also Alain Toumayan, "I More Than Others: Dostoevsky and Levinas," *Yale French Studies: Encounters with Levinas*, 62.

14. 'We might be tempted to call the Saying original or originary, but like "principle," "*arche*," or "cause," "origin" belongs to the language of ontology and is thus inapplicable to the "beyond" or "before" of beingness. To underline the exceptionality of this "precedence," Levinas uses the expressions "pre-original" or "an-archical," Peperzak, "The Anarchy of Transcendence," *Beyond: The Philosophy of Emmanuel Levinas*, 92.

15. Levinas, *Autrement qu'être ou au-delà de l'essence*, 78 ; *Otherwise than Being or Beyond Essence*, 46.

16. "Levinas's Ethical Discourse Between Individuation and Universality," *Re-Reading Levinas*, 97.

17. Levinas, *Autrement qu'être ou au-delà de l'essence*, 79 ; *Otherwise than Being or Beyond Essence*, 47. See also Edith Wyschogrod, *The Problem of Ethical Metaphysics*, where it is noted that a moral consciousness obsessed with the other person makes substitution possible. She submits that what is atypical, strange and unbalanced is what is part of the process of escaping the principled totalities of the will. She further

asserts that these atypical qualifiers are what prompt Levinas to implement the term obsession, as this word sketches and adumbrates the radical disorder always on the periphery of consciousness and being. Finally, Wychogrod mentions how obsession arrests ontology, a detention owing to memory's irrecoverability, 166.

18. Peperzak feels that essence conveys the basic urge of all beings persevering in their being, in their persisting in being. He thus infers that all beings are ego-centric and self-oriented – hence allergic to each other. Thus we are all, in a sense, in a state of war. See "The Anarchy of Transcendence," *Beyond: The Philosophy of Emmanuel Levinas*, 88.

19. Levinas, *Autrement qu'être ou au-delà de l'essence*, 15 ; *Otherwise than Being or Beyond Essence*, 4. See also Brian Schroeder, *Altared Ground : Levinas, History, and Violence*, 19.

20. Cf. Jeffrey Bloechl, *Liturgy of the Neighbor*, where it is noted that volition is restricted by an ethical relation antecedent to agency. This assertion by Bloechl in essence pronounces responsibility as 'literally and profoundly preordained.' He later affixes responsibility as 'simply my identity,' one that arrives before any sense of self-service has been established, and one which is made explicit in 'the enormous sacrifice depicted in being one-for-the-other (that) is not in the first place *willed* – for this would surly remain within the ego's attempt to reassert itself – but *imposed*,' 219, emphasis in text.

21. *Autrement qu'être ou au-delà de l'essence*, 26 ; *Otherwise than Being or Beyond Essence*, 11f. Cf. Levinas, "Dialogue with Emmanuel Levinas," *Face to Face With Levinas*, where, regarding peace and responsibility, Levinas comments that 'I seek this peace not for *me* but for the other.... I must always demand more of myself than the other; this is why I disagree with Buber's description of the I-Thou ethical relation as a symmetrical copresence. As Alyosha Karamozov says in *The Brothers Karamazov* by Dostoyevsky, "We are all responsible for everyone else – but I am more responsible than all the others." This essential asymmetry is the very basis of ethics: not only am I more responsible than the other but I am even responsible for everyone's else's responsibility. For ethics, it is only in the infinite relation with the other that God passes, that traces of God are to be found,' 31, emphasis in text. See also John D. Caputo, "*Adieu – sans Dieu*: Derrida and Levinas," *The Face of the Other and the Trace of God*, 279.

22. "Face and Revelation," *Addressing Levinas*, 135.

23. See Davis, *Levinas*, 59.

24. Levinas, *Autrement qu'être ou au-delà de l'essence*, 25 ; *Otherwise than Being or Beyond Essence*, 11.

25. See Rudi Visker, *Truth and Singularity*, 260.

26. Levinas, *Autrement qu'être ou au-delà de l'essence*, 25 ; *Otherwise than Being or Beyond Essence*, 11. Regarding this exceptional election to the good, B. C. Hutchens offers that being responsible is not a form of servitude but reflects one being 'struck' by the good before one has chosen any good: 'The Good exercises a "good" violence on the self that differs dramatically from the "bad" violence of the "being" of the ontology of power. In other words, anything that enslaves the self does so within the ontology of power, whereas the Good is beyond being and otherwise than being.' Thus, according to Hutchens, the self is elected and is 'a sacrificed hostage who has not chosen subservience, but has been elected by the Good,' *Levinas: A Guide for the Perplexed*, 81.

27. *Levinas and the Philosophy of Religion*, 154. See also Hent De Vries, *Philosophy and the Turn to Religion*, 115f.

28. Apropos of this kenotic subjection is Oswald Chambers contention that 'the good is always the enemy of the best.' Also using Abraham as exemplar, Chambers notes that 'whenever *right* is made the guidance in life, it will blunt spiritual insight. The great enemy of the life of faith in God is not sin, but the good which is not good enough.... It would seem the wisest thing in the world for Abraham to choose, it was his right.... Many of us do not go on spiritually because we prefer to choose what is right instead of relying on God to choose for us.' This insight provides a unique perspective on Levinasian thought, since 'no one is good voluntarily,' as noted above, *My Utmost for His Highest: Selections for the Year* (Uhrichsville, Ohio: Barbour Publishing, 1963) May 25th, emphasis in text.

29. Levinas, *Autrement qu'être ou au-delà de l'essence*, 187 ; *Otherwise than Being or Beyond Essence*, 118.

30. Ibid. See also Michael B. Smith, *Toward the Outside*, 98f.

31. Communication and transcendence are irreducible to codes of conduct and must be approached as promptings towards awakening. In fact, Levinas comments in an interview that 'ethics is no longer a simple moralism of rules which decree what is virtuous. It is the original awakening of an I responsible for the other,' "The Awakening of the I," *Is It Righteous to Be?* 182. See also Amit Pinchevski, *By Way of Interruptions: Levinas and the Ethics of Communication*, 10.

32. *Correlations in Rosenzweig and Levinas*, 182.

33. Levinas, *Autrement qu'être ou au-delà de l'essence*, 194f.; *Otherwise than Being or Beyond Essence*, 122f., emphasis in text. Cf. "Essence and Disinterestedness," *Basic Philosophical Writings*, where Levinas notes that 'Responsibility goes beyond being. In sincerity, in frankness, in the veracity of the Saying, in the uncoveredness of suffering, being is altered. But this saying remains, in its activity, a passivity; more passive than all passivity, for it is a sacrifice without reserve, without holding back, and therefore nonvoluntary – the sacrifice of a hostage designated who has not chosen himself to be hostage, but, possibly, elected by the Good, in an involuntary election not assumed by the elected one,' 121f.

34. See Gibbs, *Why Ethics? Signs of Responsibility*, 57.

35. Peperzak, *Beyond: The philosophy of Emmanuel Levinas*, 109. See also Rudolf Bernet, "The Encounter with the Stranger: Two Interpretations of the Vulnerability of the Skin," *The Face of the Other and the Trace of God*, 60.

36. Levinas, *Autrement qu'être ou au-delà de l'essence*, 199 ; *Otherwise than Being or Beyond Essence*, 125, emphasis in text. Cf. ibid., where Levinas defines the soul using comparable language: 'In the form of responsibility, the psyche in the soul is the other in me, a malady of identity, both accused and *self*, the same for the other, the same by the other. Quid pro quo, it is a substitution, extraordinary. It is neither a deception nor truth, but the preliminary intelligibility of signification,' 112; 69, emphasis in text.

37. *Emmanuel Levinas: The Genealogy of Ethics*, 146.

38. See Jeffrey L. Kosky, *Levinas and the Philosophy of Religion*, 95.

39. Alvin Dueck and David Goodman, "Expiation, Substitution, and Surrender: Levinasian Implications for Psychotherapy," *Pastoral Psychology* 55, no. 5 (May 2007): 603f.

40. Levinas, *Autrement qu'être ou au-delà de l'essence*, 156; *Otherwise than Being or Beyond Essence*, 99. Bernasconi notes that, within the context of responsibility, the self is challenged. He also notes that Levinas's notion of responsibility is non-conventional in the sense that one is elected to, and hence answerable, for everything to everyone. This asymmetrical responsibility is far more radically exigent than one

simply requiring one to be responsible for what one has chosen, Introduction to "Substitution," *Basic Philosophical Writings*, 79.

41. See Bergo, *Levinas Between Ethics and Politics: For the Beauty that Adorns the Earth*, 156.

42. Levinas, *Autrement qu'être ou au-delà de l'essence*, 31; *Otherwise than Being or Beyond Essence*, 15. See also Brian Schroeder, *Altared Ground: Levinas, History, and Violence*, 100f.

43. *Liturgy of the Neighbor*, 219, emphasis in text. This preordained imposition substantiates ethical antecedence for Levinas in what he calls the 'heteronomy of ethical obedience,' "Philosophy and Transcendence," *Alterity and Transcendence*, 34f.

44. "Ethics as First Philosophy," *The Levinas Reader*, 84. Cf. Bernhard Waldenfels, "Response and Responsibility," *Ethics as First Philosophy*, 43f.

45. *Self and Salvation: Being Transformed*, (Cambridge: Cambridge University Press, 1999) 47.

46. Ibid., 67. For another important text apposite to the idolatries of ontology, see Jean- Luc Marion, *God Without Being*, trans. Thomas A. Carlson (Chicago: The University of Chicago Press, 1991). It is Marion's contention that thought attached to the thinking of being is lacking in precision, and that one must pass through the divine and holy before addressing the question of being, 41.

47. Ibid., 68.

48. Ibid., 71.

49. Ibid.

50. See Cohen, *Ethics, Exegesis, and Philosophy*, 337.

51. In the interview "Responsibility and Substitution," Levinas comments that 'For me, the notion of substitution is tied to the notion of responsibility.... Here, the existential adventure of the neighbor would matter more to the I than does its own, and would thus posit the I straightaway as responsible for this alterity in its trials, as if the upsurge of the human within the economy of being overturned ontology's meaning and plot. All of the culture of the human seems to me to be oriented by this new "plot," in which the in-itself of a being persisting in its being is surpassed in the gratuity of being outside-of-oneself, for the other, in the act of sacrifice or the possibility of sacrifice, in holiness,' *Is It Righteous To Be?* 228f.

52. Levinas, *Autrement qu'être ou au-delà de l'essence*, 180f.; *Otherwise than Being or Beyond Essence*. 114f., emphasis in text.

53. "What is the Question to which 'Substitution' is the Answer?" *The Cambridge Companion to Levinas*, 241.

54. Levinas, *Autrement qu'être ou au-delà de l'essence*, 172; *Otherwise than Being or Beyond Essence*, 108.

55. Ibid., 177; 112. Cf. Levinas, "Énigme et Phénomène," *En découvrant l'existence avec Husserl et Heidegger*, 214; "Enigma and Phenomena," *Collected Philosophical Papers*, 71.

56. Ibid., 202f.; 127f.

57. Levinas, "A Religion for Adults," *Difficult Freedom: Essays on Judaism*, 16f., emphasis in text.

58. Ibid., 19. Jeffrey Dudiak finds in this ennobling courage reducible to responsibility for the neighbor one factor that disabuses Levinas's thought from that containable in a positive theology. It also 'keeps his inevitable thematization of God from believing in its theme, its *theo-logos*. What theology forgets, according to Levinas, is that the word of God is still absent from the phrase in which God is for the first

time involved in words, that the God concept does not come first, but depends for its life upon the subject saying itself to the other, the responsible subject that, qua responsibility, testifies to the glory of the Infinite. What theology forgets, in short, is the ambivalence across which the revelation of transcendence qua transcendent is possible. It is only across the interruption of the said, of active consciousness in correlation with immanent objects, [that] the regime of the *logos* and its theology, that the saying without a said, testifies – across the passivity of passivity of responsibility, entirely while remaining in the world and caught up in its "influences," and thus saying a said, but *saying it to the other* – to transcendence, to the glory of the infinite, and, without invoking the name, testifies to God,' *The Intrigue of Ethics*, 341, emphasis in text.

59. Ibid., 20, emphasis in text. According to Jeffrey Bloechl, 'The themes of individual freedom and responsibility for the other person come together in what might be called the *ethics of respect*, where the term *respect* signifies a concern with that other person *as* other,' *Liturgy of the Neighbor*, 25, emphasis in text.

60. Ibid., 22.

61. *Elevations*, 130.

62. *Sensibility and Singularity: The Problem of Phenomenology in Levinas*, 120.

63. Levinas, *Autrement qu'être ou au-delà de l'essence*, 198; *Otherwise than Being or Beyond Essence*, 124.

64. See Levinas, "A Religion for Adults," *Difficult Freedom*, 18f.

65. Levinas, *Autrement qu'être ou au-delà de l'essence*, 199; *Otherwise than Being or Beyond Essence*, 125, emphasis in text.

66. Ibid., 210; 134.

67. Ibid., 213; 136. Cf. Peperzak, who notes that 'If there is some *x* to which all beings in the beingness owe what they are, this *x* cannot "be" of the order of Being, beingness, or essence. It should "be not contaminated by being," but how can such a non-thing neither be, nor "be" nothing at all? Or, in other words, how is it possible to prove that the subordination of all thought to the comprehension of Being is a "myth" that has to be destroyed?' *Beyond: The Philosophy of Emmanuel Levinas*, 88.

68. "The Question of God," *The Face of the Other and the Trace of God*, 255, emphasis in text.

69. Levinas, *Autrement qu'être ou au-delà de l'essence*, 212; *Otherwise than Being or Beyond Essence*, 135. Cf. Levinas, *Ethics and Infinity*, where one reads: 'In this book [*Otherwise Than Being*] I speak of responsibility as the essential, primary, and fundamental structure of subjectivity. For I describe subjectivity in ethical terms. Ethics, here, does not supplement a preceding existential base; the very node of the subjective is knotted in ethics and understood as responsibility. I understand responsibility as responsibility for the Other, thus as responsibility for what is not my deed, or for what does not even matter to me,' 95, *Éthique et Infini*, 101f.

70. See Atterton, *On Levinas*, 66.

71. Ibid., 216f.; 138. In "Responsibility and Substitution," Levinas comments that 'For me, the notion of substitution is tied to the notion of responsibility. To substitute oneself does not amount to putting oneself in the place of the other man in order to feel what he feels; it does not involve becoming the other or, if he be destitute and desperate, the courage of such a trial. Rather, substitution entails bringing comfort by associating ourselves with the essential weakness and finitude of the other; it is to bear his weight while sacrificing one's interestedness and complacency-in-being, which then turn into responsibility for the other,' *Is it Righteous to Be?* 228.

72. See Chapter Two of this thesis, "Positioning." Cf. Moshe Reiss, "Abraham's Moment of Decision: According to Levinas and Rembrant," *Jewish Bible Quarterly* 35 no. 1 (January-March 2007): 57f.

73. Ibid., 218; 139. See also John llewelyn, *Appositions of Jacques Derrida and Emmanuel Levinas*, 204f.

74. According to Peperzak, Levinas is in constant quest of a peace irreducible to the calculations inherent in the politics of reason. He further notes that 'this peace is inherent to the originary relationship of unique individuals, a relationship that precedes the constitution of any state or totality based on roles and functional definitions of the participating members only,' *To The Other*, 127.

75. Levinas, *Autrement qu'être ou au-delà de l'essence*, 221; *Otherwise than Being or Beyond Essence*, 143.

76. Ibid., 222; 142. This de-substantiation prompted by a driving restlessness is exactly the enucleation and self-fissuring so prevalent in later Levinas.

77. Levinas, "The Proximity of the Other," *Is it Righteous to Be?* 212.

78. See 55f., 64, 67, 72, 74, 79, 138, 155, 191.

79. Levinas, *Autrement qu'être ou au-delà de l'essence*, p. 126; *Otherwise than Being or Beyond Essence*, 79.

80. *Levinas and Theology* (Cambridge: Cambridge University Press, 2006) 158. See also Marie Louise Baird, "Revisioning Christian Theology in Light of Emmanuel Levinas's Ethics of Responsibility," *Journal of Ecumenical Studies* 36, no. 3-4 (Summer-Fall 1999): 346.

81. Levinas, *Autrement qu'être ou au-delà de l'essence*, 224; *Otherwise than Being or Beyond Essence*, 143. One might view Levinas's mixing of metaphors as a mangling of sense, particularly here where it appears three motifs clash. Colin Davis, however, sees this as a hermeneutical device implemented by Levinas in order to challenge the reader into participation with the text. He notes that '*Otherwise than Being* is an astonishingly difficult text, and astonishment is, Levinas suggests, what the book is all about.... The boldest move made in *Otherwise than Being* is the attempt to find a textual practice appropriate to its central thesis about language. The difficulty of the work and the problems of understanding that it poses are not tangential to the point, they *are* the point. Interrogating Levinas's text becomes a process of self-interrogation, as local problems of understanding confront the reader with more fundamental questions: "What does Levinas mean by responsibility?" slips into "What is my responsibility, how am I responsible for my neighbor?" The reader makes the text, and in the process makes herself,' *Levinas: An Introduction*, 91, emphasis in text.

82. Ibid., 226; 144f. According to Jill Robbins, there are substantial risks in collating subjectivity through the face of the other with the glory of the infinite, as well as consequences involved when one considers Levinas's notion of the ethical event in light of these disturbances. Robbins notes that 'The ethical event has an ontological insecurity because withdrawal is built into the trace's presentation.' This insecurity prompts one to question whether the ethical event "happened" at all. This uncertainty prompts Robbins to add that 'Strictly speaking, it does not happen; nothing forces us to take up the obligation, the imperative of responsibility that the face delivers; the imposition is altogether without force.' This lack of coercion implies a necessary risk. However, 'without this risk, the alterity of the other drops out altogether. And this is the risk that Levinas's theology is willing to run when he asks whether religions do not come to us from a past that has never been present and when

he asserts that "the trace is the proximity of God in the face of the other,"' "Tracing Responsibility," *Ethics as First Philosophy*, 178f.

83. Ibid., 229; 146.

84. Ibid., 232; 148.

85. Ibid. See also Peter Ochs, "Holy Other: Leaving Self Behind," *Living Pulpit* 10 no. 3 (July, 2001): 16.

86. Ibid., 233; 149.

87. "Theology and Philosophy of Religion according to Levinas," *Ethics as First Philosophy*, 170.

88. Levinas, *Autrement qu'être ou au-delà de l'essence*, 233; *Otherwise than Being or Beyond Essence*, 149. See also David Michael Levin, "Tracework: Myself and Others in the Moral Phenomenology of Merleau-Ponty and Levinas," *International Journal of Philosophical Studies* 6 no. 3 (1998): 345f.

89. Ibid. For more on Levinas, God and gift, see Jacques Derrida, *The Gift of Death*, trans. David Wills (Chicago: The University of Chicago Press, 1995) 48f.; and Robyn Horner, *Rethinking God as Gift: Marion, Derrida, and the Limits of Phenomenology* (New York: Fordham University Press, 2001) 59.

90. See Hendrik Hart, "Conceptual Understanding and Knowing *Other*-wise: Reflections on Rationality and Spirituality in Philosophy,' *Knowing Other-wise: Philosophy at the Threshold of Spirituality*, 39.

91. *Levinas and the Philosophy of Religion*, 190.

92. See Roger Burggraeve, *The Wisdom of Love in the Service of Love: Emmanuel Levinas on Justice, Peace, and Human Rights*, 101.

93. Levinas, "Dieu et la Philosophie," pp. 122f. ; "God and Philosophy," p. 75. See also Alphonso Lingis, who feels that in Levinas '... there is really not anything like an evidence, or a certainty, of God. Not only is God invisible, not manifest in the cosmic order, but his command is inaudible, or audible only in my words. The force of God, the proximity of infinity, has all its inscriptions in my own voice,' Introduction to *Otherwise than Being*, p. xli.

94. Levinas, *Autrement qu'être ou au-delà de l'essence*, 237; *Otherwise than Being or Beyond Essence*, 151. See also *Ethics and Infinity*, where Levinas notes that 'The witness testifies to what was said by himself. For he has said "Here I am!" before the Other; and from the fact that before the Other he recognizes the responsibility which is incumbent on himself, he has manifested what the face of the Other signifies for him. The glory of the Infinite reveals itself through what it is capable of doing in the witness,' 109; *Éthique et Infini*, 115f.

95. Ibid., 246f; 158f. See also Catherine Chalier, who comments that 'The "break" in man's desire to be, the interruption of being that occurs when God calls and man answers – "Here I am" – are the source of [Levinas's] new way of understanding responsibility.... According to him the main question is indeed the question of the Good beyond being,' "Levinas and the Hebraic Tradition," *Ethics as First Philosophy*, 11.

96. 'It is in prophecy that the Infinite eludes objectification and dialogue and signifies as *illeity* in the third person, but according to a "tertiality" different from that of the third man, from the third that interrupts the face-to-face of the welcome of the other man, and by which justice arises,' Levinas, "Truth of Disclosure and Truth of Testimony," *Collected Philosophical Papers*, 106.

97. *Toward the Outside*, 97.

98. "Ethics," *Handbook of Postmodern Biblical Interpretation*, ed. A. K. M. Adam (St. Louis: Chalice Press, 2000) 81.

99. Levinas, *Autrement qu'être ou au-delà de l'essence*, 245; *Otherwise than Being or Beyond Essence*, 157. For more on Levinas, illeity, and the third party, see Jeffrey Kosky, *Levinas and the Philosophy of Religion*, 191f.; John Llewelyn, *Appositions of Jacques Derrida and Emmanuel Levinas*, p. 87; Richard A. Cohen, *Elevations*, 190f.; Roger Burggraeve, *The Wisdom of Love in the Service of Love*, 135.

100. According to Robert Bernasconi, 'What [Levinas] calls sincerity is rather the vulnerability which accompanies exposure. It is not a revealing of the self so much as its destruction, which occurs in the form of an interruption of the historical order,' "The Ethics of Suspicion," *Research in Phenomenology* xx (1990): 11.

Conclusion

The Least of These

Our introduction alerted one to Levinas's constant yearning for an ideal of holiness, one that would become an 'absolute value (in) the human possibility of giving the other priority over oneself.'[1] Merging holiness with the sacredness of the other's hunger, it was further noted that for Levinas this sacrifice is tantamount to an election consisting not of privilege but responsibility. Regarding this election as a 'particularism that conditions universality,'[2] Levinas thus reduces history to a moral category commensurate to an exigency, one where obligation assumes the role of an authentic Eucharist offered to a stranger.[3] Then, finding in this moral category an ethical hermeneutic attuned to the other's dereliction, we noted that Levinas, in what Hilary Putnam describes as an intentional reduction in his writings, renders all human beings Jews.[4] Hence we find that for Levinas, as notes Bernasconi, 'Judaism is a particularity that promotes universalism, conditions it.'[5]

Finding ourselves reduced to the universal Jew prepares us for Abraham's patronage, one whose clarion 'Here I am' challenges us to an openness regarding the other. According to Levinas, it is indeed this disregard for the self that, when transposed into a hyperbolic and asymmetrical concern for the other, becomes through the mystery of responsibility a channeling of the word of God. And in honoring the absolute value where the other is given priority over oneself, this channeling itself modulates into what is herein nominated Levinas's mission to the Gentiles. As notes Levinas: 'When I speak to a Christian, I always quote Matthew 25; the relation to God is presented there as a relation to another person. It is not a metaphor: in the other, there is a real presence of God. In my relation to the other, I hear the Word of God.'[6]

Hence it would appear that Matthew 25 offers a lens through which to clarify Levinas's ethical hermeneutics, which we have exegeted thus far, into a Christian perspective, one where God speaks to all of us through our relations with the other. It should be duly noted that as we issue forth this clarification our terminology will assume a more theological tone. In fact, we have already implemented in this thesis perspectives from theologians David Ford, Ted Jennings, and Michael Purcell, noting ways their theologies engaged prominent ideas found in Levinas.

Other contemporary theologians resonate with Levinas's thinking as well. Terry A. Veling asserts that the keystone of Levinas's thought revolves around responsibility for the other. In fact, according to Veling, 'on the "other side" of theology is the Other in whose name theology is called to listen, to serve, to respond.' Veling further suggests that 'theology must pay attention once again to the Other who is both the mystery of God, the Holy One, and the face of the neighbor, the stranger, the poor one.'[7] Veling's book *Practical Theology* employs the thinking of Levinas throughout, particularly as it prompts the 'latent apprehension that everything *of God* is ultimately concerned with everything *of humanity*.' Veling, moreover, sees Levinas's thought as 'preeminently practical in its deepest instinct and orientation.'[8]

Kevin J. Vanhoozer reads Levinas through a postmodern lens. In his essay "The Atonement in Postmodernity" Vanhoozer brings to the surface ways Levinas betrays a violent pretension woven in the theoretical thought of today's culture. Vanhoozer notes how Levinas contrasts 'what can be seen or explained within the limits of reason with what cannot be thought or conceptually mastered.'[9] Along these lines, Vanhoozer in another work comments upon how Levinas's thought exposes these postmodern swerves towards reductive relativism. Here he offers that Levinas's 'ethics in a postmodern key questions the knower's attempts to subdue or master the other by forcing it into a system of ideas' and thus collapsing it into 'a form of intellectual imperialism.'[10] Last, in his contribution to *The Cambridge Companion to Postmodern Theology*, Vanhoozer stays in this key, noting how for Levinas ethics 'is not about moral systems or following rules; it is rather about respecting particularity and difference.'[11]

Two theologians read Levinas from the perspective of hospitality. Hans Boersma in his *Violence, Hospitality, and the Cross: Reappropiating the Atonement Tradition* comments upon how elements in Levinas 'are useful for Christian reflection. Hospitality is, after all, a virtue with a venerable tradition, both in the biblical witness and throughout the Christian tradition.' How does Levinas, according to Boersma, emphasize this approach? He 'takes his starting point in the face of the other who is knocking on the door. The alterity of the other places me immediately under obligation of hospitality.'[12] Amos Yong, from a more evangelical stance, also draws heavily upon Levinas's notion of hospitality. Yong strives to connect the hospitality of God with a pneumatological theology 'of guests and hosts for the postmodern and pluralistic world of the twenty-first century.'[13] Yong involves Levinas with this connection, particularly where he 'points out that hospitality involves, from the point of view of the "host," a divesting of one's own concerns so as to be a "hostage" to the guest.'[14] Finally, for Yong, this divesting is so profound that is makes hospitality in Levinas unconditional.

Having thus located Levinas within a broader matrix of contemporary theology, a summary is now in order to contextualize this perspective as it moves towards more exegetical emphasis, particularly as this emphasis gains import from Matthew 25.

Reduction

Since much of Levinas's thought concerns creative and operative permutations of the phenomenological reduction, Chapter One found it necessary to portray the philosophical lineage of Husserl and Heidegger as well as the way the phenomenological reduction, a process intent on neutralizing one's perspective on lived experiences, later assumed vibrancy in Levinas's ethical hermeneutics.[15] And while the phenomenological reduction provided a method by which one could reduce thought back to what is concrete, it became apparent as Levinas studied Husserl that ontological horizons were categorically different in each realm of being – dividing existence into regions, each the object of a regional ontology. Discovering this heterogeneity led Levinas to assume that existence itself was heterogeneous and that philosophical systems based on epistemology were naïve at best.[16] This assumption would later transform into what Levinas calls 'a permanent revolution' where an ethical vigilance regarding the other takes the shape of sacrificial responsibility.[17]

As noted, Levinas found ontological predilections towards homogeneity infelicitous and totalitarian.[18] What is more, the ethical vigilance resulting from these infelicities inspired him to a more calculated analysis of subjectivity, particularly ways the operational ego involved itself through intentional interfacing with things.[19] More important, though, was the fact that missing from these interfacings were those regional horizons lost in the focus of an agential consciousness implicated through time. Hence freedom for the self, at least at this stage of the saga, simply meant an ego coincident with itself – one, in other words, experiencing freedom as solipsism. This realization for Levinas was highly significant, and it imposed an incumbency upon our analysis to focus particularly on those intentional interfacings.

A Liminal Urge

Chapter Two engaged the necessity of parsing existence and the existent, particularly through the different ways Levinas implicated various moods – states such as fatigue, indolence, and insomnia – in order to adumbrate ambient affectivities and tonalities normally unintelligible.[20] Indeed, a critical sense of these ambient moods signaled Levinas to a fundamental investigation of the upsurge of an existent into existence, a process he denoted hypostasis.[21]

Hypostasis is an essential event in Levinas, as it not only depicts the birth of subjectivity, but also depicts the drama of separation between the ego and the self. Moreover consciousness, the hypostasized corporal self, now becomes explicit to itself in inwardness, participating in the sobering up we alluded to as insomnia. This restive consciousness also exhibits an incipient leaning towards the other, one that will be inscribed later in the exilic self. Hence the insomnia and sobering-up constituting this labile self is indicative of a liminal urge toward responsibility. This compulsion will later prompt the sacrificial substitution depicted in Chapter Seven. Therefore Chapter Two allowed a proper introduction illustrating this incipient yearning away from the machinations of self, an urge that later assumes prominence as responsibility in Levinas takes on the shape of sacrifice.

Chapter Three put a face on the other, leaning heavily on Peperzak's seminal research involving the early Levinas essay "Philosophy and the Idea of Infinity." Significantly, we noted how the philosophy of autonomy, which aims to ensure the freedom or the identity of beings, uses that freedom as an assimilative violence that reduces all the elements of exteriority into totalitarian and synoptic truth.[22] However, in order for a true transcendence to be possible, the other must concern the I – while at the same time remaining external to it. We also wanted to show that the other's face is concerned with the ego while at the same time external to the ego; and to exhibit the fact that without any mediation, the face in Levinas displays an exceptional capacity to lift the subject to responsibility. Again, noting early this capacity and predilection toward radical responsibility furthered our theme by registering its provenance in the self, thus beginning the initial charting of the ego's sojourn toward the other.

Chapter Three also provided insight into the crucial Levinasian notion of infinity, noting how the I, when thinking infinity, contains the uncontained, thus exhibiting how an idea can exceed a concept – and, more importantly, how this notion of infinity has been *put* into us, thus establishing it as an experience *par excellence*.[23] This in turn led us to the preeminent theme in Levinas: 'Experience, the idea of infinity, occurs in the relationship with the other. The idea of infinity is the social relationship.'[24] This assertion alerted us to the disturbance inherent in the idea of infinity – which allowed us to move from the idea of infinity in experience, through vigilance, to the exigent responsibility inherent in ethical resistance.

What makes this move so significant to our analysis is this: awakening to the presence of ethical resistance prompts one to renounce the petty imperialisms and injustices endemic to the ego. This renunciation in turn calls our freedom into question. Thus antecedent to knowledge, the ethical relationship is objectified by this resistance. But for now one is engaged fully in ethical resistance, a resistance incited by the other and made conscious through the epiphany of language. Preliminary to knowledge, the ethical relationship thus objectifies this resistance, inundating as it does every conception of the same, and breaking as it does with cognition and commanding the self towards a purer experience.

Again, this experience is language, which is contingent on the face-to-face relation, and is — vital to our argument — an experience expressing a command and an exchange of themes.[25] Hence language itself is a preoriginal offering to the other; one, moreover, breaking the self away from it solipsistic trappings; and one ingredient to Levinas's authentic Eucharist to the other. We concluded Chapter Three by asserting that ethical resistance — the presence of infinity — was now ethical consciousness, a consciousness made real in a freedom invested by the heteronymous other, an investiture further aggravated and ennobled through responsibility.

A Responsible Self

Chapter Four provided a hermeneutical pivot by concretizing and isolating Levinas's ethical metaphysics in the figure of Abraham. By circuiting through *Totality and Infinity*, particularly its essential problematic concerning the nakedness and vulnerability of the face of the other, we analyzed Levinas's messianic eschatology through the filter of the ethical resistance presented in the previous chapter. Reducing Levinas's ethical metaphysics to Abraham was crucial in that it not only particularized the universal jewishness addressed earlier, but also provided a personal and patriarchal frame within which radical hospitality to the other could later be presented. In line with these roles and ways they thread with Levinas's mission, we noted how Jewish particularism was 'consistent with Israel having been chosen historically to preach universalism and to be an example to light the way for the Gentiles.'[26] Realizing responsibility complemented this election, specifically in ways it reflected the asymmetrical ethical onus particularized in each self. The exegetical section dealing with Abraham in Chapter Four thus anticipates our later exegesis on Matthew 25. It was our contention that responsibility assumes flesh and blood for Levinas in the person of Abraham.[27]

Thus, by alluding to Abraham while at the same time clarifying his assertion that 'the subject, while preserving itself, has the possibility of not returning to itself,'[28] Levinas is in fact submitting again that asymmetrical intersubjectivity is the locus of transcendence, and that radical ethical service convolving obligation and transcendence essentially roots ethical precedence firmly in the place of the other. We portray in fact Levinas staging an exodus away from ontological security, pairing transcendence with what is now becoming a responsible self.

This responsible self now is called to liturgy, a term that in Levinas means ethics itself.[29] As mentioned, this is a performative responsibility, one where liturgy is an ethical optics breaking contextualization through a hyperbolic vigilance for the other, a vigilance bordering on obsession. In fact, as we noted, there is no conceptual differentiation in Levinas between obsession and responsibility.[30] Finally, Chapter Four introduced us to the crucial notion of the Master in Levinas.

Towards Substitution

In Chapter Five Levinas joins discourse with desire, finding a more primordial connection with the other than that reduced to synthetic agencies. We noted how language in Levinas implies separation, thus relegating a metaphysical status to the other, one mirroring Levinas's ethical optics. This ethical optics prompts a relation commensurable with a foundational event of separation contingent on the other's inassimilable nature. Retarding the ego's proclivity towards mastery and possession, we noted how this separation emphasized and hyperbolized the asymmetrical relation of the self and the other, rendering the other precedential.[31]

Discourse with the other implicates separation without degrading into autonomy, thus breaking synoptic systems reducible to symmetry and categories of correlation. Significantly, in Chapter Five we also addressed Levinas's critical notion of freedom, particularly how, through the crucible of language, it heightens the vigilance constitutive of ethical resistance. For Levinas freedom does not have the final say. Nor is it the dominion of truth. Indeed, as noted, truth for Levinas is reflective of a relation with the other who operates as Master and who, furthermore, lifts discourse into the domain of responsibility.[32]

Chapter Five further presented the trace as a disturbance, a calling, and an invitation to exodus. Irreducible to a sign, the trace in Levinas localizes the absence in the diachrony (or breach) betraying God, allowing the face to witness to this betrayal, hence concretizing responsibility beyond intentionality through involvement with the other. This exigency beyond intentionality we noted was a sacrificial goodness where God, the other, the face and the trace merge in responsibility. This brought us to a critical crossroad, one where the subject in Levinas, disabused of its selfishness, comes to the realization that 'Man as Other comes to us from the outside, a separated – or holy—face.'[33] Welcoming the holy yet derelict face modulates obligation into hospitality, bringing us to our central tenet: 'The subject is a host.'[34] At this crossroad Abraham, the consummate host artlessly offering hospitality to God and stranger, shares signifiers with Levinas's bread offered to the stranger in *Otherwise than Being*, hence prefiguring the Authentic Eucharist offered to the Gentiles. So doing, the boundary between immanence and transcendence is rendered transparent through the giving of self and substance, a transparency localized in the face.

In Chapter Six we further presented responsibility in Levinas as rooted in ethical exigencies and the demands they make upon subjectivity. Keying in on his seminal essay "God and Philosophy," we focused on the struggle between the same and the other, between totality and infinity – particularly as it presents diachrony as breaking apart the coincidence of meaning, essence, and presence. We further noted how this fissuring allowed Levinas a breach where meaning beyond being can, through the trace, prioritize the passage of the divine in accordance with a direction irreducible to theology and philosophy. This direction, we said, reflected the ordination and command coming from the face of the other, and hence presented a third way beyond immanence and transcendence, one warped and woofed in responsibility.

Significantly, we have traced the sojourn of the self through its solipsistic permutations, now channeling disturbance into the generosity and obedience ingredient to responsibility. This creative insomnia is attributable to the fact that the self experiences a sobering contingent upon the awakening to the other. In fact, awakening to the other is commensurate with sacrifice and responsibility, both of which find logical fulfillment in Levinas's concept of substitution. We devoted our whole previous Chapter Seven to exegeting this essential motif of substitution in Levinas, implementing it as a hermeneutic portal to our concluding chapter which contextualizes and implicates Christian mission in the thought of Levinas. Chapter Seven also introduced us to the crucial notion of witnessing in Levinas, one we will now transpose into a Christian key.

Towards Christ

Christians are charged by the gospel to attend to the least and lost, a commission essentially extending the Judaic entrustment to reach out for those in need. The other encountered is reducible to the mission field, and the intentionality inherent in the desire for the other will fashion faith as phenomenological. While this proposal may seem controversial, it has significant lineage, particularly that left by Dietrich Bonhoeffer. His notion of nonreligious interpretation as well as his concern for genuine witnessing offer a methodological counterpoint addressing a new 'sphere of the church,' one where `Christ takes everyone who really encounters him by the shoulder, turning them around to face their fellow human beings and the world.'[35] As we shall discover, this turning to face the other by Christ radicalizes 'what you have done to the least of these' in Matthew 25. It also, as we shall see, draws from those witnessing Christ undertones implicit in Levinas.

Christ's mission was one of surrendering to and sacrificing for the other.[36] As Bonhoeffer noted, 'God lets himself be pushed out of the world on to the cross.'[37] For Christians this surrendering, this kenosis or emptying, was inaugurated in Christ's incarnation, initiated in his baptism, promulgated in his ministry, exhibited in his crucifixion, and is now witnessed when hands and hearts, through the Spirit, are offered to the other.[38] Today, however, 'Christendom is largely dissolved, and the peoples of Europe and North America are increasingly secular.'[39] And for those obsessed with self-interests, barraged with product, and webbed in information, a prescriptive ethos observing sacrificial concern for the other is for some a minor inconvenience; but for most it is an experiential contradiction, moving as it does contra-grain to our consumer world. Yet still some are called to other harvests: called, in fact, to the scattered lonely. These other harvests, indeed, when viewed through the lens of Christ, clarify community through the boldness of witness. In *Life Together* Bonhoeffer offers (in non-inclusive language) that 'God has put his Word into the mouth of men in order that it may be communicated to other men. When one person is struck by the Word, he speaks it to others. God has willed that we should seek and find his living Word in the witness of a brother, in the mouth of men.'[40]

For Christians using Emmanuel Levinas's metaphysical ethics as a paradigm for witnessing, a methodology proposing exclusive status to the other must be centrifugal, seeing Christ in and as the other. Thus Christians perform what they intend, all the while exemplifying an exilic progression symbolic of the escape from self emphasized so dramatically in Levinas and keynoted in this analysis. And as this escape from self is actualized through the sacrifice of self carried all the way to substitution, only a hyperbolic emphasis on the hermeneutics of vigilance can suffice. Further, one journeying to God journeys through and to the other. This encounter, moreover, prompts what Levinas calls the 'glory of the Infinite . . . substituting for the other, a responsibility ordered to the first one on the scene, a responsibility for the neighbor, inspired by the other.'[41] Gathered about this glory are a constellation of ideas, many illuminating Christian themes.

We are told by Levinas that 'Election traverses the concept of the ego' and that 'obligation calls for a unique response not inscribed in universal thought, the unforeseeable response of the chosen one.' We also find our responsibility is an 'ordination' that 'commands us to the other.' Sacrificial life permeates this language, witnessed in a 'Hospitality, the-one-for-the-other' where we are both encouraged and challenged that 'Being torn from oneself for another in giving to the other the bread from one's own mouth is being able to give up one's soul for another.'[42]

Thus for Christians Levinas offers a new discipline, one requisite of an extreme vigilance deemed insomnia-like in its obsession and one heralded as sacramental. Naturally implicit in this call to sacrifice, in this 'giving to the other bread from one's mouth,' is the Eucharist. And if witnessing Christians are called to see Christ in the other, and if (as Dietrich Bonhoeffer claims) Christ is 'the man for others'[43] – then this sacrifice tropes as 'an account of the sacraments as the earthly prolongation of Christ's glorified bodiliness' witnessed in the fact 'that the Church's sacraments are not things but encounters of men on earth with the glorified man Jesus *by way of a visible form*.'[44] Hence while the outer husks of the sacraments may have been discarded, there remains left the stranger grain worthy of bread.

A Transportable Temple

Again, while this rendering of sacrificial life as it concerns responsibility to the other may rub some as unorthodox, it nonetheless resonates sympathetically with Bonhoeffer's concept of 'nonreligious interpretation.'[45] In fact, according to Alister E. McGrath, 'Bonhoeffer's *Letters and Papers from Prison* argues for "religionless Christianity": the church exists "for others," and if it is to be relevant in a "world come of age" it must discard traditional religious expressions which have become meaningless in an age of increasing secularization.'⁴⁶ Of significance regarding this increasing secularization is this section in Bonhoeffer's prison letters. Here he asks himself

> Who is God? Not in the first place an abstract God, in his omnipotence etc. That is not a genuine experience of God, but a partial extension of the world. Encounter with Jesus Christ. The experience that a transformation of all human life is given in the fact that "Jesus is there only for others." ... Faith is participation in this being of Jesus (incarnation, cross, resurrection). Our relation to God is not a "religious" relationship to the highest, most powerful, and best Being imaginable – that is not authentic transcendence – but our relation to God is a new life in "existence for others," through participation in the being of Jesus. The transcendence is not infinite and unattainable tasks, but the neighbor who is within reach in any given situation. God in human form . . ., "the man for others," and therefore the Crucified, the man who lives out of the transcendent.⁴⁷

There is a noteworthy confluence of themes here: the exigency of obligation in Bonhoeffer dispatched towards 'the neighbor who is within reach in any given situation' interweaves with the radical urgency in Levinas's 'responsibility ordered to the first one on the scene.' Moreover, as when with Bonhoeffer the emphasis is on an encountering Christ, our new paradigm will focus on witnessing Christ – accenting all the while the Levinasian nonreciprocal nature of this engagement. (Remember our credo: the other is precedential.) Moreover, this witnessing, transposed through the one for others to the others, adumbrates Christ just as margins reveal event-horizons in phenomenology.

Here is why: If the other just as he or she is occupies a place of sovereignty and dominion, then the way I approach this other and the language I use is of vital significance. Significant also is the notion that we are *called* to this obedience to the other; that we are *responsible* beyond measure and determination; and that one's life before the other is in the accusative. As notes Peperzak, these measures prompt one to address the other thusly:

> '*Me voice*' – 'See me, here and now.' The subjectivity of this 'me' is being the one – the unique and only one – who is responsible for any other who arises in front of me. Affected by the defenseless nudity of another's face, I am exposed and inescapably delivered to an orientation that does not rest upon a choice of mine. . . . Against the dogma of an original and originary liberty, and against its total abolition of some writers today, Levinas shows that obligations of my responsibility do not stem from any decision or contact or convention originating in my or our will. Before I even think or choose or freely accept, I have become responsible. My responsibility for the others has begun before I became aware of my own being.⁴⁸

Intrinsic in this responsibility is the metaphorical and antecedent intentionality of faith. If those witnessing Christ believe that the stranger they meet is Christ, then Christ is both the way, truth, and life of this intentionality.⁴⁹ Hence access, the phenomenological road to the object, the journey of faith, and responsibility all bear within their ambit christological ramifications when viewed from the paradigm of those witnessing Christ.

Moreover, insofar as those witnessing do so with the *modus operandi* of endless donation, with an epistemology of the gift and endless leave-taking, then the place of worship stays mobile with the stranger. As Levinas was prone to assert, man can adore God 'in a transportable temple.'[50]

This centrifugal movement of Christian witness reflects as well the thought of Franz Rosenzweig, whose influence on Levinas was invaluable. Rosenzweig in fact alerted Levinas to the possibility of a symbiotic reconciliation between Judiasm and Christianity. For Rosenzweig mission was exclusively a Christian obligation, one whose task was to faithfully engage a pagan culture by spreading the light of God's word. What is more, this symbiosis promulgated a missional centrifugality where Christians shone as rays from the fire of God. Since the annunciation of peace is the transcendental base for ethical experience in Levinas, where prophecy and the ethical converge in the saying of 'Here I am,'[51] it appears one is needed to whom to extend this annunciatory offering, one who behaves as a de facto church: the church of the other.[52] Significantly, this annunciation, focused through the lens of responsibility, may be viewed as Levinas's mission to the Gentiles. Furthermore, this mission is grounded in narrative.

One For Others

Interpersonal relationships involve narrative: the encounter with the other is a narrative experience: 'It is because we all live out narratives in our lives and because we understand our own lives in terms of the narratives that we live out that the form of narrative is appropriate for understanding the action of others.'[53] Naturally narrative takes place in time. And for Levinas, time is 'the turning of the Same toward the Other.'[54] This inversion, this breaking away from the gravity of being, results in a deformalization of time, dismissing it from the logic of sequence, implicating it in the agency of encounter. Through witnessing, a contextual hermeneutic is suffused into this agency of encounter, prompting an intensified ethos in 'both conversations in particular and human actions in general' that are demonstrated through 'enacted narratives.'[55]

Interestingly, these enacted narratives offer a fresh perspective on what James E. Loder calls an 'integrated functioning of the new competence.' Loder offers that 'transposition takes place as the capacity for creative behavior is moved from actual time and actual discovery into fictive time, thus becoming the plot for transformational narratives.' Resonating with what Levinas calls a 'diachronic transcendence' where everything depends on 'the possibility of vibrating with a meaning that is not synchronized,' here with Loder we discover 'narrative forms that move from an initial lack, loss, or dilemma into a gain over the original conditions' through the provisions of 'the narrative equivalent of intuition or insight.' One finds in this process how to 'transpose transformational logic . . . into stories that tell us who we are, why we are, and what is our destiny.'[56] For Christians, our destiny is the encounter with the other, one that heralds an ecclesiological moment. Applying his logic to this moment, Loder then states that 'the Christ event is the historical paradigm of transformation.'[57]

Much here warrants unpacking. For Christians, the 'Christ event' will be what Bonhoeffer noted as participation with the 'one for others' that occurs when those in need are mercifully addressed.[58] He called this participation, when shielded in love, faith. Without this shield, however, 'such faith is not faith at all, but hypocrisy. It is of no use to anyone for someone to confess his faith in Christ if he has not gone first and reconciled himself to his brother [Levinas's "the first one on the scene"], to the reality of each of his brothers, even to the godless, racially different, ostracized, and outcast.'[59] This experience attunes those witnessing to the intuitive narratives evoked through these participatory encounters. Levinas as well offered an 'intuitionist conception of meaning' which states unequivocally that 'Intuition remains the source of all intelligibility.'[60] Seamlessly Levinas commutes this intuition towards what he calls a 'signifying intention' where 'meaning would be the very illumination of this horizon.'[61] As we have consistently offered, merged on the horizon in works of Levinas are God and the other.

For this new missional paradigm, the approach of the other is an ordination, invocation, and exposition. Moreover, for those witnessing, just as for Levinas, 'the proximity of the Other is presented as the fact that the Other is not simply close to me in space . . . but he approaches me essentially insofar as I feel myself – insofar as I am – responsible for him . . . . I analyze the inter-human relationship as if, in proximity with the Other – his face, the expressive in the Other, were what *ordains* me to serve him.'[62] Significantly, what Bonhoeffer signals as faith, as participation in this 'one for others,' Levinas signals as an intuition burgeoning intentional when ordained through the sacrificial responsibility for the other.

Liturgy

While Levinas was a Talmudic scholar and practicing Jew, enigmas abound regarding his relationship to Christianity. As noted, his reverence of Rosenzweig steeped him in the notion of Christian mission. In *Wittgenstein and Levinas*, Bob Plant alludes to Levinas's 'Catholicism.'[63] What is more, before Levinas's death Jacques Derrida, his close friend and astute critic, noted 'I can't help recall the day when, listening to a lecture by Andre Neher at a Congress of Jewish Intellectuals, Emmanuel Levinas turned to me and said, with the general irony so familiar to us: "You see, he's the Jewish Protestant, and I'm the Catholic" – a quip that would call for long and serious reflection.'[64] Added to that, Derrida in his essay "Beyond" further implicates Levinas in an insinuated Christianity.[65]

Levinas was straightforward and unambiguous, however, when directing Christians to engage Matthew 25. It is the only Gospel passage he references by name and chapter, and he does so often and emphatically.[66] This emphasis reflects his life's work of honoring the asymmetrical responsibility one has to the other. This honoring and obligation, moreover, involves witnessing Christians in what Levinas called the epiphany of the other, and again this epiphany is reducible to the face. Notes Levinas: 'One says: the face of the other. But what I say about the face of the neighbor, the Christian probably says about the face of Christ.'[67]

And Levinas witnessed to this face of Christ as embodied in the other through the text of Matthew 25. Notes Levinas:

> The teaching in them (the Gospels), and the representation of human beings in them, appeared always familiar to me. As a result, I was led to Matthew 25, where the people are astonished to hear that they have abandoned and persecuted God. They eventually find out that while they were sending the poor away, they were actually sending God himself away. I always said, after I became acquainted with the concept of the Eucharist, that the authentic Eucharist is actually in the moment when the other comes to face me. The personality of the divine is *there*, more so than in the bread and wine.[68]

Remember liturgy plays a vital role in Levinas, one we have highlighted throughout this analysis. Consider as well Michael Barnes's assertion that 'liturgy as the responsible practice of the tradition before the face of the Other provides a powerful metaphor for understanding Levinas's project.'[69] So in essence, staying true to our introduction's pledge that we will aim towards a transparency regarding Levinas's work, letting his writing carry the burden of its own proof; as well as our assertion that the other will be origin and destination, and that themes and concepts will be taken apart, examined, and then reconfigured around a Levinasian notion of responsibility; and that difficult freedom herein will be equivalent with the severe obligation Levinas calls all to pursue that devote themselves 'to service with no thought of reward' as it relates to a 'burden carried out at its own expense. . . . This is the original and incontestable meaning of the Greek word *liturgy*'[70] – indeed, staying true to this pledge we can assert that the authentic Eucharist of which Levinas speaks is this service with no thought of reward – and the burden carried would be as bread for the other.

I Was a Stranger

The pericope in Matthew referenced by Levinas engages trenchantly this liturgy, this burden carried out at its own expense. Verses 31 through 46 read as follows:

> When the Son of Man comes in his glory, and all the angels with him, he will sit on his throne in heavenly glory. All the nations will be gathered before him, and he will separate the people one from another as a shepherd separates the sheep from the goats. He will put the sheep on his right and the goats on his left. Then the King will say to those on his right, 'Come, you who are blessed by my Father; take your inheritance, the kingdom prepared for you since the creation of the world. For I was hungry and you gave me something to eat, I was thirsty and you gave me something to drink, I was a stranger and you invited me in, I needed clothes and you clothed me, I was sick and you looked

after me, I was in prison and you came to visit me.' Then the righteous will answer him, 'Lord, when did we see you hungry and feed you, or thirsty and give you something to drink? When did we see you a stranger and invite you in, or needing clothes and clothe you? When did we see you sick or in prison and go to visit you?' The King will reply, 'I tell you the truth, whatever you did for one of the least of these brothers of mine, you did for me.' Then he will say to those on his left, 'Depart from me, you who are cursed, into the eternal fire prepared for the devil and his angels. For I was hungry and you gave me nothing to eat, I was thirsty and you gave me nothing to drink, I was a stranger and you did not invite me in, I needed clothes and you did not clothe me, I was sick and in prison and you did not look after me.' They also will answer, 'Lord, when did we see you hungry or thirsty or a stranger or needing clothes or sick or in prison, and did not help you?' He will reply, 'I tell you the truth, whatever you did not do for one of the least of these, you did not do for me.' Then they will go away to eternal punishment, but the righteous to eternal life.[71]

This text behaves as a winnowing fork, leaving none to prevaricate as to who is left and who is right. We know what the passage asserts: One who attends to the other attends to Christ. We also are not unaware of some academic leanings, particularly those that depict those in need 'either as Christians in general or Christian missionaries in particular.'[72]

But why would those behaving thusly be astounded if they knew they were offering succor to those of their own stripe? Again, there is an antecedence involved, one that we have analyzed in Levinas through the lens of responsibility, and one that operates here in those proffering mercy. Notes Douglas Hare: 'The motif of astonishment is much more credible if those addressed had no notion that the persons they helped or refused to help had any relationship to the one whom Christians proclaimed as the judge of the living and the dead.'[73] Indeed, what they were called to was one's need, one's dereliction, one's difference – not one's likeness. Hence again we engage that most critical Levinasian motif of asymmetrical responsibility. Levinas felt 'I have this responsibility as soon as I approach the other man. It is in this sense that I speak of the word of God which overturns my perseverance in being into a solicitude for the other. Miracle, first miracle. The first miracle is the fact that I say *bonjour*!'[74]

Regarding a similar encounter, and one also referencing Matthew 25, Robert Mounce offers that one's 'blessedness stems from response to the needs of the deprived (the hungry, thirsty, homeless, poor, sick, and imprisoned). The righteous are unaware that in ministering to the dispossessed they have been ministering to the King.'[75] Just as with Abraham, one tending to the stranger here is tending to God and King. What is more, and this is crucial, is Eugene Boring's assertion that 'to the reader's surprise, the criterion of judgment is not confession of faith in Christ. Nothing is said of grace, justification, or the forgiveness of sins. What counts is whether one has acted with loving care for needy people.'[76]

This loving care, this liturgy, this service for the other with no thought of recompense, operates as Levinas's mission to the Gentiles. It was for him, as for us, a communion experienced in the moment the other comes to face us. And what one addresses to the face of the other – as we just noted, according to Levinas – the Christian says to the face of Christ. Thus full circle: from the exilic self in exodus toward the other; from Abraham saying 'here I am' to the stranger God through acts of radical hospitality; to one's responsibility for the other modulating into an authentic Eucharist where 'the subject is a host'[77] given to Christ himself: what is most in us is best served as bread for the least of these. This service is Levinas's mission to the Gentiles.

Notes

1. Levinas, *Entre Nous: Thinking-Of-The-Other*, trans. Michael B. Smith and Barbara Harshav (New York: Columbia University Press, 1998) 109.

2. Ibid.

3. *Is It Righteous To Be? Interviews With Emmanuel Levinas*, ed. Jill Robbins (Stanford, California: Stanford University Press, 2001) 255f. Glenn Morrison addresses Levinasian notions of otherness and passivity to critique von Balthasar's soteriological conceptions of the Eucharist. So doing, however, he transposes Levinas's motifs into the key of Balthasar's theo-aesthetics. As emphasized, we here have let Levinas speak as Levinas vis-à-vis Christianity. See "Levinas, von Balthasar and Trinitarian *Praxis*" (PhD thesis, Australian Catholic University, 2004), 3f.

4. "Levinas and Judaism," in *The Cambridge Companion to Levinas*, eds. Simon Critchley and Robert Bernasconi (Cambridge: Cambridge University Press, 2002) 33.

5. "Only the Persecuted . . ." in *Ethics as First Philosophy: The Significance of Emmanuel Levinas for Philosophy, Literature, and Religion*, ed. Adriaan T. Peperzak (New York: Routledge, 1995) 83.

6. Levinas, "Philosophy, Justice, and Love," *Entre Nous: Thinking-Of-The-Other*, trans. Michael B. Smith and Barbara Harshav (New York: Columbia University Press, 1998) 110.

7. "In the Name of Who? Levinas and the Other Side of Theology," *Pacifica* 12 no. 3 Fall (1999): 275f.

8. *Practical Theology: "On Earth as It Is in Heaven"* (Maryknoll, New York: Orbis Books, 2005) xix, emphasis in text.

9. *The Glory of the Atonement*, eds. Charles E. Hill and Frank A. James (Downers Grove, Illinois: Intervarsity Press, 2004) 368.

10. *Is There a Meaning in This Text? The Bible, The Reader, and the Morality of Literary Knowledge* (Grand Rapids, Mi.: Zondervan, 1998) 185.

11. "Theology and the Condition of Postmodernity," ed. Kevin J. Vanhoozer (Cambridge: Cambridge University Press, 2003) 16.

12. (Grand Rapids, Mi.: Baker Academic, 2004) 29.

13. *Hospitality & the Other: Pentecost, Christian Practices, and the Neighbor* (Maryknoll, New York: Orbis, 2008) 118.

14. Ibid.

15. Levinas, "Meaning and Sense," in *Basic Philosophical Writings*, 36f.

16. Levinas, *The Theory of Intuition in Husserl's Phenomenology*, 3f.

17. Levinas, "Philosophy and Awakening," in *Discovering Existence With Husserl*, 178.

18. See Levinas, *Totalité et Infini*, xf; *Totality and Infinity*, 22f.

19. See Levinas, *De Dieu qui vient a l'idée*, 49f.; *Of God Who Comes To Mind*, 25. Cf. Michel Henry, *I Am the Truth: Toward a Philosophy of Christianity*, trans. Susan Emanuel (Stanford, Ca.: Stanford University Press, 2003) where it is noted how the ego conditions initiative and action as it exercises its powers. However, Henry calls this exercise not only 'paradoxical' but a 'transcendental illusion,' 139f.

20. See Dudiak, *The Intrigue of Ethics*, 228f.

21. See Levinas, *De l'existence a l'existant*, 51 ; *Existence and Existents*, 24f.

22. See Llewelyn, *Appositions of Jacques Derrida and Emmanuel Levinas*, 88.

23. See Levinas,"La philosophie et l'idée de l'Infini," 172 ; "Philosophy and the Idea of Infinity," 54.

24. Ibid.

25. See Hutchens, *Levinas: A Guide for the Perplexed*, 50f.

26. Llewellyn, *Appositions of Jacques Derrida and Emmanuel Levinas*, 139.

27. See *Nine Talmudic Readings*, 99; *Du Sacré Au Saint* (Paris: Editions de Minuit, 1977) 19.

28. De l'existence a l' existant, 165; *Existence and Existents*, 100.

29. See Levinas, "Meaning and Sense," *Basic Philosophical Writings*, 50.

30. See Levinas, "Language and Proximity," *Collected Philosophical Writings*, 123.

31. According to David Tracy, 'Part of this return to otherness ... is the return of biblical Judaism and Christianity to undo the complacencies of modernity, including modern theology,' "Theology and the Many Faces of Postmodernity," *Theology Today* 51 v. 1 (1994): 27.

32. "My freedom does not have the last word. . . . It resides in the irreversibility of the relation between me and the other, in the Mastery of the Master coinciding with his position as other and as exterior,' *Totalité et Infini*, 74f. ; *Totality and Infinity*, 101.

33. Levinas, *Totalité et Infini*, 267 ; *Totality and Infinity*, 291.

34. Ibid., 276; 299.

35. Eberhard Bethge, *Dietrich Bonhoeffer: Theologian, Christian, Man For His Times*, ed. and revised by Victoria J. Barnett (Minneapolis, Minn.: Fortress Press, 2000) 883.

36. See Udo Schnelle, *Theology of the New Testament*, trans. M. Eugene Boring (Grand Rapids: Baker Academic, 2007) 248f.

37. Dietrich Bonhoeffer, *Letters and Papers From Prison*, the Enlarged Edition, ed. Eberhard Bethge (New York: A Touchstone Book, 1971) 188.

38. See Alister E. McGrath, *Christian Theology: An Introduction* (Oxford: Blackwell Publishers, 1997) 260. See also Michael Welker, *God the Spirit*, trans. John F. Hoffmeyer (Minneapolis: Fortress Press, 1994) 40.

39. Hunter, *Church of the Unchurched*, 23. See also Charles Taylor, *A Secular Age* (Cambridge, Massachusetts: The Belknap Press of Harvard University Press, 2007) 19.

40. Trans. John W. Doberstein (New York : Harper & Row, 1954) 22f.

41. Levinas, *Autrement qu'être ou au-delà de l'essence*, 224; *Otherwise than Being or Beyond Essence*, 144.

42. Ibid.

43. *Letters and Papers from Prison*, 382.

44. Edward Schillebeeckx, *Christ the Sacrament of the Encounter with God* (New York: Sheed and Ward, 1963) 44, emphasis mine.

45. Edwin Robertson sees this religionlessness in Bonheoffer as expressing the notion that 'what runs the world today and explains it for the majority of people is not religion. In this sense, religion has had its day. That does not mean (though) that the time of Christ has passed,' *Bonhoeffer's Legacy: The Christian Way in a World Without Religion* (New York: Collier Books, 1989) 7.

46. *The Blackwell Encyclopedia of Modern Christian Thought*, ed. Alister E. McGrath (Oxford: Blackwell Publishers, 1993) 58.

47. *Letters and Papers from Prison*, 381f.

48. Adriaan Peperzak, 'From intentionality to Responsibility,' in *The Question of the Other: Essays in Contemporary Continental Philosophy*, eds. Arleen B. Dallery and Charles E. Scott (Albany: State University of New York Press, 1989) 15f.

49. Jn. 14:6.

50. "A Religion for Adults," *Difficult Liberty*, 22.

51. See Levinas, *Autrement qu'être ou au-delà de l'essence*, p. 224; *Otherwise than Being or Beyond Essence*, 143.

52. An ecclesiology of the other is not without precedence. In fact, Veli-Matti Kärkkäinen's *An Introduction to Ecclesiology: Ecumenical, Historical, and Global Perspectives* attends extensively to the other-centric dimensions and directives regarding the church and the other, (Downers Grove, Illinois: InterVarsity Press, 2002) *passim*. See also Vincent J. Donovan's *The Church in the Midst of Creation* (Maryknoll, New York: Orbis Books, 1989), where it is asked: 'Is it possible that the true and ultimate meaning of the church, and the final meaning of the sacraments, can be found only *outside* the church, in the arena of the world, in the midst of creation?' 63, emphasis in text. Later Donavan assets that 'the sacrament must be as real as the world,' 66.

53. Alasdair MacIntyre, *After Virtue : A Study in Moral Theory* (Notre Dame, Indiana : University of Notre Dame Press, 1984) 212. See also Jonathan Culler, *The Pursuit of Signs: Semiotics, Literature, Deconstruction* (Ithaca, New York: Cornell University Press, 1981) 185-187; Reynolds Price, "The Origins and Life of Narrative" in *A Palpable God* (Pleasantville, New York: The Akadine Press, 1997) 37.

54. "Thinking About Death," in *God, Death, and Time* (Stanford, California : Stanford University Press, 1993) 111.

55. MacIntyre, 211.

56. Loder,*The Transforming Moment* (Colorado Springs: Helmers and Howard, 1989) 129f. ; Levinas, "Enigma and Phenomenon," in *Basic Philosophical Writings*, 67.

57. Ibid, 149; See also Pheme Perkins, *Resurrection: New Testament Witness and Contemporary Reflection* (Garden City, New York: Doubleday & Company, 1984) 26; E. P. Sanders, *Jesus and Judaism* (Philadelphia: Fortress Press, 1985) 340.

58. Cf. Stanley Hauerwas, *Performing the Faith: Bonhoeffer and the Practice of Nonviolence* (Grand Rapids: Baker, 2004) 24.

59. "Only Love Keeps Us from Being Rigid" in *A Testament to Freedom: The Essential Writings of Dietrich Bonhoeffer*, eds. Geffrey B. Kelly and F. Burton Nelson (San Francisco: Harper & Row, 1990) 263.

60. "Meaning and Sense," in *Basic Philosophical Writings*, 35f.

61. Ibid., 36.

62. *Ethics and Infinity*, 96f., emphasis in text.

63. Robert Plant, *Wittgenstein and Levinas: Ethical and Religious Thought* (Oxford and New York: Routledge, 2005), 136.

64. *Adieu to Emmanuel Levinas*, 12.

65. See *The Gift of Death*, trans. David Wills (Chicago: The University of Chicago Press, 1995), where Derrida states: 'For argument's sake let us follow the hypothesis that in what they say in general Heidegger and Levinas are not Christian, something that is far from being clear,' 49.

66. See *Entre Nous*, 110; *Is it Righteous to Be?* 52, 255. For more on Levinas and Matthew 25, see Glenn Morrison, "Jewish-Christian Relations and the Ethical Philosophy of Emmanuel Levinas," *Journal of Ecumenical Studies*, 3 vol. 8:2-3 (Spring-Summer) 326.

67. *Is it Righteous to Be?* 280. Regarding Levinas's reduction of God, Christ, and the other to the face, William C. Placher, following a similar critique found in Jean-Luc Marion's "The Voice without Name," in *The Face of the Other and the Trace of God*, 227, notes that 'I worry that Levinas sometimes too nearly simply identified God and the human other, and regret that he was so unwilling to consider any other context for talk of God *except* the ethical,' *The Triune God: An Essay in Postliberal Theology* (Louisville: Westminster John Knox Press, 2007) 34, emphasis in text.

68. Ibid., 256, emphasis in text.

69. *Theology and the Dialogue of Religions* (Cambridge: Cambridge University Press, 2002) 114.

70. Levinas, *Difficult Freedom*, p. xiv, emphasis in text. Liturgy for Levinas is commensurate with ethics, as it 'designates the exercise of a function which is not only totally gratuitous, but requires on the part of him who exercises it a putting out of funds at a loss. . . . (As) a work that is effected in the complete dominations of and surpassing of my time, liturgy is not to be ranked alongside of "works" and ethics. *It is ethics itself*,' "Meaning and Sense," in *Collected Philosophical Papers*, trans. Alphonso Lingis (Pittsburg, Pennsylvania: Duquesne University Press, 1998) 92f.

71. NIV.

72. David L. Turner, *Matthew: Baker Exegetical Commentary of the New Testament* (Grand Rapids: Baker Academic, 2008) 605. For more on advocates of this perspective, see Craig L. Blomberg, *Matthew* (Nashville: Broadman, 1992) 377f.; Robert H. Gundry, *Matthew: A Commentary on his Literary and Theological Art* (Grand Rapids: Eerdmans) 514f.; Craig S. Keener, *A Commentary on the Gospel of Matthew* (Grand Rapids: Eerdmans, 1999) 604.

73. *Matthew: A Bible Commentary for Teaching and Preaching* (Louisville: John Knox Press, 1993) 290. Cf. Jacques Ellul, *The Ethics of Freedom*, trans. Geoffrey W. Bromiley (Eerdmans: Grand Rapids, 1976) 321.

74. *Is it Righteous to Be?* 59.

75. *Matthew* (Peabody Ma.: Hendrickson Publishers, 1991) 236.

76. *The New Interpreter's Bible*, VIII (Nashville: Abingdon, 1995) 455.

77. Levinas, *Totalité et Infini*, 276 ; *Totality and Infintiy*, 299.

Bibliography

Atterton, Peter and Matthew Calarco. *On Levinas*. Belmont, CA: Thomson Wadsworth, 2005.
Badiou, Alain. *Ethics: An Essay on the Understanding of Evil*. Translated by Peter Hallward. London: Verso, 2001.
Baird, Marie Louise. "Revisioning Christian Theology in Light of Emmanuel Levinas's Ethics of Responsibility." *Journal of Ecumenical Studies* 36, no. 3-4 (Summer-Fall 1999): 31-48.
Barber, Michael D. "Alma Gonzalez: Otherness as Attending to the Other." In *The Question of the Other: Essays in Contemporary Continental Philosophy*, edited by Arleen B. Dallery and Charles E. Scott, 119-126. Albany, NY: State University of New York Press, 1989.
Barnes, Michael. *Theology and the Dialogue of Religions*. Cambridge: Cambridge University Press, 2002.
Barth, Karl. "The Gift of Freedom." Translated by John Newton Thomas. Essay 2 in *The Humanity of God*. Atlanta: John Knox Press, 1960.
Batnitzky, Leora. "Encountering the Modern Subject in Levinas." In *Yale French Studies: Encounters with Levinas*, 6-21. New Haven, CT: Yale University Press, 2004.
Bauman, Zygmunt. *Postmodern Ethics*. Oxford: Blackwell, 1993.
Benso, Silvia. "Levinas – Another Ascetic Priest?" *The Journal of the British Society for Phenomenology* 27, no. 2 (May 1996): 137-156.
Bergo, Bettina. "Is There a Correlation Between Rosenzweig and Levinas?" *Jewish Quarterly Review* 96, no. 3 (2006): 404-405.
———. *Levinas Between Ethics and Politics: For the Beauty that Adorns the Earth*. Dordrecht, The Netherlands: Kluwer, 1999.
Bernasconi, Robert. "The Ethics of Suspicion." *Research in Phenomenology* 20 (1990): 3-18.
———. Introduction to *Existence and Existents*, by Emmanuel Levinas. Pittsburgh: Duquesne University Press, 1978.
———. "Failure of Communication as as a Surplus: Dialogue and Lack of Dialogue Between Buber and Levinas." In *The Provocation of Levinas: Rethinking the Other*, edited by Robert Bernasconi and David Wood, 100-135. London and New York: Routledge, 1988.
———. "Levinas and Derrida: The Question of the Closure of Metaphysics." In *Face to Face with Levinas*, edited by Richard A. Cohen, 181-202. Albany: State University of New York Press, 1986.

———. "Levinas Face to Face with Hegel." *Journal of the British Society for Phenomenology* 13, no. 2 (1982): 267-276.

———. "Levinas: Philosophy and Beyond." In *Philosophy and Non-Philosophy Since Merleau-Ponty*, edited by Hugh Silverman, 232-258. New York: Routledge, 1988.

———. "No Exit: Levinas' Aporetic Account of Transcendence." *Research in Phenomenology* 35 (2005): 47-55.

———. "'Only the Persecuted...': Language of the Oppressor, Language of the Oppressed." In *Ethics as First Philosophy: The Significance of Emmanuel Levinas for Philosophy, Literature, and Religion*, edited by Adriaan T. Peperzak, 77-86. New York: Routledge, 1995.

———. "Rereading *Totality and Infinity*." In *The Question of the Other: Essays in Contemporary Continental Philosophy*, edited by Arleen B. Dallery and Charles E. Scott, 23-34. Albany, NY: State University of New York Press, 1989.

———. "The Silent Anarchic World of the Evil Genius." In *The Collegium Phaenomenologicum: The First Ten Years*, edited by John C. Sallis, Giussepina Moneta, and Jacques Taminiaux, 257-272. Dordreche: Kluwer Academics Publishers, 1988.

———. "What is the Question to which 'Substitution' is the Answer?" In *The Cambridge Companion to Levinas*, edited by Simon Critchley and Robert Bernasconi, 234-251. Cambridge: Cambridge University Press, 2002.

———. "Who Is My Neighbor? Who Is the Other?" In *Emmanuel Levinas*, edited by Claire Elise Katz, 97-109. Vol. 4, *Critical Assessments of Leading Philosophers*. London: Routledge, 2005.

Bernet, Rudolf. "The Encounter with the Stranger: Two Interpretations of the Vulnerability of the Skin." In *The Face of the Other and the Trace of God: Essays on the Philosophy of Emmanuel Levinas*, edited by Jeffrey Bloechl, 43-62. New York: Fordham University Press, 2000.

———. "Levinas's Critique of Husserl." In *The Cambridge Companion to Levinas*, edited by Simon Critchley and Robert Bernasconi, 82-99. Cambridge: Cambridge University Press, 2002.

Bernstein, Richard J. "Evil and the Temptation of Theodicy." In *The Cambridge Companion to Levinas*, edited by Simon Critchley and Robert Bernasconi, 252-267. Cambridge: Cambridge University Press, 2002.

Bethge, Eberhard. *Dietrich Bonhoeffer: Theologian, Christian, Man for His Times*. Edited and revised by Victoria J. Barnett. Minneapolis: Fortress Press, 2000.

Blanchot, Maurice. *The Writing of the Disaster*. Translated by Ann Smock. Lincoln: University of Nebraska Press, 1980.

Bloechl, Jeffrey. *Liturgy of the Neighbor: Emmanuel Levinas and the Religion of Responsibility*. Pittsburgh: Duquesne University Press, 2000.

Blomberg, Craig L. *Matthew*. Nashville: Broadman, 1992.

Blum, Roland P. "Emmanuel Levinas' Theory of Commitment." *Philosophy and Phenomenological Research* 44 (1983): 145-168.

Boersma, Hans. *Violence, Hospitality, and the Cross: Reappropriating the Atonement Tradition*. Grand Rapids, Mi.: Baker Publishing, 2004.

Boothroyd, David. "Responding to Levinas." In *The Provocation of Levians: Rethinking the Other*, edited by Robert Bernasconi and David Wood, 15-31. London and New York: Routledge, 1988.

Bonhoeffer, Dietrich. *Letters and Papers from Prison*. Enlarged ed. Edited by Eberhard Bethge. New York: Touchstone, 1971.

———. *Life Together*. Translated by John W. Doberstein. New York: Harper & Row, 1954.

———. "Only Love Keeps Us from Being Rigid." Chapter 37 in *A Testament to Freedom: The Essential Writings of Dietrich Bonhoeffer*, edited by Geffrey B. Kelly and F. Burton Nelson. San Francisco: Harper & Row, 1990.
Bouckaert, Luk. "Ontology and Ethics : Reflections of Levinas' Critique of Heidegger." *International Philosophical Quarterly* 10 (1970): 402-419.
Brody, Donna. "Levinas and lucan: Facing the Real." In *Levinas and Lucan: The Missed Encounter*, edited by Sarah Harasym, 56-78. Albany: State University of New York Press, 1998.
Brogan, Michael. "Nausea and the Experience of the Il Y A: Sartre and Levinas on Brute Existence." *Philosophy Today*, July 2001. http://www.highbeam.com/doc/1P3-75424066.html (accessed Oct. 23, 2007).
Brueggemann, Walter. "From Anxiety and Greed to Milk and Honey." *Sojourners* 23, no. 2 (2009): 33-39.
———. *Theology of the Old Testament: Testimony, Dispute, Advocacy*. Minneapolis: Fortress Press, 1997.
Burggraeve, Roger. "The Bible Gives to Thought: Levinas on the Possibility and Proper Nature of Biblical Thinking." In *The Face of the Other and the Trace of God: Essays on the Philosophy of Emmanuel Levinas*, edited by Jeffrey Bloechl,165-183. New York: Fordham University Press, 2000.
———. *From Self-Development to Solidarity: An Ethical Reading of Human Desire in Its Socio- Political Relevance According to Emmanuel Levinas*, edited by Tina Chanter, 53-
77. Leuven: Center for Metaphysics and Philosophy of God, 1985.
———. "Violence and the Vulnerable Face of the Other: The Vision of Emmanuel Levinas on Moral Evil and Our Responsibility." *Journal of Social Philosophy* 30. No. 1 (Spring 1999): 29-45.
———. *The Wisdom of Love in the Service of Love: Emmanuel Levinas on Justice, Peace, and Human Rights*. Translated by Jeffrey Bloechl. Milwaukee: Marquette University Press, 2002.
Burke, John Patrick. "The Ethical Significance of the Face." *Proceeding of the American Catholic Philosophical Association* 56 (1982): 194-206.
Busch, Thomas W. "Ethics and Ontology: Levinas and Merleau-Ponty." *Man and World* 25, no. 2 (1992): 195-202.
Caputo, John D. "*Adieu – sans Dieu*: Derrida and Levinas." In *The Face of the Other and the Trace of God: Essays on the Philosophy of Emmanuel Levinas*, edited by Jeffrey Bloechl, 276-312. New York: Fordham University Press, 2000.
———. *Against Ethics: Contributions to a Poetics of Obligation with Constant Reference to Deconstruction*. Bloomington, IN: Indiana University Press, 1993.
Carey, Seamus. "Embodying Original Ethics: A Response to Levinas and Caputo." *Philosophy Today* 41, no. ¾ (Fall 1997): 446-459.
Casey, Edward. "Levinas on Memory and the Trace." In *The Collegium Phaenomenologicum: The First Ten Years*, edited by John C. Sallis, Giusepina Moneta, and Jacques Taminiaux, 241-255. Dordrecht: Kluwer Academic Publishers, 1988.
Chalier, Catherine. "Ethics and the Feminine." In *Re-Reading Levinas*, edited by Robert Bernasconi and Simon Critchley, 119-129. Bloomington, IN: Indiana University Press, 1991.
———. "Levinas and the Talmud." In *The Cambridge Companion to Levinas*, edited by Simon Critchley and Robert Bernasconi, 100-118. Cambridge: Cambridge University Press, 2002.

———. "The Messianic Utopia." Translated by Andrew Slade. *Graduate Faculty Philsophy Journal* 20,21, no. 2-1 (1998): 281-297.

———. "The Philosophy of Emmanuel Levinas and the Hebraic Tradition." In *Ethics as First Philosophy: The Significance of Emmanuel Levinas for Philosophy, Literature, and Religion*, edited by Adriaan T. Peperzak, 3-12. New York: Routledge, 1995.

Chambers, Oswald. *My Utmost for His Highest: Selections for the Year*. Uhrichsville, OH: Barbour Publishing, 1963.

Chanter, Tina. "Levinas and Impossible Possibility: Thinking Ethics with Rosenzweig and Heidegger in the Wake of the Shoah." *Research in Phenomenology* 28 (1998): 91-109.

———. "The Question of Death: The Time of the I and the Time of the Other." *Irish Philosophical Journal* 4, no. ½ (1987): 94-119.

———. "The Temporality of Saying: Politics Beyond the Ontological Difference." *Graduate Faculty Philosophical Journal* 20-21, no. 2-1 (1998): 503-528.

———. "Traumatic Response: Levinas's Legacy." *Philosophy Today* 41 (Supplement 1997): 19-27.

Ciaramelli, Fabio. "Levinas's Ethical Discourse Between Individuation and Universality." In *Re-Reading Levinas*, edited by Robert Bernasconi and Simon Critchley, 83-108. Bloomington, IN: Indiana University Press, 1991.

Cohen, Richard A. "Absolute Positivity and Ultrapositivity: Husserl and Levinas." In *The Question of the Other: Essays in Contemporary Continental Philosophy*, edited by Arleen B. Dallery and Charles E. Scott, 35-46. Albany, NY: State University of New York Press, 1989.

———. *Elevations: The Height of the Good in Rosenzweig and Levinas*. Chicago: The University of Chicago Press, 1994.

———. "Emmanuel Levinas: Happiness is a Sensational Time." *Philosophy Today* 25 (1981): 196-203.

———. *Ethics, Exegesis, and Philosophy: Interpretation after Levinas*. Cambridge: Cambridge University Press, 2001.

———. Introduction to *Ethics and Infinity: Conversations with Philippe Nemo*, by Emmanuel Levinas. Pittsburgh: Duquesne University Press, 1985.

———. Introduction to *Time and the Other*, by Emmanuel Levinas. Pittsburgh: Duquesne University Press, 1987.

———. "Non-in-Difference in the Thought of Emmanuel Levinas and Franz Rosenzweig." *Graduate Faculty Philosophy Journal* 13, no. 1 (1988): 141-153.

———. "What Good is the Holocaust? On Suffering and Evil." *Philosophy Today* 43, no. 2 (Summer 1999): 176-183, edited by Caroline Bayard and Joyce Bellous.

Comay, Rebecca. "Facies Hippocratica." In *Ethics as First Philosophy: The Significance of Emmanuel Levinas for Philosophy, Literature, and Religion*, edited by Adriaan T. Peperzak, 223-234. New York: Routledge, 1995.

Critchley, Simon. *The Ethics of Deconstruction*. Edinburgh: Edinburgh University Press, 1999.

———. "*Il y a* – A Dying Stronger Than Death." *Oxford Literary Review* 15, no. 1-2 (1993): 110-113.

———. Introduction to *The Cambridge Companion to Levinas*, edited by Simon Critchley and Robert Bernasconi, 1-32. Cambridge: Cambridge University Press, 2002.

———. "Prolegomena to any Post-Deconstructive Subjectivity." In *Deconstructive Subjectivities*, edited by Simon Critchley and Peter Dews, 13-46. Albany: State University of New York Press, 1996.

———. Review of *On Being with Others: Heidegger-Derrida-Wittgenstein* by Simon Glendinning. *Mind* 109, no. 434 (Apr. 2000), http://www.jstor.org.stable/2660149 (accessed March 3, 2008).

Culler, Jonathan. *The Pursuit of Signs: Semiotics, Literature, Deconstruction*. Ithaca, NY: Cornell University Press, 1981.

Davies, Paul. "A Fine Risk: Reading Blanchot Reading Levinas." In *Re-Reading Levinas*, edited by Robert Bernasconi and Simon Critchley, 201-228. Bloomington, IN: Indiana University Press, 1991.

———. "On Resorting to an Ethical Language." In *Ethics as First Philosophy: The Significance of Emmanuel Levinas for Philosophy, Literature, and Religion*, edited by Adriaan T. Peperzak, 95-106. New York: Routledge, 1995.

Davis, Colin. *Levinas: An Introduction*. Notre Dame, IN: University of Notre Dame Press, 1996.

de Boer, Theodore. "An Ethical Transcendental Philosophy." In *Face to Face with Levinas*, edited by Richard A. Cohen, 83-116. Albany: State University of New York Press, 1986.

———. "Theology and the Philosophy of Religion According to Levinas." In *Ethics as First Philosophy: The Significance of Emmanuel Levinas for Philosophy, Literature, and Religion*, edited by Adriaan T. Peperzak, 161-172. New York: Routledge, 1995.

Degnin, Francis Dominic. "Laughter and Metaphysics: Interruptions of Levinas and Nietzche." *Philosophy Today* 39, no. 1 (1995): 31-46.

de Greef, Jan. "Skepticism and Reason." In *Face to Face with Levinas*, edited by Richard A. Cohen, 159-180. Albany: State University of New York Press, 1986.

Derrida, Jacques. *Adieu To Emmanuel Levinas*. Translated by Pascale-Anne Brault and Michael Nass. Stanford, CA: Stanford University Press, 1999.

———. "At This Very Moment in This Work Here I Am." In *Re-Reading Levinas*, edited by Robert Bernasconi and Simon Critchley, 11-50. Bloomington, IN: Indiana University Press, 1991.

———. *The Gift of Death*. Translated by David Wills. Chicago: The University of Chicago Press, 1995.

———. "Violence and Metaphysics: An Essay on the Thought of Emmanuel Levinas." In
Writing and Difference, translated by Alan Bass. Chicago: University of Chicago Press, 1978.

Descartes, Rene. *Meditations on First Philosophy* III. In *The Rationalists*, translated by John Veitch, 45-68. Garden City, NY: Dolphin Books, 1960.

Desmond, William. *Being and the Between*. Albany: State University of New York Press, 1990.

Devlin, Keith. *Goodbye Descartes: The End of Logic and the Search for a New Cosmology of the Mind*. New York: John Wiley and Sons, 1997.

de Vries, Hent. "Adieu, à dieu, a-Dieu." In *Ethics as First Philosophy: The Significance of Emmanuel Levinas for Philosophy, Literature, and Religion*, edited by Adriaan T. Peperzak, 211-222. New York: Routledge, 1995.

———. *Minimal Theologies: Critique of Secular Reason in Adorno and Levinas*. Baltimore: The
Johns Hopkins University Press, 2005.

———. *Philosophy and the Turn to Religion*. Baltimore: The Johns Hopkins University Press, 1999.

Donovan, Vincent J. *The Church in the Midst of Creation*. Maryknoll, NY: Orbis Books, 1989.

Drabinski, John E. *Sensibility and Singularity: The Problem of Phenomenology in Levinas*. Albany, NY: State University of New York Press, 2001.

Drazenovich, George. "Toward a Levinasian Understanding of Christian Ethics: Emmanuel Levinas and the Phenomenology of the Other." *Cross Currents* 54, no. 4 (Winter 2005): 37-54.

Dudiak, Jeffrey. *The Intrigue of Ethics: A Reading of the Idea of Discourse in the Thought of Emmanuel Levinas.* New York: Fordham University Press, 2001.

Dueck, Alvin and David Goodman. "Expiation, Substitution, and Surrender: Levinasian Implications for Psychotherapy." *Pastoral Psychology* 55, no. 5 (May, 2007): 601-617.

Duns, Ryan G. "Being in the Face of Nameless Mystery: Levinas and the Trace of Doctrine." *Heythrop Journal* 49, no. 1 (Jan 2008): 97-109.

Durie, Robin. "Speaking Time ... Husserl and Levinas on the Saying of Time." *The Journal of the British Society of Phenomenology* 30, no. 1 (January 1999): 35-58.

Ellul, Jacques . *The Ethics of Freedom.* Grand Rapids, MI: Eerdmans, 1976.

Eagleston, Robert. *Ethical Criticism: Reading After Levinas.* Edinburgh: Edinburgh University Press, 1997.

Ehman, Robert M. "Emmanuel Levinas : The Phenomenon of the Other." *Man and World* 8, no. 2 (1975): 210-220.

Farley, Edward. *Deep Symbols: Their Postmodern Effacement and Reclamation.* Valley Forge, PA.: Trinity Press International, 1996.

Farley, Wendy. 'Ethics and Reality: Dialogue Between Caputo and Levinas." *Philosophy Today* 36, no. 3 (1975): 141-145.

Floyd, Wayne W. "To Welcome the Other: Totality and Theory in Levinas and Adorno." *Philosophy and Theology* 4 (1989): 145-170.

Ford, David. *Self and Salvation: Being Transformed.* Cambridge: Cambridge University Press, 1999.

Foshay, Toby. "Resentment and Apophasis: The Trace of the Other in Levinas, Derrida, and Gans." In *Shadow of Spirit,* edited by Philippa Berry and Andrew Wernick. New York: Routledge, 1992.

Franck, Didier. "The Body of Difference." In *The Face of the Other and the Trace of God: Essays on the Philosophy of Emmanuel Levinas,* edited by Jeffrey Bloechl, 3-29. New York: Fordham University Press, 2000.

Fretheim, Terrence E. "The Book of Genesis: Introduction, Commentary, and Reflections." In *The New Interpreter's Bible* 1:319-674. Nashville: Abingdon Press, 1994.

Froman, Wayne. "The Strangeness in the Ethical Discourse of Emmanuel Levinas." In *Addressing Levinas,* edited by Eric Sean Nelson, Antje Kapust, and Kent Still, 52-60. Evanston, IL.: Northwestern University Press, 2005.

Fryer, David Ross. *The Intervention of the Other: Ethical Subjectivity in Levinas and Lacan.* New York: Other Press, 2004.

Gadamer, Hans-Georg. *Truth and Method.* Translated by Joel Weinsheimer and Donald G. Marshall. New York: Continuum, 1989.

Gans, Steven. "Ethics or Ontology: Levinas and Heidegger." *Philosophy Today* 16, no. 2 (1972): 117-121.

———. "Levinas and Pontalis: Meeting the Other as in a Dream." In *The Provocation of Levinas: Rethinking the Other,* edited by Robert Bernasconi and David Wood, 83-90. London and New York: Routledge, 1988.

Gibbs, Robert. *Correlations in Rosenzweig and Levinas.* Princeton, NJ: Princeton University Press, 1992.

———. "Height and Nearness: Jewish Dimensions of Radical Ethics." In *Ethics as First Philosophy: The Significance of Emmanuel Levinas for Philosophy, Literature, and Religion,* edited by Adriaan T. Peperzak, 13-24. New York: Routledge, 1995.

———. *Why Ethics? Signs of Responsibility*. Princeton, NJ: Princeton University Press, 2000.
Golomb, Paul. "A Matter of Time: The Jew, Christian, and Muslim in Conversation."
    Cross Currents 54, no. 4 (Winter 2005): 18-24.
Greisch, Jean. "The Face and Reading: Immediacy and Mediation." Translated by Simon Critchley. In *Re-Reading Levinas*, edited by Robert Bernasconi and Simon Critchley, 67-82. Bloomington, IN: Indiana University Press, 1991.
Grob, Leonard. "Emmanuel Levinas and the Primacy of Ethics in Post-Holocaust Philosophy." In *Ethics After the Holocaust: Perspectives, Critiques and Responses*, edited by John K. Roth, 1-48. St. Paul, MN.: Paragon House, 1999.
Guibal, Francis. "Cultural Significations and Ethical Sense: On Emmanuel Levinas." Translated by Diane Perpich, and Somervell Linthicum. *Graduate Faculty Philosophy Journal* 20, 21, no. 2-1 (1998): 189-219.
Gundry, Robert H. *Matthew: A Commentary on His Literary and Theological Art*. Grand Rapids: Eerdmans, 1982.
Gunning, Meredith. "About Face: Altered States of Subjectivity in Levinas." PhD diss., Fordham University, 2006.
Handelman, Susan. "Facing the Other: Levinas, Perelman and Rosenzweig." *Religion and Literature* 22 (1990): 61-84.
Hansel, George. "Emmanuel Levinas (1906-1995)." *Philosophy Today* 43, no. 2 (Summer 1999): 168-175, edited by Caroline Bayard and Joyce Bellous.
Hare, Douglas. *Matthew: A Bible Commentary for Teaching and Preaching*. Louisville: John Knox Press, 1993.
Harris, Chris. "Toward an Understanding of Home: Levinas and the New Testament." *Religious Education* 90, no. 3 (Summer/Fall 1995): 433-444.
Hart, David Bentley. *The Beauty of the Infinite: The Aesthetics of Christian Truth*. Grand Rapids, MI: Wm. B. Eerdmans Publishing Co., 2003.
Hart, Hendrik. "Conceptual Understanding and Knowing Other-Wise: Reflections on Rationality and Spirituality in Philosophy." In *Knowing Other-Wise: Philosophy at the Threshold of Spirituality*, edited by James H. Olthuis, 19-53. New York: Fordham University Press, 1997.
Hatley, James. "Beyond Outrage: The Delirium of Responsibility in Levinas's Scene of Persecution." In *Addressing Levinas*, edited by Eric Sean Nelson, Antje Kapust, and Kent Still, 34-51. Evanston, IL: Northwestern University Press, 2005.
Hauerwas, Stanley. *Performing the Faith: Bonhoeffer and the Practice of Nonviolence*. Grand Rapids: Baker, 2004.
Heidegger, Martin. *Being and Time*. Translated by John Macquarrie and Edward Robinson. New York: Harper and Row Publishers, 1962.
———. *Poetry, Language, Thought*. Translated by Albert Hofstadter. New York: Harper and Row Publishers, 1971.
———. *The Question Concerning Technology and Other Essays*. Translated by William Lovitt.
    New York: Harper and Row Publishers, 1977.
Held, Klaus. "Husserl's Phenomenological Method." In *The New Husserl: A Critical Reader*, edited by Don Welton, 3-31. Bloomington, IN: Indiana University Press, 2003.
Henry, Michel. *I Am the Truth: Toward a Philosophy of Christianity*. Translated by Susan Emanuel. Stanford, CA: Stanford University Press, 2003.
Hodge, Joanna. "Ethics and Time: Levinas between Kant and Husserl." *Diacritics* 32, no. 3/4 (2002): 107-134.
Horner, Robyn. *Rethinking God as Gift: Marion, Derrida, and the Limits of Phenomenology*. New York: Fordham University Press, 2001.

Horton, Michael Scott. "Meeting a Stranger: A Covenantal Epistemology." *Westminster Theological Journal* 66, no. 2 (Fall 2004): 337-355.
Howells, Christina. "Sarte and Levinas." In *The Provocation of Levinas: Rethinking the Other*, edited by Robert Bernasconi and David Wood, 91-99. London: Routledge, 1988.
Hunter, George G. *Church of the Unchurched*. Nashville: Abingdon, 1996.
Husserl, Edmund. *Ideas Pertaining to a Pure Phenomenology and to a Phenomenological Philosophy, First Book*. Translated by F. Kersten. The Hague: Martinus Nijhoff, 1982.
Hutchens, B.C. *Levinas: A Guide for the Perplexed*. New York: Continuum, 2004.
Irigary, Luce. "The Fecundity of the Caress." In *Face to Face with Levinas*, edited by Richard A. Cohen, 231-246. Albany: State University of New York Press, 1986.
———. "Questions to Emmanuel Levinas: On the Divinity of Love." Translated by Margaret Whitford. In *Re-Reading Levinas*, edited by Robert Bernasconi and Simon Critchley, 109-118. Bloomington, IN: Indiana University Press, 1991.
Iyer, Lars. "The Unbearable: Trauma and Witnessing in Blanchot and Levinas." *Janus Head: Journal of Interdisciplinary Studies in Continental Philosophy, Literature, Phenomenological Psychology and the Arts* 6, no. 1 (2003): 37-41.
Izzi, John. "Proximity in Distance: Levinas and Plotinus." *International Philosophical Quarterly* 38. No. 1 (March 1998): 5-17.
Janicaud, Dominique. "The Theological Turn of French Phenomenology." Part I in *Phenomenology and the "Theological Turn": The French Debate*. New York: Fordham Press, 2000.
Jennings, Ted. "Transcendence, Justice, and Mercy." In *Rethinking Wesley's Theology for Contemporary Methodism*, edited by Randy Maddox, 65-83. Nashville: Kingswood Books, 1998.
Jonas, Hans. *The Imperative of Responsibility*. Chicago: The University of Chicago Press, 1984.
Jopling, David. "Levinas on Desire, Dialogue and the Other." *American Catholic Philosophical Quarterly* 65, no. 4 (1991): 405-427.
Karfikova, Lenka. "God of Philosophers: The Idea of God in A.N. Whitehead and E. Levinas." *Communio Viatorum* 48, no. 2 (2006): 77-84.
Kärkkäinen, Veli-Matti. *An Introduction to Ecclesiology: Ecumenical, Historical, and Global Perspectives*. Downers Grove, IL: InterVarsity Press, 2002.
Katz, Claire Elise. *Levinas, Judaism, and the Feminine: The Silent Footsteps of Rebecca*. Bloomington, IN: Indiana University Press, 2003.
———. "Raising Cain: The Problem of Evil and the Question of Responsibility." *Cross Currents* 55, no. 2 (Summer 2005): 215-233.
———. "Reinhabiting the House of Ruth: Exceeding the Limits of the Feminine in Levinas." In *Feminist Interpretations of Emmanuel Levinas*, edited by Tina Chanter, 145-170. University Park, PA: Penn State University Press, 2001.
Kearney, Richard and Emmanuel Levinas. "Dialogue with Emmanuel Levinas." In *Face to Face With Levinas*, edited by Richard A. Cohen, 13-34. Albany: State University of New York Press, 1986.
Keenan, Dennis King. "Reading Levinas Reading Descartes' *Meditations*." *The Journal of the British Society for Phenomenology* 29, no. 1 (January 1998): 63-74.
———. *Death and Responsibility: The "Work" of Levinas*. Albany: State University of New York Press, 1999.
Keener, Craig S. *A Commentary on the Gospel of Matthew*. Grand Rapids: Eerdmans, 1999.

Kelly, Andrew. "Reciprocity and the Height of God: A Defense of Buber Against Levinas." *Sophia* (Australia) 34, no. 1 (1995): 65-73.
Kemp, Peter. "Ricoeur Between Heidegger and Levinas: Original Affirmation Between Ontological Attestation and Ethical Injunction." *Philosophy and Social Criticism* 21, no. 5/6 (1995):41-61.
Kosky, Jeffrey L. *Levinas and the Philosophy of Religion*. Bloomington, IN: Indiana University Press, 2001.
Kovacs, George. "The Question of Ultimate Meaning in Emmanuel Levinas." *Ultimate Reality and Meaning* 14, no. 2 (1991): 99-108.
Kunz, George. *The Paradox of power and Weakness: Levinas and an Alternative Paradigm for Psychology*. Albany: State University of New York Press, 1998.
Large, William. "On the Meaning of the Word in Levinas." *The Journal of the British Society for Phenomenology* 27, no. 1 (January 1996): 36-52.
Lee, Jung H. "Neither Totality Nor Infinity: Suffering the Other." *The Journal of Religion* 79, no, 2 (April 1999): 250-263.
Lesser, Harry. "Levinas and the Jewish Ideal of the Sage." In *Facing the Other: The Ethics of Emmanuel Levinas,* Edited by Sean Hand, 141-152. Richmond, Surrey: Curzon Press, 1996.
Levin, David Michael. "Tracework: Myself and Others in the Moral Phenomenology of Merleau-Ponty and Levinas." *International Journal of Philosophical Studies* 6, no. 3 (1998): 345-392.
Levinas, Emmanuel. *Alterity and Transcendence*. Translated by Michael B. Smith. New York: Columbia University Press, 1999.
———. *L'au-Delà du Verset: Lectures et Discours Talmudiques*. Paris: Minuit, 1982.
———. *Autrement qu'être ou au-Delà de l'Essence*. The Hague: Martinus Nijhoff, 1974.
———. "Bad Conscience and the Inexorable." In *Face to Face with Levinas,* edited by Richard A. Cohen, 35-40. Albany: State University of New York Press, 1986.
———. "Beyond Intentionality." Translated by Kathleen McLaughlin. In *Philosophy in France Today,* edited by Alan Montefiore. Cambridge: Cambridge University Press, 1983.
———. *Beyond the Verse: Talmudic Readings and Lectures*. Translated by Gary D. Mole. London: Athlone Press, 1994.
———. *Collected Philosophical Papers*. Translated by Alphonso Lingis. Pittsburg: Duquesne University Press, 1998.
———. *De Dieu Qui Vient a l'Idée*. Paris: Librairie Philosophique J. Vrin, 1986.
———. *De l'Existence a l'Existant*. Paris: Librairie Philosophique J. Vrin, 1986.
———."Dialogue with Emmanuel Levinas." In *Dialogues with Contemporary Continental Thinkers,* edited by Richard Kearney. Manchester: Manchester University Press, 1984.
———. *Dieu, la Mort et le Temps*. Paris: B. Grasset, 1993.
———. *Difficult Freedom: Essays on Judaism*. Translated by Seán Hand. Baltimore: The Johns Hopkins University Press, 1990.
———. *Discovering Existence with Husserl*. Translated by Richard A. Cohen and Michael B. Smith. Evanston, IL: Northwestern University Press, 1998.
———. *Du Sacré au Saint*. Paris: Editions de Minuit, 1977.
———. *Emmanuel Lévinas: Basic Philosophical Writings*. Edited by Adriaan T. Peperzak, Simon Critchley, and Robert Bernasconi. Bloomington, IN: Indiana University Press, 1996.
———. *En Découvrant l'Existence avec Husserl et Heidegger*. Paris: Librairie Philosophique J. Vrin, 1967.

———. *Entre Nous: Thinking-Of-The-Other*. Translated by Michael B. Smith, and Barbara Harshav. New York: Columbia University Press, 1998.
———. *Ethics and Infinity: Conversations with Philippe Nemo*. Translated by Richard A. Cohen. Pittsburgh: Duquesne University Press, 1985.
———."Ethics as First Philosophy." In *The Levinas Reader*, edited by Seán Hand, 75-87. Oxford: Blackwell Publishers Ltd., 1989.
———."Ethics and Politics." Translated by Jonathan Romney. In *The Levinas Reader*, edited by Seán Hand, 289-297. Cambridge: Basil Blackwell, Inc., 1994.
———. *Existence and Existents*. Translated by Alphonso Lingis. Pittsburgh: Duquesne University Press, 1978.
———."God and Philosophy." Translated by Richard A. Cohen and Alphonso Lingis. In *The Levinas Reader*, edited by Seán Hand, 167-189. Cambridge: Basil Blackwell, Inc., 1994.
———. *God, Death, and Time*. Translated by Bettina Bergo. Stanford, CA: Stanford University Press, 2000.
———. *Humanism of the Other*. Chicago: University of Illinois Press, 2006.
———."Ideology and Idealism." Translated by Sanford Ames, and Arthur Lesley. In *The Levinas Reader*, edited by Seán Hand, 235-248. Cambridge: Basil Blackwell, Inc., 1994.
———. *In the Time of Nations*. Translated by Michael B. Smith. Bloomington, IN: Indiana University Press, 1994.
———. *The Levinas Reader*. Edited by Sean Hand. Cambridge: Basil Blackwell, Inc., 1994.
———. *Nine Talmudic Readings*. Translated by Annette Aronowicz. Bloomington, IN: Indiana University Press, 1990.
———. *Of God Who Comes to Mind*. Translated by Bettina Bergo. Stanford, CA: Stanford University Press, 1998.
———. *On Escape*. Translated by Bettina Bergo. Stanford, CA: Stanford University Press, 2003.
———. *Otherwise Than Being: Or, Beyond Essence*. Translated by Alphonso Lingis. Pittsburg: Duquesne University Press, 1998.
———. *Outside the Subject*. Translated by Michael B. Smith. Stanford, CA: Stanford University Press, 1993.
———."The Primacy of Pure Practical Reason." Translated by Blake Billings. *Man and World* 4 (1994): 445-453.
———. *Proper Names*. Translated by Michael B. Smith. Stanford, CA: Stanford University Press, 1996.
———. *Quatre Lectures Talmudiques*. Paris: Editions de Minuit, 1968.
———. "Secularization and Hunger." Translated by Bettina Bergo. *Graduate Faculty Philosophy Journal* 20,21, no. 2-1 (1998): 3-12.
———."Simulacra: The End of the World." Foreword in *Writing the Future*, edited by David Wood, 11-16. London and New York: Routledge, 1990.
———. *The Theory of Intuition in Husserl's Phenomenology*. 2d ed. Translated by André Orianne. Evanston, IL: Northwestern University Press, 1995.
———. *Time and the Other*. Translated by Richard A. Cohen. Pittsburgh: Duquesne University Press, 1987.
———. *Totalité et Infini: Essai sur Extériorité*. 4th ed. The Hague: Martinus Nijhoff, 1971.
———. *Totality and Infinity: An Essay on Exteriority*. Pittsburgh: Duquesne University Press, 1969.
———. "The Trace of the Other." In *Deconstruction in Context: Literature and Philosophy*, edited by Mark C. Taylor, 345-360. Chicago: The University of Chicago Press, 1986.

———. "Useless Suffering." Translated by Richard A. Cohen. In *The Provocation of Levinas: Rethinking the Other*, edited by Robert Bernasconi and David Wood, 156-167. London and New York: Routledge, 1988.
———. "Wholly Otherwise." Translated by Simon Critchley. In *Re-Reading Levinas*, edited by Robert Bernasconi and Simon Critchley, 3-10. Bloomington and Indianapolis: Indiana University Press, 1991.
Lichtigfeld, A. "On Infinity and Totality in Hegel and Levinas." *South African Journal of Philosophy* 2 (1983): 31-33.
Lingis, Alphonso. "The Elemental Imperative." *Research in Phenomenology* 18 (1988): 3-21.
Llewelyn, John. *Appositions of Jacques Derrida and Emmanuel Levinas*. Bloomington, IN: Indiana University Press, 2002.
———. *Emmanuel Levinas: The Genealogy of Ethics*. London: Routledge, 1995.
———. "Levinas and Language." In *The Cambridge Companion to Levinas*, edited by Simon
    Critchley and Robert Bernasconi, 119-138. Cambridge: Cambridge University Press, 2002.
Loder, James E. *The Transforming Moment*. Colorado Springs: Helmers & Howard Publishers, 1989.
Lyotard, Jean-François. "Levinas's Logic." In *Face to Face with Levinas*, edited by Richard A. Cohen, 117-158. Albany: State University of New York Press, 1986.
MacAvoy, Leslie. "The Other Side of Intentionality." In *Addressing Levinas*, edited by Eric Sean Nelson, Antje Kapust, and Kent Still, 109-118. Evanston, IL: Northwestern University Press, 2005.
MacDonald, Michael J. "'Jewgreek and Greekjew': The Concept of Trace in Derrida and Levinas." *Philosophy Today* 35 (1991): 21-30.
MacIntyre, Alasdair. *After Virtue: A Study in Moral Theory*. Notre Dame, IN: University of Notre Dame Press, 1984.
Mack, Michael. "Franz Rosenzweig's and Emmanuel Levinas's Critique of German Idealism's Pseudotheology." *Journal of Religion* 83, no. 1 (2003): 56-78.
Malka, Salomon. *Emmanuel Levinas: His Life and Legacy*. Translated by Michael Kigel and Sonja M. Embree. Pittsburgh: Duquesne University Press, 2002.
Manning, Robert John Sheffler. *Interpreting Otherwise than Heidegger: Emmanuel Levinas's Ethics as First Philosophy*. Pittsburgh: Duquesne University Press, 1993.
Marion, Jean-Luc. "From the Other to the Individual." In *Transcendence: Philosophy, Literature, and Theology Approach the Beyond*, edited by Regina Schwartz, 43-60. New York: Routledge, 2004.
———. *God Without Being*. Translated by Thomas A. Carlson. Chicago: The University of
    Chicago Press, 1991.
———. "A Lucan Kenosis? Luke's Concept of Truth as an Ethics of Service." *Journal of Philosophy and Scripture* 6 (2009): 1-8.
———. "A Note Concerning the Ontological Indifference." *Graduate Faculty Philosophy Journal* 20, no.1 (1998): 2-21.
McClendon, James Wm., Jr. *Systematic Theology: Ethics*. Nashville: Abingdon Press, 1986.
McGrath, Alister E. *Christian Theology: An Introduction*. Oxford: Blackwell Publishers, 1997.
Morrison, Glenn. "Jewish-Christian Relations and the Ethical Philosophy of Emmanuel Levinas." *Journal of Ecumenical Studies* 8, no. 2-3 (Spring-Summer 2001): 316-329.
———. "Levinas' Philosophical Origins: Husserl, Heidegger and Rosenzweig." *Heythrop
    Journal* 46, no. 1 (2005): 41-59.

———. "Levinas, Von Balthasar and Trinitarian Praxis." PhD thesis, Australian Catholic University, 2004.

Mounce, Robert. *Matthew*. Peabody, MA: Hendrickson Publishers, 1991.

Moyn, Samuel. *Origins of the Other: Emmanuel Levinas between Revelation and Ethics*. Ithaca, NY: Cornell University Press, 2005.

Natanson, Maurice. *Edmund Husserl: Philosopher of Infinite Tasks*. Evanston, IL: Northwestern University Press, 1973.

Niebuhr, H. Richard. *Christ and Culture*. New York: Harper Torchbooks, 1956.

Ochs, Peter. "Holy Other: Leaving Self Behind." *Living Pulpit* 10, no. 3 (July 2001): 31-39.

O'Connor, Noreen. "Who Suffers?" In *Re-Reading Levinas*, edited by Robert Bernasconi and Simon Critchley, 229-233. Bloomington, IN: Indiana University Press, 1991.

Olthuis, James. "Face to Face: Ethical Asymmetry or the Symmetry of Mutuality?" In *Knowing Other-Wise: Philosophy at the Threshold of Spirituality*, edited by James H. Olthuis, 131-158. New York: Fordham University Press, 1997.

Orianne, André. Forward to *The Theory of Intuition in Husserl's Phenomenology*, by Emmanuel Levinas. Evanston, IL: Northwestern University Press, 1973.

Peperzak, Adriaan Theodoor. *Beyond: The Philosophy of Emmanuel Levinas*. Evanston, IL: Northwestern University Press, 1997.

———. "From Intentionality to Responsibility: On Levinas's Philosophy of Language." In *The Question of the Other: Essays in Contemporary Continental Philosophy*, edited by Arleen B. Dallery and Charles E. Scott, 3-55. Albany: State University of New York Press, 1989.

———. "Presentation." In *Re-Reading Levinas*, edited by Simon Critchley and Robert Bernasconi, 51-66. Bloomington, IN: Indiana University Press, 1991.

———. *To the Other: An Introduction to the Philosophy of Emmanuel Levinas*. West Lafayette, IN: Purdue University Press, 1993.

Perkins, Pheme. *Resurrection: New Testament Witness and Contemporary Reflection*. Garden City, NY: Doubleday, 1984.

Phillips, Gary A. "Levinas." In *Handbook of Postmodern Biblical Interpretation*, edited by A.K.M. Adam, 154-160. St. Louis: Chalice Press, 2000.

Pinchevski, Amit. *By Way of Interruption: Levinas and the Ethics of Communication*. Pittsburg: Duquesne University Press, 2005.

Placher, William C. *The Triune God: An Essay in Postliberal Theology*. Louisville: Westminster John Knox Press, 2007.

Plant, Bob. *Wittgenstein and Levinas: Ethical and Religious Thought*. London: Routledge, 2005.

Pohl, Christine. *Making Room: Recovering Hospitality as a Christian Tradition*. Grand Rapids: Wm. B. Eerdmans, 1999.

Price, Reynolds. "The Origins and Life of Narrative." In *A Palpable God*. Pleasantville, NY: The Akadine Press, 1997.

Purcell, Michael. *Levinas and Theology*. Cambridge: Cambridge University Press, 2006.

Putnam, Hilary. "Levinas and Judaism." In *The Cambridge Companion to Levinas*, edited by Simon Critchley and Robert Bernasconi, 33-62. Cambridge: Cambridge University Press, 2002.

Raffoul, François. "Being and the Other: Ethics and Ontology in Levinas and Heidegger." In *Addressing Levinas*, edited by Eric Sean Nelson, Antje Kapust, and Kent Still, 138-151. Evanston, IL: Northwestern University Press, 2005.

Reiss, Moshe. "Abraham's Moment of Decision: According to Levinas and Rembrant." *Jewish Bible Quarterly* 35, no. 1 (January-March 2007): 41-49.

Ricoeur, Paul. *Oneself as Another*. Translated by Kathleen Blamey. Chicago: University of Chicago Press, 1995.

———. "Otherwise: A Reading of Emmanuel Levinas's *Otherwise than Being or Beyond Essence*." In *Yale French Studies: Encounters With Levinas*, 82-99. New Haven, CT: Yale University Press, 2004.

Robbins, Jill, ed. *Is It Righteous to Be? Interviews with Emmanuel Levinas*. Stanford, CA: Stanford University Press, 2001.

———. "Tracing Responsibility in Levinas's Ethical Thought." In *Ethics as First Philosophy: The Significance of Emmanuel Levinas for Philosophy, Literature, and Religion*, edited by Adriaan T. Peperzak, 173-184. New York: Routledge, 1995.

———. "Visage, Figure: Reading Levinas's Totality and Infinity." *Yale French Studies* no. 79 (1991): 135-149.

Robertson, Edwin. *Bonhoeffer's Legacy: The Christian Way in a World Without Religion*. New York: Collier Books, 1989.

Rolland, Jacques. "Getting Out of Being by a New Path." Introduction to *On Escape*, by Emmanuel Levinas. Stanford, CA: Stanford University Press, 2003.

Rosenzweig, Franz. *The Star of Redemption*. Translated by William W. Hallo. Boston: Beacon Press, 1972.

Sacks, Jonathan. *The Dignity of Difference*. London: Continuum International Publishing Group, 2002.

Sallis, John. "Levinas and the Elemental." *Research in Phenomenology* 28 (1998), http://www3.baylor.edu/American_Jewish/everythingthatusedtobehere/resources/jphil_articles/levinas-elemental.doc (accessed December 9, 2008).

Sanders, E.P. *Jesus and Judaism*. Philadelphia: Fortress Press, 1985.

Schnelle, Udo. *Theology of the New Testament*. Translated by M. Eugene Boring. Grand Rapids, MI: Baker Academic, 2007.

Schroeder, Brian. *Altared Ground: Levinas, History, and Violence*. New York: Routledge, 1996.

Schwartz, Regina M. "Revelation and Revolution." *Cross Currents* 56, no. 3 (Autumn 2006): 376-382.

Schweiker, William. "Disputes and Trajectories in Responsibility Ethics." *Religious Studies Review* 27, no. 1 (January 2001): 18-20.

Scott, Charles E. "A People's Witness beyond Politics." In *Ethics as First Philosophy: The Significance of Emmanuel Levinas for Philosophy, Literature, and Religion*, edited by Adriaan T. Peperzak, 25-38. New York: Routledge, 1995.

Scruton, Roger. *A Short History of Modern Philosophy*. London: Routledge, 1995.

Schwartz, Regina, ed. *Transcendence: Philosophy, Literature, and Theology Approach the Beyond*. New York: Routledge, 2004.

Schillebeeckx, Edward. *Christ the Sacrament of the Encounter with God*. New York: Sheed and Ward, 1963.

Sikka, Sonia. "Questioning the Sacred: Heidegger and Levinas on the Locus of Divinity." *Modern Theology* 14, (1998): 299-323.

Smith, Michael B. "Levinas: A Transdisciplinary Thinker." In *Addressing Levinas*, edited by Eric Sean Nelson, Antje Kapust, and Kent Still, 61-74. Evanston, IL: Northwestern University Press, 2005.

———. *Toward the Outside: Concepts and Themes in Emmanuel Levinas*. Pittsburgh: Duquesne University Press, 2005.

Smith, Steven G. *The Argument to the Other: Reason Beyond Reason in the Thought of Karl Barth and Emmanuel Levinas*. Chico, CA: Scholars Press, 1983.

———. "Reason as One for Another: Moral and Theoretical Argument." In *Face to Face with Levinas*, edited by Richard A. Cohen, 53-72. Albany: State University of New York Press, 1986.

Spengler [pseud.]. "Christian, Muslim, Jew: Franz Rosenzweig and the Abrahamic Religions." *First Things*, no. 176 O (2007): 29-33.

Steinbock, Anthony J. "Face and Revelation: Levinas on Teaching as Way-Faring." In *Addressing Levinas*, edited by Eric Sean Nelson, Antje Kapust, and Kent Still, 119-137. Evanston, IL: Northwestern University Press, 2005.

Tallon, Andrew. "Nonintentional Affectivity, Affective Intentionality, and the Ethical in Levinas's Philosophy." In *Ethics as First Philosophy: The Significance of Emmanuel Levinas for Philosophy, Literature, and Religion*, edited by Adriaan T. Peperzak, 107-122. New York: Routledge, 1995.

Tanner, Kathryn. *Theories of Culture: A New Agenda for Theology*. Minneapolis: Fortress Press, 1997.

Taylor, Charles. *A Secular Age*. Cambridge, MA: The Belknap Press of Harvard University Press, 2007.

Taylor, Mark C. *Alterity*. Chicago: The University of Chicago Press, 1987.

———. Introduction to *Deconstruction in Context: Literature and Philosophy*, edited by Mark
C. Taylor. Chicago: University of Chicago Press, 1986.

Toumayan, Alain. "'I More Than Others': Dostoevsky and Levinas." In *Yale French Studies: Encounters With Levinas*, 55-66. New Haven, CT: Yale University Press, 2004.

Tracy, David. "Theology and the Many Faces of Postmodernity." *Theology Today* 51 (1994): 104-114.

Turner, David L. *Matthew*. Baker Exegetical Commentary of the New Testament. Grand Rapids: Baker Academic, 2008.

Valevicius, Andrius. *From the Other to the Totally Other: The Religious Philosophy of Emmanuel Levinas*. New York: Peter Lang Publishing, Inc., 1988. Vanhoozer, Kevin J. *Is There a Meaning in This Text?* Grand Rapids, Mi.: Zondervan, 1998.

Veling, Terry A. "In the Name of Who? Levinas and the Other Side of Theology." *Pacifica* 12, no. 3 (October, 1999): 275-292.

_____. *Practical Theology: "On Earth as It Is in Heaven."* Maryknoll, N. Y.: Orbis Press, 2005.

Vetlesen, Arne Johan. *Perception, Empathy, and Judgment: An Inquiry into the Preconditions of Moral Performance*. University Park, PA: Pennsylvania State University Press, 1994.

Visker, Rudi. "The Price of Being Dispossessed: Levinas's God and Freud's Trauma." In *The Face of the Other and the Trace of God: Essays on the Philosophy of Emmanuel Levinas*, edited by Jeffrey Bloechl, 243-275. New York: Fordham University Press, 2000.

———. *Truth and Singularity: Taking Foucault into Phenomenology*. Boston: Kluwer, 1999. Volf, Miroslav. *Exclusion and Embrace: A Theological Exploration of Identity, Otherness, and
Reconciliation*. Nashville: Abingdon Press, 1996.

Waldenfels, Bernhard. "Levinas and the Face of the Other." In *The Cambridge Companion to Levinas*, edited by Simon Critchley and Robert Bernasconi, 63-81. Cambridge: Cambridge University Press, 2002.

———. "Response and Responsibility in Levinas." In *Ethics as First Philosophy: The Significance of Emmanuel Levinas for Philosophy, Literature, and Religion*, edited by Adriaan T. Peperzak, 39-52. New York: Routledge, 1995.

Ward, Graham. "The Revelation of the Holy Other as the Wholly Other." *Modern Theology* 14, no. 2 (1993): 159-180.
Watson, Stephen H. "Reason and the Face of the Other." *Journal of the American Academy of Religion* 54, no. 1 (Spring 1986): 33-57.
Webb, Mary-Ann. "Eros and Ethics: Levinas's Reading of Plato's 'Good Beyond Being.'" *Studies in Christian Ethics* 19, no. 2 (2006): 205-222.
Weber, Elisabeth. "Persecution in Levinas's *Otherwise than Being or Beyond Essence*." In *Ethics as First Philosophy: The Significance of Emmanuel Levinas for Philosophy, Literature, and Religion*, edited by Adriaan T. Peperzak, 69-76. New York: Routledge, 1995.
Welker, Michael. *God the Spirit*. Translated by John F. Hoffmeyer. Minneapolis: Fortress Press, 1994.
Welz, Claudia. "God – A Phenomenon? Theology as Semiotic Phenomenology of the Invisible." *Studia Theologica* 62 (2008): 4-7.
Westphal, Merold. "Levinas's Teleological Suspension of the Religious." In *Ethics as First Philosophy: The Significance of Emmanuel Levinas for Philosophy, Literature, and Religion*, edited by Adriaan T. Peperzak, 151-160. New York: Routledge, 1995.
Williams, Bernard. *Descartes: The Project of Pure Enquiry*. Middlesex, England: Penguin Books, 1978.
––––. "Descartes." In *The Great Philosophers: An Introduction to Western Philosophy*, edited by Bryan Magee, 85-88. Oxford: Oxford University Press, 1987.
Wood, Barry and David Woodruff Smith. Introduction to *The Cambridge Companion to Husserl*, edited by Barry Wood and David Woodruff Smith. Cambridge: Cambridge University Press, 1995.
Wood, David. "Some Questions For My Levinasian Friends." In *Addressing Levinas*, edited by Eric Sean Nelson, Antje Kapust, and Kent Still, 152-169. Evanston, IL: Northwestern University Press, 2005.
Worthen, Jeremy. "Beginning Without End: Christianity in Franz Rosenzweig's *Star of Redemption*." *Journal of Ecumenical Studies* 39, no. 3-4 (2002): 348-352.
Wyschogrod, Edith. "Derrida, Levinas, and Violence." In *Derrida and Deconstruction*, edited by Hugh J. Silverman, 177-194. New York: Routledge, 1989.
––––. *Emmanuel Levinas: The Problem of Ethical Metaphysics*. 2nd ed. New York: Fordham University Press, 2000.
––––. "God and 'Being's Move' in the Philosophy of Emmanuel Levinas." *The Journal of Religion* 62, no. 2 (April 1982): 145-155.
––––. *Saints and Postmodernism: Revisioning Moral Philosophy*. Chicago: The University of Chicago Press, 1990.
Yamada, Frank M. "Ethics." In *Handbook of Postmodern Biblical Interpretation*, edited by A.K.M. Adam, 76-85. St. Louis: Chalice Press, 2000.
Yong, Amos. *Hospitality & the Other: Pentecost, Christian Practices, and the Neighbor*. Maryknoll, N.Y.: Orbis Press, 2008.
Zizioulas, John D. *Communion & Otherness: Further Studies in Personhood and the Church*, edited by Paul McPartlan. London: Continuum, 2006.

www.ingramcontent.com/pod-product-compliance
Lightning Source LLC
Chambersburg PA
CBHW031710230426
43668CB00006B/168